Anyone Can Grow Up

How George Bush
and I Made It to the
White House

SIMON & SCHUSTER

New York • *London* • *Toronto* • *Sydney* • *Singapore*

SIMON & SCHUSTER
Rockefeller Center
1230 Avenue of the Americas
New York, NY 10020

SIMON & SCHUSTER and colophon are registered trademarks
of Simon & Schuster, Inc.
For information about special discounts for bulk purchases,
please contact Simon & Schuster Special Sales:
1-800-456-6798 or business@simonandschuster.com

Designed by Leslie Phillips
Manufactured in the United States of America

10 9 8 7 6 5 4 3 2 1

Library of Congress Cataloging-in-Publication Data
Carlson, Margaret.
Anyone can grow up : how George Bush and I made it to the White
House / Margaret Carlson.
p.   cm.
Includes index.
1. United States—Politics and government—1993–2001.
2. United States—Politics and government—2001–   3. Presidents—
United States—Election—History—20th century.   4. Political campaigns—
United States—History—20th century.   5. Political culture—United States.
6. United States—Social conditions—1980–   7. Carlson, Margaret.
8. Women journalists—United States—Biography.   I. Title.
E885.C368 2003
973.929—dc21   2003042461
ISBN 0-684-80890-0

For Courtney

Contents

Anyone Can
Grow Up

PART ONE

Personal or Family Matters

MY STORY DOESN'T BEGIN WITH TALES of working on *The Harvard Crimson* or memories of evenings gathered around the dinner table discussing the issues of the day. In the Bresnahan household, we sat around the dinner table all right. Eating was a major pastime. But the issues of our day ran more to the progress of my mother's projects for fixing up the house (a more sophisticated toolbox and she could have built us a new one), under what conditions my father would be allowed to attend the weekly poker game (my mother, whose Irish father died from drink, worried over the amount of beer consumed at these get-togethers), and trying to get Jimmy, my older brother, who was having a hard go of it, to say how school had gone that day. There were four of us back then, my stay-at-home mother, my father, who worked at the nearby military depot, Jimmy, and me. The setting was typical, the paneled station wagon in the driveway of the cookie-cutter postwar house. The chatter at dinner was incessant but rarely about the news. My parents loved John Kennedy (he was Catholic) and didn't love Richard Nixon (he wasn't, and picked on Helen Gahagan Douglas, who was). Politically, that was about it.

Yet my parents propelled me toward journalism as surely as if they'd had the Alsops over for cocktails every night. My brother had suffered serious brain damage at birth, and their struggle to give him a normal life stamped my view of the world. I learned quickly to dislike those who slight the weak or different or unlucky. I learned that when no one is looking, those who think of themselves as the best people can behave like the worst. It wasn't the pale kid with asthma who taunted my brother, it was the tall, good-looking one with the Schwinn three-speed and the Ted Williams bat. From an early age, I kept a list of "People Who Must Be Stopped." Like some tiny, pigtailed Mike Wallace, I tracked down the parents of kids who didn't play fair and squealed on them. I had a moral purpose in becoming an annoying tattletale, but that didn't make me less annoying. It was a wonder I had any playmates at all.

By the time I arrived, the two high school sweethearts, Mary Catherine McCreary and James Francis Xavier Bresnahan, already knew the life they blithely assumed would be theirs was over. Two years earlier, soon after my father returned from the war, they had brought their first child, deprived of oxygen in a difficult delivery at an army hospital, home. There was no testing then for developmental problems. Only gradually did they discover how severe the damage was. Decades later, in the blissful two weeks my parents visited after my daughter was born, my normally taciturn father told me of the morning when I was four and Jimmy was six and he'd been trying for months to get my brother to sound out the letters on the back of the corn-flakes box. I'd absorbed every bit of that tutoring, at the same time it bounced off my brother. One morning I sat down and read off how many box tops were needed, how the contest was void where prohibited, and that the employees of Kellogg were not eligible to compete. He told me that that night in bed, he and my mother cried themselves to sleep, half in sorrow, half in relief.

Yet as a small child I sensed little of their grief. Jimmy was talkative and could ask a hundred questions: Where's my Davy Crockett hat? Can I make Jell-O? Did you see the Sauers got a riding mower? When's Grandma coming? Unlike families whose children know what they don't know and are filled with longing for what they cannot have, Jimmy wasn't self-aware enough to complain. That, in its way, was a gift, and it saved us.

My mother wanted our lives to orbit around Jimmy's, which turned her into a manic Martha Stewart and my already sweet-tempered father into a saint. It made me uncommonly devoted at first—I liked being in the thick of things, my brother's protector, my parents' fallback, my own counsel—but remote and rebellious later. I was a bookworm by nature, but "sticking my nose in a book" when I could be joining in kneading bread, banging in stakes for the tomato plants, making pottery, or holding up a piece of knotty-pine paneling for my mother to measure was discouraged.

In the morning, my mother would try to teach Jimmy practical things: how to brush his teeth (that was successful), tie a tie (that wasn't), or put a belt through his pant loops (a semisuccess: back loops, no; front loops, yes). Since she was so much more intelligent than the tasks at hand, my mother restlessly gave over her afternoons to organizing the Altar Guild, halfheartedly learning bridge and generally bending the house to her will, including the walls and pipes.

Neither of my parents was born handy with tools, yet my mother was reluctant to hire a carpenter or a plumber, so my father became bad at both. After we moved from a row house in Washington to a Cape Cod in Camp Hill, Pennsylvania, a suburb of Harrisburg, my mother nagged my father into laying flagstone for a patio, then screening in the flagstone patio, then putting a door between the kitchen and the porch. One day I came home from school to find that my mother had knocked out the new door and wall entirely and maneuvered the table around the remaining studs onto the porch. What had once been a patio was now, apparently, a dining room. She announced we would be eating there from then on. It was summer, so my father had time to rough in windows and install insulation before the first frost.

We didn't eat on that porch for long. As soon as it was finished, it filled with equipment: a pottery wheel and a kiln for my mother's pots, a sewing machine (and a dress form), gardening tools (we grew tomatoes, peppers, zucchini, and onions), and a stack of oven bricks to make her homemade bread rise properly. Mom did not work alone. "Are you sick?" she would ask, feeling my forehead for a fever if she caught me sitting down. She lined three walls of the basement with shelves filled with enough canned goods to survive six months. She built a long sewing table with slots underneath for bolts of fabric she got wholesale. She bought a deep freezer at a garage sale, so she would no longer be constrained in her baking by what we could consume in a day. Had the nuclear catastrophe we crouched under our desks in preparation for come to pass, the neighbors would have rushed to our house.

It was the perfect childhood if I'd wanted to grow up to be a contractor, an interior decorator, or a survivalist. And I was mostly happy in it, although the only place I could read in peace was the bathtub, where, to trick my mother, I would make occasional swishing sounds in water turned icy cold so I could finish the latest Nancy Drew mystery. My friend Joanne coveted Nancy Drew's roadster. I coveted her calm household.

It felt as though we went out a lot, but we had quite a few restrictions. My father flew for his job, but my mother was phobic about flying—loudly so—and made Jimmy phobic, too. (When he saw the Pan Am crash in Lockerbie, Scotland, on CNN he said, "Mom was right.") We never went anywhere my brother couldn't go—not to a movie, a museum, or a play. We went to the beaches or mountains we could reach by car (or in the RV we briefly owned). My first trip by air was to Paris for a junior year abroad. I was in college before I set foot in a museum.

Most Saturday nights we went to dinner at my dad's parents'. My stern grandfather was a butcher, and back when a steak was a steak, he brought sirloins home. What a feast! We ate well at our house, but the menu ran to stews and pot roasts, not your very own cut of meat. My father's mother, Gertie, had a braid of red hair down her back, smoked butts during Lent when she gave up cigarettes, drank Pabst Blue Ribbon, and let us kids stand on a stool to put nickels in the slot machine at the Rod 'n Reel down the street from our cottage at Chesapeake Beach.

While the rest of us had mashed potatoes and wedges of iceberg with Thousand Island dressing, my grandfather was served boiled potatoes and peas in a separate dish by my doting grandmother. This seemed an exotic form of married love to me, and I wondered if it was that tender gesture to Granddad, not my grandmother's swearing and drinking, that made her such an annoyance to my mother. After we tired of watching the adults play cards, the cousins would head down to the basement to run around like maniacs until we collapsed in a sweaty heap of sleep on the coats piled on the sofa. I slept on the lining side, my brother on the wool.

When I was little, I didn't resist my mother's urgings to "go out and play and take your brother with you." I chose Jimmy for my side ("If you want me, you have to take him"), and I tried to guide the games toward large motor skills that he could manage (hide-and-seek) and away from small ones he couldn't (marbles, pogo sticks). Because Jimmy was never to be left alone, I urged the neighborhood kids to come over to my house. They loved coming. It wasn't just the scrumptious food or the home-churned ice cream that they had never thought of coming from anywhere but the freezer section of the A&P that pulled them in. It was the messy, kid-centered chaos of it.

Although my mother always seemed to be cleaning like a madwoman, our house wasn't orderly, so if you found yourself in the middle of Parcheesi, you could put the board in the corner under the card table with the jigsaw puzzle on top and be sure it would be there when you came back—as would the jigsaw, for years at a time. Jimmy loved jamming straight-edged pieces into the middle. Once when we at last finished a harbor scene without losing any pieces, my mother shellacked it and hung it above the piano.

My parents took care of everything inside the house. I was left to patrol the perimeter, where I administered rough justice. Twisting the training wheels on Jimmy's bike (he never learned to ride without them) was a minor sport among the bullies. Frustrated, I went to Patrick's house and told his father that his son was the ringleader of the bunch. I was met with a blank stare and the bang of the screen door as he turned to yell for his wife to come downstairs. She never came. So the next time, I threw a rock and bloodied Pat's nose. Years later, my daughter got her hands on my old report cards and was delighted to learn that I got an F in deportment—with the note from Mother Marita Joseph that I was to leave the summary executions to her.

I still get furious when someone makes fun of Jimmy. Not long ago, a guy in a three-piece suit got in the elevator in my office building with Jimmy and me. Unfamiliar with high-rise etiquette, Jimmy made inappropriate eye contact. When Mr. Lawyer got off, he looked back and said, "Weirdo." I returned to his floor, hunted him down at his law firm, and told his secretary what had happened—to a blank stare. I tried to bloody his nose in a letter to the senior partner at the firm what had happened. I never heard back.

Because Jimmy demanded constant attention, I grew up partly in a state of benign neglect, which is vastly underrated by today's parents as a child-rearing technique. I didn't lack for affection and approval: the simplest thing I did was a joy to my parents. But I wasn't overmanaged. The only time I remember parental intervention was in seventh grade, when my father helped me bend a plant toward the light so I would have a plausible example of photosynthesis for entry in the science fair.

This was no doubt the most unethical thing he ever did—this man who never got so much as a parking ticket, who lifted his thumbs off the steering wheel every few miles to check the speedometer to be sure he was abiding by the posted limit—unless you count résumé inflation. When I was going through papers to organize my brother's life after my father's sudden death, I came across Jimmy's application to work at the naval depot. Under "Previous Job Experience," Dad wrote "Dishwasher at the country club." That much was true. Under "other duties," he added: "Assisted in the bar." That was a stretch. I knew the bartender. He wanted Jimmy nowhere near the maraschino cherries, much less the glassware.

The Church of the Good Shepherd was school, country club, and social center. My father was an usher at Sunday mass, and my mother ironed the linens for the altar; they chaperoned bowling nights and knew all my classmates. Like my dad (a non–college grad who used his GI credits to land a white-collar job as a contract specialist for the navy), most of the fathers in our parish worked in low white- or high blue-collar jobs.

The nuns taught as if each of us might win a Nobel Prize, and if they gave them out for long division or diagramming sentences, I'd have one under my belt by now. Their horizons didn't stretch much beyond the Susquehanna River. While others worried about Sputnik, we took up collections for pagan babies and went to see only those movies acceptable to the Legion of Decency. Our class trip was *always* to Hershey Park, where, after watching chocolate being made and stuffing ourselves with free samples, we rode the roller coaster. There was no slow track: each of us had a soul to be saved, so each of us had a brain to be honed. I never saw the nuns hit a student. We feared detention, censure, disappointment, but not the ruler. Step out of line and you would be ostracized, not just by Sister Mary William, but by the whole class. We'd all be deprived of crossword puzzles and spelling bees for a week.

But even the nuns' expansive idea of who could be taught wasn't enough to encompass Jimmy. What were my parents to do? Their main point of reference was the Kennedy family, which suggests that all the money and all the experts in the world is not enough. Ashamed of his eldest daughter, Rosemary, who had been deprived of oxygen at birth, Joe Kennedy, without telling his wife, had her lobotomized. She had lived at home before but was shipped off afterward to a school in Wisconsin for "exceptional children." Our small town had no schools for exceptional children, and surely if it meant living there, my brother would not have gone. Instead he started going to a "sheltered workshop" nearby, where the production of lanyards and pot holders outstripped local demand, but which occupied him. He looked around and didn't understand why he was there at first. "I'm not handicapped," he kept saying. But soon he was engaged in the activities. At dinner, he gave a blow-by-blow of his day, which was exactly like every other day, which was why he came to like it. We were thrilled by every word.

*   *   *

The dynamic of our family changed when I went off to Bishop McDevitt High School. Before then, I'd been a child of limited means but endless possibilities. We had everything I could think of—a shiny Chevrolet, a TV, summer vacations, a big lawn with a volleyball net, and *Reader's Digest* condensed books. We fit into our neighborhood with houses so similar that you could practically walk into someone else's kitchen and open the refrigerator before realizing it wasn't yours.

Suddenly I entered a new world. McDevitt had a modest tuition, which many of my former schoolmates' parents couldn't pay. Soon I had a group of new friends I didn't want to explain to my parents, and parents I didn't want to explain to them. I became aware of class distinctions. I met the children of doctors and lawyers from Camp Hill I hadn't known before because they went to private school, and a new set of kids who lived on the other side of Harrisburg, which was flourishing with new development. There were builders' and bankers' kids with big houses and their very own cars.

In this world, most everyone knew—and cared—what your dad did. By no means was McDevitt as status-conscious as my daughter's sixth grade at National Cathedral School, where kids could discern the difference between an undersecretary and assistant secretary of commerce. But gross distinctions could be drawn. The kids from the aptly named Steelton, where mills were closing, were left behind in the stampede to hang with the kids whose parents were bankers and builders, lawyers and doctors, and who lived in the Father Knows Best neighborhoods. Their dads went off to corner offices with secretaries who brought them coffee and made deals that yielded your own car when you were sixteen and a backyard pool.

I got this sickening feeling my father had a job and not a career. What we had came from scrimping, not from my father landing a new client. It never entered my mind to ask if he liked going off to a desk and requisition forms each morning, just as it never entered his mind to tell me he didn't. When he retired the first minute he could, I thought it was only so he could take care of my mother who was ill by then. But it also must have been to end the drudgery. When he was suddenly so full of energy and good humor, I realized how deadening worrying over parts for aircraft carriers for thirty years must have been. Even if I'd understood as a kid that he'd droned away so I wouldn't have to, I couldn't have explained it to my ninth-grade gym class.

So I kept my mouth shut and concluded that to succeed in this new world, I would have to fail at home. I no longer had enough time to keep Jimmy amused. I stopped having friends over (there was that pool and a centrally located diner to hang out at) and was out as much as I could be, which wasn't nearly enough. My parents were opposed to extracurricular activities because they kept me out too late and also included members of the opposite sex, some of whom had never been altar boys. Not that there was much chance to be boy crazy. At McDevitt, there was a boys' tower and a girls' tower (how medieval is that?), which made me both a protofeminist (without alpha males around all the time, we could be high achievers) and a party girl (we didn't see enough of boys not to go a little batty when we did). I wanted to be a cheerleader, play basketball (I was taller then), and be in the school play. I made the cheerleading squad but couldn't try out for the play because I wasn't allowed to take the city bus home after dark. I sewed the costumes without ever tipping my hat to my mother for teaching me how.

Nothing was more crucial to my teenage happiness than summer afternoons at the country club pool. A whiff of Coppertone and chlorine can transport me back to that Promised Land, where all-important social transactions took place. An ice-cold Coke, "Teen Angel" on the transistor radio, and the boys from the tennis team dropping by our blanket were heaven on earth.

Although I'd been relieved of Jimmy duty by then, on the hottest days my mother would suggest that I take him swimming. This was the mountaintop of my years as a teenage reprobate, so I huffed around as if I'd been asked to give Jimmy my kidney. "How could you ask such a thing?" I said. "Why don't you take him?" Of course, we didn't belong to a pool and he could only go on my guest pass. Long gone was the impulse I had as a kid to say "If you want me on your team, you have to take my brother." I was determined not to miss out on the afternoon's fun or to be excluded from the evening's plans, since arrangements weren't made on the phone but at the snack bar by those present. I begged to go alone and won.

As evidence that we sometimes pay for our youthful indiscretions, I now beg Jimmy to go swimming with me, and lose every time. He's either afraid of drowning, or reminded of those sweltering days he was left behind. He won't as much as stick a toe in the water.

My poor parents didn't know what hit them. They fought back as they saw me become a second-class student and a first-class social butterfly. There were no signs yet that I was headed to Washington. There were no signs yet that I was headed anywhere. I was still a bookworm, and the nuns taught us Catholic writers first (I have an uncommon knowledge of the works of G. K. Chesterton and Hilaire Belloc) and others like Theodore Dreiser (they must have thought *Sister Carrie* took place in a convent). *Catcher in the Rye* was sweeping the country, but I didn't hear of it until I was a freshman in college. As with Henry Adams, "my education had not yet begun."

Despite my social aspirations, I never became the belle of the ball. I had a lot of friends for someone who was by no stretch cool. I didn't have a car, I didn't even have a license until I was eighteen, and there were strict rules about whose car I could ride in. I was still dressing as if my mother had veto power. When I got cut from basketball (I wasn't as tall as I thought), I sublimated my disappointment by going out with the captain of the boys' team, which made for an odd sight since we were separated by more than a foot in height. Yet my parents approved. Victor had been an altar boy at St. Theresa's.

I spent a lot of time trying to make my parents presentable. Because my mother was such a fanatical homemaker, we had some touches of the gentility I aspired to: linen napkins with hand-sewn handkerchief borders, Nouvelle Cuisine (when it was Old), a garden full of vegetables, fresh bread every day. But I obsessed over her deficiencies: Why didn't we get *The New Yorker*? (A nun had given me a copy, and I took to reading it in the library.) When could we go skiing? I was grateful the shellacked jigsaw puzzle had migrated to the basement, but why did we have a tacky picture of

John Kennedy on the wall? I begged my mother to get highlights in her hair so it wouldn't look as though she'd colored it with shoe polish. (By the time she did, she was a teacher's assistant at my little brother's nursery school and one of the children shrieked, "Mrs. B., Mrs. B., you finally washed your hair!") If she wanted me to wear anything she made, I announced, she would have to give up crocheting, learn how to knit, and remove from her fabric stash all but 100 percent natural fibers.

For the first few years of high school, I had the cockeyed idea that even though my easygoing father didn't say much, he was secretly on my side. The way I saw it, he was piggybacking on me. On a car trip, I would never say I had to use the bathroom, because that would be siding with my mother, who was always agitating to stop. When my mother thought up some new project, I'd come down on the side of not doing it, reasoning that any sane person would prefer watching the ball game on TV to wallpapering. In return, I was certain that when my mother grounded me for one month because I didn't make it home at nine P.M. from a basketball game to stay with Jimmy so my parents could go play bridge, my father was silently thinking that it was cruel and unusual punishment.

The summer I worked at the naval depot with my father, I broached the subject of Mom's crazed approach to life when we were in the car one morning, fully expecting him to agree. But it turned out that "Margaret, listen to your mother" was not code for "I'm on your side but not at liberty to say so."

How could my father love someone who could be so rigid and demanding? Like all marriages, theirs had its mysteries. Though my mother didn't make my father special servings of potatoes and peas like Grandma, he relied on her for a life he couldn't have lived on his own. My father gave my mother an anchor and an easygoing, willing presence, while my mother gave my father wings. He was the saint, but he might have rested on a pedestal without her.

What saved us all from the toxic shock of me was that my mother had a baby when I was a junior in high school. Aside from my adolescent reaction ("What *were* they thinking?"), I was so enthralled by Edmund that I took a U-turn back to being a homebody. I stood by the crib staring, willing him to wake up so I could give him his bottle.

The baby transformed my mother. With Jimmy to tend to every minute of the day and monitoring my progress to make sure lightning hadn't struck twice, I doubt she had the ease to enjoy me. With this third child, I discovered the woman she must have been when she assembled the white spool crib excitedly expecting her first child—warm and relaxed and a little bit lazy. She let things go just to play with the baby. Of course, every home improvement that could be made had been made, but she stopped a lot of the optional activities as well. She moved the kiln to the basement, closed the sewing machine and used it as a desk, cooked on demand, not as a hobby, and, in general, mellowed out. I don't recall her ever again yelling, "Margaret, get in here, I mean it, come here right now or I'm going to kill you." She had been given another chance to get it right. She read Dr. Spock about when Edmund should be learning the alphabet. She wasn't worried he never would.

I rediscovered Jimmy, too, who was launched on a fulfilling career. He went to work at the navy depot (thanks to that inflated résumé), where my father found him a set-aside job unloading and breaking down color-coded boxes. He was sometimes taken advantage of and learned words my mother never said in her lifetime, but his boss, Rod Hagy, looked after him closely enough that the twenty years he worked there were better than we could have hoped for when he was weaving placemats. Jimmy won awards, not just the standard kind for never taking a day of sick leave, but also for coming up with ways to move boxes more efficiently. When I hear people (or myself) complain about too many handicapped spaces at Safeway, I want to tell them about Jimmy. The Americans with Disabilities Act is a godsend.

Just because my mother was happier than I'd ever seen her didn't mean she was going to let me be. Although she'd stopped asking, "Was he an altar boy?" she still insisted, "I want you at a Catholic college." The Ivy League, if my parents even knew what it was, was out of the question, but so was Penn State, my choice. It was too far away, too big, and too heathen. My mother loved pointing out that the Newman Club, where Catholics socialized and went to mass, was the tiniest building on campus. When it came time to send off applications, my mother simply neglected to mail the ones she disapproved of. I didn't find this out until I won an essay-writing contest that offered a scholarship to Penn State, which had no record that I'd applied. I hurriedly filled out the forms and went off to Penn State in a huff.

College yielded no hint that I would end up in journalism. Although I majored in English, I was too lazy to join the school paper, and although I didn't like football, I did like football parties. On weekends, I rarely cracked a textbook. I was as self-satisfied as George Bush at Yale, and about as productive, pleased with myself just for being at Penn State rather than at a convent school. Finally able to curl up with a book at any time of day or night without fear of being asked to move furniture, I got by. But Mom had a point about it being too big and too anonymous. I still get mail from my high school nuns; I doubt one professor from Penn State remembers me.

After graduation, the counterculture was roiling around me, but my boundaries were so closely drawn, I didn't have to go very far to rebel. Simply being against the war and joining the March on the Pentagon was enough to alarm my parents. Tear gas! Arrests! Would it go on my record, they wanted to know? I wasn't a trust fund kid. They didn't want me to turn my back on the Establishment before I was even in it.

Much good came out of this period—an end to the war, skepticism about government, greater tolerance for others. And that's not to mention organic food and dress-down Fridays. My ambivalence was particular to the lower middle class hoping to move into the upper middle class. My friends were questioning the values I'd grown up with, and I wanted to be part of them. But I wasn't ready to reject my parents, who celebrated those values. Indeed, the bourgeoisie looked a lot like the people I grew up with. Our neighbors answered the siren of the volunteer fire department, my father and his friends were in the military, and we had several policemen in the neighborhood. They were hardly pigs to me. My parents weren't hopelessly bourgeois, they were full of hope about becoming so.

I wish I'd tuned in and turned on a little more, and had explained to my friends how my parents had some Sixties values before it was cool. As Dorothy Day Catholics, my parents were part of a parish that took care of one another. We had a phone tree and when bad things happened to anybody, my parents were the first ones there with a casserole, a pan of brownies, and an open wallet. My father didn't know much about house repairs, but thanks to my mother's harassment, he knew more than most and was on call from Father Simpson to fix up the falling-down apartments he found for poor parishioners. It doesn't seem like much in the retelling but the year right after he retired, my father became a surrogate father to a child traumatized by the sudden death of his own father by simply showing up every morning to drive him to school.

The two years after graduation were my own experiment in living. I tried out a few things, including a federal government management program where I spent three months at four different cabinet departments learning how government works (or doesn't).

The best part of that year was living with my grandmother, not Gertie on my father's side but Nellie McCreary on my mother's side. Since my great grandmother O'Connor had died, my grandmother was living alone in Anacostia, a neighborhood in Washington that had once been a beautiful, leafy haven but had slipped so badly that her block on Yuma Street was notorious as the site of the slaughter of two FBI agents who'd been trying to bust a band of drug dealers.

Like most grandmothers, mine went easy on me when compared to my mother. When we came to Washington to visit, which was nearly every weekend when I was a youngster, we stayed with my mother's mother when we went for Saturday night dinner across town to Gertie's. I was told to be quiet when I pleaded with Grandma McCreary to come with us. My parents didn't acknowledge that the two grandmothers were cordial to each other but only came together on the largest occasions. Grandma McCreary explained to me that she got her fill of people who drank, swore, and gambled during the week as a nurse's aide at St. Elizabeth's, the mental hospital in southeast Washington. She could do without craziness on the weekends. She didn't smoke and objected to secondhand smoke before we knew there was such a thing.

At her house, it was lights out by nine P.M. (she was up at six) and martial order: all beds were made by eight A.M., after which we appeared dressed and scrubbed for a full breakfast of eggs, bacon, ham, home fries, and biscuits. Like my mother, she kept us busy: her frame house with a big porch always needed something, as did the big garden with a large stand of trees that dropped an extraordinary number of branches, limbs, and leaves. My favorite part of the weekend was the bonfire. Because she was too impatient to wait for the trash to be picked up, she threw all the debris from the yard and the alley (a minor dumping ground) into a wire basket and set it on fire with such satisfaction I worried she harbored the heart of an arsonist. We smelled like soot all the way back to Pennsylvania.

By the time I moved in, my grandmother had retired from the hospital and was working at the Hotel Washington, a block from the White House. Like my mother, my grandmother was pure energy and efficiency, common sense and spunk. On little more than minimum wage, she'd raised two children in a bungalow that cost ten thousand dollars and was upgraded by elbow grease to *House Beautiful* status.

At work, she made lifting a heavy mattress to make a hospital corner look like a high calling. She kept an iron on her cleaning cart to touch up any pillowcase that might get creased. She held the indoor speed record for completing her floor. I never smell a freshly laundered sheet without thinking of her, or tucking it in extra tight.

My grandmother started out as a night maid and rose to head of housekeeping, but after a few months, she gave up her management job. She liked the women she worked with and she saw she'd only been chosen to supervise them because she was white. She was no firebrand or organizer or even Democrat, other than having an Irish Catholic's tribal affection for John Kennedy. She saw that her selection was unfair, and she didn't like it.

But she was no bleeding heart liberal, and she didn't want to take a pay cut. She had struck up a chatty relationship with Clare Boothe Luce, a regular guest, who sent postcards to my grandmother that she tucked in the mirror above her dressing table (although she never looked in that mirror, doing no more each morning than brush her thick white hair). After hearing her story, Luce suggested that she offer to split her time: half making up rooms, half managing the linen and supply closet. It worked.

What didn't work was Luce's other suggestion: that maids lobby for a line on hotel bills, similar to the one on restaurant tabs which makes it easy for business travelers to tack on a tip and expense it later. Hotel workers still haven't nailed that one.

Most people would find living with their grandmother a complete non-starter, but I'd always loved her to pieces. When she came to visit us, I'd hide her purse hoping she'd miss the Greyhound home. Aside from running a tight ship, she was quite a bit of fun, nonjudgmental, and best of all, treated me like an adult. She could talk to Luce, she could talk to the teenagers who tossed beer cans in her garden, she could talk to me. It never bothered her when I had my nose in a book, my door closed, or company. She wasn't a cooking monster like my mother, but we always ate well. I still make her version of home fries with cabbage, onions, and leftover ham. Small things were to her small miracles. When twice as many tulips as usual poked through the frozen ground, when wool was two skeins for the price of one, when she completed her settings of blue willow china on lay-away one piece at a time, she was thrilled. Those plates she left me are so chipped and warped now I never pass an estate sale without looking for replacements.

What especially endeared her to me was her total love for my mother, coupled with her complete disapproval. Unlike my father, my grandmother took my side in everything: about when I should learn to drive, about my curfew, about my dating. My grandmother had divorced my sodden grandfather years earlier and so had been officially excommunicated, rendering her far less enamored of altar boys and the Church than my mother. Mom held the divorce against my grandmother something fierce, more than Father Joe did. I thought we were going to have a modern day Inquisition when my grandmother went to communion at my cousin's wedding. Father Joe had given his blessing but my mother thought she was a higher authority on canon law. They didn't speak for nearly a year.

Every Thursday when the stores downtown stayed open until nine P.M., I met my grandmother for dinner at Reeves, an old-fashioned bakery with lemon meringue pies in the window. We went to Murphy's and Woodward & Lothrop, where my grandmother would study the latest advances in knitting, crocheting, and embroidery before spending the large sum of ten dollars.

Well into her seventies, she would come visit me and when I came home from the office, I would see that the light fixture on the back porch would be scraped, sanded, and painted with Rust-Oleum, the thicket of weeds behind the garage chopped down, wallpaper stripped—all done in a house-dress with an apron. No matter how much climbing or stretching the job called for, she never wore pants.

After I left, I talked her into accepting my parents' pleas to come to Pennsylvania. I was afraid the police would soon just build bars around her whole block to contain the crime. She refused to live with my mother and bought her own place a few blocks away. She and my father fixed it up. They became the best of friends.

After what I think of as my year with my grandmother as opposed to my year with the Department of Labor, I wanted to do something worthwhile and went off (after a summer in Europe) to teach third grade in the Watts section of Los Angeles. The school system was so troubled I didn't need a teaching certificate and I was free to follow the syllabus of the nuns (phonics and multiplication tables) without being reproached for ignoring modern instructional methods.

One night in L.A. I went to a lecture at USC to hear Ralph Nader and was captivated. He fit my idea of making the world a fairer place, reining in the big guys who enlarged themselves at the expense of the little ones. I went up to him afterward, and he scribbled his phone number on a scrap of paper. I took a year to dial it, but when I did, Nader picked up the phone himself. He offered me $75 a week to work on auto safety. I've never toiled so hard for so little to so much purpose. I so admired Nader that I signed up for the LSATs and enrolled at George Washington University Law School. I would spend thousands on tuition and many hundreds of hours of boredom before I grasped that "Unsafe at Any Speed" wasn't a legal brief, it was a story about a company that cut corners on safety to make a buck. Although Nader had a law degree, he worked as a journalist.

Still, it seemed crazy to waste so much effort—I'd passed the bar exam—so I got a job as a lawyer at the Federal Trade Commission during the Carter administration, when Chairman Mike Pertschuk (a friend of Ralph's) was giving the cereal makers, children's TV producers, and car-makers a fit. That job ended when Carter did, and after a few weeks of interviewing at law firms, I knew my brilliant career as a lawyer was going to be short. Representing anyone who walked in the door needing someone to help him comply with (or get around) government regulations would be lucrative but unsatisfying. It was time to start over.

I'd recently started over at home as well. I got married when I was in law school in 1972 to a reporter for UPI, a world-class sailor and an absent-minded intellectual. Gene Carlson had taken classes at the Julliard School of Music, read Japanese haiku, preferred movies with subtitles, and rarely watched television. His family lived in Seattle, where his mother was head of the garden club and his father, Eddie, had chaired the 1962 Seattle World's Fair and conceived the Space Needle with a doodle on the back of a napkin. Eddie had risen from bellhop to chairman of Westin International Hotels and then chairman of United Airlines, after Westin merged with it in 1970. This was back in the day when CEOs put their pants on one leg at a time and didn't pay themselves a king's ransom. Gene had a wonderful younger sister who looked so much like me, we could be siblings.

Even accepting the theory that opposites attract, my friends were surprised by the match. When I try to explain, I keep coming back to the fact that Gene and his family were so . . . quiet. They didn't mind if I stuck my nose in a book—that's where Gene's was much of the time. They ate breakfast on the good china with the grapefruit sectioned. The well-polished Steuben bird never moved from its perch on the credenza. The lamps may have been glued to the end tables. Gene talked to his parents about golf and a new jib for the sailboat, and I came to talk about such things as well. In all my years with the Carlsons—and I stayed unusually close—I never heard a raised voice, not even when I ran over Gene's mother's foot with a cart carrying a one-hundred-pound block of ice intended for the galley fridge.

I had so much fun with the Carlsons on their sailboat that I agreed to go sailing on my honeymoon. The good news was also the bad news: We were alone, but a 40-foot ketch is not meant to be crewed by two people, one of whom is a committed landlubber. Gene had a destination in mind—we started in Seattle, and he wanted to get to Princess Louisa inlet, far up the coast of British Columbia. It was a forced sail where we were up at dawn and hauling sails until midnight in a quest to reach a distant harbor. We never got there.

Back on shore, it occasionally occurred to me that in addition to not being meant to sail boats, we weren't meant to be married. But I stopped having any such thoughts once Courtney was born. I was transported to a galaxy of such bliss that I could have been married to Ted Bundy for all it mattered. As time went on, Gene and I were sufficiently respectful of being parents not to split apart, but insufficiently drawn to each other to live together. When Gene got a Neiman Fellowship in 1975, he went off to Harvard and visited on the weekends. When the next year he got a job offer from *The Wall Street Journal,* he went off to Hong Kong and couldn't visit on the weekends. With deep family discounts on United, he came back often enough to remain a critical part of Courtney's life.

Real estate finally separated us. We sold our big house. Gene leased an apartment in Hong Kong and I bought a colonial in disrepair in Washington. Because the breakup had been so gradual and we had no financial entanglements other than the house, it took less than a half hour answering questions posed by an administrative judge to sever the bonds of matrimony. I walked down the aisle of a D.C. courtroom and out the door, struck that in its dissolution, marriage has no equal and opposite reaction. No drama marked the occasion.

Who better to provide the missing drama than parents? We had to move our parents away from the comfortable fiction that work was keeping us apart and introduce the reality that it was the two of us who were doing it. Divorce produced an onus of sin (mortal and excommunicative like my grandmother) and banishment. When an older cousin told my grandfather she was getting divorced, he lowered the venetian blinds and sat in darkness for the rest of the day, saying he would never see her again. He relented, but the black cloud never lifted. That my parents initially objected to Gene's reserve and Protestantism didn't matter. Marriage was a sacrament. Ours took place at the church in which I was baptized. Once they made their peace with Gene for not being an altar boy and keeping a statue of Buddha in his office, they wouldn't hear any talk of it not working out. Years passed and they never acknowledged I was divorced.

The Carlsons were equally disappointed and silent, since that was their way. But Eddie did write me a letter, describing how devastated he'd been when his own parents divorced, which made this all the more devastating for him. If I was no longer his daughter-in-law officially, he wrote, he would treat me like a daughter. His own daughter, Janie, was sweet enough to share. His devotion never wavered.

After rejecting the life of associate at a downtown law firm, I went to work at the *Legal Times,* a halfway house for fallen-away attorneys, writing about the legal profession instead of being in it. It paid poorly, and one day Eddie was waiting for me to go to lunch and overheard an intense auto repair conversation about how long a leaky water pump could last and the life expectancy of the radiator. That night he took me to get a new car. He was buying, but with my parents whispering in my ear, I convinced him what I really wanted was a used Honda.

For a couple of years, I saw so much of my father-in-law, you'd think he lived around the corner. The airlines were being deregulated, and Eddie had two or three visits to Washington a month to testify before Congress or appear before the Federal Aviation Administration. I was renovating my first house Mom's way, which meant as many unskilled volunteers and as few pros as possible. When he wanted to see a lot of Courtney and me,

Eddie had to don a painter's cap. By day he was a CEO in a Paul Stuart suit, by night he was Joe Six-Pack, eating pizza out of a box, wielding a Red Devil scraper to strip wallpaper, and pulling up hundreds of tiny nails out of the hardwood floor that had been holding down shag carpet. My mother was on to something with her hammer and power drill. All the hours in that falling-down house brought Courtney and me to a closeness with Eddie that lasted until he died in 1990.

After the *Legal Times* and writing freelance pieces, I got a job at *Esquire* magazine as its Washington bureau chief, which meant wielding huge power over a bureau of one (me) at my own kitchen table. The high point of that job was when editor Adam Moss lit on the idea of compiling an *Esquire Register*—a collection of profiles of up-and-coming men under forty. For the length of that assignment, I was never lonely. After a small item appeared in *The Washington Post*'s gossip column about the project, I even got a note from the father of one potential candidate, who wanted me to know his son was so brilliant, he could say "cow" and "moon" at a very early age.

Spurning the law was bad for my bank account but good for Courtney. Piecework fit nicely with motherhood. In the morning, I could roll out of bed to drive the car pool dressed like a grad student who'd overslept instead of a striving junior associate in a suit and heels. I wrote anywhere, anytime—on a yellow legal pad, sitting in the bleachers watching soccer, on a laptop in the pediatrician's office, at midnight at home. Editors, unlike senior partners, approve of you being a mile wide and an inch deep and don't feel cheated if you're not at the office until all hours, as long as you produce the requisite 1,500 words. The goal is not to master the minutiae of the Sherman Antitrust Act, but to master the issue at hand for as long as it takes to write about it that week.

I was usually home after school to claim the lost hours before dinner, when I turned the kitchen into a playground, sometimes letting Courtney roller-skate from the counter to the table, carrying plates. She started cooking by making pancakes, then scrambling eggs, then omelets. Before long, with the help of my mother, she learned to make pie dough, which still eludes me. My mother taught her so well that Courtney became the head baker at the Red Door Café at Kenyon College. When Courtney was eighteen, she won the Bloomingdale's cooking contest for baking one of my mother's desserts.

In the mid-1980s, I joined a start-up called the *Washington Weekly,* which seemed too good to be true, and was. It folded after a year.

Just when I needed a lifeboat, my friend Michael Kinsley needed a managing editor at *The New Republic*. Having written there over the years, I knew the ropes. While editing, every few weeks I found time to write the back page "Diarist," which caught the attention of *Time*'s political editor, Walter Isaacson. Walter was dismayed to see *Time* lose good women writers—among them Maureen Dowd and Michiko Kakutani, who went on to win Pulitzer Prizes at *The New York Times*. When he became *Time*'s "Nation" editor, he set out to make the magazine sound more like America than like Yale and Harvard circa 1925.

So he flew down to Washington to recruit me. But it was not an easy sell. In the 1980s, *Time* was still a place where the good jobs of correspondent, writer, and editor were held by men, while the lesser jobs of researchers and librarians were manned by women. Relations between the two were similar to those between pilots and stewardesses or doctors and nurses—different pay and different status, with one meant to serve the other. They worked in a closed, intimate environment with clear gender lines of demarcation where at least two nights a week everyone was expected to stay late. There was no Hugh Hefner walking around in pajamas, but it felt like party time, with premium liquor and rare roast beef served by white-jacketed waiters. There were more affairs than weddings, and the tales of top editors keeping cars purring at the curbs racking up hundreds of dollars in fares were the source of ribbing, not ridicule. Two top editors married researchers. Jason McManus, editor in chief, married three. One senior editor, between marriages, plastered *Playboy* centerfolds around the cubicle of one researcher, a prank typical of the frat house atmosphere. It didn't improve the condition of women at the magazine any more than bra burnings did the condition of women generally, but the females on the staff were nonetheless grateful when B. J. Phillips showed up without her blouse at story conference the next morning.

Time still had a peculiar division of labor: reporters from the many bureaus would send "files" to New York at the end of the week to be chopped and diced by hard-drinking, late night writers, who then sent them on to be pureed by hard-drinking, late night editors. I told Walter no.

But then Walter, like a good reporter, tracked me down in Pennsylvania on Thanksgiving. The Bresnahans were encamped at Holy Spirit Hospital, visiting my mother who had just had surgery. We carted turkey and fixings (and a jigsaw puzzle) to the solarium. It wasn't a time to be doing career planning.

Being home did make me think about my relationship with my parents. It hadn't had just one turn, from child to adult, but from good child, to bad child, to semi-good child in college, to adult with a checkered career. The best thing I'd done was make them grandparents. They were glad I'd settled on journalism finally, but they didn't know if *The New Republic* was a good job or a bad one. My parents dutifully subscribed, but it was as foreign to them as *Le Monde Diplomatique*. They had no interest in Michel Foucault's deconstruction or parsing the meaning of meaning.

Walter, who would become the centerpiece of my professional life, was more convinced that I was meant to be at *Time* than I was convinced I wasn't. But what really moved me was how much the idea of their daughter working at a magazine on Ed McMahon's Publisher's Clearing House list pleased my parents. It was mainstream and middlebrow, had currency at the bridge table and in Good Shepherd parish hall. I moved to *Time* and my parents soon were displaying each issue like a coffee-table book.

But if the idea of *Time* appealed to them, big-time journalism did not. There came to be a gap between us, not of my making and not as large as the one that existed when I was a teenager pretending to be an orphan, but it was big enough to trouble me. My parents would never say, "You're putting on airs," or "too big for your britches," as they did when I was a kid. But I could tell they didn't feel entirely at ease with a life they didn't feel part of. They'd made a lot of adjustments downward, giving up on "my daughter, the nun," and "my daughter, the teacher." They were ready to settle for "my daughter, the lawyer," until I snatched that away from them. My daughter at *Time* was something else again.

Washington journalism had come to symbolize that I had left the old neighborhood and wasn't coming back, even though I came back all the time. I couldn't get them to Washington short of threat of a nuclear meltdown—literally. One of their rare visits took place during the leakage from the reactor at nearby Three Mile Island when they came to stay with me for three weeks—long enough to turn my household into a replica of theirs, right down to their sulking if I wanted to go out.

I wanted my parents to be proud of me, but not too proud. I preferred they be somewhat blasé, like the parents of my fellow journalists who took it for granted that their offspring would get White House invitations. They were either horrified (how much I paid for my house in Georgetown, and Georgetown itself), or too thrilled ("You had dinner with who?"). Once again I kept secrets. I would hang on the phone with my mother discussing meat loaf recipes, but not say who I was making the meat loaf for. They weren't familiar with the notion that if you hang a lamb chop in the window, they will come. It doesn't even take meat loaf to get Senator John McCain.

When my mother was sicker than ever, it didn't matter who was coming to dinner or what my schedule was. I was home most weekends. I talked to my father several times a day. In a way we got closer, but as for quality time, there was little. Since we spelled each other (there was no household help), when I came, he would catch up on his sleep and errands. We passed in the night.

In the spring of 1991, a neighbor came over to stay with my mother so that Dad could join the group he'd played cards and golf with for thirty years. He hadn't been able to play even once the year before. Just as the first hand was being dealt and the beer was being poured at the 19th hole (he'd overruled my mother on the drinking question), my father said he didn't feel well and a minute later, keeled over. He was playing on a public course, not a country club, and there was no doctor nearby. CPR wasn't enough to keep him from slipping into a coma before the ambulance arrived.

When I got a call from the emergency room doctor at the hospital and he said my father was there, I was sure an overworked, sleep-deprived intern had gotten it wrong. "You mean my mother, don't you? Could you put my father on?" I was there in two hours and didn't leave for seven days. I'd watched too many hospital dramas to leave my father alone unconscious. If his daughter was there, there was a better chance he'd be treated like someone's father. I hired a nurse for my mother and moved in, showering in the doctor's lounge and sleeping on two chairs. My main goal was to make sure they didn't leave him uncovered and exposed or mix up IV bags. The doctors agreed to reduce his morphine to see if they could get any response. That night, thinking he might be able to hear, I talked for hours. By the next morning, the doctor was convinced there was no chance he would regain brain function and said we should say good-bye.

Until then, Jimmy had not visited. He'd stubbornly refused to accept that Dad could walk out of the house with a cooler of beer and his clubs and not come back. Edmund forced Jimmy into the car, and minutes after he came and said good-bye, we removed the respirator. My father died without my ever saying good-bye.

As an adult, Jimmy had become closer to my father than to my mother. They ate breakfast together, packed their lunches, and drove off to the depot every morning for twenty years. They worked together on the weekends as well. With Dad's supervision, Jimmy's fascination with cars became a wash-and-wax business. Obsessively clean, Jimmy would take Q-tips to the vents of the air conditioner. Everlastingly forgetful, he would neglect the ashtray. My father spent a lot of time in the driveway with a checklist.

Jimmy was dry-eyed until little cracks in his fragile world began to appear. Money from his car washing was piling up and Dad wasn't around to sort the money into paper packets with him. Finally I drove him to the bank, which automatically sorted it. I told him I'd hired someone to live with him and drive him to work and he'd have to get lunch at the commissary. He knew life as he'd known it was over. I said, you miss Dad, don't you? His chin quivered. "What do you think, Margaret? He was my buddy."

My mother died of lung cancer a few months later. She'd been in bed for a year on oxygen and steroids, unable to bark orders and rearrange furniture—and unable to get the kind of comfort from me she'd gotten from my father. I came to visit most weekends for the better part of a year with Courtney, serving as buffer. Every child is a blessing, but I got one that compensated for my deficiencies. Courtney has my mother's energy and resilience, my father's steadiness and sweetness. Fairness demanded that my teenager should inflict on me a dose of my own medicine, but other than a brief period her sophomore year, when she had a friend I didn't like (imagine that!), she manifested none of my adolescent angst. Going with me to Camp Hill was an imposition on the social life of a sixteen-year-old only partly ameliorated by my teaching her to drive at a nearby parking lot late at night. My mother was luckier in her grandchild than in her child. Courtney was willing to go through the jewelry box and listen to a story about each item, to cut my mother's nails, to just sit, while I busied myself around the house so I wouldn't have to.

Every child is sad when a parent dies. I was panicked. I'd gotten Courtney to the point where she spent less time at home than I did and was about to go off to Kenyon College. But now I would have to look after Jimmy, and worry about Edmund, who was only in his early twenties. I had a premonition of what it would be like to be the adult in the family at Edmund's wedding in October. My mother was too sick to go to the rehearsal dinner, which she had planned down to the amount of sweet versus bittersweet chocolate in the dessert. Nor could she go to the wedding, where I tried to be mother and father of the groom. I broke character only a few times, when I couldn't resist slinking off to the kitchen of the Hershey Hotel to catch a glimpse of the Clarence Thomas hearings a few of the wait staff were following. I fulfilled my main purpose: to nod in agreement the hundred times my brother said to me, "Well, at least Dad knew Colleen and I were getting married." And unlike my marriage, Edmund's is perfect.

My mother had her own panic. Pumped up on steroids, her brain beginning to fail from lack of oxygen, she called a lawyer and wrote a codicil to her will, appointing the local bank as executor of her estate and of Jimmy. At the last minute, she either wanted to save me from the responsibility, or she doubted me. The first thing the bank wanted to do was sell the house to assure there would be funds to pay its fee, the very thing my mother most dreaded. It would take three months, and dusting off my law degree, to undo the catastrophe of Jimmy having to move.

In those first awful months, I learned that my parents had left very little money but had bequeathed me a raft of friendships. I felt like Harrison Ford in the movie *Witness* when at the sound of the bell clanging for help, the Amish farmers from miles around flocked to his side. The neighbors rushed in to take over when I needed it.

By then, my professional life had been transformed from part-time piecework at the kitchen table to more than full-time commitments at *Time* and on TV. At *The New Republic* I went as far as Capitol Hill to cover politics. For *Time*, I flew all over the country to cover campaigns, conventions, and primaries. I was also out and about, working Washington's second shift, the cocktail and dinner party circuit. It was fun, like high school with money. I justified the Holly Golightly routine by telling myself that it's easier to get Colin Powell to return a call if I'd sat next to him at Sally Quinn's dinner table the week before.

After a few years at *Time*, when I was White House correspondent, I got a call from Bob Novak at CNN to fill an open seat on *The Capital Gang*. I was not his first choice. He'd invited Maureen Dowd to breakfast at the Army and Navy Club to ask her to join the panel. When she turned him down, he called me, and didn't have to buy me eggs and bacon to get me to say yes. Novak offered to keep this our little secret. But unlike Salieri when Mozart came to town, I feel honored to play second fiddle to Maureen.

In 1993, Jim Gaines, editor of *Time*, asked me to come to Le Bernardin in New York for a get-acquainted lunch. I was confident enough the meeting would not be ulcer inducing to take full advantage of the culinary opportunity, ordering wine, salmon tartare, risotto, and tiramisu. As I was capturing the last morsel of rice, Gaines asked how I would feel about becoming the first woman columnist at *Time* magazine. Even if it was a case of affirmative action to break *Time* out of its old boy shell, I felt just dandy about it. (Later I would occasionally be asked if it hurt my self-esteem to have *Time* touting me constantly as "Margaret Carlson, the first woman columnist at *Time*." No, it didn't. It would have hurt my self-esteem not to have gotten a crack at the job.) After five dry runs and much hemming and hawing over what to call it (trivia answer: "Public Eye"), the column kicked off in 1994. What a gift!

My friends didn't change from year to year, but their jobs did. It was Michael Kinsley (my friend before he was my boss at *TNR*) who first took me to dinner at the big, intimidating mansion of Katharine Graham, the reigning queen of Washington and publisher of *The Washington Post*. Every few weeks, when Henry Kissinger or Barbara Walters was stuck on the tarmac at LaGuardia, I would get a late call asking if I'd like to fill in. Following the Meg Greenfield rule—call anytime before the main course—I always said yes. Eventually, I would go as me. Like the rings on a tree, my evenings with Graham chart my evolution from rookie journalist to old timer. One day Mrs. Graham complained that she'd never been asked to my house. A few months later, I was giving a going-away party for Kinsley, who'd been wooed to be editor of Slate.com by Microsoft's Bill Gates. It seemed the perfect occasion to hide behind. She came, she tossed salad, she scooped ice cream. She became a fixture at my house.

But it took more than dinners for us to become such good friends. My empty nest coincided with the death of her best friend and *Washington Post* editor, Meg Greenfield. I lived just across the street and loved to cook. She couldn't boil the proverbial pot of water, so whenever the French chef was off, I would take over dinner and a video. Since she didn't drive, we carpooled to many a book party. On Sundays, we would join a larger group of friends who went to an early movie and for Chinese food in the neighborhood.

When Courtney decided to get married in 2000, Kay asked if she would get married in her garden, and that began a wedding my mother would have been proud of. I didn't make Courtney's wedding dress, as my mother (and I) had made mine. She preferred one by Vera Wang, proving there can be progress from one generation to the next.

But Courtney did let me choose her husband, whom I'd met when he worked as press secretary to the mayor of Philadelphia, Ed Rendell. When Rendell took over chairmanship of the Democratic National Committee, he called to tell me David was moving to Washington. "Could you introduce him to a few people his age?" he asked. The first of the few people his age I introduced him to was my very own daughter. I had her join us for lunch on the premise that she was interested in politics, too. After that three-hour meal, I backed off (I swear), and they managed to fall in love on their own.

Every silver lining has a cloud, and eighteen months later, I found myself up to my ears in wedding planning and at war with my only child. I was in a bind. I wanted to have the most beautiful wedding in the world (misplaced compensation for not staying married myself), but without becoming a captive of the wedding industry. I was opposed to hiring a wedding planner on the grounds that you don't seek expert advice on matters people have been tending to on their own for hundreds of years. This—and my sense that the reception would be just a bigger version of the kind of dinner where you turn on the oven an hour ahead of time—terrified the bridal monster my daughter had become. She pictured overcooked chicken and a seating plan scribbled in the margin of the newspaper.

Like me, she was willing to cut a corner, but unlike me, she wasn't willing to take it on two wheels. I was mystified. How could someone so level-headed and lighthearted—in short, someone so much like me—be poring over a two-foot stack of bridal magazines designed to make every young woman yearn to be Princess for a Day?

With over 150 people due to arrive in Mrs. Graham's garden for the ceremony concentrating my mind, I finally turned into the mother of the bridal monster. I hired a band that agreed not to play so loud that we couldn't talk, a caterer that would let me bake fifty loaves of bread, and a photographer from the Senate press gallery who promised not to take more than five staged shots. With two days to spare, I found a dress. I had cooked Chris and Kathy Matthews's rehearsal dinner twenty years earlier, so they returned the favor. We couldn't work out the Catholic-Jewish divide, so the mayor's wife, federal judge Midge Rendell, performed the ceremony. For the wedding dinner, I finished the seating plan forty-five minutes before people were expected to sit, with my artistic friend Eden Rafshoon, who serves on the Fine Arts Commission, writing out the place cards in her perfect script. With moments to spare, we finished arranging the centerpieces from the twelve buckets of roses Courtney's father and I had picked up at a wholesaler's the night before.

It would make a better story if some disaster occurred, but none did, unless you count the orange roses in Courtney's bouquet, which, since I had extra flowers in Mrs. Graham's basement, I was able to yank out and replace. We had no rain plan, so it didn't rain. We had no air-conditioning, so it wasn't hot. Chris Matthews sang " 'A' You're Adorable, 'B' You're So Beautiful" so off-key, it was adorable. Gene was such a good father of the bride, I decided that a marriage lasting forever should not be the only measure of success. Mrs. Graham said, "We launched the jolliest bride I ever did see."

During the wedding toast, I said, "My work is done." But luckily, it wasn't. A few months later, moments after the happy couple settled on their first house in Philadelphia, where David returned to work for gubernatorial candidate Rendell, Courtney and I picked up sledgehammers and crowbars and demolished the wall between the kitchen and dining room. Within two weeks, with five thousand dollars and the intermittent intervention of skilled labor, we renovated the kitchen complete with Corian counters (from a wholesaler), cabinets rubbed with milk paint, and hardwood floors (hiding under the linoleum). My son-in-law, who didn't know my mother, was surprised to find that marrying a Carlson meant embracing the building trades.

And, of course, my work with Jimmy will never be done. He hadn't adjusted to going to work without my father right away, so he came to Washington for an extended stay. It was wrenching for him, but he took some comfort in the fact that I'd morphed into my mother, becoming the same volatile mix of Betty Crocker and Judge Judy I'd inveighed against, cleaning with a toothbrush, making curtains (I mean window treatments), baking bread, and disciplining my daughter like a drill sergeant.

At first, Jimmy, who'd never once been left alone, went everywhere I went. One morning, he put on his funeral suit and I took him to a small breakfast for reporters with presidential candidate Pat Buchanan at a downtown hotel. The reporter next to Jimmy asked, "Who are you with?"

"My sister," said Jimmy.

"Who's your sister with?" the reporter asked.

"She's with me," Jimmy said quizzically. When the waiter came around with OJ and coffee, he asked for a stack of blueberry pancakes—and got them.

Jimmy remembered that morning so that when Michael Kinsley resumed doing *Crossfire* with Buchanan after his presidential run, his most faithful viewer, Jimmy, said to him, "I see you're doing the show with your boss now." Kinsley knew that debating John Sununu, who'd filled in for Buchanan, was a piece of cake compared to wrangling with Buchanan every night. He didn't know how obvious it was until Jimmy pointed it out. He toughened up.

When I gave my yearly brunch after the White House Correspondents Dinner, at which the *Time* editors down from New York mingle with Washington folks like George Stephanopoulos, Alan Greenspan, and Dee Dee Myers, Jimmy answered the door at eleven A.M. to find Walter Isaacson, an hour early. I was in my nightgown, the first egg yet to be cracked, so I shoved Walter upstairs to my room to use the phone. When he came down, Jimmy said, "Do you know my sister wants to kill you?"

In those first weeks with Jimmy, I came to see how frustrated my mother must have been. Every day she would try to find a friend for Jimmy; every day she would fail. Every day she would teach him how to dial 911 and tie his sneakers, and every day he would forget. How did she retain any cheerfulness in the face of constant failure? It's easier for me, what with speed dial, Velcro, and clip-on ties. But it still behooves me to keep the projects rolling and not stick my nose in a book. Opening the *Times* at Sunday breakfast is like putting a barbed-wire fence between us. Jimmy knows he is going to get hurt trying to go over it, but he can't help nattering on about people I don't know doing things I don't care about. When I snap at him, he says, "Just making conversation," which is also his reply when he turns around to talk to me in the midst of washing a car and hoses me down.

Eventually, I set Jimmy up according to his wishes, with my parents in mind. He wanted to keep his job at the depot and live in my parents' house, which he has done for eleven years with a succession of caretakers (some of whom should be shot, others canonized). He is indispensable to the neighborhood. You have leaves on your lawn? He's got the leaf blower. Mail to be picked up? He's your man. Your dog needs walking? He's there.

I should have reassured my mother that I would put myself in assisted living before I'd put Jimmy there. I stubbornly didn't, because I thought she should trust me. It took me a long time to realize how right she'd been about so many things: she was right, of course, that if she didn't make Jimmy part of our lives, he might have no life at all, that it was possible to have a household that accommodated Jimmy's limitations and my ambition. Jimmy doesn't take away from my household, he enriches it.

I finally learned that lesson a few days after the disaster at the World Trade Center. Jimmy always comes to Washington for his birthday on September 16, but because of the general chaos after September 11, none of the family could come. So I called on my friends to make the day festive, even though most of them were drained and exhausted from working round the clock. Instead of a decorous "No gifts, please," I shouted "Gifts! Please!"

Jimmy set the menu: pizza made with Mom's bread dough, German chocolate cake, and ice cream. The guests—a congressman, an anchor, a cabinet secretary, a publisher—were people he'd met over the years, although he relates to them by their cars, not what they do. "Claire [Shipman], why'd you get rid of your Saab?" he asked, checking out the new SUV before the new baby. My parents might have been flustered to meet Senator Joe Lieberman. Jimmy just wants to know if his car's dirty.

They brought the ideal presents: microwave popcorn, Turtle Wax, chamois, two CDs with a mix of country songs, a sweatshirt, and enough cans of pretzels, potato chips, and peanuts to give Dr. Atkins a heart attack. Given the week everyone had had, crooning "Happy Birthday" felt like singing "America, the Beautiful." I've never thrown a better party.

At breakfast the next morning, my brother pushed a stack of white envelopes at me and said, "Why don't you take a look at these?" He'd been so poised the night before that I had forgotten he didn't know which card went with which gift, except by making conversation with his guests. As I read each one, he nodded, as if the treacly sentiments of Hallmark had been written just for him.

And in a way they were. Jimmy had given my friends an outlet for their best impulses and most generous sentiments after a singularly devastating event. He had reminded all of us that a tightly knit network of family and friends can buoy you up, if ever you should need it. Those cards are now lined up on the dresser in his bedroom in the house where we grew up. In a way I couldn't imagine when I was trying so hard to get away from it, my parents built a house sturdy enough to shelter us forever.

Mom's Way and My Way

It's hard to know who came out ahead

Where's the girl that once I was? I hear that sentiment frequently from friends approaching midlife. But I never heard it from my mother or the women in the neighborhood, and that wasn't just because they didn't go around paraphrasing Broadway musicals. Unlike baby boomer women, dear old Mom just soldiered on without theorizing too much about it. She didn't look for meaning in a diaper, or make distinctions between quality vs. quantity time. She wished she were not so plump, but it would have never entered her mind to take two hours out of her day to jump around to an exercise video. Rocky marriages were talked about over coffee perked in a Farberware pot. But most women didn't expect to find the moon and stars in another human being, or to perfect the institution of marriage. My parents had the good sense not to *look* for so much from each other that they couldn't *stick* with each other.

When '60s daughters became '80s mothers, though, we looked back and saw our moms as chumps. They didn't have it all, or even enough. We'd run banks, law firms and corporations while raising picture-perfect children who would like us, as well as love us. We'd find husbands who would treat us as equals and not call it baby-sitting when they stayed home to watch the kids. So as Hillary Rodham Clinton and her cohort of leading-edge baby boomers turn 50, it's time to take stock. Women are no longer forced to decide between children and careers (although our salaries are still only about 70% of men's). The kids survive; some thrive, despite the time bind of two parents running from work shift to home shift. We're tired—studies find women sleep fewer hours a week than their husbands—but happy.

Or are we? Fathers today talk a sensitive game, but why do so few take paternity leave? The yuppie dad will put the baby in the Snugli, pick up a steak and light the grill Saturday, then post a piece about it on the Internet.

Many more of us are divorced now. Our kids have their clothes and hearts in separate houses. Middle age remains less forgiving to women than to men—and no women's movement will ever change that. Our dads may have tuned out in their La-Z-Boy recliners, but fewer of them dumped a first family for second wives and second lives. Women may now have the means to leave dead marriages, but few go on to collect trophy husbands or start new families.

Some days I look in the mirror, see my mother looking back and, after the shock passes, give in to it. Why was I so sure I could do it better? As Letty Cottin Pogrebin says in *Getting Over Getting Older,* it's not so much our fading youth we worry about as our fading future. Hillary may have talked wistfully about adopting a child just as Chelsea was planning to leave home, not for the family-values vote, as cynics suggested, but to duplicate her one unambiguous triumph, the most important enterprise of her life.

Every summer my parents rented a cottage at the shore, lugging Melmac plates and jelly glasses, setting up a beach encampment by day, playing cards by night, always with the same families. Part of the pleasure of those vacations came from there being ever more children and grandchildren—and the same spouses. All wasn't sweetness in my family: doors were slammed, tears shed, dreams thwarted. With her energy and brains, my mother might have run General Motors. Instead she ran us, and felt there was no greater happiness. As we race from boardroom to courtroom, soccer practice to PTA, with hardly a moment to savor any of it, it occurs to me she may have been right.

October 20, 1997

Why It Was More Than a Game

So much that is wonderful about being a woman in 1999 is embodied in the U.S. women's soccer team: their sticking with it, their unassuming ways, their heart. The first time my daughter and I saw that captivating Nike commercial, the one in which four teammates—and the dentist's nurse—ask to have two fillings because one of the players has to, we burst out laughing and then blinked back tears.

When I was young in the Dark Ages, I played field hockey with a stick that had duct tape around its base. The nun who coached us would pin up her long blue sleeves, hold an instruction manual in front of her and pray. We sewed numbers on old gym suits to make them look like uniforms, while the guys wore miracle-fabric football jerseys over molded plastic sufficient to protect them in the event of a nuclear attack. I look back to those days and wonder what the dads devoted to Little League and their sons' football were thinking. Didn't they feel slighted that their daughters weren't in on the fun, not to mention getting their characters built as all that teamwork was supposed to do? I was a tomboy, and my father spent countless hours playing catch with me. But he never expected that there would be organized softball for girls and he might have been anxious if there were. There was a part of him that overworried about my infrastructure. Girls have babies, after all! When my brother got a detached retina playing tackle, my parents didn't blanch. One day I came home with a bloody nose, and I thought my father was going to faint.

No one was used to seeing girls throwing, batting, kicking and catapulting themselves around the place. Because girls didn't see other girls doing it, we didn't know what we were missing. Even pros had it hard. Bobby Riggs advised the queen of women's tennis, Billie Jean King, that when playing doubles she should "stand in the alley, and don't hit anything that doesn't hit you first."

But by the time my daughter was in grade school, Title IX had kicked in. I found myself becoming a soccer mom before pollsters knew there was such a thing. Courtney became a Stoddert Stomper, playing on the team at the neighborhood school. There she was in a bright gold mesh-and-Lycra uniform and shoes with cleats. Much of the time, it wasn't pretty; the kids all went where the ball was. But there they were, sprinting, passing, lunging and kicking with abandon, just like the boys. I stood there amazed. A child I hardly recognized as my own hurled herself toward the goal, squealing like a maniac at the satisfaction of competing like the boys, and delighted at how much fun it was to get covered in mud without any consequences. I think it was then that the seeds of putting more of her bones in jeopardy by playing college rugby were planted.

My parents came to the last game of the season—they were quantity-time grandparents and would have come to watch her sleep if I had let them—when the Stompers had almost congealed into a team, intermittently sticking with their positions, occasionally getting a goal. We would have many other touching times together, but it is hard to think of a happier moment than watching my father cheer as his granddaughter went splat into the ground trying to block a goal. If he cringed, he kept it inside. No after-game drink of Gatorade has ever been so sweet.

So thanks to the U.S. women's soccer team, to Hamm and Scurry and Chastain and Foudy. Courtney and I will have two fillings.

July 19, 1999

Hail, Mary and Regina

The Roman Catholic nuns were really on to something

If I ever win an award and get to give an acceptance speech, I will start by thanking first my parents and second Mother Marita Joseph. She and the Immaculate Heart of Mary nuns prepared me to go to college, win frequently at Trivial Pursuit and strive, although mostly fail, to do good rather than simply do well.

Everyone knows the stereotypes: altar boys scared to death of girls, repressed virgins in plaid jumpers, the kids who win spelling bees and know their multiplication tables but not their inner child. But the fact is that the nuns I had for 12 years made the life I came to live possible. And that's not just because Sister Alma Doloros gave me my first copy of *The New Yorker* in sixth grade, which, speaking of overcrowding, was housed in the vestibule of the church. The nuns were single-mindedly devoted to the task of enlarging our minds and saving our souls in the belief that we were all God's children—the doctor's daughter and the plumber's son; the 150 IQ and the dyslexic. Having no families, they spent most of their time with us, pinning up their long sleeves and tucking away their crucifixes to coach a team or set up booths for the school fair. I heard that boys occasionally got their ears boxed, but "the look" was usually enough. The nuns administered the original version of tough love with the utter certainty that they knew what was best for us.

And so they did. A parent rarely sided with a child against a teacher, as often happens now. You prayed your mother wouldn't find out that Sister Mary William had kept you after school because you would be punished again at home. Truth be told, my parents were probably a little afraid of Sister Mary William too.

I assumed that the order in the Catholic schools came from the nuns. In their flowing black robes, they embodied moral authority and seemed to live on spirit alone, since we never saw them eat or drink. Since nuns no longer prevailed in Catholic schools (which were no longer single-sex) by the time my daughter came of age and my first experience with a lay teacher involved spitballs and passing notes, I didn't see the point of Catholic school for Courtney. So I sent Courtney to an all-girls Episcopal school.

But I was wrong. In checking out schools for this piece, I saw a secular version of my own education. At Nativity Academy, test scores are high, dropout rates near zero. Yet only three nuns teach there. The principal credits "continuity of teachers, consistency of rules, and parents signing an agreement to back us up." At Holy Trinity, so redolent of Murphy's Oil Soap it could be my old school, uniformed students raise hands respectfully, say "yes, sir" and "yes, ma'am," and face detention for slight infractions. And like the nuns, teachers teach because they love it.

Time is running short for an Oscar or Pulitzer, so let me say to Mother Marita Joseph, and Sisters Mary William, Justin and Regina, thanks a lot, for my putting "i" before "e" except after "c," and so much more.

September 23, 1996

Clothes Make the Kid

It's Saturday, Labor Day weekend. Sensible people are enjoying the last four-day weekend of the summer. But not me. With only a few shopping days left until school starts, I'm at Bloomingdale's, the young teen section.

You can smell the anxiety in the air. It has something to do with the 10-minute wait for a dressing room, but it also has to do with the free-floating anxiety that attaches to being a parent these days. All around, the equivalent of the gross national product of Chad is being frantically spent on back-to-school wardrobes. Historian and former Librarian of Congress Daniel Boorstin has said that this decade will be remembered as one in which people formed themselves into communities not by what they believe, but by what they own. Ronald Reagan's "Morning in America" means getting to Neiman Marcus when the doors open at 10 a.m.

Many baby boomer parents postponed childbirth until their income level reached the upper brackets and they'd bought a houseful of consumer durables. With enough disposable income, birth is another buying opportunity, a whole new human being to be consumed for. Child psychologist Neil Bernstein says baby-boomer parents equate success with what they can buy. "You've put together the perfect life, you want a perfect child. The easiest way to create that illusion is with things." He also sees a new anxiety among today's parents, the first generation to sense that their children might not do as well as the generation before. "The pressure is much greater now than during the last baby boom. The world was expanding in the '50s. Now the baby boomers see shrinking possibilities—that it is going to be a lot harder for their kids. It's not just keeping up with the Joneses, it's getting ahead of the Joneses' kids."

To that end, a couple can spend $60,000 in the first two years of a baby's life. At the junior high school level, there are parents who admit—in school meetings and on national television—to spending as much as $4,000 a year for kids' clothes. Spend a few hours shopping and you will see how.

Over at the watch boutique, novel and expensive ways of keeping time are proliferating faster than new strains of Adidas. There are watch faces as big as a chocolate chip cookie and ones as tiny as a nickel; there are clip-on watches and ones that attach to a sock. All make a fashion statement; none tell the time. One boy has just bought four different watches. He can be late for class in all four time zones.

How have we come to the point where spending $100 on a kid's sweater is thinkable? The younger generation's need to conform and peer pressure have always been factors—no one wants his child to be the one sitting alone over a steam-table hamburger because he dresses like a dork. But psychologists and school officials see a new factor at play: parents themselves. In the old days parents acted as a countervailing force against children's acquisitiveness. A parent could place a limit at one pair of penny loafers, muttering all the while about the importance of sturdy arches, and could count on other parents to mutter the same thing. Now what you can count on is kids showing up with an entire wardrobe of pricey sneakers. Restraint has disappeared along with the refrain that kept the universe intact: "I don't care what Caroline is buying, I'm your mother and I say one pair of shoes is enough."

Manipulation, says Bernstein, is one product of materialism. "We didn't have everything handed to us and we didn't even know to ask for elite things. Now a 13-year-old will say to a parent, 'Don't lay a guilt trip on me about buying a $100 sweater when you own a Mercedes.' " Susan Blumenthal, M.D., a psychiatrist at the National Institute of Mental Health, calls this the "precociously sophisticated stage, when a child who has been fulfilling the status needs of his parents comes to feel entitled to whatever he wants." Even if parents see this for what it is, they are often not equipped to deal with it. "These parents are used to spoiling their kids," says Blumenthal. "Both frequently work and they don't want what little time they have to be filled with conflict—so they give in."

Prof. Carol Seefeld of the University of Maryland's Institute for Child Study sees a kind of parent inflation, too many acquisitive adults chasing too few legs-up for their children, the legs-up all being superficial.

Indeed, it's parents, not adolescent pressure, bidding up the ante on infant accouterments. Consider strollers, all hundred imported varieties of them. Among the most popular status items for newborns is an Aprica canopied convertible with rollbar, soft leather interior and steel-belted radials, roomy enough to command two lanes in your gourmet grocery. It costs close to $400. With dealer incentives, and 1.9% APR financing, you can pay it off before the bill for the first pair of Topsiders rolls in.

Across the aisle in Bloomingdale's infant section, parents are scooping up the accouterments of the "Bloomie's Baby." Now, a Bloomie's Baby is going to run you a lot more than, say, a Sears Baby, what with the Naf-Naf coverall, the Absorba undershirt, the Dior booties, the Petit Bateau pajamas and the Je Suis sleepsack ($50) for that Cartesian youngster born pondering dualism. The Bloomie's Baby does not appear to be made-in-the-USA. Bloomingdale's may be the only store that needs its own foreign policy.

But that's child's play compared to the hours and money invested in the wardrobe once the baby enters the fast lane in nursery school. Your little tyke can't possibly network with the right people at pre-K if he's wearing a poly-cotton blend from J. C. Penney. Bernstein points out that the whole school exercise—the fear that if your child doesn't get into the right prekindergarten he will never get into Harvard and end up in a gutter some-where—plays a big part in parent spending.

The whole category has become so lucrative that a raft of designers has begun cutting kids' clothes—Ralph Lauren, Gloria Vanderbilt, Calvin Klein, Georges Marciano (Guess), Izod, Dior and Giorgio Armani—and they are using the same success-and-sex hype in the child market that they use for adults. Brooke Shields in her Calvin Klein seems mildly jaded to today's bored and boring kids advertising Jordache jeans on prime-time television. Upscale publications like *Vanity Fair* and *The New York Times Sunday Magazine* feature page after page of pouty, world-weary children leering at the camera in enough layers of designer-wear to clothe a family of four in a temperate Third World clime. Sophistication, not innocence, sells. In the Georges Marciano Guess ads, the leering kid models seem to be asking for it.

Neither the Old Child, who would spit up mashed carrots on that blazer no matter how much it cost, or the Old Parent, who thought a little permanent-press never hurt anybody, is much in evidence in glossy ads.

Even so, there may be a limit. Perhaps with the $200 Giorgio Armani sweater for a 6-year-old, we have reached an intermediate top, a pause in the Shopping Wars where nostalgia for a bygone era will kick in. Do we really want a generation of children who will never hearken to the words "Attention Kmart shoppers," or experience vinegar in large bottles without raspberries? As adults, we can at least remember a day when liver had a life of its own outside pâté.

I wish I could go against the culture, pick up a wardrobe for Courtney at

Kmart and say the hell with it. I believe Harvard child-development expert Dr. T. Berry Brazelton when he warns parents against giving children too much because soon, no matter how often you tell them they are privileged, and no matter how much footage of starving Ethiopian children you show them on the nightly news, they will come to feel entitled. And therein lies a generation of spoiled brats with fallen arches. But it's hard enough to send a child off to a new school without making her be the Gandhi of junior high. I may rant about how things have gone too far, but can I ask her to do it? Having a child makes you do things you never thought possible; your life pre-child is like the world beyond the Hudson in the Saul Steinberg New York poster. It hardly exists anymore.

So until the day when parents adopt a mutual non-aggression pact—I won't let my kid do it if you won't let your kid do it—I head back to the mall. We buy some things, not as much as most kids, but more than enough. We hover in the lowest three figures you can hover in, but that's without new shoes or socks.

October 4, 1987

Why I Said No

Time columnist Margaret Carlson tells why she, as a parent, was strict about marijuana

Like most yuppie parents, I read Dr. Spock for crucial information, like what to do about projectile vomiting and earaches. But unlike many of my contemporaries, I ignored him on discipline. As a captive of the permissive '60s, he could be of no help to baby boomers, already hopelessly ambivalent about authority. Better to rely on the example of my own parents, who believed their children's happiness in the future was dependent on their being sharply disciplined in the present.

If you adhere to that philosophy during the terrible twos, it doesn't surprise your kids if you stick with it through the ticklish questions of sex, drugs and alcohol. It's at these times that children are uppity enough to ask, and some parents are foolish enough to reveal, what they did as adolescents. This is a big mistake in the drug wars. I asked myself: "Did hypocrisy matter when Courtney was little?" Absolutely not. Without any reference to my own early years of experimenting with electricity, I insisted that she not stick her curious fingers into electric sockets. Don't grab

Johnny's sand bucket, I would tell her, although I'm sure I was a poacher at the beach. Don't eat with your fingers, I instructed. Well, I still do that.

When my daughter started asking what I did and when I did it as we proceeded to the dicey teenage years, I thought, O.K., honesty is the best policy. Well, what's the second-best policy? Omission, because kids are so much better off not knowing everything about you. Authority flows more easily when there is some mystery about who you were as a child, as opposed to who you are as the older and wiser parent they now know.

It's so tempting to give up that distance prematurely, because, well, there is so little distance after you put the Map of the States puzzle together, say, a million times. I watched many a soccer game whose rules I only dimly grasped, and was a favorite car-pool mom without ever getting chummy. When your offspring is crossing over from the things of a child to the things of an adult, it's easy to speed the process and encourage openness. But I ruled out exchanging any confidences in the crossover areas of drugs, drink and sex, except for advising there should be none of the latter until true intimacy attaches, or at age 25, whichever comes later.

Yes, I knew Courtney wanted to hang with the kids who were most likely to be fast-tracking every experience. She wanted to do what everyone else was doing, to which a parent can sometimes only say, "No, you can't," and to the follow-up "Why not?," "Because I'm your mother, and I say so." It might not stop her, but it slowed her down. I didn't go the confession route, either. If you let them confess and you don't put them under house arrest, you are admitting your own waning authority. Kids don't want to know you have limited options to track and punish them before they are ready to run their own lives.

I revealed expurgated versions of my life, about term papers handed in late and unchaperoned parties, enough so that she wouldn't completely discount me as a dork sitting alone every Saturday night. We made it through adolescence without disaster and have entered a period when the perils of parenting have given way to the joys of it. And I've yet to tell her what I really did during the '70s. My own mother was fond of sighing deeply and saying, to explain anything I didn't like, "You'll understand when you have a child of your own." On the day she first heard me say to Courtney, "Because I'm your mother, that's why," she was as happy as a mother can be.

Much later, because we had waited, we became friends.

December 9, 1996

Why I Said Yes

Her daughter, Courtney, explains that she did get the message but smoked anyway

BY COURTNEY CARLSON

As a recent college graduate, I'm pretty certain my next job will not require Senate confirmation. But because I live in a world where the depth of a breath is the difference between the President and the guy who asks, "You want fries with that?" this confession makes me nervous. Mom, Dad, you loved me, you paid attention to me, and you told me not to smoke marijuana—but I did anyway. I wasn't experimenting. I was taking deep gulps and inhaling.

My mother's generation says, "It was the '70s," as if sex, drugs and rock 'n' roll were O.K. before the Surgeon General got involved. But I was born in the '70s and inhaled in the '90s. By then, I knew the implications and the potential repercussions. I heard Nancy Reagan tell me to "just say no," but I eagerly said yes. Unlike people of my parents' generation, I can't blame my experimentation on a decade.

Now, my mom is no dummy. She spent her evenings at home, where "quality time" was making homemade bread and propaganda, indoctrinating me about the dangers of everything that sounded like fun. The conversations evolved from Cheerios are better for you than Froot Loops to no sex before marriage, no drinking to excess and certainly no drugs. I was the last of my friends to endure a midnight curfew; I always had to be home for dinner; and if I was going out, I had to leave a phone number.

A lot of these messages sank in. Cheerios is my breakfast food of choice. I know that drinking too much gives me a hangover and that sleep before midnight is the most valuable kind. Yet under my parents' watchful eyes, I still managed to find an illegal drug more than once by the time I was a senior in high school. I had a sense of adventure, and I certainly didn't want to be in the library all the time. I sought out others who felt the same way. And in my age of invincibility, none of the tragic stories seemed like they could happen to me.

My parents' warnings did make a difference. Parents who talked about their flower-child days and getting wasted at Woodstock seemed to give tacit consent by fondly relating the experience. They didn't want to be hypocrites, and their children tended to go further because they felt less guilt. They were the kids who took bong hits instead of seminars.

By contrast, guilt nipped my fun right in the bud. Yes, I went on to disobey my mother, but only so much. I felt O.K. in doing so because on most other fronts, I went along with her. "Thou shalt not smoke pot" is not the 11th Commandment, I rationalized. Armed with that perspective and the sound of my mother's voice in my head, I could tinker with the rules and push the boundaries without being afraid I would cross them. So, Mom, it was your fault after all.

But despite what politicians say, marijuana was not my gateway to heroin and a crack pipe. I have not used other drugs, and I don't plan to. Aside from the occasional roll through a stop sign, I am a law-abiding citizen. As I write these words, I have this sense of shame that makes me hope that my first-grade teacher and my best friend's parents don't read this issue of *TIME*. They still think I'm a good kid. Fortunately, my mother didn't know about my behavior until I had more or less turned out all right.

As a California voter, I cast a ballot to legalize marijuana for medical use. So perhaps by the time I'm ready for Senate confirmation, the nonsense about who did and who didn't will be over.

December 9, 1996

A Dinner @ Margaret's

Having 30 for supper? Let the Internet stock your pantry (just don't count on having goose)

What a delicious assignment: Invite 12 people to dinner at my Washington house, come up with any menu I want, hire someone to serve and clean up, and charge the whole feast to the company. I could hear the Champagne corks popping.

There were a few hitches. Everything had to come from the Internet, there could be no trips to the grocery store, and I would have to write about it. There's no such thing as a free dinner.

Immediately, I e-mailed an invitation to our local Internet hero, America Online CEO Steve Case. A reply came by phone: Would we mind faxing the information?

Not at all, but if Mr. You've Got Mail regresses to old tech, can e-commerce really be that easy? With Case on board, and *TIME*'s "Person of the Year" issue to dangle before guests, I pursued a Noah's Ark theory of who else to invite: two members of Congress, two teachers, two candlestick makers. I warned everyone they would be *TIME*'s guinea pigs. But when you're having Alan Greenspan to dinner, you realize the repercussions of a dyspeptic entree. Who wants to serve the meal so bad that it ends the longest economic expansion in peacetime history?

With the party set for Sunday night, the plan was to give myself a week to order, always starting online but resorting to 800 numbers in a pinch, to find a middle ground between ordering the totally exotic (alligator meat) and the reliably prosaic (ham) and default to vendors in California when in doubt, figuring those geeks in Silicon Valley surely have figured out how to stuff a turkey through a modem.

First things first: I needed a new salt shaker (more than one coffee drinker had got a nasty surprise spooning salt out of the makeshift sugar bowl I keep it in) and a tablecloth that actually fit. I ordered both from Williams-Sonoma. This is where I first felt screen rage, a risk at many sites. This arises after you've just filled in every last scrap of personal data, except your shoe size and SAT scores, and the screen freezes on you. Don't think that Mr. Internet has saved the information you've already provided. (If God is a woman, then the Web is a man, silent and indifferent, with a short attention span.) You have to start over. And over.

Getting great coffee was a comparative breeze. I went directly to the sources—a Hawaiian plantation for Kona and bluemountaincoffee.com for Jamaica's Blue Mountain beans. This is also when I became a Coffee Bore. At most sites it's easier to get in than to get out, since Webmasters tend to fill all the space available, which online is infinite. Did you know that Kona beans thrive in the dark volcanic soil, sunny mornings and cloudy afternoons of Hawaii? I didn't either, but now I've brought it up at three parties. I've turned into the kind of person I used to avoid.

For real food I thought holiday season and went hunting for a goose. At goose.com I found I could acquire a rifle for the purpose—it's an outdoors store. This is when I fell in love with Jeeves, the fictional British butler who helped Bertie Wooster put his pants on one leg at a time, reincarnated in cyberspace as a cheerful search engine that sorts through all the others at AskJeeves. As in life, you need a friend of whom you can ask anything: What is love? What's the GDP of Monaco? Where can I buy a goose? The easily distracted might choose to go elsewhere, for there are no nonstop flights at AskJeeves. The whimsical Jeeves served up Mother Goose, along with the chance to hear one (a nasal honk right out of your laptop) and a recipe (Remove stray pinfeathers. Place orange rind and celery leaves under the loosened skin. Truss). That was enough goose for me.

The encyclopedic Jeeves brought me to goose liver, which led me to foie gras, which took me finally to France Gourmet Traditions, a Parisian grocer that could get the foie gras to me on time—if I were in the Paris bureau. At its site a Strasbourg charcuterie posted this bad news: "Cannot at this time ship. USDA does not return our calls." Funny, I have that very same problem with government agencies.

A few more clicks, and I found the same pâté at GreatFood.com, a luxurious site with Hollywood-studio visuals. You can't touch, smell or squeeze the merchandise on the Web, so pictures, however doctored, are essential. It was at GreatFood that I met temptation in the form of dinner for 24 at the click of a mouse. But the meat worked out to about $40 a pound and . . . it would have been wrong.

GreatFood had a link to Omaha Steaks, which had a scrumptious picture of beef Wellington—very festive, very holiday, very Savoy Hotel—with a bonus gift of six 4-oz. sirloins. Maybe there is such a thing as a free dinner, after all.

I went to Napa Valley at the eponymous Wine.com (what luck to nail down that name), proved I was 21 and ordered better wine than I'd ever served. Since I was already in California anyway, I called up Patisserie Lambert where I'd eaten in real time—I mean, real life. It's remarkably cybersophisticated, with visuals so good you could almost smell the madeleines. And there it was, the cake of my dreams, Chocolate Fantasia, three layers of chocolate caramel mousse cake with ladyfinger biscuits soaked in espresso. A dramatic dessert can redeem many a main-course sin, so I went for it. But Lambert quickly replied that a three-tiered cake was too dicey to ship. Then send the layers separately, I said. Some assembly required? No problem. Then came word that this was actually a wedding cake. Hey, pal, no problem. I'll have someone get married. One of these government officials will preside—captain of the ship, quick ceremony, that type of thing. Just send the cake.

There is no grocery website that delivers to my zip code, so fresh vegetables are hard to come by—thank goodness. I find the very sight of raw broccoli and cauliflower on a buffet table dispiriting. I don't go to parties looking to balance my diet with the four major food groups or to consume the recommended daily allowance of fiber. For my own soiree, I hit Cajun Joey's Specialty Foods, where sugar is the fifth major food group. Joey hasn't met a vegetable that can't be mashed, pureed, creamed or souffléed—Beechnut meets Le Cirque. The carrots, corn, spinach and artichokes looked great and ended up tasting like candy. I was thrilled.

I can't pinpoint just when the task of foraging for food on the Web finally began to overwhelm me. It might have been when I found out that because of liquor laws in Washington, the wine would take at least 10 days for delivery. But wait . . . fast delivery was possible to West Virginia. The political columnist in me wanted to know why: the power of Senator Robert Byrd? Some anomaly in the jurisdiction of the Bureau of Alcohol, Tobacco and

Firearms? But the Martha Stewart in me just wanted the wine. A round trip to West Virginia would take more time than I had left, yet I needed a case of Merlot to ensure that my guests were slightly desensitized to the cellophane and cardboard from which their meal had so recently been liberated. I needed a way around the rules. What if I could find a local store with a website but faxed the order? My seven years covering the Clintons were coming in handy. How do I get a case of wine to my doorstep by Saturday? Don't ask, don't tell.

The trouble didn't necessarily end with delivery. When I sampled the beef Wellington, although remarkably juicy and delicious, I realized it wasn't going to slice cleanly into pieces suitable for lap dining (fearful everyone would be busy during Washington's party-gridlock season, I had let the guest list swell to an SRO crowd of 30). I was worried enough to e-mail my editors in New York City: How about a backup ham, that mainstay of Irish funerals? "Boring," they replied.

But not as boring as going hungry. Dinner by committee was my worst idea yet; by a committee composed of editors, deadly. Through Jeeves, I reached the Smithfield Collection and despite the pretentious name for a company that slaughters pigs, I got delivery of a crusty, honey-soaked ham in an ice chest left under the porch, per my instructions, in one day's time.

At this point, I realized I needed a real-life Jeeves. Who better to serve food with snootiness sufficient to obscure its Internet provenance than an English butler? Ironically, my virtual Jeeves couldn't produce a human one. He did tell me of a school in the Netherlands where I could "learn the true art of butling." Smarty pants. I located a domestic agency in Beverly Hills on my own, but its best price for a footman in a morning coat was $500, minimum. In a panic, I called the caterer *TIME* uses, which has an online site. A waiter from an online site would come. Was this breaking the rules? Let's just say there's no controlling legal authority.

There are many outlets for flowers, but it is hard to get just what you want—pale peach, but please, no pink—if your screen, like mine, bleaches the colors. The good news is that the roses I ordered arrived fresh and on time. The bad news is their color roughly matched that of the ham.

On Saturday, calling frantically for items that hadn't arrived, I lived out the sorry fact of modern life that at any given moment one in five Americans is on hold for the next available customer representative with the added indignity of having to endure endless rounds of "Jingle Bell Rock." Not to single out Williams-Sonoma—because it happens just about everywhere—but when you get your stuff depends on what a company's definition of "submit now" is. You submit, they process, and depending on the distributor, or the manufacturer, the popularity of your item, or who's out with the flu that day, you will get it overnight—or in a week. The customer service representative at Williams-Sonoma sent me an apron and refunded my shipping costs. I guess there's such a thing as a free apron.

Since the tablecloth would come too late for the party, I sponge-ironed the creases out of my old one until it almost fit. The foie gras, sourdough and olive Pugliese breads from San Francisco did not arrive until Tuesday. I became a culinary Luddite, baking two dozen rolls. On the day of the dinner, the waiter called in sick at 4 p.m. Well, that's why God made daughters—and editors visiting from Manhattan who know their way around a corkscrew.

Dinner and a good time were had by all, confirming my belief that people go to restaurants for good food and to friends' houses for good company. There were lots of leftovers (I had e-mailed a Maryland caterer and got a shrimp appetizer and a spare filet). And the ham was the size of an aircraft carrier. The morning after, I staggered to my desk and clicked my way to D.C. Central Kitchen, which recycles food to homeless shelters. A team came right away and wiped out all traces of My Cyberdinner.

My effort cost more than $2,000. That's not exactly a value meal, due partly to the fact that it's not the food but the shipping that kills you. But when I read that during the week I was dining à la Web, Internet users spent more than double what had been spent the preceding week, I felt pleased that in this little piece of Web history, I had played a part. Next time I have people over, I'm likely to revert to my old ways. I could have crawled to Safeway and back in the time it took to make an Internet dinner. But it was nice meeting Jeeves, even though he didn't work out in the end, and getting my Mac to honk.

All in all, a virtual success.

December 27, 1999

The Child Bride

Getting married means growing up. Planning the wedding means learning to be 16 again

BY COURTNEY CARLSON

For the past eight months I have ceased to be my parents' daughter. I am known simply as the bride. My new title brings with it some interesting contradictions. Having made a major decision about the course of the rest of my life, I am an adult, and yet this process catapults me back to childhood. After a good five years of being on my own, I find that I have to plead my case with my parents about even the smallest of details. Who knew each of my parents and I would have a strong opinion about which musical instrument should be playing during the procession? Me, trumpet; Mom, flute; Dad, violin.

I am thrown back to the days of negotiating for a later curfew when my mother pronounces that my groom, David, and I should make an early grand exit from the wedding. We suggest we just might want to stay out late at our wedding and have fun with our friends. Six months ago my mother and I rehashed a seventh-grade Guess jeans drama when I assured her that all brides are wearing strapless dresses and it is not inappropriate. I actually seem to be getting worse at this. The outcomes? In 1986, age 12, yes to the jeans. In 2001, age 26, no to the strapless dress. As the only child of divorced parents, I have always dreaded my parents' being in the same room, not because they fight but because I have learned to deal with them independently, and I prefer the simplicity of that arrangement. I like them to keep their distance. Well, so much for that. The two of them are now as thick as thieves, e-mailing guest lists, announcements, sample menus, rendering useless my usual role as go-between. I'm a little confused. Are they getting friendly for the sake of their child, or have they grown up too?

The invitation list, to no one's surprise, has been the greatest source of difficulty. I wanted a small wedding, and so did everyone else—in theory. But when you divide a small list into six portions, as we did, the parcels become unbearably tiny. David and I each had a list, and then the two of us had a sublist of mutual friends each felt should be included in the other's count. My separate parents each had a separate list. Then, in the greatest irony of the wedding, familial functionality turned out to be a detriment for David's happily married parents, because they only got one list between them.

There is a theory that no wedding is complete without one massive family fight, preferably one that exhumes old slights, hurts and differences. That gives us something to strive for in the next two weeks. In the meantime, my plan is to keep everyone busy. I deployed my dad to review photographers and find chamber music. My mom is arranging flowers and baking bread for the reception. I am overseeing the food, as I look forward, after five months of austerity, to finally being able to eat once I get the dress on. David, relieved that I have stopped cutting his list, is writing the ceremony. So far, the scheme is working, giving me the odd sensation that as the bride I've actually found a footing somewhere between self-absorbed teenager and budding adult. I have also learned that the purpose of weddings, aside from the obvious one, is to reconnect you with the family you have and prepare you for the one you hope to produce yourself.

April 30, 2001

Why Quayle Has Half a Point

When last we saw Baby Brown's father, it was shortly after conception and well before birth. He's off now saving the rain forest, having opted out of Lamaze class and changing diapers. He may come back, but the show's premise is built around the notion that he won't; a woman who has made it in a man's world without a man can make it as a parent without one as well. The lack of a dad is not an accident but a running joke. For the successful, glamorous woman who has everything: Now, live from Hollywood, your very own baby. Father optional.

Dan Quayle weighed in on the right side of a touchy issue. There is nothing new about having babies without getting married. What's new is society's attitude, which has gone from punishing it, to tolerating it, to celebrating it. Ah, Murphy Brown, she is too darn busy and successful to have a baby the old-fashioned way, and anyhow, men are jerks. This is not about mothers who sadly find themselves doing it alone. In any event, with her high income, Brown seems a poor vehicle for examining that dilemma.

Yet she has more in common with the inner-city teenager than we might think. The 14-year-old gets pregnant as a way to give her life meaning. Murphy Brown was looking for meaning as well and a tiny version of her nearly perfect self filled the bill. Among other things, being a Murphy Mom means having postponed childbirth until your salary has reached the upper brackets and you have sufficient disposable income to employ a full-time muralist and buy enough Scandinavian furniture to induce existential dread.

But even at the upper end, where the career track is fast and the dress code is for success, there can come the nagging feeling that this might not be all there is. By then, of course, the flexibility to tolerate a big lug leaving his dirty socks on the floor—and the luxury of having time to find the big lug—are in short supply. It's a tiny leap for those accustomed to satisfying every whim to see a baby as one more choice. It is a way to turn a lifestyle into a life in nine months.

Babies also fit into the new stay-at-home. Shopping for the layette has replaced comparing a $400 Gaggia cappuccino maker to the Braun. People who own fish poachers now wonder what in the world they were thinking of when they can consume practical items, like English prams and French nappies. Cloning oneself opens up a whole new buying opportunity.

But single pregnancy (as opposed to those households where the father remains active in the child's life) is not necessarily glamorous for the child, even at the upper-economic end. Has anyone ever met a child happy not to know who his father is? In the projects, the boy with a father is king. In the wider world, children may end up being moral relativists, but in their formative years, they adhere to a code of conduct more traditional than the decor at Williamsburg, Va. Single pregnancy commingles the worst of the Me decade—let's have more of Me—with extreme feminism—let's do away with men.

It's completely unfair that men have such an edge in childbearing, able to marry women 60 years their junior and reproduce themselves into dotage. Unfortunately, there is no legislation to correct this injustice.

But Quayle was only half right in denouncing single motherhood if he wants to make criminals of those single women who find themselves pregnant but unprepared and unsuited to be mothers. Having both a mother and a father is an ideal to strive for. Shouldn't abortion be available when that can't be the case? Coming into the world with one parent is a handicap, no matter how mature and moneyed the mother may be, or how young and poor. Imagine if men decided that motherhood was equally expendable. Sated with their corner offices and home gyms, guys of a certain age could go around paying women to have babies for them. The howl of feminists over such selfish, macho pigs could tie up talk-radio for years. Fatherhood may take moments, motherhood nine months, but doing it right takes the lifelong commitment of both parents. Just because fatherhood can be reduced to 20 seconds, or dispensed with altogether by tapping into Nobel Prize winner sperm banks, does not mean it *should* be.

Mothers, single and otherwise, are heroic in the ways, large and small, that they make up to their children for absent, negligent or destructive fathers. Children can thrive in many circumstances. But there is a danger in the current attitude that plays down the deficit with which a child enters the world with half a family and that places a woman's self-fulfillment first. Hard as it is to hear the biological clock ticking and not be able to do anything about it, gratifying the yearning to have a child is not the same as

satisfying the other aspects of having it all. Some yearnings in life go unful-
filled. What is socially and emotionally acceptable to a woman may not be
so to a child purposefully brought into the world with a hole at the center of
his life where a father would be.

June 1, 1992

Here's a Precious Moment, Kid

What helps teens the most? A federal study reveals a commonsense truth

On Wednesday, all of Washington woke up to an above-the-fold banner
headline in the *Post* blaring the news LOVE CONQUERS WHAT AILS TEENS.
Gee, all this time I thought it was Guess jeans and $140 Air Jordans. What
kind of love are we talking about? Parental, rock-star, tough or backseat?

When I found out it was the kind a mother can give, I thought it was
news after all. How sweet, how wholesome, and what a relief. There were
times when my love for my own particular teenager seemed capable of cur-
ing very little, much less whatever ailed her. For one three-month period,
she so preferred the company of her best friend's family that I feared they'd
claim her as a dependent on their income tax return.

The survey, the first part of a long-running, $25 million study, inter-
viewed 20,000 teenagers. It found that kids who have a strong sense of connection to their parents were less likely to be violent or indulge in drugs,
alcohol, tobacco or early sex. The opus, paid for by 18 federal agencies,
probably got the attention it did because it offers so much comfort to parents whose little Mary doesn't make a move without calling her pal Molly,
while treating Mom like a potted plant. Peer pressure isn't as pressing as I
thought. "The power and the importance of parents continue to persist,
even into late adolescence," says University of Minnesota professor
Michael Resnick, the lead author of the survey.

A reassuring finding: although your child may seem to ignore you, she is
living off the remnants of the bond built during the years before getting her
ears pierced was the most important thing in her life. The study, published
last week in the *Journal of the American Medical Association,* is a little fuzzy
when it comes to just what builds that magic bond, saying it's neither time
nor activities but simply the intensity of the involvement. "It's more than
the physical presence of parents, the number of hours a day they're in the
home. It's their emotional availability," says Resnick.

Uh-oh. Are we spending $25 million to recycle the old saw about quality time, the one that says to the parent trying to make partner at the law firm, "Don't worry if you spend more time with your clients than with your child. Just bear down like a freight train during those precious moments you're actually there"? And they say our tax dollars are wasted.

Without putting an hour figure on it, the survey singles out mealtimes as important, which can eat up hours if you do it right. I had to give up on breakfast, which was consumed, if at all, in the car out of a can. Dinner was a battle, but I won. Many of Courtney's friends were allowed to graze like hunter-gatherers at mealtime, with full carry-out privileges and access to expense-account restaurants that had their parents' credit card on file. I was so depressed by the thought of kids' eating out of a carton, like Woody Allen, or high off the hog, like a lobbyist, that I insisted that mine eat at home, even when I was heating up Stouffer's.

The survey cites the fact that parents spend 10 to 12 hours less per week at home than moms and dads did in 1960. Perhaps the next phase of the study will look at carpooling as the underrated source of both quality and quantity time that it is. It yields the absolute best inside information for the parent who wants to keep up with what's going on but can't pry the information out in any other setting. In a car you might as well be a cabdriver, unfamiliar with English, for all the kids will notice you. They're irrepressible, so intent on conducting their business they convince themselves you aren't there. Carpooling at night, though the leading cause of teenage sulking, is the very best type. Pick up the kids after movies, parties or ball games, and you're an eyewitness to history. You know who's drinking, who's smoking, who's about to peel off from the group and get pregnant. With the early-warning system of late-night driving, you have the chance to go on high alert when the occasion warrants. Of course, you have to give up some of your own social life and have a thick hide for this. My own teenager wondered loudly, Why couldn't she take a taxi? Why couldn't she get a ride with the older kids? Why couldn't I get lost for a few years?

I didn't get lost, and neither did she. Love does conquer an awful lot. But it's inescapable that love takes time. The kids in the survey might be better off if the government gave their parents $25 million to buy back those lost 12 hours.

September 22, 1997

What's Love Got to Do with It?

Wellesley's unease over wife and mother Barbara Bush renews the
debate about women's divided loyalties

How can women pick on Barbara Bush? If anything, the feminist police
should give her an award for resisting pressure from every side to slim
down, work out, dye her hair, hide her wrinkles or wear clothes no grandchild would dare drool on. Instead the First Lady must be feeling a little
like Henry Kissinger, who attracted protests nearly every time he was invited to a college campus.

But it's not the secret bombing of Cambodia that has a quarter of the
senior class at Wellesley College objecting to the First Lady as speaker at
this year's graduation. It is simply that she is married to George Bush and
has no career of her own. "To honor Barbara Bush as a commencement
speaker is to honor a woman who has gained recognition through the
achievements of her husband, which contradicts what we have been taught
over the past four years," the students wrote in their petition.

Being First Lady may be an automatic disqualification at an all-women's
college where graduates aspire to be President, not a President's wife; to
run the country, not the house; and where previous speakers have included
Shirley Chisholm, Gloria Steinem and Dukakis campaign manager Susan
Estrich. Barbara Bush wasn't Wellesley's first choice this year; that honor
went to Alice Walker, black author, single mother and Pulitzer Prize winner, who declined. To women in cap and gown who have worked hard to be
able to make it on their own, having a wife and mother on the podium may
feel too diminishing, like getting on *Nightline* and then having to wave to
your mom.

What the protest over Bush really displays is not disrespect but uncer-
tainty. Women, after all, have always known they could be mothers. It is the
opportunity to have full-strength, male-like careers that is relatively new
and, therefore, tenuous. What makes it frightening is the assumption that
they can play both roles well. Bush has acknowledged that being a woman
was easier in her day. In a speech last year at Smith—the school she
dropped out of in 1944 at 19 to marry George Bush—she told the students,
"You have so many options that it must be difficult . . . women are often
expected—especially by themselves—to be all things to all people, and to
be perfect in every role."

Therein lies the rub. Women know that the hard-won choice to work has
somehow turned into an imperative to do so, but without the support at
home that makes it feasible. The professional classes paper over the short-

fall by hiring a small army of parental surrogates, by accepting a reduced idea of the emotional needs of family life and by lobbying for flextime and expanded day care. But no act of Congress will ever allow a parent to be in two places at once.

Despite two decades of feminist victories, only women seem to feel the emotional schizophrenia that comes with having children. The fact that "working father" and "daddy track" have not worked their way into the language is instructive, if not disconcerting. So is the survey that shows that wives put in an extra month of work at home each year, time their male counterparts can spend at their desks or, unfairer still, sleeping. If a woman has a fulfilling career, she still yearns for more time with her child. If she stays home, she is bound to wish for some of the excitement and perks that come with a job.

On commencement day, few college graduates want to be reminded of the dilemma; at 22, motherhood is easy to devalue. The rush that comes from closing a million-dollar deal, getting the corner office or winning the respect of your colleagues has an immediate appeal that mountains of diapers and 12 years of PTA do not. Many women have come to believe that the only jobs worth pursuing are paid and the only accomplishments worth having are ones that enhance a resume.

Bush may be the perfect antidote to this culture, which economist Sylvia Hewlett, author of *A Lesser Life*, says has "taught young women to almost despise the nurturing role." Indeed, now that Barbara Bush is on her own, she is holding her own. Rather than hype fashion designers or choose new White House china, Bush spends her days drawing attention to the homeless, AIDS patients, the poor and those whose lives have been so impoverished they never learned to read. For Wellesley students, Bush has all sorts of wisdom about what half of their lives will be—of the victories of motherhood, small and evanescent, which occur largely behind closed doors with results apparent in the next decade, not the next deal. It is a profession in which almost nothing happens day by day but everything is won or lost over time. Important stuff for these women who, if they are lucky, will graduate to more than a paycheck.

May 7, 1990

Does He or Doesn't He?

Have husbands really evolved from hunters and gatherers into nurturers and helpmates? I don't think so. A yuppie dad I know puts Junior in the car seat, hits the gourmet market, lights the grill and then boasts of fixing dinner and tending baby. Poke Superdad in the middle of the night and quiz him on his kids' shoe sizes, their birthday-party preferences or Sara's science-fair entry. Tops, he nails two out of three.

It's women who still expend the psychic energy that keeps a household going (Is Dave & Buster's right for Ethan's birthday? Christmas here or at my sister's?). As for chores, let's define the term. A chore is the thing that has to be done right now or all hell breaks loose. A chore is putting in an extra load of laundry or cleaning up after the kids before you get rec-room Pompeii. It's not installing an antique doorknob, planting tomatoes or grilling salmon for company. That's fun. Hobbies, surfing the Web, working out, tinkering with the sound system are not housework simply because they're done at home.

Author Arlie Hochschild, who visited 50 families over several years, wrote in *Second Shift* that sleep-deprived women work an extra month at home each year. More recently, University of Maryland sociologist John Robinson found that mothers still spend about four times as much time with children as fathers do. Psychologist Carin Rubenstein, author of *The Sacrificial Mother,* found that twice as many moms as dads are involved at school. Soccer moms make up a third of soccer coaches. When the real crunch comes, 83% of mothers stay home with a sick child, compared with 22% of fathers.

It may be ever thus. Women realize that they have five decades to make law partner but only two to raise a child. A mother's triumph may seem small, occurring in the kitchen over strained peas, with the results apparent not in the next quarter but the next generation.

So we married someone whose nose can discern the vintage of a Merlot but can't smell a dirty diaper when it's right in front of him. It's easier to change the diaper than to argue over who changed the last one. So we're a little more tired, and men are pulling a fast one on these gullible pollsters. In the end, we're the ones who just might turn out to have it all.

April 27, 1998

Underwear Update

It looks to me as if we are headed for economic hard times, and that's not based on reading Ravi Batra or keeping track of M-1. It's a close reading of the country's lifestyle reporters, all breathlessly pursuing stories on how to remain stylishly acquisitive without any money. Until a few weeks ago, these same reporters were painstakingly comparing the merits of sushi-making machines and Biedermeier chairs. The current articles run to making a casserole look like a soufflé, organ meats palatable, and a little bit seem like a lot. I'm reminded of the articles my mother used to clip from *Family Circle* on how to disguise a cut-up fryer by pouring a can of mushroom soup over it, adding a cup of sherry and serving the result on your best wedding china. My favorite appeared in the Sunday *Washington Post* under the headline FAKING IT: A CRASH COURSE IN ELEGANT BUT INEXPENSIVE ENTERTAINING, and contained this helpful hint on how to entertain elegantly but cheaply: "To create the aura of lobsters without the expense, simply serve your fish dishes on a lobster-motif serving platter, with a lobster-shaped potholder or while wearing a lobster-decorated tie or undershorts."

I would rather eat Chicken of the Sea alone than risk a stunt like this. Where's the percentage in taking a group of people, not lobster-averse but with lobster the last thing on their minds as they arrive (at least at my house), and turning them into a bunch of salivating, lobster-obsessed monsters before serving them a nice casserole?

We should have known lifestyle reporting would one day sink to features on men serving cheap fish in lobster-covered underpants. The genre has been wearing thin for a while, especially in our newspaper of record, which has an entire section to fill every week with drivel for the Y-people. Even so, they try to maintain an aura of seriousness, using the same portentous headlines in the "Living" section that are used on the op-ed page. Last week's lead article on what to serve at gatherings to watch football games was subtitled "Beyond Chips and Dip." It can only get worse as writers strain for ways to reach that consumer who once thought nothing of dropping $200 on a rowing machine but is now sunk into his couch holding onto a remote control device, too tired and too poor to go out.

I had a big Life Choice to make last weekend: whether to take a job in New York. So I spent most of the weekend mindlessly at the movies—four in 36 hours. Fortunately, two of the movies were set in New York, which was some help—more than my few trips there each year when I get to know a few offices and runway six at LaGuardia. From *Three Men and a Baby* I learned that in New York it takes three high-income males to swing the rent for an apartment on the Upper West Side and to do what most mothers do alone. Like Dustin Hoffman, who bonded with his son after learning what grade he was in only to have Meryl Streep return and reclaim him, the three men get attached to Mary only to have Mom return and take custody. Think of this as *"Kramer* vs. *Kramer, Kramer & Kramer."*

Wall Street was even less illuminating. Most of the movie is talk, and most of the talking is done by men on the phone. One man shouts into the phone; another shouts back into the phone. When the tension really mounts, whole roomfuls of men shout into the phone.

It's not at all encouraging about Manhattan. It suggests that if you want to move out of a dark, one-room apartment in a questionable neighborhood, you have to sell your soul and your father to a greed-besotted investment banker who shouts into the phone even when he's on the beach. Then there are the masses of people yearning to get from A to B but having difficulty. The scene where Bud Fox is tailing the English takeover specialist in the lift suggests that if the city gets any more crowded, people will soon be forced to book space on elevators during peak travel periods. Women don't have much to say in this movie, perhaps because they don't carry cellular phones. It's just as well; Daryl Hannah barely made it as the spacey stargazer in *Roxanne.* She's been out of her depth since she took the fin off.

Broadcast News had more to say about New York, even though it's set in Washington. Network news people remain New Yorkers even when posted here, running at 78 rpm to our 45. They live in apartments, turn on their stoves only for warmth, and insist on meeting friends at alien, Manhattan-type restaurants serving hostile food in small portions. If only Washington, where kids can go to school without a .38-caliber pistol and the subway is safe, were filled with the likes of Albert Brooks.

As always, sitting in the dark among strangers in a seat lousy with popcorn and Coke only feeds decision gridlock. Perhaps I could steal a scene from Woody Allen in *Annie Hall* and buttonhole strangers on the street, to see what they think. I ran into some New Yorkers waiting to get into the theater. They said not to do it, even if I get dental.

Polls show that Gary Hart's high negatives are coming from women. A lot of men attribute this to single-issue politics: that women won't vote for him simply because he had an affair. I suspect that the men shouting about this at dinner tables are talking with their glands; that they are trying to settle, once and for all, their right to have an affair and still run for president. We'll soon find out, but I don't think all this noise is going to translate into pulling the Hart lever in the secrecy of the voting booth. As for women, I don't think we eliminate men as friends or candidates because of an affair.

Hart's affair was an event that exposed Hart in a way few candidates ever are. He couldn't rehearse his reaction and turn it into a sanitized sound bite for the evening news. He had to go naked into the bright lights, without the shroud of position papers and new ideas, and he was revealed as embittered and arrogant. It's also been said that criticizing Hart for lying is just a cover for criticizing him for adultery; that his lies were trivial—why he wasn't home at night, his name and his age—compared with the lies of Nixon and Bush about what country was being bombed and whether arms for hostages was a good idea. Be fair. Give Hart a chance. He just hasn't had the opportunity to lie about affairs of state yet.

January 25, 1988

Less Than Uplifting

Women want to be attractive to men; men want to be attractive to women. This will ever be so. But why must women, after three decades of working toward equality, still spend countless hours and endure pain to that end, while men get off with a shave and a shine? The latest instruments of female torture are contraptions with names like Wonderbra and Super-Uplift that force a woman's breasts, however small, into a harness, creating cleavage of the sort enjoyed by Dolly Parton. The maker of Super-Uplift describes its product as a feat of engineering (constructed with 46 separate components and underwires, a "gate back" for anchoring, and ridged shoulder straps to prevent the "embarrassing jellies-on-a-plate look"), but it is actually a feat of marketing. Convincing women that the absence of breasts holds them back is as easy as forcing hemlines up or down: it is only a few fashion shows, press releases and glossy-magazine features away. When Super-Uplift went on sale at Manhattan's Saks Fifth Avenue two weeks ago, 489 were bought the first day.

Why are liberated women willing to buy the successor to the corset? It does not hurt, but neither is it comfortable. Like shoes that never stop rubbing the back of your heel, it is always there, doing what nature did not intend, with wires sufficient to hold up a suspension bridge and pads that would protect a linebacker. And for what? To be more appealing? A few minutes ago, the Kate Moss waif effect was all the rage, together with its requisite minimizer bra—a contraption that could raise your voice an octave.

There is a postfeminist argument for the Wonderbra: Liberation means that women can dress any way they want. No more the little bow tie and the boxy gray suit or the Sears orthopedically correct underwear beneath it. Women should feel free to be sexy in the boardroom as well as the bedroom. Fine. But the Wonderbra sends the message: Notice my breasts before you notice my recommendation to go long pork-belly futures.

Replacing dress-for-success with dress-for-sex is no leap forward. Men don't wear tight pants to get a promotion or a new client. By contrast, women lighten, heighten, straighten, curl, iron and bleach their hair—and that's the hair they want. Unwanted hair is ripped out by its roots with hot wax, electrolysis and depilatories. Bound feet may never have caught on here, but high heels that force the entire body weight onto the tip of the big toe are a cause of daily anguish.

Women have endangered themselves with many kinds of surgery. It is some comfort that three companies—Dow Corning, Bristol-Myers Squibb and Baxter Healthcare—agreed last week to pay $3.7 billion over 30 years to women claiming they were injured by silicone breast implants. But that settlement, the largest ever for a class-action suit, does nothing to alter the mentality that led as many as 2 million women over the past quarter-century to seek the operation in the first place. Only a male model or a body builder would think of surgically enhancing a bicep, and only in a few cases of dealing with male-pattern baldness has a Senator or actor succumbed to scalp-piercing follicle transplants. Otherwise, machismo allows for vanity, if at all, in terms of toupees and dentures. The Wonderbra is not what most women were thinking about when they talked about getting control of their lives.

April 4, 1994

Divorce, Corporate-Style
Her job was his career, so she wants half the loot

What's a wife worth, anyway? She's priceless, of course, spiritually. But financially, we still don't know, when it comes to that rare species, the stay-at-home spouse of the corporate tycoon. When nonwealthy couples divorce, the assets are generally divided equally. But for the wealthy—unless you're in a 50-50 community-property state—when love fades, the wife's value is inversely calculated: the richer the household, the less, pro-portionally, she gets.

One such wife, Lorna Wendt, 53, has decided to fight that principle. She returns to court in Stamford, Conn., this week, having turned down a $10 million offer from her husband Gary Wendt, 54, the chief executive of General Electric's GE Capital. "I view marriage as a partnership," says Lorna, who contends that Gary has made roughly $100 million (his lawyer claims it's less than half that), "and I was actually quite surprised to find out that my husband does not believe that, nor, possibly, do the courts." "This isn't a matter of what Lorna needs but of return on investment," says Stanford economist Myra Strober, who testified on her behalf. The Wendts started out with a net worth of $2,500, counting all their wedding gifts, and she gave up her job as a music teacher shortly after helping to put him through Harvard Business School. (Lorna has introduced into evidence her Ph.T., a "Put Hubby Through" degree, awarded by the dean back then.) They proceeded to hit it big.

Men argue that they spend countless hours at the office, missing their children, and bear all the corporate stress. Robert Epstein, Gary's lawyer, says the offer "far exceeds anything she ever dreamed of when she first mar-ried. Equitable does not mean equal." Without denying her contribution, he told *The New York Times* it was "de minimus."

One of her lawyers, Sarah Oldham, notes that Lorna packed up and sold five houses and took primary responsibility for the two kids. She created what William H. Whyte Jr., author of *The Organization Man*, once called an island of tranquillity that would "liberate her husband's total energies for the job." Eight days after the Wendts' first child was born, according to Oldham, "Lorna got a call from Mr. Wendt's secretary saying, 'Your hus-band has decided to have a dinner party tonight. There will be 12 people ar-riving at 7.'"

Not every corporate spouse is selfless—there's the cartoon figure who di-vides her time between the country-club tennis pro and the hairdresser. But women like Lorna are often the difference between the guy who is stuck as vice president of human resources and the president. It's hard to feel sympathy for someone asked to scrape by on a mere $10 mil, but given her superior performance, shouldn't she share the spoils of reaching the top slot?

In California, courts have begun putting value on the social trappings of a high-end marriage: the A-list party invitations and the good table at Spago. Given what awaits a 53-year-old divorcée in Stamford who may be lucky to be invited to a potluck supper with a game of Scrabble afterwards,

Gary Wendt's decision to spin off Lorna after 31 years should get her half and then some.

February 3, 1997

The Mummy Diaries

A sparkling novel about juggling marriage, kids and job (and getting some sleep)

Sleep is the new sex. That's what it's come down to for the heroine of Allison Pearson's *I Don't Know How She Does It* (Knopf; 338 pages). A hedge-fund manager and frazzled mother of two, Kate Reddy aches for sleep, fantasizes about it and contrives how to get more, largely by avoiding sex with her husband.

Nearly every female lucky enough to have both a child and a byline—and I plead guilty—has strip-mined Pearson's theme: how to squeeze babies, marriage and a high-powered job into a day that cannot be stretched beyond 24 hours. But Pearson's Kate, a brisk, sardonic, loving world beater, has made it all fresh again. The book's title, when uttered by a member of the Muffia—the nonworking mums—is not a compliment. They send thank-you notes for play dates, needle Kate about when she will go part-time and snap up the best party clowns, leaving Kate with one who specializes in twisting balloons into phallic designs. Kate sees both sides of the mother divide: "The non-working mother looks at the working mother with envy and fear because she thinks that the working mum has got away with it, and the working mum looks back with fear and envy because she knows that she has not."

Pearson, a star columnist at the *London Evening Standard,* makes Kate one of those superwomen who think they would like a wife. But when Kate's husband, Rich, a low-energy architect, picks up the household slack, she loses interest in him. She is hard-wired to want a hunter-gatherer and nearly has an affair with one, an alpha millionaire client. But she cheats on her boss instead, stealing "Illicit Mummy Time," which requires "the same lies to get away for the tryst, the same burst of fulfillment and, of course, the guilt."

Kate adores Jill, a stay-at-home mom dying of cancer, who poignantly captures family life in instructions she leaves for her husband (the water temp for socks, Christmas gifts for the next two years, advice to kiss the boys even when they grow tall). Unlike Jill, though, Kate is a bit player in her own household, which is run by a nanny wielding absolute power. Kate doesn't know her daughter's best friend or how much her son weighs. She's a victim of reverse intimacy; her associates soak up so much time that she stays in touch with her real friends through increasingly heartfelt messages in which she cancels plans yet again. Like many professionals who leap a social class, she wonders—when her child demands pasta instead of canned SpaghettiOs—if "I've traveled this far . . . only for my kids to grow up as jaded and spoiled as the people I was patronized by at college."

Kate has been called Bridget Jones five years later. But Kate is a grown-up, sharp and observant yet wise and sentimental, something Bridget can never be. Feminists may hate the fact that Kate quits her job after deciding that you can't have it all. But, by the way, it's not male or female but merely childish to think otherwise. Pearson says she has sackfuls of mail from women who reject what they have seen in the boardroom. "Who wants to sit at ludicrous meetings in some testosterone jungle," Pearson asks, "and think of our children as problems to be handled?" She didn't make Kate a journalist like herself because, she says, "it's not ball breaking enough. I wanted a place where Human Resources has a policy for dealing with mothers similar to their one for dealing with cocaine users, except they believe there's a cure for drug addicts."

Pearson is married to *New Yorker* film critic Anthony Lane, whom she squarely places in the hunter-gatherer category. He pitches in, she says, but "until they program men to notice you're out of toilet paper, a happy domestic life will always be up to women."

During the months when she was writing, Lane "loaded the washing machine, cooked dinner, read *Owl Babies* 300 times and even found time to write the odd film review." Pearson concludes, "I don't know how he does it."

October 7, 2002

The Crying Game

No female stereotype is too familiar or out of date for Virginia Military Institute, fighting to stay all male

Do you ever get the feeling that the men in the world might not care if the office door closed and there were no women in the room? Ever suspect many men still think that when a woman argues a point she's being combative, while a man is being analytic; that women are motivated by emotions and the need to be loved, while men are driven by facts; that when a woman asks for a raise, she is grasping and greedy, while male breadwinners are simply collecting their due?

Well, have I got validation for you. Several of the country's most powerful lawyers, in briefs and in oral argument before the Supreme Court last week, trotted out those stereotypes and more in a last-ditch attempt to save the 157-year-old, state-supported Virginia Military Institute as an all-male preserve. According to VMI's argument, women respond more naturally to an "ethic of care" than to an egalitarian "ethic of justice," and those few women who are confident need to go to a women's school to be "reminded" that female "leadership" carries "the hazard of being oppressive." In lower court, VMI had solicited the expert testimony of retired Harvard sociology professor David Riesman, who warned that a young woman's "aspirations" to marry are "still in the South very common," and that men still divide women into the "good girls and the bad girls"—and you know which kind would want to attend a military school. Besides, noted Riesman, even "macho" women cry.

VMI also argued that a leadership program it set up at Mary Baldwin College in Staunton, Virginia, although separate, is entirely equal. A traditional women's school that features Apple Day and genteel residence halls with brass chandeliers, carpeting and cable, Baldwin offers two hours of ROTC a week for freshmen, but none of the character-building deprivation or bonding possibilities of barracks life. There is also no bachelor of science degree or alumni network similar to VMI's, which has always been touted as the key to cracking the Virginia establishment. Last week VMI put itself in the ridiculous position of lowballing its worth, pointing out that only one member of the Virginia General Assembly was a grad and, in effect, questioning why any woman would want to go to such a dump.

Although the VMI ruling will also decide the pending Citadel lawsuit, this case has attracted far less attention because the plaintiff was anonymous. Anonymous's weight and hair were not nearly so much fun to ridicule as the huffing and puffing Shannon Faulkner, whose dropping out to the cheers of cadets was carried live by CNN.

During oral argument, Deputy Solicitor General Paul Bender grabbed the rapt attention of the Justices when he harked back to a certain law school that refused to admit women, claiming they would run in tears from the lecture hall, unable to cope with the harsh Socratic method, the legal version of hazing. Five of the Justices recognized the school as their alma mater, Harvard Law. Justice Ruth Bader Ginsburg, one of the first women to get there, seemed to hold back a smile. VMI and the Citadel might want to start building those women's bathrooms now.

January 29, 1996

Is This What Feminism Is All About?

By playing out a male fantasy, *Thelma & Louise* shows Hollywood is still a man's world

So few movies place women at their center that when one does it is held up to the light and turned every which way for clues about the state of the gender. Not since *Fatal Attraction* has a movie provoked such table-pounding discussions between men and women. Along partisan lines, men attack the movie as a male-bashing feminist screed, in which they are portrayed as leering, overbearing, violent swine who deserve what they get, from a bullet in the heart to being stuffed in a trunk. Women cheer the movie because it finally turns the tables on Hollywood, which has been too busy making movies about bimbos, prostitutes, vipers and bitches—and glamorizing the misogynists who kill them—to make a movie like *Thelma & Louise*. Yet for all the pleasure the film gives women moviegoers who want to see the worst of the opposite sex get what's coming to them, it can hardly be called a feminist movie. As a bulletin from the front in the battle of the sexes, *Thelma & Louise* sends the message that little ground has been won. Thelma and Louise are so trapped that the only way for them to get away for more than two days is to go on the lam. They become free but only wildly, self-destructively so—free to drive off the ends of the earth.

They are also free to behave like—well, men. For all the talk that *Thelma & Louise* is the first female buddy movie, it is more like a male buddy movie with two women plunked down in the starring roles. The heroines are irresistibly likable: the gentle, bewildered Thelma, married to a smug, philandering salesman who wears more gold jewelry than she does, and for whom she leaves dinner on a child's partitioned plate in the microwave; and Louise, the world-weary, wised-up waitress who has waited too long for her lounge-singer boyfriend to marry her. But rather than finding their way with their female natures intact or even being able to reach out to the one decent man who could help them, they become like any other shoot-first-and-talk-later action heroes.

Thelma and Louise act out a male fantasy of life on the road, avoiding intimacy with loud music, Wild Turkey, fast driving—and a gun in the pants. The movie has almost as many chase scenes per reel as *Smokey and the Bandit*. The characters don't confide in each other as women do, nor are they able to just have fun with each other, now finally free of the men who hem them in. Thelma is still the teenager at the slumber party who gets bored and has to call a few boys to come over. Less than an hour out of town, she talks Louise into stopping at a raunchy bar, where she dances with a creep who then tries to rape her in the parking lot. The women are sympathetic enough characters by this time so that we leap over the hurdle many adventure movies present—Why didn't they call the police?—and rationalize what might be a cold-blooded murder as an act of self-defense. That way we can climb into that green Thunderbird, put down the roof and go along for the joyride.

But it becomes harder and harder to root for the heroines, who make the wrong choice at every turn and act more like Clint Eastwood than Katharine Hepburn. The day after her near rape, Thelma is begging Louise to pick up a hitchhiker. It requires a breathtaking somersault of faith to believe Thelma would be eager to take up with another stranger so soon, that she would let him into her motel room and go limp with desire after he admits he robs convenience stores for a living.

The turning point of Thelma's character rests on one of the most enduring and infuriating male myths in the culture: The only thing an unhappy woman needs is good sex to make everything all right. After a night of knock-over-the-nightstand sex with the hitchhiker, Thelma comes down to the coffee shop suffused with satisfaction and tells Louise, "I finally understand what all the fuss is about." Thelma is transformed, more confident and buoyant than she has ever been, reducing her angst to the simplistic notion that she was stuck with a husband who was insufficiently accomplished in the bedroom.

Despite such flaws, long after the movie is done entertaining, it stirs up questions about why men and women remain mysteries to each other. It has its small triumphs. Susan Sarandon makes Hollywood a little safer for older actresses; she fearlessly plays next to someone 10 years younger. And at least Thelma and Louise stop short of emulating Butch Cassidy and the Sundance Kid, who use their remaining ammunition to go out in a blaze of testosteronic glory. The movie may not have the impact of *Fatal Attraction*, but next time a woman passes an 18-wheeler and points her finger like a pistol at the tires, the driver might just put his tongue back in his mouth where it belongs.

June 24, 1991

The Ultimate Men's Club

As pampered denizens of a virtually all-male bastion, many senators
were slow to grasp the seriousness of the sexual-harassment issue

There may be no better place in America for a referendum on male domi-
nation than the U.S. Senate. All white, mostly over 50, cosseted by fawning
aides and uninhibited by women, the Senate may be the most visible con-
centration of full-frontal prefeminist thinking left.

If it weren't for that, the Judiciary Committee might have found a way to
evaluate Professor Anita Hill's charges against Judge Clarence Thomas
confidentially. But it was easier to consign her to the category of she-devils,
like Fanne Foxe, Elizabeth Ray, Tai Collins, Donna Rice, who rise from a
public official's past to bring down a man simply for being, well, a man. In
this postgraduate Skull and Bones, most of whose members hardly need to
worry where their next million is coming from, it is hard to empathize with
someone worried enough about her career that she would overlook offen-
sive conduct until it became literally a federal matter. Senators don't inter-
act with women as colleagues—they have only two—and most of the other
women they come in contact with are subservient. According to a 1991
study by the Congressional Management Foundation, women hold 31% of
the top four positions on Senate staffs. Among those, women account for
24% of the very top post of administrative assistant. They earn 78 cents to
every dollar their male counterparts pull in. Still, the preponderance of females is found in the catchall legislative jobs, where, as one staff member
says, "taking good notes and neatness count."

When the Senate is not operating like a men's club, it behaves like a family—a patriarchal, dysfunctional one. Not only does the Senate have all the
institutionalized forms of sexism common in the corporate suite, but by
dint of its privileges and power it is one of the few places where acting like
a cross between a rock star and the dictator of a banana republic is tolerated. During orientation, congressional spouses are instructed on how to
live with a celebrity. It's an atmosphere, says former Missouri Lieutenant
Governor Harriett Woods, who now heads the National Women's Political
Caucus, where "Senators prey on women as if they were groupies." One
wife has remarked that a reason members spend so much time at the office
is the adoring staff. There's too much reality at home.

The offices resemble living rooms. There are 14 dining rooms, a gym
with a sauna and steamroom, and a pool; the women's facility, by contrast,
has been described as "six hair dryers and a Ping-Pong table."

In the absence of production quotas or a bottom line, the only measure of performance in the Senate is how much one pleases the boss. Much of the work is servile, not intellectual or history-making. Getting coffee is not a courtesy but part of the job description; being sent to the boss's house to pick up a tux and a change of underwear is all in a day's work.

Although the Senate has no shortage of clerical staff, female professionals are still expected to act as hostesses, showing a constituent, a defense contractor or a contributor around. In a Senate dining room, a young aide delivering papers to Senator Strom Thurmond was asked to remove her jacket so that a constituent could get a better look. She did. To someone operating in that atmosphere, perhaps, as Senator Arlen Specter said at Friday's hearing, talk of "women's large breasts" hardly seems such a big deal.

While the Senate is full of selfless older women, happy to substitute the life of the office for a life, it also has a huge contingent of postfeminist younger women, who think being asked to walk the dog and clean up after the mutt is the price one pays for invaluable experience. Says an aide to a Democratic Senator on the Judiciary Committee: "You know what the code is, and if you want to be involved, you know what you have to tolerate. It's happened to me, and I never call anyone on it. You have to show you are tough enough to take a certain kind of harassment."

After it became impossible to ignore Hill's charges, the Senate's major preoccupation, like that of an exclusive club, was an infraction of its by-laws. Senator John Danforth, Thomas' chief handler, harrumphed, "The cloud of doubt was created by a violation of the rules of the U.S. Senate"; so Danforth maintained that the doubt was not valid. Anyway Thomas had given Danforth his gentleman's word, and that was enough for him. Says Woods: "It's the male, Yale, class response. It's infuriating to women because it's the club they never belonged to."

When a contingent of seven House members marched down the marble halls of the Senate to the Democratic caucus room to ask for a meeting about sexual harassment, they were told they couldn't come in. Said California Congresswoman and Senate candidate Barbara Boxer: "What could be more symbolic than that closed door?" Some Senators "got it" better after some sensitivity training at home. Senators Daniel Patrick Moynihan and Jim Exon said they didn't realize how serious the issue was until they talked to their wives. Said Boxer: "If there were more women in the Senate, they wouldn't need to rely on spouses to tell them what's important to 51% of the American population."

The rules of Congress are arcane, often unwritten, and demand a lifetime of male bonding to understand. It's bad form to call one's deepest philosophical enemy anything but "my distinguished colleague," or to continue a political argument after hours. When cries went up for a list of Capitol Hill check bouncers, House Speaker Tom Foley protected Democrats and Republicans alike, as does the Ethics Committee. So ingrained is the clubbiness that partisanship often seems like a Hulk Hogan spectacle, faked for the C-SPAN audience.

But something happened last week that may, for better or worse, permanently destroy all that comity. Senator Hatch opened the hearings in disgust, saying that if the Democrats had only asked for a closed executive session, the committee would have been spared its Friday circus. Senator Alan Simpson, who usually manages to hide his meanness behind an Andy Rooney facade, warned Hill that she would be "injured, and destroyed and belittled and hounded and harassed—real harassment, different from the sexual kind, just plain old Washington-variety harassment." What debates over the budget, arms control, abortion or the Gulf War did not destroy was finished off by televised hearings that stripped bare the sensibilities of two witnesses and the Senators who questioned them. The club may never be the same again.

October 21, 1991

Liar, Liar, Pants on Fire . . .

Even people unknown to the tabloids have trouble being honest about sex

It's not the adultery, it's the lying; so goes the argument of various keepers of the public morality. Well, that's a lie, akin to saying it's not the winter, it's the cold that bothers me.

No, it's sex, in and of itself, that occupies us, the lying is a less entertaining collateral offense.

A visitor from another planet reading the papers recently about First Lieut. Kelly Flinn, Marv Albert, Frank Gifford, Michael Kennedy and Paula Jones would think that our national pastime was not baseball but the Playboy channel. The day after the Supreme Court ruled that Paula Jones' lawsuit could go forward, the story led most major newspapers, above the announcement by Boris Yeltsin at the NATO summit that he would no longer target nuclear missiles at the Western alliance. Peace is at hand, so what? We've got a woman here saying once again that Clinton came on to her in a hotel room six years ago.

This preoccupation wouldn't be so troublesome if sex, or lying about it, wasn't such a growth sector, spawning lawsuits, dishonorable discharges, job losses, book contracts and political meltdowns. It's one thing to be amused by whether Marv Albert had to remove his hairpiece when being booked on charges he bit a woman in his hotel room and quite another matter to make sexual allegations grounds for court-martialing a female B-52 pilot who didn't fully own up to a relationship, winnowing potential political candidates and crippling a President.

If sexual behavior were the only measure of a man, Richard Nixon would be one of our best Presidents and Franklin Roosevelt one of our worst. One's sexual behavior as a component of character used to count for nothing (President Kennedy's assignations were not covered while he was alive), which was wrong; now it counts for far too much. Gary Hart was no prize, but should his 12 years as a Senator and 39-year marriage be blotted out by his dalliance with Donna Rice?

Any sexual encounter is subject to self-delusion, and that's when it turns out well. Sexual lies may be the most common form of lying in the U.S., after "That hat looks good on you" and "Let's have lunch." Even the most scientific sex surveys are subject to criticism for the inherent unreliability of people's recounting of their sexual experiences. In the massive 1994 study *Sex in America: A Definitive Survey,* the authors conjecture that men may exaggerate or women may understate the number of sex partners they have had. At a routine level, men lie to get women in bed ("You're beautiful," "My wife doesn't understand me"), lie when they are there (witness the hilarity that greets Jim Carrey's "I've had better" to a postcoital inquiry in the movie *Liar Liar*), and lie afterward ("I'll call you in the morning").

When there's no happily ever after, revisionism can really set in. What was ill-advised can in retrospect look involuntary. If you meant not to, wished you hadn't, know you shouldn't have, maybe you didn't; maybe you were coerced. You're not lying. Who knows?

Some forms of withholding information are sanctioned. Alcoholics Anonymous, which otherwise insists on brutal honesty, allows an exception for not telling your spouse about affairs. Annulment, when an applicant says he lacked due discretion to enter into marriage, is a form of sanctified lying about sex.

By stalling the Paula Jones case until after the '96 election, Bob Bennett, Clinton's attorney, won the crucial political war at the lesser cost of losing before the Supreme Court. If the case isn't dismissed, the President's best hope now is that Jones is indeed in it for the money. Then he can give her a small enough amount so as not to look like a payoff yet enough to fortify her against pressure from her political supporters, for whom airing the charges is the goal.

And who thinks the truth will ever be known? While it is hard to believe Jones is making it all up, it is not at all hard to believe that in the hands of right-wing zealots, rabid Clinton haters and a local lawyer who got a piece of any subsequent television, movie or jeans deals, she became a lot more emotionally distressed than she was at the time. It is just as hard to believe Clinton when he says nothing happened in the hotel, although when he denies her story in its possibly embellished form, he may have stumbled onto the truth.

The state trooper who places Clinton at the scene also says Jones emerged unshaken and hopeful of being the Governor's girlfriend. On the other side, six of her friends back her account. We've been building to this sexual peak for decades, through scandals concerning bold-type names from stage, screen and sports, Congressmen, Senators and presidential candidates. And now, live from the capital, it's the President. As the ultimate celebrity trial goes forward, there's little hope of truth and every chance we'll all be diminished. As for nuclear disarmament, never mind. We're busy with sex over here.

June 9, 1997

Even Feminists Get the Blues

At 57, Gloria Steinem finally comes to terms with her childhood and realizes what she has been missing

For all those women who wailed, "How could she do it?" when Gloria Steinem, the world's most famous feminist, began keeping company with demibillionaire real estate developer and publisher Mort Zuckerman in the late '80s, *Revolution from Within: A Book of Self-Esteem* (Little, Brown; 377 pages; $22.95) will serve as belated explanation. She did it for the car.

This wasn't just any car she fell for but a warm, chauffeur-driven cocoon of transit dispatched by Zuckerman to meet her as she returned to LaGuardia Airport late one night from yet another fund-raising trip, so exhausted that the auto's "sheltering presence loomed out of all proportion."

There she was, approaching 50, a burned-out crusader for women's causes who had not had time in 20 years to unpack the boxes in her bare apartment. She was nearly eligible for a senior citizen's discount before she bought her first sofa. Despite her confident demeanor, she felt so plain she wondered who that attractive, articulate woman impersonating her on television was. Thin as a pinstripe, she nonetheless felt one Sara Lee cheesecake away from Weight Watchers. Once a lively writer who impersonated a Playboy Bunny to expose Hugh Hefner's cheesy idea of sex appeal and quipped that if men could menstruate they would brag about how long and how much, she had produced very little since her collection of essays, *Outrageous Acts and Everyday Rebellions*, in 1983. *Ms.*, the magazine she co-founded in 1972 and edited from crisis to crisis ever since, was spinning out of her control. What was worse, the younger generation winced at the word *feminism*, while those who had never supported the idea were blaming it for everything from male impotence to global warming. By the time she sank into the soft leather interior of the car that night at LaGuardia, she was insecure as a junk bond, without energy, without hope and without enough self-esteem to resist this inappropriate but eager suitor. "This relationship," she writes, "became a final clue that I was really lost."

By the time she is back to hailing cabs for herself several years later, she is well into her search for her lost self and a 12-point recovery program that includes imagery, hypnosis, meditation, unlearning, relearning and the universal "I." She traces her loss of self to the day her 300-lb. father, an itinerant salesman, abandoned her when she was 10 in a rat-infested, dilapidated farmhouse fronting on a major highway in Toledo. Left to care for a loving but mentally ill mother who heard voices, she was forced to grow up too soon, to be mother to her mother. She escaped to Smith College but never escaped the trap of being the caretaker. Once she became involved in the movement, there was no campus, community group or benefit so small that she wouldn't hop on a plane and raise money for it. At times it seemed as if she had taken personal responsibility for every oppressed woman in America.

It is not surprising that this loss of childhood would catch up with her and that at fortysomething a parent substitute would come along in the guise of a knight in shining sedan, "someone," she writes, "I couldn't take care of." Overscheduled women everywhere will recognize themselves in her surrender to a decision-free zone of well-appointed houses and someone to clean them. "I found this very restful," she writes of the period. "I was just so . . . tired."

She mistook fatigue for love for only two years, but that was long enough to give rise to a rumor more virulent than the Asian flu that she was racing around Manhattan to fertility specialists trying to get pregnant. The sad truth is that she was consulting cancer doctors who saw her through breast surgery for a malignant tumor.

There were lots of reasons for the throw weight of the rumor. If true, it gave the lie to her belief that the single life was worth living, that a family consists of the people we are tied to by the work we share and friendship as well as by blood. If false, it was still an excellent occasion for schadenfreude by those who suspected, without proof, that she was a cunning hypocrite and who, incidentally, resented the way she could blast men as a group for their piggishness but nevertheless attract a succession of highly appealing ones who adored her but didn't expect her to pick up their sweat socks.

When Steinem, now 57, pours a second cup of coffee and writes like she talks, there is no one more fascinating. The only comparable figure in public life is Ralph Nader, and he doesn't manage the trick of combining her monastic commitment with unapologetic glamour that gets her waved past the velvet ropes at clubs on both coasts. Strangers come up to her on the street and tell her, "You changed my life," and cleaning women at the airport find a nook where she can take a nap.

Fortunately, one of the world's most interesting women is incapable of writing an uninteresting book, even when she summarizes most of the extant literature on the inner child. A $700,000 advance can buy a lot of self-esteem. But if that's not enough, if only the women whose lives were touched by Steinem were to buy the book, it would be a best-seller. Here, Gloria, is $22.95. Buck up, and thanks for everything.

January 20, 1992

A Woman of Substance
Katharine Graham, 1917–2001

Katharine Graham told the story of her life so well and with such raw candor in her 1997 autobiography, the Pulitzer Prize–winning *Personal History*, that retelling it here seems redundant. It was the tale of a fretful rich girl who married the dazzlingly brilliant Philip Graham. It was her father who owned *The Washington Post*, but her husband was given majority control of the paper on the theory that no man should ever work for his wife. When she found the manic-depressive Graham dead of a gunshot wound in the bathroom of their country house in 1963, this "doormat wife" at 46 was thrust into running the company. Men in suits thought they would be able to wrest it from someone so crippled by anxiety that she practiced saying "Merry Christmas" before giving her first staff party. But she was a brainy graduate of the University of Chicago with common sense who hired good people and learned to fire those who weren't. She bet the farm on editor Ben Bradlee, who had Phil's manic brilliance without the depression. The *Post* went from a decent, dull paper to a crackling, moneymaking one. She was not a natural skeptic but a natural, principled truth teller, shaking the Establishment of which she was a pillar. Against the wishes of financial advisers worried about the *Post*'s imminent IPO, she published the Pentagon papers. Alone among publishers, she followed the facts in Watergate. With the creation of the paper's irreverent "Style" section, Graham had to face at night the very powers that Sally Quinn was skewering by day. Graham never killed a story, although she occasionally rolled her eyes in sympathy with a deflated pol. At the paper she was a regular presence in the newsroom, even taking classified ads during the violent pressmen's strike of the mid-'70s. She visited the child-care centers she funded, folding her 6-ft. frame into many a kiddie-size chair. Last week, at an elite retreat in Sun Valley, Idaho, after lunch with Tom Hanks and before dinner with Mexican President Vicente Fox, she fell and lost consciousness. She died on Tuesday.

By then, Katharine Graham was the most powerful woman in America, no longer shy and awkward but regal and utterly imposing. With an ever more influential newspaper, with *Newsweek*—which Phil had acquired in 1961—and with an ever more influential salon at her house on a hill in Georgetown, she was Walter Lippmann and Perle Mesta rolled into one. Much has been made of evenings at Mrs. Graham's—the network stars, the Vice Presidents, the gray eminences. But her reach was deeper. She was the connective tissue for the permanent substratum of the capital— the one layered with beat reporters, academics and junior Senators yet to head a committee. She never babbled and showed little patience for those who did. I was scared to death when I met her. She was quick to judge someone a bore, though ready to reverse the call on receipt of evidence to the contrary. I'd been at her house for dinner 50 times before she wondered whether she might be invited to mine. "I don't mind lap eating," she said. Having missed the bustle of a happy family life, she was thrilled to pitch in and toss the salad. She drew the line at busing dishes.

She never got sentimental. But she sat with her best friend, Meg Greenfield, op-ed editor of the *Post*, through almost every chemotherapy treatment in a losing battle with cancer. She talked with her old friend Nancy Reagan almost every week after the former President fell ill. No one quite took care of friends the way Kay Graham did. One night she shared Chinese food with me and my daughter as Courtney and I argued over the propriety of a strapless wedding gown. "Now, Courtney," Kay said, "this is your wedding. You're the one wearing the dress. You should get exactly what your mother tells you."

When it came time to pass the baton to her son Donald Graham in 1991, she did it seamlessly and gracefully, which is not always the case with dynastic successions. She still asked the first question at editorial lunches. But she kept out of her son's hair by spending six solid years writing her book. If there was any interference, it took place during their weekly Sunday walks around Dumbarton Oaks. By then, an artificial hip was slowing her. She never complained about getting old. At parties she would plant herself on a chair and let the room come to her. She kept in touch by going to the movies, even the bad ones, and she'd always ask for the senior discount.

She invariably wrote out her toasts and delivered them with shaking hands, as she did at a February dinner for President George W. Bush. But on her 84th birthday in June, in her house on the hill, she had no notes. The room had seen its share of kings and princesses, but the event on that evening meant the most to her. "When you live alone," she concluded, "you're married to your friends." She wasn't trembling at all.

July 30, 2001

ISSUES

Children Without Souls

Adoption, the church doorstep: anything but this

About the time most prospective parents are obsessing over what color to paint the nursery, Amy Grossberg and Brian Peterson Jr. were acquiring a gray garbage bag with yellow drawstrings and a map of Newark, Del., to help them find a Comfort Inn off the highway, where birth and death could come and go in a moment. Was there ever a second when one of them was shocked by the horror of it all and said, "No, we can't do this. Have we lost our minds?" only to be talked back into it by the other? Did they hear a cry or blurt out, "It's a boy"? Afterward, they slept for a few hours and took the car to the White Glove Car Wash.

When a poor, black 13-year-old from the Bronx leaves her newborn to die, we go on about our business, but we are gripped when two affluent white teenagers do the same thing. Yes, there's race and class. But there is also our belief that it is society in its dysfunctional state that yields ruthless behavior, not society when it is giving kids the best of everything, including private help when things go wrong. Of course, the dark side of kids who have everything is that they cannot tolerate a blemish on their smooth lives.

Pro-life advocates seized upon the crime as the logical end to the slippery slope of abortion rights. It offered an occasion to revisit the effort to close a "health of mother" loophole that allows partial-birth abortions, not just for women in dire straits but teenagers who have changed their minds. You don't have to be persuaded that the difference between what Amy and Brian did and a third-trimester abortion is only time (a couple of weeks) and place (a $56-a-night motel rather than a clinic) to retreat to a dark corner of your conscience and fathom what is right.

Certainly watching a father turn his son in because that son has killed his grandchild is heart wrenching. So was the sight of Barbara Peterson hiding her head in her son's soft fleece jacket as she walked him into the courthouse, one she may have bought for him to wear on cool November days as co-captain of his soccer team. But perhaps his conscience had been warped somewhere along the way by these same parents. His mother's week-long reaction was to keep her son from authorities and consider helping him escape punishment altogether after he admitted, minimally, to putting the baby into a plastic bag and hurling it into a Dumpster. She may have been modeling herself after the parents of another privileged teenager who provided their son Alex Kelly with a life of European ease after he was accused of rape. Surely a lion must protect her cub, but there's a point when instinct must give way to morality.

By week's end, Baby Boy Grossberg was being reclaimed from the morgue by his grandparents, who will name him before burying him. Defense lawyers are urging us not to rush to judgment, which is surely a prelude to a rush to explain and a plea to excuse. One attorney said, "Brian, the individual, the human being, the nice, normal kid, has been displayed, and I think that it gives the public a different perspective, and I think it's helpful." Helpful to whom? Not to a moral life. There are monsters among us who, with wealthy parents and a battalion of lawyers, tap a culture ready to forget the victim and forgive the accused, especially if they remind us of ourselves. But not this time, not this evil.

December 2, 1996

Partial-Truth Abortion

He lied, she lied, they lied, we all lie, to ourselves and one another, in hearings and in print, at dinner and on *Nightline*, lest we give one inch in a war over abortion that rages on. Occasionally a lie is recanted, as happened when abortion-rights lobbyist Ron Fitzsimmons said that there are many more D&E procedures than he had admitted. With the "partial birth" abortion bill coming to the House floor this week for the second time, and with every chance of passage, even partial truth on the subject is elusive.

The truth eludes not just those on the extremes but also those in the middle. Every mother who is pro-choice knows to keep her mouth shut when the subject of late-term abortion comes up. Those of us who have been happily pregnant have pored over the pictures in *A Child Is Born,* amazed that a creature still months away from filling the Jenny Lind crib in the nursery is so human. We know there's a life's worth of difference between a 20-week-old fetus and a 24-week-old one. A 1991 study shows that 34% of babies delivered at that point live. This puts *Roe's* trimester construction on a collision course with our own eyes.

But that knowledge is tamped down because the stakes are so high. To voice any doubts might jeopardize our tenuous hold on first-trimester abortions and could give aid and succor to the other side, which ranges from morons who kill doctors to the rank and file who would protect zygotes. Give those people a month and they will take nine. It will be you, your doctor and Jesse Helms at the sonogram.

Most people find the debate over D&E discomfiting for its grisly details (though, in fact, all surgical abortions are gruesome) and for what we don't know—the number of procedures and the medical circumstances. But it is also disturbing because it forces us to confront when and why these procedures happen. Most of us assume that later-term abortions are rare, indeed prohibited, except in the gravest circumstances. We're wrong.

The third-trimester exceptions permitted by the court for the "health of mother" are wide enough to allow a healthy teenager, eight months pregnant and carrying a healthy baby, to squeeze through the clinic door. Most times, the reasons for a late-term abortion are as tragic as those endured by the women Clinton introduced at his press conference when he vetoed the ban last spring. But, in addition to physical health, courts have allowed "emotional, psychological, familial" factors to be considered, as well as "the woman's age." We fool ourselves if we don't acknowledge that these exceptions have been extended to women too poor, too young, or too dysfunctional to care for a child—or obtain a timely abortion. When Clinton asks for a "health of mother" exception in the current bill, without specifying physical health, he is saying there should be no change in the status quo.

It's a terrible thing to force a 12-year-old who lives in chaos, poverty and hopelessness, with a boyfriend who has disappeared or an abusive uncle who hasn't, to have a baby. But it's a worse thing to let her abort it when she comes so late for help that the only difference between the baby's being born alive or dead is whether she gives birth in a maternity ward or a clinic. This doesn't happen often, but even one time is too many to defend.

March 24, 1997

Prom Nightmare
A dead baby in the wastebasket, a debate gone awry

Depravity was defined downward last week, six months after two New Jersey teenagers—who had been given everything but a conscience—delivered a baby boy and briskly disposed of him in a Dumpster before heading to the White Glove Car Wash to rinse off the blood. Now we have Melissa Drexler, who slipped into the bathroom at her senior prom, delivered a 6-lb.-6-oz. baby boy and tossed him in the trash basket with the soiled paper towels in time to get back to the party. She asked the disc jockey to play her favorite Metallica song and danced with her boyfriend. A student told a reporter later, "She seemed to be enjoying herself." Cleaning up after themselves, as Amy Grossberg and Brian Peterson did, seems like a quaint gesture of guilt next to a hasty return to the prom for a postpartum spin around the dance floor. There's not a flicker of humanity in these cases, and there are more of them being reported, if not more of them happening. No one keeps comprehensive statistics on abandoned babies, but in Los Angeles County last year, there were 10 newborns left to die; two summers ago, three were discarded in Southern California beach communities. In Monmouth County, N.J., where Drexler left her baby, there were 12 abandoned babies in the past 10 years. But four New Jersey teenagers have abandoned babies in the past six months alone.

Whenever these grisly abandonments occur, right-to-life proponents argue that we've arrived at the bottom of the slippery slope they've been warning us about since *Roe v. Wade* in 1973. As usual, Newt Gingrich goes too far when he talks about a culture of Dumpster babies, but why couldn't Melissa have wrapped the baby in a cloth and left him, as panicked girls used to do, someplace safe like the church steps, or turn to the Yellow Pages, filled with "pregnancy counseling" and "abortion alternatives" to find a foster home.

The newspaper ads suggesting that girls were having third-trimester abortions because they couldn't fit into their prom dresses remain pro-life hyperbole, but the Roman Catholic bishops who ran them are right when they say there is almost no difference between the prom mom and a woman having a third-trimester abortion, except for location and a few days.

The bishops lost moral high ground, however, when they tossed in the Dumpster the best chance to restrict late-term abortions since abortion was made legal. An astonishing thing happened during the debate over a bill to ban partial-birth abortions, which has no chance of actually becoming law, and wouldn't result in even one less abortion even if it did. Alarmed to learn of the many third-trimester abortions performed after six months, under milewide exceptions for vague reasons of mental health, Democratic Senator Thomas Daschle introduced a bill that would have banned all abortions in which the baby could have lived outside the womb, which these days means after about 23 weeks. Yet Republicans preferred to cling to their own doomed bill rather than give up a potent political issue or accept Daschle's exception for women whose pregnancies could cause "grievous physical injury"—even though that closes the mental-health loophole. If it's disregard for life that turns girls like Melissa into murderous monsters, then the Republicans need look no farther than themselves for someone to blame.

June 23, 1997

The Silver Fox

And now for something completely different: a down-to-earth First Lady

I had a small crisis this week.

I was staying at a very stylish hotel in New York City where I knew they always had a bathrobe in the closet, so I left mine at home. I had called room service for coffee, then discovered there was no robe. When the coffee came, I took a sheet off the bed and wrapped it around myself toga style to answer the door. I can imagine what the waiter thought. I can just see him going back to the kitchen and saying, "You'll never guess what I saw in Room 1712!"

—From the campaign diary of Barbara Bush.

America, meet Barbara Bush, taking center stage in national life just in the knick of time. Nancy Reagan had many good qualities, but she was, well, something of a strain: those rail-thin looks, that hard-edged show-biz glitter and no children or grandchildren around to mess things up. The country may be ready for a First Lady who is honest about her size (14), her age (63) and her pearls (fake). She sports sweats on the weekends with no intention of jogging, does her own hair, likes take-out tacos, devours mystery novels, poaches at the net in mixed doubles, teases her husband and speaks her mind. When she is home near her own bathrobe, she wears it outside to walk the dog.

Barbara Bush knows that the two-mile move from the Vice President's 1893 Victorian mansion on Embassy Row to 1600 Pennsylvania Avenue is more than a change of zip codes. As she puts color-coded stickers on the furniture to signify what goes, what stays and what gets tossed out, she is already nostalgic over life as Second Lady. "I got away with murder," says the woman who allowed as how Nancy Reagan should have simply replaced the White House china a piece at a time instead of buying a whole new set, and who suggested that her husband strip down to disprove rumors that he was wounded during a tryst. As she prepares for her new post, she says, "I'm now slightly more careful about what I say." (Pause.) "Slightly."

On its face, First Ladyhood looks easy enough: one gets to live in a big house with a large yard, travel a lot and throw fancy dinner parties. Someone else cleans up. But the job—unpaid and with no days off—has its pitfalls. The person a pillow away from the presidency is held up to an undefined ideal; she bears all America's conflicting notions about women as wives, mothers, lovers, colleagues and friends. A First Lady should be charming but not all fluff, gracious but not a doormat, substantive but not a co-President. She must defend her husband and smile bravely when he says stupid things. She must look great, even fashionable, when a shower and clean clothes would suffice for anyone else; possess perfect children though such critters do not exist in nature; and traipse around the globe in a suit and sensible pumps when she would rather be home with a good book. She has both a day and a night job, but is not allowed a profession of her own. Hardest of all, she has to appear to love every minute of it.

Yet, in an era when the concept of First Lady seems like a stuffy anachronism, Barbara Bush may prove to be the right woman in the right place. She has projects—literacy, cancer research, education—that predate her husband's bug for politics. As she heads for 64, with no regrets about having poured her energies into raising her family, she seems to have enough heart left over to suffer fools gladly but enough wit not to indulge them. Years of good works behind her, she may embody the kinder, gentler world that her husband so gauzily evoked during the campaign.

Like many political wives, Barbara has devoted her life to her husband, the first man she ever kissed, with whom she has survived a wartime separation, 44 years of marriage, 29 moves, the death of a child, public rumors of his infidelity and the rigors of three national campaigns. Through it all, she has remained defiantly independent. Her Secret Service code name— Tranquillity—belies the fact that she has several hot buttons. Criticism, particularly of her husband, moves her to anger, as it did in 1984, when she suggested to reporters questioning the Bushes' wealth that a word that rhymes with rich might be an appropriate label for Geraldine Ferraro. She can cut off an interview with a wave of the hand, having been burned by those who talk sweetly but interview harshly (as when Jane Pauley asked her, "Your husband is a man of the '80s, and you're a woman of the '40s. What do you say to that?").

She refers to Ann Richards, who delivered a stinging critique of her husband at the Democratic National Convention, as "that woman." As for Ted Kennedy's famous "Where was George?" line, Barbara can only say, "He shouldn't even say George Bush's name." Though she has spent much of her life in Texas, this product of tony Rye, N.Y., can still summon a patrician bearing to cut the uppity down to size. The next President says she is "more direct" than he is. Says campaign manager and Republican Party chairman Lee Atwater: "She can spot a phony a mile away." Her children have a nickname for her: the Silver Fox.

Barbara and George Herbert Walker Bush have striking yet compatible differences. He hates to quarrel; she once liked it. She kids him about being too big for his britches, especially his style of britches. She particularly goes after the cowboy boots he sports for both day and evening wear. "They've got his initials in gold on the side—just two of them, not four of them—and the Lone Star State star. In color." He kids her about suspending the usual rules of conduct when it comes to her English springer spaniel, Millie. "That dog literally comes between us at night," he complains. "She wedges right up between our heads, and Bar likes it. She was better with the kids than she is with the dog."

George grumps about having to pack a few boxes to be shipped to the summer house in Kennebunkport, Maine; Barbara meticulously plans every move and every trip. While other people throw mementos from trips into a box, Barbara has arranged hers in a series of more than 60 giant scrapbooks. It's a wonder she doesn't have more enemies.

Having five children close together made Barbara more than a one-minute manager. It gave her a sense of humor, a playful, teasing manner (the secret of a strong marriage, she says), and a casual attitude toward how many people the pot roast can feed. She loves to have her five children and 10 grandchildren around her; she is flexible about George's 5,000 closest friends dropping by. On a few hours' notice two weeks ago, Bush brought Senator Nancy Kassebaum, Treasury Secretary Nick Brady, Senator Lloyd Bentsen and lawyer-Democrat Bob Strauss home to dinner. One of the best things about moving to the White House, Barbara says, is guest rooms. "Now I'm going to have a lot more."

The humor has served her well in politics. In her campaign stump speech, she regularly poked fun at herself, telling audiences that, if recognized at all, she is confused with Mrs. George Shultz. After the Ferraro crack, she opted for an immediate apology and told reporters that "the poet laureate has retired." Though public criticism of her hair, weight and wrinkles have hurt her, she has turned such remarks to her advantage. After her hair turned white in her early 30s, she began dyeing it "warm brown," although it was a nuisance for someone who swam frequently and shampooed every day. "One time," recalls Marvin, "I came home, and it was brown and orange, and it was like, 'Whoa, Mom, what happened?' " Eventually, she just gave up the coloring—"It was ridiculous," she said.

Barbara's clothes are attractive, but she will never be known, as her predecessor was, by her designer affiliation. As for weight, well, she enjoys eating too much ever to be svelte. She laments that the campaign added 13 lbs. to her 5-ft.-8-in. frame. During the Bushes' Florida post-election vacation, photos appeared of her swimming in the type of bathing suit popular with matrons in the '50s. Later, she jokingly asked photographers to cap their lenses—"My children are complaining all over the country." When she told a reporter that her trademark pearls were $90 fakes worn to hide her wrinkles, it was a comment on the universal regret at aging and the hopeless human foible of trying to hide it.

Barbara Bush has been training for her new job as long as her husband has been prepping for his. The third of four children of a father who worked his way up the ladder to become president of the McCall Corp., which among other things owned *McCall's* magazine, and a mother happy to entertain and garden in suburban Rye, Barbara attended public and private schools. She finished at Ashley Hall, a South Carolina prep school where neglecting to wear white gloves was a punishable offense. At a party in Greenwich, Connecticut, during Christmas break her senior year, she met George Bush, recently graduated from Andover. A generic dancer— she complains that whatever the tempo, he does the fox-trot—George asked her to sit out a waltz.

They sat and fell in love. The two became engaged that summer in Kennebunkport. It was a secret engagement since Barbara was still in school, Bush says, meaning "The German and Japanese high commands weren't aware of it." But after Bush was shot down over the Pacific in September 1944, Barbara dropped out of Smith in her sophomore year to marry him at the First Presbyterian Church in Rye. "I married the first man I ever kissed," she says. "When I tell this to my children, they just about throw up."

After Bush graduated from Yale in 1948, the couple packed up their Studebaker and with their son George headed west to make their way in the oil fields of Texas. The first stop was Odessa, and a one-bedroom apartment where they shared a bathroom with a mother-daughter team of prostitutes. Then it was Midland, where Bush would make a small fortune by Texas standards. After moving to Houston in 1958, he sold his stake in Zapata Off-Shore in 1966 for $1 million. While in Texas, Barbara suffered her biggest losses. In 1949 her mother died in a freak accident: her father, trying to keep a cup of coffee from spilling off the dashboard, lost control of the car. Then one day in the spring of 1953 the Bushes' second child, Robin, 3, woke up feeling too tired to go out to play. The doctors diagnosed leukemia and gave her two weeks to live. She hung on eight months, with Barbara, whose hair began turning white, sitting by the bedside at Memorial Hospital in New York City and Bush commuting on weekends. Friends say they handed their grief back and forth, acting alternately as mourner and supporter. Barbara says, "George held me tight and wouldn't let me go. You know, 70% of the people who lose children get divorced because one doesn't talk to the other. He did not allow that." By then they had the two boys, George, born in 1946, and Jeb, in 1953. Three more children in quick succession—Neil, 34, Marvin and Dorothy, 29 (all her children, she emphasizes, were planned)—helped ease the pain.

There would be two terms for Bush in Congress, from 1967 to 1971, a lost race for the Senate, and a stint at the U.N. in 1971 before Barbara developed her public persona. Until then she was so shy she once cried over having to speak to the Houston Garden Club. Sunk deep in diapers and dishes for so long, she lacked confidence. "George was off on a trip doing all these exciting things," she said, "and I'm sitting home with these absolutely brilliant children who say one thing a week of interest." By contrast, when Bush was appointed U.S. envoy to China in 1974, she became an important part of the enterprise. For the first time without car pools and PTA meetings, she could give everything to the post.

After China, the return to Washington, where Bush would head up the CIA, was something of a letdown. Barbara went from being included in everything to being shut out. "Why would he tell me any secrets," she joked, "when he says I begin every sentence with 'Don't tell George I told you this, but . . .'?"

Living over the store as First Couple, the two will once again be spending a lot of time together. Barbara will not have to find a cause since she already has many, in part as a result of events in her own life. Robin's leukemia got Barbara involved in medical activities. She has been on the board of Atlanta's Morehouse School of Medicine since 1983, and she spearheaded a $15 million fund-raising drive there. Her son Neil's dyslexia first got her interested in fighting illiteracy. In 1984 she wrote a book, C. Fred's Story, a surprisingly wry look at Washington life as told by her first dog. C. Fred could have been a disaster, but Barbara's wit and candor made it work. "I didn't have to squeeze it out of her. There was no ghostwriter," says editor Lisa Drew. "And it came in on time."

Barbara will probably never sit in on Cabinet meetings à la Rosalynn Carter or get people fired, as Nancy did. But a spousal "Dear, I wouldn't do that if I were you," delivered with a raised eyebrow, can often defeat a stack of position papers.

Long before President Bush begins his official day by conferring with top aides or national security advisers, he will already have had his first briefing of the day—in bed. Each morning, as they have for years, the Bushes awake to country music a little before 6 a.m. and take coffee, juice and the papers in bed while they watch the news shows. Together they discuss the hot news of the day, and she weighs in on everything from policy to personnel.

Barbara has been most influential on issues that concern her deeply or where her husband is behind the curve, like AIDS, the homeless, civil rights and education. In the late 1950s, she battled segregationist innkeepers who refused to let the family's black baby-sitter stay with them in the same hotel. She was instrumental in the appointment of the only black in Bush's Cabinet.

Barbara tries to mask her views where they differ from her husband's. Her preferred line on abortion is, "I'm not going to tell you my opinion," a perhaps pointedly transparent admission of her pro-choice views, since if she agreed with Bush, she would presumably say so.

Some staffers credit Barbara with getting George to suddenly pledge cleaner campaign tactics at a fund-raiser last fall at Bob Hope's Hollywood spread. The announcement so stunned aides that they disappeared on purpose afterward. But Barbara wasn't all softball. When Bush was resisting advice to air the now famous "straddle ad" in New Hampshire that showed Iowa caucus victor Robert Dole flip-flopping on taxes, Barbara finally chimed in, "I don't see anything wrong with that ad." It ran, and Bush took the state by 10 points.

No First Lady escapes microscopic scrutiny, and before the new family pictures are hung in the second-floor family quarters at the White House, Barbara Bush is likely to offend someone or other, perhaps for her informality, perhaps for her patrician noblesse oblige. Yet First Ladies are more than the sum of their good works. They offer a glimpse into the heart of a President—if she loves him, he can't be all that bad—and they often reflect the culture of the times. After eight years of new-money flash and glitz, of astrology and donated designer gowns, of friends over family, Barbara Bush's unspoken message may be as important as anything she may do: There is honor in motherhood; it is O.K. to be a size 14; a lined face is the price of living; and growing old is nothing to get frantic about. No small contribution, that.

January 23, 1989

A Story Better Left Untold

Coverage of the Bush twins' drinking shows why First Families need privacy

When the story broke about the Bush twins' being cited for drinking at a restaurant in Austin, Texas, I hoped it would fade before my deadline. I remember all too well when I was 19, although not as well as I would have if I hadn't gone in for a good deal of underage drinking. More recently, I remember being the parent of a 19-year-old and worrying about her underage drinking. I would have been a lot more concerned, however, had I thought a bunch of outsiders would be judging her as a teenager or me as a parent.

It's fair game to take after George W. Bush for his policy on the environment. It's less fair to take after him for his policy on his daughters, especially since we don't know what that policy is. The weekend at Camp David was going to be hard enough for the extended Bush clan without a couple of hundred nosy press people volunteering their uninformed opinions. So it was a surprise when Grandma Barbara Bush said in a speech on Friday how interesting it was to have known the President in his unpresidential days, adding dryly—and pointedly—that George was now "getting back some of his own." The crowd roared in a we've-been-there sort of way. Barbara found a middle ground between where Bill Clinton would be—calling Jesse Jackson in to pray and harking back to his alcoholic father—and the total silence of her son George. Calling it a "private matter," White House press secretary Ari Fleischer scolded reporters. "Do you want the American people to know that you're asking about private conversations that took place between the President of the U.S. and his child?"

Yes and no, Ari. People don't want to ask those questions, they dislike the press for asking them, but boy, do they gobble up the newspapers and magazines that provide the answers! Though a majority of Americans say they're pleased that honor and dignity have been restored to the White House, it is only human to gawk when a crack appears in the marble of 1600 Pennsylvania Avenue, especially if we've stepped on the same crack. Yes, it's part voyeurism, but it's much more I-wonder-how-they'll-deal-with-this.

The arc of these stories guarantees a long life. The tabloids go big first (JENNA AND TONIC, bleated the *New York Post*), thereby laundering the story for the rest of the media, which then cluck over the tabloids' distressingly low standards. How long will it be, I wondered, before the first JENNA'S CRY FOR HELP story appears? Not long enough. See Friday's *New York Daily News*. And yet the coverage so far has been more restrained than it would have been if the name on the police report had been Chelsea Clinton. Conservatives lie in wait for evidence of feeble family values and general Democratic decadence. Newt Gingrich blamed the squishy morals of the Left when Susan Smith drowned her two young sons in a South Carolina lake. The press gave Chelsea Clinton a lot of room when she arrived at the tender age of 13. Even harsh Clinton critics concede she was one good kid (adding in the next breath, of course, that she was compensating for her dysfunctional parents). Unfortunately for the twins, they are older; one is blonder; both make good copy; and they are highly recognizable. Jenna could hardly have asked for salt on her margarita before the bartender began dialing 911. The Secret Service was nearby, of course—close enough to protect the girls from physical attack but not close enough to protect them from themselves.

Teenage drinking is too common, regrettably, to be news, and Bush's daughters must hate the press for making such a big deal of theirs. But it's also the press that makes it impossible for Dad to claim that in his day he never did such a thing. Friends and family happily volunteer the story of young George arriving home, feeling no pain, running his car into trash cans and confronting his father with the taunt, "Wanna go mano à mano?" Then there's the famous D.U.I. that came out at the end of the campaign. Just two weeks ago at Yale, Bush wore the no-sweat saunter of the frat guy who was so smart (or elite) that he could party and succeed. Bush grew up to become a Governor who drastically increased the penalties for teenage drinking in his state. Once upon a time, I was a little like the young W. But now I want my daughter to do what I say, not what I did. I suspect Bush feels the same way.

June 11, 2001

Same Substance, Different Style

For Republicans, the real issue is temperament and personality

They should certainly not be invited to the same dinner party. The Senate chamber, for that matter the entire country, sometimes seems too small a place to absorb the personal antagonisms of George Bush and Robert Dole, the two front-runners for the Republican presidential nomination.

Theirs is hardly a tension born of an ideological split. On substance, Bush and Dole differ so little that in debates they seem like two wrestlers faking it for the crowd. If Dole gets exercised when Bush charges that he would raise taxes, it is precisely because he knows their views on taxes are nearly identical. Both are pragmatic conservatives, men molded by political realities rather than burning convictions.

But the similarity in outlook only heightens the deep differences in personality and style. In manner, temperament, perspective on life—that amorphous bundle of characteristics that define a person—Bush and Dole are like aliens from separate planets despite years traveling in the same orbit. It is no accident that the two sit at opposite ends of any platform; any closer, and the friction could set the place on fire. When Bush lapses into his gee-whiz optimism, that rosy outlook that comes from having everything dropped into his lap, Dole looks as if he wants to stuff a sock in the vice president's mouth. When Dole makes one of his sardonic asides that let observers know he is above the low company he is temporarily keeping, Bush appears so offended by the impropriety of it all—no one made sharp remarks at the Bush family dinner table—that he is momentarily speechless.

Bush and Dole have reached the very pinnacle of Republican politics by vastly different paths. Bush's road was smooth and privileged, Dole's unrelentingly difficult. While Bush was being chauffeured to Greenwich Country Day School and going off to Andover and Yale, Dole was walking to the public schools of Russell, Kans., and working his way through the University of Kansas at Lawrence and Washburn University of Topeka. As Bush went to prove his manhood in a West Texas oil field with a family stake of $500,000, Dole was serving as county attorney of Russell, where an unhappy part of his job was approving welfare payments for his grandparents.

Bush has seldom been without a safety net. When he gave up his congressional seat in 1970 in an unsuccessful bid for the Senate, Nixon made him U.N. Ambassador. Other appointments followed: the Republican National Committee in 1973, liaison to China in 1974 and director of the CIA in 1976. In fact, it was Dole who had to move aside as chairman of the Republican National Committee in 1973 to make room for Bush.

Even heroism came to the Vice President at less of a price. Bush received the Distinguished Flying Cross after being shot down during World War II. A harrowing experience, to be sure, but he was soon rescued and left the service with no disabling wounds. Dole too was decorated in World War II, but the war left him crippled. He spent three years in hellish convalescence, moving from one hospital to another, deprived of therapy for so long that the injury to his right arm became a disfiguring handicap.

Dole's hard knocks have in some ways made him more appealing. Unlike Bush, he has a forceful personality, an appearance of calm that inspires confidence. Dole's sense of humor can be savage, sarcastic and sardonic. Sometimes, when he has it under control, he can direct it gently at himself. At other times it merges with his mean streak.

Dole expects his staff to keep his own punishing 14-hour-a-day, six-day workweek. Building staff morale is for sissies. A former aide says, "You don't go to his house to have Thanksgiving dinner or watch football on television."

In contrast, Bush has solicited and taken advice from virtually the same team for seven years. He stays in touch with most of the politicos he's met and worked with. Bush spends much time writing notes and making phone calls. He is, in a word, nice.

Dole's family seems to be an adjunct to his driving ambition. He left his first wife one day without any explanation. His second marriage, to Elizabeth Hanford, a Democrat turned Republican from North Carolina who was serving as a member of the Federal Trade Commission, seems more like a merger. He is curiously distant from his only child, Robin, a daughter from his first marriage; when he arrives at a podium, he will give his wife a kiss and his daughter a handshake. Dole and his second wife, who have no children, live in his former bachelor apartment at the Watergate. They rarely have time for dinner together, and when they do they joke about thawing Lean Cuisine.

When three generations of the tightly knit Bush family gather at their summer home in Maine, they spill off the veranda like an all-American tableau. Barbara Bush, mother of five, grandmother of 10, helpmate of 43 years, has the expectant look of a First Lady in training, holding the Nancy Reagan gaze before there was a Nancy Reagan gaze.

The only question that seemed to stump Dole on a recent Sunday talk show was what he did in his spare time. The Senator finally listed reading newspapers and magazines, and watching TV news shows. Almost as an afterthought, he added having dinner with his wife. When the Doles travel to their Florida apartment, they socialize little and participate in few activities other than tanning by themselves. When Bush and his wife go to Florida to visit their son, they see old friends and political leaders. Bush likes to pursue his hobbies, which tend to be of the upper-class sort, such as sailing boats and fishing with flies, although he does like gunning across the bay in his down market cigarette boat.

Dole charges, with some justification, that Bush tries to look decisive but that in his years as Vice President he has made only one real decision: to support Reagan on every issue. Dole, on the other hand, has been a forceful and decisive legislative activist, taking risks when necessary but also knowing when to compromise.

Dole's main challenge now, as it has been for years, is to keep his dark side under control. Aides joke about his demeanor. Playing off *Doonesbury*'s conceit that George Bush has an invisible "evil twin" Skippy, Dole staffers joke that their candidate has an invisible "happy" twin. Even after Dole knew he had won Iowa, he was slow to celebrate. When he finally accepted his victory, breaking into a genuine smile, Iowa voters must have got a special lift, having made this sad man happy for a moment. Before the week was out, the happy twin had disappeared.

Bush faces a far different challenge: overcoming the impression that he has never been truly tested, that he knows little about the earthy struggles of daily living and that he has been sheltered from life's hard knocks. Where Dole projects a brooding quality, Bush sometimes exudes a disconcerting shallowness. He is almost stunningly incapable of expressing himself emotionally. Walking through Auschwitz last fall, he made jarring comments like "Boy, they were big on crematoriums, weren't they?"

But Bush's problem may be less a lack of feeling than a well-bred inability to effectively express it. In his stump speech, Bush says his failure to articulate his emotions does not mean he lacks deep passion. When it comes to family and friends, Bush's loyalties run deep.

The campaign is not likely to become any less intense. For Dole at 64 and Bush at 63, this may be the last chance to run for the office they so desperately want. Having overcome all the adversities life has thrown at him, Dole sees the presidency as one more challenge to conquer so as to make the pain go away. Bush, for his part, sees a President every time he looks in the mirror, and has ever since he was a schoolboy.

Campaigns, according to the civics texts and good-government groups, are supposed to be about issues and ideas, ideology and vision. Focusing on personality and manner is trivial. Yet this year, the fight for the Republican nomination involves something far more important than artificial differences on oil-import fees or taxes. It is a struggle between styles and temperaments that go to the heart of the kind of President each would be.

February 29, 1988

A Tale of Two Childhoods

Dukakis and Bush: upper-middle-class drive vs. patrician noblesse oblige

Each summer of his childhood, George Bush went with his family to a sprawling shingle-and-stone cottage in Kennebunkport, Maine, joined by assorted cousins and friends who could always find a spare bedroom, an extra tennis racket. Days were crammed with sailing and tennis at the River Club, fierce games of backgammon at night. After Prescott Bush Sr., the imposing (6-ft.-4-in.) patriarch, arrived by sleeper car from Manhattan on the weekends, he would recruit a vocal quartet from the assembled company for after-dinner harmonizing. Family friend Bill Truesdale describes those summers: "It's hard to imagine anything better."

One vacation that the Dukakis family embarked on when Michael was growing up lasted less than a day. Euterpe Dukakis had persuaded her husband, a doctor, to rent a house on the Massachusetts shore for a week. The day the family arrived, Panos Dukakis got word that one of his patients had gone into labor. The family immediately headed back to Boston. They never planned another long vacation.

The contest between Dukakis and Bush will be less about ideas and ideologies than about clashing temperaments and styles. Assessing such traits is always tricky, and never more so than in a campaign that provides little more than snippets of carefully programmed candidates. But the puzzle can sometimes be pieced together by examining the contenders' backgrounds, including the values and formative experiences of childhood. From their earliest days, Bush and Dukakis were very different. Bush was the outgoing, eager-to-please son to whom athletics and grades came easily; Dukakis was a serious, hardworking achiever. Bush always wanted to be liked and would do just about anything toward that end; Dukakis was willing to settle for respect and may have preferred it. Bush joined every social club that would have him (most would); Dukakis spurned them.

Bush has an easygoing disposition and a raft of friends he swamps with notes and phone calls. Generous to a fault, he once opened his cramped apartment at Yale to a former Andover teacher beset by alcoholism. Dukakis is frugal to the point of cheapness. He has never made many friends; two school chums he did have were sacrificed to his career. In high school, Dukakis cared so little for peer approval that he went around scolding fellow students for not putting milk cartons into the trash bin. His yearbook calls him "Chief Big Brain-in-Face." He did not have his first date until the second half of his senior year. Sandy Cohen, the girl he wanted to take to his senior prom, went with one of his rivals, so he checked coats instead.

Both Bush and Dukakis were blessed with families that could afford to give them every advantage. But among the blessed, Bush occupied a more exalted perch; he was a prime specimen of the WASP Wall Street elite that once dominated the Eastern establishment. The second of five children, he grew up in a nine-bedroom house in Greenwich, Conn., an enclave of wealth and power an hour from New York City. A chauffeur took him to Greenwich Country Day School; he played tennis and golf at the Flossy Field Club. Recalls his mother, Dorothy Walker Bush: "Life was very easy in those days. We had a lot of help. All the children had a lot of friends who were always swarming around the house."

Christmases were spent in South Carolina at the plantation owned by Dorothy's family; summers at the Kennebunkport house, where college friends remember being met after a late-afternoon swim by servants bearing warm towels and cold drinks. Both families were well heeled. Prescott Bush, the son of a Midwestern industrialist, went to Yale in 1913 (where he was tapped for Skull and Bones, the most exclusive of the secret societies) and eventually to Wall Street, where he became managing director of Brown Brothers Harriman. After his children were in college, he ran for the Senate and served 10 years, distinguishing himself for his incorruptibility and his early opposition to Joseph McCarthy. He died in 1972.

Dorothy Bush, now 86, was the daughter of a St. Louis dry-goods wholesaler, George Herbert Walker, who founded his own investment firm. She was the disciplinarian in the family, determined that her children would not grow up spoiled. Lights were turned off in unoccupied rooms, long-distance telephone calls were circled on the family bill, Cokes at the tennis club were prohibited (they could be had more cheaply at home). Possessions were downplayed; Bush offspring remember never boasting about a new car.

A onetime national women's tennis finalist, Mrs. Bush used sports to teach her brood the value of team play above any individual achievement. When George would run home to tell about his stand-up double in a baseball game, his mother would quickly interrupt, "Weren't there other boys on the team?" Young George's first nickname, "Have-Half," came from his unfailing willingness to share.

But Dorothy Bush was also a blithe spirit, always happy to hit a bucket of tennis balls with a child or swim two miles off Kennebunkport in water that rarely got above 70 degrees. Prescott Bush played a smaller part in family life, as fathers catching the early train from Greenwich did in those days. Most weekends found him swinging a 9-iron at the Round Hill links.

George was always the star of the family, a natural athlete, no intellectual but a good student, liked by everyone, especially the adults. Somehow
the other kids did not want to short-sheet his bed for this. "They accepted
from the start that George was going to be the best in whatever activity," his
mother says. "Someone asked me, 'Wasn't it hard for Pres that his younger
brother was able to do everything so well?' But George never boasted, so it
was all part of the family performance." The category that Bush's parents
monitored most closely at Greenwich Country Day School was "claims no
more than his fair share of time and attention." George excelled.

Dukakis' upbringing was not as privileged. But despite his current em-
phasis on being the son of immigrants, he had all the advantages an upper-
middle-class life could provide. Within 12 years of arriving in America at 16
with $25 in his pocket, Panos Dukakis, the candidate's father, had learned
English and graduated from high school, Bates College and Harvard Medical School, the first Greek immigrant to do so. Michael's mother, Euterpe
Boukis, a Phi Beta Kappa, was graduated from Bates 12 years after her arrival from Greece. Although the two had crossed paths briefly a decade earlier, it was not until Panos finished his residency that he asked Euterpe for
a date. It was a no-nonsense courtship. Their second time out, Panos proposed.

By 1933, when Michael Stanley* Dukakis was born, Panos had a thriv-
ing medical practice and could afford a frame house in Brookline, a well-
to-do Boston suburb. The Dukakises prospered, but they are remembered
by friends as close but not joyful, never relishing success as much as building on it. Panos had few distractions; he never swung a baseball bat or shot
a basketball with his kids. Says Michael: "My dad was not an intellectual.
His two passions in life were medicine and his family, in reverse order."

Michael (he was never called Mike) was a model son. He recalls, "My father was an Old World father in many ways. You had a series of things to do
and you just did them." For Michael, they included bringing home A's,
doing chores without being asked, earning his own spending money from
his paper route, becoming an Eagle Scout and working hard enough to
make first-string point guard on the basketball team.

Assimilating was extremely important to Euterpe Dukakis. She remembered the humiliation of being turned down for a teaching job because she
was Greek. Michael would stand before a mirror, practicing his pronuncia-
tion.

Adolescence, if Bush and Dukakis had any, has been blacked out by both
families. No teenage escapades, no bad skin, no sullen rebellions. Says

* In honor of Stanley Gray, Euterpe's mentor in elementary school.

Mrs. Bush: "I used to wonder why people had problems with their children. I just never did." Mrs. Dukakis has to go back to toddler days to recall any acting up, a refusal by young Michael to change mismatched socks.

Michael adored his brother, Stelian, who was three years older—shooting basketball in the driveway, happily wearing his hand-me-downs—but the relationship became troubled and competitive. If Stelian made the honor society, Michael was president. If Stelian was picked for the tennis team, Michael would be named captain. Euterpe describes them as close but intense siblings. During Michael's senior year in high school, Stelian suffered a nervous breakdown and came home from Bates College. While at home, he attempted suicide. Eventually, with medication and counseling, Stelian was able to finish college. But for the next 20 years, he was chronically unstable, aggressively hostile toward his younger brother, going so far as to distribute leaflets urging people to vote against his re-election as a state representative. In 1973, at the age of 42, Stelian was hit by a car while riding his bike; he slipped into a coma and died four months later.

Whatever sorrow this caused, Dukakis has kept it to himself. To this day, Dukakis will not acknowledge Stelian's suicide attempt, although his mother confirms it.

George Bush followed lockstep in his father's path: prep school, Yale, stalwart of the baseball team, Skull and Bones. Dukakis, on the other hand, broke with the expected pattern, deciding against Harvard in favor of Swarthmore, a small Quaker college near Philadelphia. A D in physics dissuaded him from studying medicine. Instead, he threw himself into politics, working for the 1951 election of Philadelphia reformist Mayor Joe Clark, his first taste of squeaky-clean government. Dukakis still did not have much of a social life—no one remembers a steady girlfriend—and he did not join any fraternities because they blackballed people. He became a minor legend in college, setting up a dormitory barbershop to serve Nigerian students, whose hair the local barbers refused to cut. It was a perfect Dukakis enterprise: high-minded and lucrative at the same time.

Both Bush and Dukakis were Big Men on Campus. But Dukakis, by nature less popular, had to campaign and occasionally lose. Bush did not seek election so much as accept it. Despite a miserable batting average, he was elected captain of the Yale baseball team. When it came time for his pledge class at his Skull and Bones to elect its president, Bush was quickly nominated, and elected unanimously. "Leadership," says Yale classmate Stu Northrup, "always came to him."

Bush and Dukakis both joined the military, Bush on his 18th birthday in 1942, just after finishing Andover, Dukakis after finishing college in 1955. Although Dukakis talks about being in the "rice paddies in Korea," the war was over by the time he joined up. He served guard duty and used his free time to study Korean. During his two and a half years in the Pacific during World War II, Bush was shot down, won the Distinguished Flying Cross and formed lifelong attachments. At a campaign stop in San Diego last month, reporters asked Leo Nadeau, Bush's turret gunner, what kind of pilot the Vice President was. Nadeau said, "The best. I'd go back up with him right now if he wanted to go."

Strong wives have replaced strong mothers in both candidates' lives. Neither man wasted much time looking around. George met Barbara Bush, a student at Smith College and the debutante daughter of the president of McCall's publishing house, when they were 17. Two weeks after George came home from the war, they wed.

Dukakis' marriage, on the other hand, was a pairing of opposites. Katherine Ellis Dickson (nicknamed after Kitty Carlisle), daughter of the first violinist of the Boston Symphony Orchestra, is emotional where he is repressed, profligate where he is cheap, high-strung where he is calm. Kitty, divorced with a 3-year-old son, was not the Dukakis family's ideal choice for Michael. But they relented, and the two were married in 1963, when Dukakis was 29.

Bush is still decent to his core, like the child who could not sit by and watch a fat classmate teased or endure dissension for very long. His self-effacement and gentility, however, may conflict with the immodesty and occasional crassness required in the real world of 1988 politics. Dukakis has no such problem. He remains aloof and utterly in control, wedded to the work ethic and the conviction that he is destined to achieve. He can cut down friends when they get in his way, suffering no pangs of loss in the process. Each man has parlayed his own distinctive personality into a particular political style. This election voters may have to choose between a candidate with too soft a heart and another with one too cool.

June 20, 1988

PART TWO

Presidential Material

GEORGE W. BUSH

I NEVER THOUGHT WE'D SEE such conclusive proof that anyone can grow up to be president as we did in the 2000 election of George W. Bush.

An optimist would say that what it takes to be president keeps evolving, a pessimist that it keeps sinking. In 2000, Americans elected the least experienced, least intellectual candidate since Calvin Coolidge. At the same time, the country (or the Supreme Court) rejected a candidate with solid credentials—a sitting vice president who'd served in the House and Senate, written two serious books, and been working toward the office since age sixteen. Leaving aside Florida (although many never will), Americans ended up with the candidate who was by far the less substantial and experienced of the two.

In electing a president, we are unable to take the measure of the man or the breadth of the task. In fact, we often measure the wrong thing. If there was discussion about a stateless enemy without a standing army wreaking unimaginable devastation on America, or that the stock market would implode, I didn't hear it. What I heard from the Bush side was, "He sighed, I heard him," and from Gore's side, "You mean a candidate running for president doesn't know what's in the Dingell-Norwood bill?"

A president is elected partly on intangibles: Does he share my values? Does he care about people like me? Of less concern is whether he knows which countries are part of NATO or how to pronounce the names of Middle Eastern emirs, anomalies for which George W. Bush must be grateful. Bush's knowledge of foreign affairs was scant and he had little appetite for study. Other than to Mexico, Texas's good neighbor to the south, Bush had traveled very little outside the United States. On a rare trip abroad to visit his parents when his father was ambassador to China, he joked that he was only going "to check out the girls."

What voters care about, perhaps inordinately, is whether they like the man who would be president. They concluded that Gore knew everything, but that Bush, the guy they liked better, knew enough.

Bush enjoyed a substantial honeymoon by modern standards, given that Clinton was nearly chased out of town in his first few months over Nanny-gate, gays in the military, and an energy tax. By contrast, Bush's early months were placid. He didn't come to Washington to do anything much (he joked he didn't see anything wrong with gridlock). As promised, he restored honor and dignity to the Oval Office, going to bed most nights by 9:30—and with his wife, thus proving that unlike Clinton, he could be trusted with your daughter. Unfortunately, thanks to those unstimulating tax cuts, he proved he couldn't be trusted with your job. Unemployment and deficits rose, and Bush's response was still: More tax cuts! If you asked him for the cure of the common cold, it would be: Tax cuts! Problem is wealthy people aren't going to stimulate the economy with the cash they get back. They already have all the appliances they need. Even economists sympathetic to the administration damn his tax cuts with faint praise. Does anyone think Bill Gates is going to buy something as a result of a spare few million? My bet is he has all the Sub-Zero refrigerators he needs.

Bush took credit for Senator Ted Kennedy's education bill, announced a limit on stem cell research so restrictive that Nancy Reagan quietly worked against it, and then headed off to his ranch for a vacation long enough to merit a name, "Returning to the Heartland."

It wasn't much to show for nine months, and some things, like those tax cuts and the limit on stem cell research, were damaging. But those issues would drop out of sight in September when Bush was back in the Oval Office barely a week, confronted with the gravest crisis since the Japanese bombed Pearl Harbor. Instead of Roosevelt at the helm, however, the country had the most inexperienced leader in modern memory. Had we made a terrible mistake in thinking we had the luxury of electing the class clown, rather than the class nerd, when the world, as we knew it, no longer existed?

It was hard to know those first hours after the attacks. In fact, it was hard to know where he was after he left the school in Sarasota, Florida. After saying he was ordering a massive investigation "to hunt down the folks who committed this act," Bush disappeared, leaving the country Home Alone for twelve hours. Even congressional Republicans were anxious, not knowing if the first bombs of World War III had been detonated that morning. Ushered to a holding room at the Capitol Hill police station, they knew no more about what was going on than TV anchors who knew nothing. The vice president had been taken to an undisclosed location, the bunker in the basement of the White House. There wasn't a peep out of him. The highest White House official seen all day was Communications Director Karen Hughes.

Late in the afternoon, aboard Air Force One, Bush asked that the cabin be cleared and had the signal operator place a call to the last person who had had to grapple with the decision of whether to go to war. After he talked to his father, Bush got his bearings. He decided to address the country that night from the Oval Office. Air Force One returned, and twelve hours after the first plane hit the World Trade Center, Bush gave a reassuring, although not inspiring, speech to the nation, calling the attack on America an "act of war."

The speech would have been better had White House aides not stepped on it by insisting that Bush had remained away from Washington because of "credible evidence" that the White House was a target of the attackers. This put the Secret Service and FBI in a terrible bind, pressured to back up a story the administration had to later concede was hyped. Flight 93 was aiming for the Capitol. The other planes hit their targets.

That was the last time Bush would be caught flat-footed, as he transformed himself into what he hadn't been before: informed, decisive, reassuring. He enlisted allies in a global coalition against al-Qaeda, ordered $20 billion in emergency funds to New York, issued a "play ball" to Major League Baseball and the National Football League, and within two days won authority to retaliate from both houses of Congress. Criticism vanished, except from one source. After the president remarked that he wanted Osama bin Laden "dead or alive," Laura Bush pulled him aside and said, "Bushie, are you gonna git 'em?"—a warning, she told me, that he should tone down the cowboy talk.

Before 9/11, Bush staffers mocked Clinton as the weepy minister in chief. They swore you'd never catch Bush feeling anyone's pain. After 9/11, there was so much pain, he had to feel some of it. The cowboy had to become Minister-in-Chief, to engage in rituals he'd previously derided, in a vernacular that was unfamiliar, in a setting that was formal.

His big moment came that Friday. When President Bush arrived at the National Cathedral for the day of remembrance, you could see why the staff had always gone to such lengths to keep Bush senior out of sight. It's hard for any child to look as though he's in charge when a parent, much less one who's been president, is in the room. Seeing him there, nervous, fidgeting, I thought back to a funeral for shooting victims in Texas when he had mugged for reporters like a squirming child in need of a stern word from his parents. He was looking as if Mom, seated in the same pew, had minutes earlier smoothed his hair and straightened his tie. It would have seemed natural for the elder Bush to rise and go to the altar to speak, leaving his son to listen.

But, of course, it was the son who rose to speak. With four former presidents looking on, Bush spoke solemnly and emotionally, calming a shaken country, reaching out to the devastated families, joining them in "a kinship of grief." When he returned to his seat, his father, gaze staying straight ahead, reached his arm across Laura to grasp his son's hand.

Sometimes Bush's feelings are too raw, as in the "dead or alive" line, but more often, they're dead on. Bush has the capacity to express feelings without resorting to Clinton's lip-biting or Gore's melodrama. During his first visit to New York after 9/11, Bush looked small as he climbed atop the jerry-built platform at Ground Zero, insubstantial in that cloth jacket, so much slighter than the firemen in their greatcoats and hardhats, until someone shouted that they couldn't hear him. Spontaneously, he stuck a bullhorn up toward the sky, put his arm around a retired firefighter, and shouted, "I can hear *you*. The people who knocked down these buildings are going to hear all of us soon." Bush had become commander in chief.

*   *   *

If Bush proved himself the man for 9/11, he is yet to show he's a man for all seasons. His instincts served him well as he met the country's massive emotional needs, promising he would go after the savages who attacked us. He routed the Taliban and broke up al-Qaeda's camps in Afghanistan, despite predictions that the United States would be stymied there as the British and the Soviets had been. A huge majority of Americans—nearly 90 percent, not the scant 49 percent who elected him—approved of how he performed.

Yet a year later, the president had lost the coalition that had swiftly prevailed in Afghanistan. He'd gone from having nearly the whole world with him as he struck al-Qaeda, to having nearly the whole world against us, as we prepared to strike Iraq.

Compared to the world Bush faces now, Afghanistan was checkers. The complex, interlocking situation in the Middle East is chess. At the outset of his administration, the president ignored growing violence in Israel, in part because he disapproved of Clinton's intense obsession with brokering a Mideast peace. Bush wanted America to go it alone and act in its own self-interest. Treaties were optional; the UN for sissies.

During the campaign, Bush's lack of foreign policy experience was flicked away with the promise that he would have the best advisers Dad's administration could produce, people who had served previous presidents, not the rookies Clinton brought in. No one mentioned what would happen if those advisers disagreed, as they did throughout the summer of 2002 in full view and hearing of the world.

On one side was Defense Secretary Donald Rumsfeld (and his brilliant but single-minded deputy, Paul Wolfowitz) and Vice President Cheney. They believe Saddam Hussein is a power-mad monster one aluminum tube away from having nuclear weapons and that he has ties to al-Qaeda. The United States had to get him or he would get us. On the other side were Secretary of State Colin Powell and Republican senators, such as Chuck Hagel and Richard Lugar, concerned that the United States needed to build a coalition and work through the United Nations if it was going to take on Saddam Hussein and govern Iraq. The goal, they said, should be to disarm Saddam; toppling him would be a bonus.

In fact, in October Powell said, "Disarming Hussein is the equivalent of regime change." Powell was also adamant that consideration be given to who would come to power post-Hussein and how the region would realign itself absent Hussein. Is the United States prepared to have a Marshall Plan for the Middle East? Bush never squarely faced the question of how much treasure and troops the country would expend in the cause of an Iraqi democracy. We've expended almost none in the cause of an Afghan democracy. Iraq will never be Iowa, but without nation building, it could splinter into warring sects that will make Afghanistan resemble Switzerland. National Security Adviser Condoleezza Rice, who aides joke is the daughter Bush never had, is his Pentium processor, giving intellectual infrastructure to Bush's visceral feeling that Hussein must go. Smart as she is, the task became more difficult after North Korea's Kim decided to act like a full-fledged member of the axis of evil. He kicked out weapons inspectors (Iraq was swarming with them), reneged on the Nuclear Non-Proliferation Treaty and boasted of a nuclear arms program one aluminum tube away from launch. Still, he could get no respect. Bush refused to rattle a saber in his direction.

Indeed, Bush specifically took military action against North Korea off the table in favor of negotiations, dispatching New Mexico Governor Bill Richardson, former UN ambassador, to meet with North Korean diplomats. The meeting went well, if normalizing relations between Santa Fe and Pyongyang were the goal. But it did little to walk Kim back from the brink.

True, there's some reason to give Kim more kid-glove treatment than

Saddam: He could wipe out Seoul and some 37,000 American troops in a blink. Still, it is hard to justify such disparate treatment of two similarly awful regimes. Bush makes the distinction that Saddam having gassed his own people is much worse and that the world community should give democracy a chance to flower in a region of the world just waiting to be saved.

His arguments persuade more than half of Americans, according to polls, and Britain's Tony Blair, but not other members of the Security Council, who think the U.S. should follow international law. The recalcitrant countries worry over a Saddam Hussein with nothing left to lose unleashing whatever weapons he does have upon the world, and leaving the international community with a destabilized Middle East, and a mess of religious sects to clean up after the military finishes its part. They point to Afghanistan as a case in point, where warring tribes, not peacekeepers, control the country and its mountainous border with Pakistan, which harbors the world's most dangerous terrorists. If Osama is alive, he may well be happy that Bush is distracted by Saddam, and not the least bit disturbed by his demise.

Skeptics also wonder if other factors, not present in North Korea, are clouding the president's judgment: Iraq is the one place the U.S. can fight back, since terrorists have no country and finding bin Laden to punish is akin to looking for the proverbial needle in a haystack. What's more, Hussein controls a quarter of the world's oil, and he tried to assassinate Bush's father. They worry over inflaming Muslims against the invading infidels from America.

Democrats opposed to taking on Iraq alone did a miserable job of making their case. Of course, the case against is harder to make. Saddam is bad (no argument there) and wants to acquire nuclear weapons (who among the bad guys doesn't?). They were stuck arguing a mishmash of nuanced points, none of which had the advantage of wiping a bad guy off the face of the earth. Waiting is hardly ever an appealing argument to make when the country is scared to death, which is what opting for intrusive inspections under the aegis of the lumbering United Nations means. Building a coalition of countries beyond Britain and fostering opposition groups that might govern an Iraq without Hussein sounds like the solution of the ninety-seven-pound weakling when Bush is channeling Patton. Clinton nailed the Democrats' dilemma and Bush's appeal. "People prefer someone who is strong and wrong to someone who is weak and right."

Bush got the House to vote in favor of broad powers to take on Iraq, with only the modest requirement that he certify to Congress that all diplomatic efforts had been exhausted before a first strike. The Democratic Senate was more resistant to such a blank check. But a commander in chief is hard to turn down. After getting some modest concessions, the Senate passed the resolution overwhelmingly.

Bush had his way, and we could only hope that he wouldn't someday regret getting what he wished for. Bush showed no qualms. His version of grace under pressure was to brag that his running time had never been as good as it was once he began fighting the war on terror, nor had he ever slept better. Laura Bush told me how, during the night of 9/11, the two of them were wakened in the middle of the night by an anxious Secret Service and led to a bomb shelter in the basement of the White House. Bush had no desire to sleep on a pullout couch without his feather pillow and insisted on returning to bed upstairs. Bush told friends he felt like Truman, who after he ordered the bombing of Hiroshima slept a dreamless sleep. But should life, as usual, go on? Wouldn't we all sleep sounder if Bush slept a little less? Secretary Powell says he sleeps like a baby, too. Every two hours, he wakes up screaming.

*   *   *

Iraq was a tough nut to crack for the opposition party. But shouldn't Democrats have been able to make a case that Republicans had destroyed the robust economy they were handed?

That's where Iraq comes in again. The old Jack Benny skit in which the skinflint was asked "your money or your life" was played out in the country in the fall of 2002. Benny amusingly hesitated, but Americans were too scared to play it for laughs, more frightened for their lives than they had been since the Cuban missile crisis. Fear, rekindled by the prospect of a preemptive strike on Iraq, kept them from noticing their money was gone.

Republicans couldn't be happier that no one was paying attention to the economy. Since they were put in charge, the stock market had lost a third of its value, a drop not seen since the Hoover administration. Bankruptcy, joblessness, and deficits were up; consumer confidence and savings were down. The country had been hit by a wave of corporate crime not seen since robber baron days.

In the go-go nineties, CEOs hid costs, created sham companies, took out massive loans with no intention of repaying them, sold stock inflated by false profits, and awarded themselves, with the complicity of sweetheart boards, a king's ransom in mansions, jets, and Impressionist art. Retirees, employees, and shareholders were left holding the bag after the plundering drove some companies like Enron, Tyco, and WorldCom to bankruptcy or its brink. Turns out men in three-piece suits had stolen billions of dollars when no one was looking, not even the accountants entrusted with doing so.

Bush's gut could be no help. He was pals with CEOs who'd grabbed monster pay and perk packages (salaries have risen from forty times workers' pay to five hundred times). As a few CEOs and their top executives were hustled off in handcuffs to be fingerprinted and arraigned, Bush mumbled all the wrong things about accounting laws not being "black or white" and a few "bad apples" spoiling the barrel. He gave a speech on Wall Street, with a backdrop "Corporate Responsibility" repeated three hundred times, as if an errant accountant had been forced to stay after school and write his lesson on the blackboard. The speech was so weak that by the end of it, the Dow Jones had dropped three hundred points. He and his former SEC chairman, Harvey Pitt (who'd promised a "kinder and gentler" agency at his confirmation hearings), recommended that people see the implosion of the market as a buying opportunity. Anyone who took the advice took a bath.

As close as Bush came to identifying with the workers at Enron was to harp on his mother-in-law's $8,000 stock loss, without mentioning that the employees, shareholders, and retirees were left penniless while Kenneth "Kenny boy" Lay kept his $7 million Houston penthouse. Tyco's chairman, Dennis Kozlowski, had three mansions furnished at company expense with fripperies like $6,000 shower curtains and a $15,000 umbrella stand. Indeed, the scandal is not what's illegal, it's that much of what left corporate chiefs rich and employees impoverished *was* legal. Kozlowski will likely go to jail, not for sumptuary excess but for failing to pay sales tax on his excesses, a little like Al Capone getting caught for mail fraud.

Bush's gut told him that if risk-taking entrepreneurs like himself were going belly-up and stranding employees and shareholders, it wasn't their fault. After all, nothing that went bad in his business career was his fault. In the late 1980s, Bush, who'd never been successful by Texas standards, needed some money. He'd done the schmoozing and backslapping to get the Texas Rangers to come to town. But he still needed some cold, hard cash to buy into the syndicate for which he was the front man, a fraction of the $86 million others were investing, but still $600,000.

That's where Harken Energy, on whose audit committee and board he sat, came in. It took just a few of the moves now familiar to us from congressional hearings to raise the money: buy a company with a loan from your company, sell the company back to your company, grossly minimize the purchase price and grossly inflate the sales price, and sell the stock before anyone catches on. Report the sale not within ninety days, as the SEC requires, but anytime you feel like it, if your dad is president.

Without that Harken deal, Bush couldn't have bought a stake in the Texas Rangers and wouldn't be the wealthy man he is today. The Texas Rangers, with the help of a bond referendum and new taxes, got a sparkling new stadium and attracted a well-heeled buyer, Tom Hicks, a Bush friend. Bush was entitled to $2.8 million from the sale but got almost $13 million for his "sweat equity." Baseball was very, very good to Bush.

Little of this came out during the campaign when Bush and Cheney touted their business accomplishments. Bush campaigned as much on stewardship of the Texas Rangers as on the stewardship of his state (wise, since the lieutenant governor and land commissioner have as much power as the governor). And Dick Cheney crowed about his record in the corporate suite: "By any measure you want to use, Halliburton has been a great success story." Not exactly. Cheney's decision to take over Dresser Industries, with its huge asbestos liability, was a disaster that nearly ruined the company. Halliburton got clobbered, its stock falling 75 percent. It earned its own SEC investigation over accounting practices put in place by Cheney, the kind used by Enron and Global Crossing that boosted the stock price by inflating revenue.

But to admit that the orchard, not just an occasional apple, is rotten would mean Bush would have to do something about it. In Bushworld, regulation, especially the alphabet soup of agencies that tormented his pals in the oil patch, is the enemy. He likes government more than he used to, since it was government firefighters and rescue workers on civil service salaries without expense accounts who walked into burning buildings to save strangers, but only slightly more.

When he caught on that if people realize the game is rigged, the game is over, Bush sent the message "I care." He belatedly supported a watered-down bill to reform the accounting industry. He interrupted his August 2002 vacation in the "Heartland" (on his way to Crawford, he got off a crack at the Clintons by remarking that "normal Americans don't sit in Martha's Vineyard swilling white wine") to chair a hastily arranged but minutely choreographed economic summit at Baylor University in Waco. Bush invited campaign contributor Charles Schwab (author of Bush's $300 billion dividend tax cut) to share the stage with him the very day that Chuck, listed among *Fortune* magazine's "Greedy Bunch," was laying off four hundred Schwab & Co. employees.

As Bush was telling the handpicked entrepreneurs and grandmothers, "We've got the best tax policy in the world. I mean, we got a lot going for us," the Federal Reserve Board issued a bleak report predicting a slowdown prolonged by a loss of faith in government's ability to punish wrongdoers and root out corporate corruption. Joking that he had a hall pass from former Treasury Secretary Paul O'Neill, Bush said, "Gotta go," and left early. The Dow dropped another 206 points, which suggests that one way for Bush to help would be to never, ever mention the market again.

Bush's upside is he can't fake it. The downside is that he can't fake it. After his big win in the midterm elections in 2002, Bush lurched further in the direction of protecting those who have, against those who don't. He sought yet other massive tax cuts tilted to the wealthy and stinted on funding his own Homeland Security bill. So much for those firefighters he hugged. Where's moral clarity when he needs it? Is Bush Two destined to follow in the footsteps of his father, who failed to grasp the problems of the little people because he was blinded by the big ones?

Corporate malfeasance or as Bush pronounces it, "corporate malfeee-ance," is not a victimless crime. My company AOL Time Warner is under federal investigation and has admitted under pressure to falsely inflating revenues by $190 million. Employees have lost about 70 percent of the value of their 401(k)s, with no recovery in sight. We would be better off if Steve Case had come into our offices in a ski mask carrying an Uzi. He would have walked off with our wallets, not our life's savings. In the deal, Time Warner got a pile of worthless stock. AOL got Time Warner. Two guys who liked each other thought it would be fun to merge. The only folks to benefit from the synergy of that merger are the executives who got huge bonuses for making it. Bush should treat corporate execs like evildoers and put them in debtors' prison until they make restitution to the people they've impoverished.

You might think the country would be ready for a Democrat who could make the case against economic laissez-faire? By rights, Al Gore should have been that person, as the winner of the popular vote in 2000. Gore's shrill populism looks prescient: fat cats have run amuck, Alaska is melting (even Bush's EPA had to admit it), the Middle East deteriorated into greater violence, and a demented tax cut has plunged the country back into debt. Yet check the clips. The most coverage Gore got since his loss was when he grew a beard, and when he shaved it off.

For a while in 2002, Gore looked like a man who was running, with increasing attention to grooming, book writing, and weight loss sufficient to get his wedding ring back on. After a self-imposed exile, he gave three speeches and went on a binge of TV. As the opposition leader, Gore proved to be no Comeback Kid. When he talked, no one listened.

*   *   *

I miss George Bush. Sure, I see him every day up on a podium, breezing into a fund-raiser, or walking across the South Lawn to Marine One. True, I was only a few dinner plates away from him at Katharine Graham's house and within joking distance at the White House Christmas party, where he charmed my goddaughter.

But once a man is president, he changes, you change, and the situation changes. He's Mr. President ("Trailblazer" to the Secret Service). Anyplace you might see Bush up close is now off-limits. He's surrounded by men in black talking into their wrists and driving armored Chevy Suburbans with gunwales. He travels on Air Force One. You travel on the press charter behind him, unless you're one of five reporters in the pool, and then you're sequestered in the back, lucky to get a few words with an underling. He works in the Oval Office and lives upstairs in the White House. You rarely get past the lower press office.

The campaign, or specifically the campaign plane, is the last time the press gets to see the man who would be president more closely than an attentive viewer of C-SPAN. Bush didn't like campaigning, so he treated the time on the plane like recess, a chance to kick back between math and chemistry classes. He was seductive, playful, and most of all, himself. It's a failure of some in the press—well, a failure for me—that we are susceptible to a politician directing the high beams of his charm at us. That Al Gore couldn't catch a break had something to do with how he was when his hair was down. Only it never was.

Bush wasn't just any old breezy frat brother with mediocre grades, a short attention span, and a career that didn't start until he got religion and stopped drinking at age forty. He was proud of it. The modern political campaign, long on Oprah-type qualities and short on specifics, played more to Bush's easygoing, genial characteristics than to Gore's Type A traits. Bush neutralized Gore's résumé by letting Gore be Gore, a tense technocrat intent on proving he was the smartest kid on the planet.

Gore elicited in us the childish urge to poke a stick in the eye of the smarty-pants, while Bush elicited self-recognition. Former governor Ann Richards lost to Bush when she hammered him for "being born on third base and thinking he hit a triple." Bush has never choked on the silver spoon in his mouth. Rather than hide his gentleman Cs and his excessive devotion to body over mind that working out two hours a day requires, Bush honed his laissez-faire approach to life into a potent tool for bonding with the goof-off in all of us.

While reporters had to go searching for Al Gore and Bill Bradley grades (surprisingly mediocre), Bush wore his as a badge of honor. In Bedford, New Hampshire, speaking to a group of schoolchildren, he joked about how he was living proof that "if you get a C average, you can end up being successful in life." The press took out after him for sending the wrong message to suggestible third-graders, but their voting parents didn't seem to mind. Speaking at Yale University commencement, he hit the point even harder. He'd always had a love-hate relationship with the school his father and grandfather, Senator Prescott Bush, had attended. A president of Deke House who didn't make any team (he played intramural sports), and a ten o'clock scholar at best, he was cheered in May 2001 when he told the graduates, "To those of you who received honors, awards, and distinctions, I say: Well done. And to the C students, I say: You, too, can be president of the United States."

Could a candidate who knew so little and was so unapologetic about it go the distance? Shouldn't a late bloomer who didn't break a sweat have had the sense to cover it up, *or* catch up, pull all-nighters to learn who ran Pakistan and that there was already a multinational force of peacekeepers in Bosnia? It would have shown sensitivity in the use of the awesome power over life and death if he'd voiced concern over the large number of death row inmates released when DNA evidence showed the system had convicted the wrong man, a number that had grown to 110 as of August 2002.

Up against Gore, who should have won handily, Bush's debits were neutralized by the deficits of Mr. Know-It-All. Successful politicians know that a country has emotional needs as well as global ones. It accounts for Bush senior's triumph over Massachusetts governor Michael Dukakis and his subsequent loss to I-feel-your-pain Clinton. Everyone knew Dukakis had a brain but couldn't tell if he had a heart. In the first presidential debate, CNN's Bernard Shaw lobbed a loopy pitch to the governor, asking what he would do if his wife, Kitty, were raped. He calmly gave a disquisition on criminal law rather than say he would want to see the man swinging from the highest tree.

Voters could sense that Gore's brain, like Dukakis's, was his most important organ, to paraphrase Woody Allen. Listening to your head is essential, but the door to your emotions needs to be kept open. Had Gore been faced with the catastrophe of 9/11, he might have given a treatise on international law, the proper role of NATO, the history of the Soviets in Afghanistan, all coated in slow-motion diplo-speak. But he would not have been able to connect with the Dirty Harry within. Had Gore waited as long to bomb Afghanistan as Bush, he would have been subject to much more carping from the public, deprived of the rhetorical satisfaction Bush dished up. Oscar Wilde said nothing worth knowing can be taught, which is one more break for Bush. If how to lead the country in the aftermath of the first attack within its own borders had been in a book, Bush wouldn't have had a clue what to do.

*　　*　　*

It's not hard to dislike Bush's policies, which favor the strong over the weak. But it *is* hard to dislike Bush. His first words to me during the campaign were, "You haven't suffered enough." He was referring to the fact that I was dropping in on his campaign plane as a "Big Foot," as opposed to being assigned to him permanently and thus condemned to live out of a suitcase and drink coffee made by strangers in the morning. For that I didn't deserve a nickname like "Dulce" (for CNN's Candy Crowley) or "Stretch" (for the very tall David Gregory of NBC). Bush explained his refusal by pointing out that I got to go home at night to sleep in my own bed on my own pillow—a commodity so special that he carried his own feather version on the campaign trail.

The pillow came to symbolize how much Bush hated breaking with his routine. He liked to start late, go to bed early, and catch a nap in between. His schedule was tightly scripted by a staff who knew that for Bush to play at the top of his adequate but not brilliant game, he needed to have all his ducks in a row, and not too many ducks at that.

Like a kid at camp, he often complained how much he missed Laura, the twins, the dogs Ernie and Spot, his familiar jogging route in Austin, and his own kitchen, where he could have peanut-butter-and-jelly sandwiches whenever he felt like it (one of the few times he lost his cool was when a newcomer on the plane ate a PB&J set aside for him). In 1984, former vice president Walter Mondale famously admitted how awful campaigning was and derided anyone who would spend hundreds of nights at a Holiday Inn—and lost. Bush was unapologetic—and won. Air Bush kept banker's hours, wheels down in Austin by four P.M. Friday afternoon, the candidate out running around the lake and settling in for dinner at home with Laura before sunset.

Bush didn't try to become something he wasn't. He faked it once, claiming during a debate to be reading a Dean Acheson biography. When pressed to summarize it, he lapsed into campaign boilerplate, which suggested that he'd *meant* to read it, but had not actually done so. He soon stopped pretending. Some saw that as a mark of maddening smugness, others as engaging authenticity.

What Bush didn't know is that I had suffered before. If I was a "Big Foot" in 2000, I'd traveled as a small foot for a long time with Michael Dukakis and Jesse Jackson and Bob Dole, with Steve Forbes and Jack Kemp and Dan Quayle. Watching Jack Kemp arm-synch throwing a football for the one hundredth time, as if being a Buffalo Bill were the major requirement for higher office, is a form of suffering, as is watching Dan Quayle jumping up and down like a puppy, inflating his accomplishments.

The least serious major candidate most of us had ever covered (I'm leaving out crank candidates like Donald Trump), Bush was a metacandidate, making fun of the process at the moment he was engaged in it, eliminating many of the rituals between the press and the candidate (he wasn't any good at pressers and Q&A at a podium anyway) in favor of informal encounters. A tongue-tied and uninspiring speaker, he relied on a good nature, a reliable gut instinct, and a playfulness developed at the dining room table of a large family. His willingness to look silly, he says, comes from the year when he tried to cheer his mother up after the death of his four-year-old sister, Robin, from leukemia. I'd never seen a candidate so happy for the chance to goof off in front of an audience, never known one to take a steaming hot towel from the steward and play peekaboo in an effort to get Frank Bruni of *The New York Times* to laugh. "Frankie boy," as Bush called him, did.

No candidate who isn't naturally prankish should try this. The political field is littered with consultants who tried to give their clients quirks they shouldn't have (remember Naomi Wolfe trying to dress Gore and make him the daddy candidate?). Phony is a label that sticks: Jimmy Carter carrying his garment bag and wearing cardigans, Richard Nixon walking on the beach in his wing tips.

Personal traits matter more in a presidential campaign than campaigns for lesser office. There's a reverse gravity at work: the higher the office, the less specific voters are about definable skills. It's why the pop quiz Bush failed didn't matter. Mayors are required to know street grids and zoning ordinances, the names of fire chiefs and school board members. By the time you compete for the presidency, whether a candidate sighs during a debate and invades the other guy's space can have more lasting significance than whether he can muster the details of health care reform. A good nature frequently trumps a good brain. At every juncture when Gore was determined to show he was the smartest guy running, Bush was wise enough to let him.

Reverse gravity operates with more force in boom times. In 2000, the Cold War was won. Peace was at hand. The very economic cycle seemed to have been halted (though it wasn't, as we learned after the election). In such a golden era, the country could indulge its preference that the guy you'd prefer to live next door to is the guy who should be in the White House. Would you rather fire up the backyard grill and have hamburgers with Bush or Gore? Who'd let you borrow the garden shears and not leave you snarky notes if you didn't return them on time?

Bush's aides quietly conceded that Bush hadn't traveled the world or mastered its problems, but it didn't matter, because he would have advisers for that. Since nothing bad was going to happen to the most powerful, most prosperous nation on earth, why worry? Good times can absorb a good-time guy. Bush and his political wizard, Karl Rove, understood that less could be more. Together, they shrunk the presidency to Bush's size.

Bush is a guy's guy, and he favored them on the plane, even former enemies like George Stephanopolous, aka "Georgie Boy," with whom he exchanged running times. He explained to Georgie Boy how he didn't hold a grudge against him for helping Clinton beat his father in 1992 because grudge-holding can slow you down.

I was able to get a little guy treatment because he liked to tease me about my close friendship with his cousin John Ellis, a former political analyst at NBC. His favorite gambit is to pit outsiders like himself against insiders like me. After slowly explaining to me the difference between a farm and a ranch, how he toured his six hundred acres in a pickup, and how many head of cattle he had, he aimed his eyes on my notebook and said slowly, "For the city slicker, that's spelled h-e-i-f-e-r."

Bush likes an easy room to work, and his inner child hovers near the surface. As he propped his rolled-up sleeves on the seat back in front of me, his body leaning into the conversation, he waggled his eyebrows up and down like Groucho Marx, mugging across the aisle to attract a larger audience. He took off on "pundits who drop in on the campaign and then get it wrong on TV." Bush knows how to push the buttons of high school insecurity, couching an insult (I resent you on behalf of your harder-working colleagues) inside a play on your vanity (I've seen your show).

Bush throws himself into a conversation, all cylinders and facial expressions firing. He likes every kind of snack and chews with his mouth open. If you're used to your presidents from history books, he is a bit of a shock. Bush liked to pat bald heads with the booming Elmer Gantry exhortation "Heal." It wasn't that he did it well, but that he imitated Austin Powers at all. You can't picture Harry Truman head-butting a reporter, or FDR making faces at church, or Eisenhower trying to engage Tony Bennett in conversation rather than joining in the singing of carols at a televised Christmas concert. Would they have called former KGB man and Russian president Vladimir Putin "Pootie-Poot" or chief political adviser Karl Rove "Turd Blossom"?

Being president of Deke House, and enjoying it, is excellent training for a campaign plane which is a lot like an intensive care unit, where all one's bodily needs are met in exchange for being totally confined, a state brilliantly captured on HBO's *Journeys with George*. The staff herds the press from event to event in a universe parallel to the candidate's, but entirely separate. There's no hopping into a car with a candidate (unless his name is John McCain) and going from hamlet to hamlet. Nowadays, we reporters clamber onto a bus to board a charter plane to hop from tarmac to tarmac.

That makes the food on the plane crucial. Like the army, the press travels on its stomach and in this regard, Gore was no match for Bush. Gore wanted the snacks to be environmentally and nutritionally correct, but somehow granola bars ended up giving way to Fruit Roll-Ups and the sandwiches came wrapped and looked long past their sell-by date. On a lucky day, someone would remember to buy supermarket doughnuts. By contrast, a typical day of food on Air Bush (going from Philadelphia to Pittsburgh to Newark to East Brunswick to Austin) consisted of five meals with access to a sixth, if you count grazing at a cocktail buffet. Breakfast one was French toast, scrambled eggs, bacon, sausage, hash browns, and fruit, followed by a midmorning breakfast of spinach-and-tomato omelets. Lunch one was grilled chicken and beef with mashed potatoes, and lunch two was mushrooms stuffed with crab, shrimp kebabs, and pizza. There were Dove Bars and designer water on demand, and a bathroom stocked like Martha Stewart's guest suite. Dinner at seven (traveling with Bush was like being a retiree in Boca Raton, the early bird special followed by bed at nine) featured lobster ravioli, grilled vegetables, and fruit cobbler with ice cream.

But lobster wasn't what Air Gore lacked. It was a candidate comfortable with himself. Gore relaxed with the press as if he'd been told it was time to take his medicine and it was slotted into his schedule: "Three P.M., talk about last night's Mets game with press pool."

Bush wasn't an intellectual and didn't try to be. Gore wasn't a wild and crazy guy, but occasionally he did try to be. When Gore tried to play well with others on the plane, he draped a starched white napkin over his arm and served poached salmon, impersonating a stiff waiter, which relaxed no one.

Gore's major social event of the year, hosting a Halloween party at the vice-presidential mansion, was perfect Gore fun—staged, stylized, with costumes to hide who you really were. At a party filled with children, Gore's normal cadence, which is to speak as if he's addressing a class of kindergartners, was suitable. In 1999, he dressed as Frankenstein, which allowed him to spend the night aping the movements and speech pattern of a slow, wooden monster.

Even with candidates like Gore, reporters scramble to get on the plane. There's value in just being there. The candidate might show a little leg, make a fool of himself, or keel over (the death watch is a macabre but essential part of the job). Barring any of those things, it is also fun, since reporters harbor a bit of the Deke House ethos, and a campaign is as close as an adult can get to duplicating college life. Few settings can compete with the hothouse of a campaign for falling in love. CNN's Judy Woodruff married *The Wall Street Journal*'s Al Hunt; CBS's Susan Spencer married PBS's and *The Boston Globe*'s Tom Oliphant; ABC's Claire Shipman married *Time*'s Jay Carney.

But editors don't authorize huge travel expenses for Jack to find Jill or for reporters to have fun as if we're back at Bishop McDevitt High School. There's a lot of pressure to find the candidate's hidden side, which arises from every editor's belief that there *is* one. In 1988, it was urgent to find another side to Michael Dukakis since no editor wanted to run another piece on good jobs at good wages. And sometimes when you think you are glimpsing an unscripted moment, you're being had. The press originally played catching Governor Dukakis dancing with his wife at Logan Airport's baggage carousel as a spontaneous whimsical touch, like a later long-lens snapshot of Hillary and Bill dancing on the beach in the Virgin Islands. But both "moments" occurred when the principals were aware that the press was hovering and when such a picture would be very helpful. The Clintons' twirl happened at the height of the Monica mess. Dukakis's was when the two candidates had begun pawing their spouses for public consumption. Dukakis in the tank was the real Dukakis.

Reporters have learned not to take at face value the happy tableau candidates put on display: the spectacle of the one-minute Al-Tipper clutch at the 2000 convention and indiscriminate and constant spousal handholding. When Bush reached for Laura's hand at a photo-op during the summit in Russia in the spring of 2002, Vladimir Putin shocked his wife by grabbing hers. Calculated displays of affection have gone global.

Women reporters are given to the notion that the way a man is with his family (not just when he's showing them off like steers at the county fair) tells you something about him. In the old days, none of that was discussed. My colleague Hugh Sidey, who wrote the White House column for twenty-five years, recalls the press corps splashing in the Kennedy pool in Palm Beach while a few feet away JFK entertained various young things in the cabanas. It was gossiped about, chortled over, even admired by some, but never written about.

Neither Bush nor Gore had anything to fear on the woman front, except that Gore seemed to be as saddled with Monica as if he were the one who'd invited the intern for a late night pizza. Vice presidents have a hard time shucking the guy who brung them and look shaky when they try to do so. The more Gore ran from Clinton, the more Bush treated them as the same person, calling Clinton Gore's shadow. Every time Bush claimed he would restore honor and dignity to the White House, he scored a twofer. It reminded people of what they hated about Clinton, and it tied Gore up in knots: he was angrier at Clinton over the whole Monica business than Hillary was, but he couldn't respond without dropping the pretense that Clinton didn't exist.

The Clinton-Gore now-you-see-them, now-you-don't became a running story. In the Rose Garden, Gore pronounced Clinton one of the greatest presidents in history, and then adopted a schedule to make sure he'd never be caught in the same camera shot with one of the "greatest presidents" again. Gore made sure Clinton and his Rocky-like walk through the underground of the Staples Center at the Democratic convention would be long over before Gore arrived. As a result of all these maneuvers, Monica stuck to Gore. The good economy did not.

Even during the Florida recount, poor Gore couldn't catch a break. The state was controlled by the other guy's brother, and he was being robbed in broad daylight by Florida secretary of state Katherine Harris, who doubled as Bush's campaign chair. But Gore came off looking like a sore loser. He made mistakes: if he hadn't made so many bad decisions during the campaign, he wouldn't have lost his home state. If he'd been a steadier person, he wouldn't have changed campaign guises so many times. If he hadn't been so clever, he wouldn't have asked for recounts only in Democratic counties (a full state recount and he might have won). And if he didn't think he was smarter than everyone else, he wouldn't have acted as his own recount counsel, with voter registration spreadsheets and law books stacked all over his dining room table. Bush left his dirty work to Jim Baker. Partly because Bush stayed above it all, his ugly win was quickly forgotten by most Americans.

The first chance voters had the opportunity to weigh in on the Bush presidency since the troubles in Florida was in the midterm elections. He campaigned across the country, raised more than $100 million, and went to some states three times (to Florida, for his brother Jeb, a dozen times). Bush turned the election into a referendum on his administration and got a resounding vote of confidence.

Imagine if positions were reversed. Imagine if Gore's daddy had appointed the Supreme Court judges who subsequently delivered the presidency to him on a golden 5-4 platter. We'd still be hand-wringing over whether Gore had the legitimacy to govern. The old joke about Gore remains true: If Bush and Gore drove through a car wash with the top down, only Gore would get wet.

The Cheshire Candidate

What's lurking behind Bush's smirk? Maybe an attitude problem

"A smile is just a smile," the song goes, but with polls showing Governor George W. Bush falling behind in the New Hampshire primary, and after two underwhelming debate performances, the smile with enough wattage to light the national Christmas tree has devolved into the smirk. It is actually a full-body tic: a pressing together of the upturned lips with a shrug of the shoulders and a preening tilt of the head that signals the Governor is awfully pleased with himself.

For a while, Bush's facial expression was chronicled only in print. *The Wall Street Journal* wrote about Bush frozen in a grin as a counselor at a Christian pregnancy center told the sad tale of her secret abortion. Earlier, Tucker Carlson of *Talk* magazine described the smirk Bush wore as he mimicked a convicted murderer. The smirk is much more harmful now that it's been captured on videotape. (Imagine if we had footage of Forbes eating caviar or McCain losing his cool.) The most telling moment in last Monday's debate grew out of Bush's earlier assertion that he was reading a biography of Dean Acheson. You might have thought he would then take the time to skim the dust jacket, at least. When CNN's Judy Woodruff asked what he had learned from Acheson, Bush neither placed the former Secretary of State in an administration or with a policy, but blithely clutched at rote nostrums about "the incredible freedoms we understand in the great land called America."

And then he smirked, a reaction that is actually the polar opposite of the deer-in-the-headlight look that overcame Dan Quayle when he realized he'd exposed his ignorance. No matter how remote Bush's answer to the question at hand, he thinks he's pulled the wool over the teacher's eyes, that with his innate smarts and abundant charm, he will not flunk History 101. After all, it's been arranged. He's going to be President.

The smirk may be a manifestation of an inner lightness that protects Bush from feeling inadequate. He seems undisturbed that he has no opinion on Boris Yeltsin's chosen successor, but "will if I'm President"; that he doesn't know much about controlling nuclear arms but will hire people "who know a heck of a lot more about the subject than I do"; or that he spouts gobbledygook ("It is not only the life of the unborn . . . it is the life of the living").

Message: I'm winging it. This may satisfy Bush, but other people have grown concerned. After he grinned through his recent foreign-policy speech, callers to C-SPAN spent more time weighing in on "the alleged

109

smirk," as Brian Lamb put it, than on his hard line on China. Last week a New Hampshire voter asked Bush, gingerly, if he were "intellectually curious." It's always better, Bush replied, to "be underestimated."

Well, no problem there. At Haley Barbour's Christmas open house last Thursday night, clogged with devoted Bushies, there was an admission that Bush's lackluster performances had raised the bar for subsequent debates (which he would clear), a concession that New Hampshire may go to McCain and an acknowledgment of the smirk only to the extent that it would be gone by the time voters pay attention.

Republicans are right when they say he can get rid of the smirk—but only if he can lose the attitude. Watching Bush spew his canned responses is as discomfiting as seeing your child straining for the high notes of "Silent Night" at the school pageant. Most kids know enough to exit the stage gracefully while vowing never to skip practice again. Bush's response to a near midair collision is to lay down more foam on the runway. Having coasted through Andover and Yale, and to a major league baseball team that employed his formidable people skills without unduly taxing his mind, he may believe he can also coast to the presidency. He's so insouciant that he told a group of schoolchildren, "No, I didn't want to be President when I was little. I'm not even sure I wanted to be President when I was big, until recently."

In search of an attitude correction, party elders have urged more intense tutorials, a speech coach and mock debates. But when Montana Governor Marc Racicot showed up to help Bush prepare for the Manchester debate, studying and dinner were both wrapped up for a 10 p.m. bedtime.

The focus on the smirk may be just one more example of that crazy thing called life, where a once endearing trait suddenly turns sour, a winning smile and blasé demeanor transmogrify overnight into a Cheshire grin and cluelessness. Perhaps it will flip again. While reporters are now intent upon finding clever ways to ask Bush if he's too dim to be President, it was just one news cycle ago they were obsessed with finding new ways to ask John McCain if he was nuts. Bush said last Thursday that it wasn't all bad that "I've got a heck of a race on my hands." No one really believes that, but he wasn't smirking when he said it.

December 20, 1999

In the Name of Their Fathers

As famous sons, McCain and Bush reveal much about their character

At dawn on the day he launched his official presidential-announcement tour, Senator John McCain went home again to the U.S. Naval Academy, where he promised 4,000 cheering midshipmen that, win or lose, he would "keep faith with the values I learned here. I hope I make you as proud of me as I am proud of you." He sounded the same theme before a noontime crowd in Nashua, N.H., as he conjured up the moment when a President has to divine "the reasons for, and the risks of, committing our children to our defense." He reminded those gathered that "no matter how many others are involved in the decision, the President is a lonely man in a dark room when the casualty reports come in."

This is the marker McCain is laying down in his quest to be President: his life. He doesn't spell out that he knows what it is like to be that lonely man, even though he spent 5½ years as a prisoner of war in Vietnam, half of it in solitary confinement. His book, *Faith of My Fathers*, tells the story of how he aspired to follow in the footsteps of his father and grandfather, both four-star admirals. As such, it is a bayonet aimed straight at the candidacy of George W. Bush, more evocative of the baby boomer who currently occupies the Oval Office than Admiral McCain. Bush blew off his foreign-policy shortfalls (referring to Greeks as "Grecians," confusing Slovenia with Slovakia) by suggesting he could hire people for that sort of thing. Even conservative columnist George Will has fretted publicly about Bush's "lack of gravitas . . . born of things having gone a bit too easily so far."

The difference between McCain and Bush is evident in how they have handled being the sons of accomplished men. Last Monday a powerful Republican former Speaker of the House in Texas testified in an obscure lawsuit that he had pulled strings to get the young Bush into the state's Air National Guard, though he had not been directly pressured to do so by Bush's father. However he did it, Bush was able to avoid Vietnam, like so many sons of the well-connected, while McCain became a POW, having his teeth and head and broken bones smashed until, fevered and racked by dysentery, he considered suicide. Imagine that this could all be made to stop by your father, the commander of the Pacific fleet at the drop of a word. McCain's captors wanted the p.r. advantage. But McCain refused special treatment and spent another 4½ years in prison.

It's no sin to take Daddy's help, but Bush, who received it at every turn, concedes only grudgingly that his success had anything to do with it, saying, "Being George Bush's son has its pluses and negatives." His father's name and connections were crucial, from his stake in the oil fields of Texas to his run for Congress to getting first crack at buying the Texas Rangers. If McCain's book is titled *Faith of My Fathers,* Bush's should be called *Friends of My Father.*

Bush provided fresh contrasts to McCain last week. While McCain blasted fellow Republican Pat Buchanan for arguing that America did not have to take on Hitler, Bush appeased him, explaining that he needed all the votes he could get. While McCain says he is running "because I owe America more than she has ever owed me," Bush sometimes seems motivated by a need to redeem his father's defeat. He keeps bringing it up in a way that suggests it has been his life's deepest wound. Last Wednesday he said that Buchanan's 1992 candidacy had had a role in derailing his father, and suggested that Ross Perot carried a "vendetta" against his family. In McCain's story his father comes across as a source of humility and as inspiration for public service. Bush, on the other hand, seems to have inherited a sense of entitlement and, after his father's defeat, an ongoing personal cause.

A week ago Saturday, Governor Bush could be found with Dad at the Ryder Cup golf tournament, having skipped the tedium of the California Republican Party's convention. To spur the American team on to its jingoistic, fist-pumping victory, Bush gave a pep talk in which he compared the brave golfers fighting to win a noisome corporate-infested sporting event to the brave men who fought to save the Alamo—the use of the profound in service of the mundane.

McCain is no saint (he will tick off the reasons he isn't, if you don't beg him to stop), but he is the natural, solid alternative should there be second thoughts about Bush's preemptive coronation. Many people at the rally in Nashua clutched McCain's book and approached him for his signature with something like reverence. One man carefully removed his copy from a Ziploc bag to get the Senator's autograph, then carefully tucked it back in the bag. He didn't want any smudges or dog-eared pages. It's not a coffee-table book, but that's where he planned to display it.

October 11, 1999

Bush's New Fraternity Brothers

The front-runner could have no better protectors than the Republican governors

I was at the heart of the Stop McCain movement recently, as a guest speaker at the Republican Governors Association at La Costa, a luxurious California resort with clay tennis courts, milk baths and valets dressed like footmen.

In exchange for being on the program, I got more face time than usual with the Governors, including late-night margaritas and brandy. While I was fascinated by their discussion about taxing sales on the Internet, what I was really looking for was any crack in their preemptive, granite-hard support for their colleague Governor George W. Bush. Lately, he had given off a slight whiff of Dan Quayle, and his first debate was imminent. Senator John McCain was showing surprising strength. And surely there must be some Oval Office envy, given that one of their own had left them in the presidential dust. Stare in the mirror now, and at best there's a Vice President staring back. I was certain there would be some hurt feelings when Bush dissed the meeting entirely. But when Bush sent word—"Love ya, but can't get there"—there wasn't a whimper.

There's no establishment like the Republican Establishment. These guys don't complain; they don't wobble; they won't entertain the notion that Bush is slighter than many others in their exclusive club. Bush has advantages the rest of them don't—lineage, family crest and primogeniture—not to mention that modern tool of war, a massive treasury. He also wooed them, as if he were back at his fraternity house. And he still does: he arm squeezes and bear hugs; he calls; he has them to the mansion. He gives each one a nickname. What does it matter if he isn't the wonkiest among them? These are can-do guys who admire a winner and want more than anything to regain the throne lost to an illegitimate king in 1992. They're in love. Pennsylvania Governor Tom Ridge says Bush is the first candidate "to absorb the Governors' organizations so completely into his own."

If the Governors squabble among themselves, it's over who will throw up the best firewall should McCain wound Bush in New Hampshire or South Carolina. "I'm solid asbestos," Michigan Governor John Engler crows. "I'm not conceding anything to McCain in New Hampshire, but when he gets to Michigan on February 22, he runs into a state where I've got an organization that has won for me three times, where the legislature is overwhelmingly for Bush, where 65% of county chairmen are already lined up."

So what do the Governors get out of Bush for their fealty? Attention, as he triangulates against the less popular Republicans in Congress; money, as he promises to send more to the states; and the possibility that one of them will be his Vice President. At the Iowa straw poll in August, Bush squealed, "Tommy T., you're the best," to the Wisconsin Governor on the short list. In June, Bush ran along the Susquehanna River with Pennsylvania's Ridge during a two-day swing through that state and joked that he "would make a great jogging mate." His campaign has registered Bush-Ridge on the Internet, but also Bush-Engler, Bush-Pataki and Bush-Whitman.

So life for Bush remains a lot like rush at the Deke House. With peace and good times, he's not worried about the talent contest. He's already won Mr. Congeniality.

December 13, 1999

Death, Be Not Proud

Nothing is as certain as the pace of executions in Bush's Texas

George W. Bush has at least one distinction as Governor: Since he took office in 1995 his state has seen more executions—119—than any other. Just as he was beginning his presidential campaign in 1998, the case of convicted murderer Karla Faye Tucker came up for review. Religious leaders from Pat Robertson to the Pope pleaded with Bush to spare Tucker. Like Bush himself, she had found Christ in midlife. He could have issued a 30-day reprieve and signaled to the parole board that Tucker should be granted clemency. He didn't. Although he said he was anguished by the decision, in an interview in *Talk* magazine, writer Tucker Carlson described Bush mimicking the woman's final plea for her life. " 'Please,' Bush whimpers, his lips pursed in mock desperation, 'don't kill me.' "

Swaggering past the death house still works in Texas, where crowds gather outside the Huntsville death chamber to cheer on the executioner. But lately more Americans, including some Republicans, are questioning how just the practice is. Governor George Ryan of Illinois, a conservative Republican, halted all executions in his state on January 31, after concluding the system was "fraught with error." Thirteen people scheduled for death in Illinois had been exonerated. Three of them were freed after a journalism class at Northwestern University proved someone else had committed the crimes. One of the three came within two days of dying. Of

12 others who were executed, one is now believed to have been innocent. That was enough for Ryan. "Until I can be sure with moral certainty that no innocent man or woman is facing a lethal injection," he said, "no one will meet that fate."

After Ryan's action, Bush said he has no such qualms. "Everybody who's been executed [in Texas] is guilty of the crime of which they've been convicted," he said, adding that all the convicts had had "full access to the courts."

But that just isn't so. Death in Texas, where there are about 450 capital cases pending, is swift. The postconviction review office was shut down five years ago, and there is no public-defender service to speak of. Judges, most of them supporters of the death penalty, tend to appoint poorly trained and poorly paid lawyers. Rarely is there money for investigators. Justice is so blind that some defense lawyers can sleep undisturbed at trial: George McFarland's lawyer dozed throughout his in 1991, yet his verdict was upheld. Bad lawyering is so notorious in Texas that the legislature, not known for coddling criminals, last year unanimously passed a bill to modestly improve counsel for indigent defendants. Bush vetoed it.

Americans still support the death penalty, but not with the ferocity they felt when it was an abstraction, or when softheaded judges were letting murderers walk on a technicality. Movies like *Hurricane* and *Dead Man Walking* show the awful drama behind the practice.

People have also watched as the guilty go free and innocent men get sent to death row. The country saw O. J. Simpson, who many thought was the "real killer," get off with the help of expensive lawyers. Eighty-five once-doomed men who were fortunate enough to have their cases taken up have been saved from the death chamber, according to Yale's Steven Bright, who directs the Southern Center for Human Rights. "That number," he says, "should shake the criminal-justice system to its core."

All this may not have slowed Bush, but others are taking a second look. The Roman Catholic Church, recognizing its prior inconsistency, now defends the life of the felon along with the life of the fetus. As crime rates have fallen, legislation has been introduced in six states that would put a moratorium on further executions. Last week Senator Patrick Leahy proposed a bill that would force states to provide competent counsel along with DNA testing in capital cases.

It is curious that Bush, who seems ambivalent about so many things, would be so unflinchingly sure of himself when it comes to carrying out the death penalty. In Texas, where speed and efficiency are highly valued, allowing a moral struggle to slow down the process might be viewed as weak. But as Bush goes about the country campaigning for the presidency, show-

ing a little doubt in the face of life-and-death decisions would lend weight
to his claim to be a compassionate conservative.

February 21, 2000

The Joe That I Know

The senator is a genuinely nice guy, but he must be careful about
one thing

Joe Lieberman is a good guy. How many times have you heard that this
week? Even George Bush said so, adding that it made Lieberman just like
him! Lieberman dispatched that one with the old chestnut about thinking
the veterinarian and the taxidermist are alike since both give you back your
dog. How like a good guy to tell such a lame joke with such obvious delight.
Rubber-faced, slow-talking, yet irrepressibly exuberant, Lieberman at his
introduction in Nashville, Tenn., was already rubbing off on the usually
constrained Gore, who nearly scampered about the stage handing Lieberman a handkerchief to wipe his sweating face.

The good-guy part of Lieberman wouldn't be worth mentioning if Republicans weren't striving to be the Good Guy Party. The Bush campaign is
premised almost exclusively on the strength of Bush's personality and the
perceived weakness of Gore's and the behavior of You-Know-Who. Now
Gore has seen the Republicans' Barney-ness and raised them one. Former
Connecticut Comptroller Bill Curry, who sat beside him in the Connecticut state legislature, enlisted Lieberman in his fight against substandard
nursing homes, which meant bucking the power of the Democratic Governor. "Once Joe saw it was the right thing to do, I never had to look over my
shoulder to make sure he was still with me," Curry says.

Lieberman's off-duty persona is much like his on-duty one, the same
mixture of great calm and boundless energy, whether in black tie at the
Kennedy Center, cheering at a Washington Mystics game or in his flannel
shirt in line at the Safeway. Close readers of this column will remember
when I was required by pesky editors to order dinner for 50 entirely off the
Internet, including a person to help serve. When that person, like so much
else, didn't show up, the Senator got his own drink, and Hadassah rolled up
her silk sleeves to lug the ham and side dishes to the table, never mentioning that there was nothing Kosher she and Joe could eat. She keeps him
from holding forth in the Great Man way, having told him one time long

ago that "there was one less Great Man in the world than he might think." Hadassah was once a fast-track yuppie executive, but now raises their 12-year-old daughter while working part-time. She cheerfully blames her husband for "ruining my career." He calls her at every turn and brings her flowers every Friday. They have the marriage I would wish for my daughter.

Democrats say Lieberman's winning a Funniest Celebrity in Washington contest shows he's not as dull as he once seemed. I was a judge, and, yes, he brought a cynical crowd to peals of laughter, but that was because of a dry, droll, double-take delivery suited to a small room. Lieberman's self-deprecating wit is unlikely to turn the Cheney-Lieberman debate into must-see TV.

But it is his gentle humor, his sideways look at life that partly explains why, in a fiercely backstabbing world, it was hard to find material to write Lieberman: The Dark Side. I called Republicans. I called people who knew him back when. On the theory that no man is a hero to his valet, I called his driver. No luck. Jimmy O'Connell, an Irish cop in New Haven, Conn., drove Lieberman on weekends for a decade without getting paid. O'Connell explains that he "liked his company." And he tells how Lieberman dropped everything to fly up to O'Connell's bedside after the ex-cop suffered a heart attack, how Joe helped get him off booze, how he's become family. Lieberman called him last week to complain that "the Secret Service won't let me ride up front." Republican Senator Fred Thompson tells how, during campaign-finance hearings, the ranking Democrat, Lieberman, was "the one who stuck with me the whole time" because he was convinced the system was corrupt and was steadfast in resisting intense White House pressure. Republican Bill Bennett, who scolds Democrats for a living, once said that what the country needed in a President was "a good role model, like George Washington . . . or Joe Lieberman. I'd vote for Joe Lieberman." The two grew close while scolding Hollywood. At a recent event, Bennett recalled Lieberman's asking him to quit going around referring to himself as "Joe's rabbi." "Yeah," Bennett said, "I bet your Democrat friends don't like it." "No," Joe drawled, "it's my rabbi who doesn't like it."

Until this week, Lieberman was among the most religious people I know—and religiously subdued about it. His Judaism first became news when he lost the lieutenant governorship in 1978 after not showing up at a convention held on the Sabbath. Such selfless observance of faith is impressive, but what was background is now headline—with 13 mentions of God in one speech. Enough already. Lieberman's warm reception allowed Democrats to defuse the Republicans' Good Guy strategy. But it's a risk to turn around and run on it. Moral piety is no more attractive in Democrats than it is in Republicans. Woe unto those seen to be on high. How tempting a target they make for those who would bring them down to earth.

August 21, 2000

I Won't Dance, Don't Ask Me

Cheney signed on as the heavyweight. No wonder he isn't light on his feet

When Dick Cheney arrives in a state, he comes with instructions. Don't send him to a rally—he doesn't like crowds. Don't send him to a county fair—he doesn't like shaking hands. And no one wants a repeat of the "polka incident," when a woman at a Polish festival grabbed a grimacing Cheney for a dance. He'll go to fund-raisers, but don't expect any schmoozing. Last Wednesday night at the Senate's annual dinner for major donors, he sat with lobbyists at a table guarded by the Secret Service and then slipped away without slapping one back. At a Labor Day parade in Illinois, as George W. Bush careened from side to side pressing the flesh, Cheney kept in formation like a drill sergeant.

You're a lot more likely to catch Dick Cheney on the campaign trail if you're a 7-year-old. The man likes a school and listening to his wife, Lynne, read *The Very Hungry Caterpillar*—a captive audience under adult supervision, and no rope line. Cheney's staff quickly penciled in a school last week when they realized they would be in Pennsylvania for two days doing nothing but fund-raisers. Cheney was preceded onstage by a onetime Veep contender, Governor Tom Ridge, who spoke more than twice as long as the candidate did, and with 10 times the animation. When his brief turn came, Cheney ventured out from behind the lectern with a hand mike, which gave him the air of an infomercial host faking enthusiasm for his product. A student asked Cheney what he would do first if the President were to die. Cheney said he would make sure the guy was dead. "You don't want to take the oath of office and find out the report was wrong."

He wasn't joking, and it was as off-key in its own way as Dan Quayle's response in 1988 that the first thing he would do was pray. Cheney has an uncompassionately conservative record, voting no on everything from Head Start to college-student aid to the Older Americans Act, which offers support services to the elderly. When *The New York Times* examined his stint at Halliburton, it found that he was more an ambassador attracting business

Mary Catherine McCreary and James Francis Xavier Bresnahan in their engagement photo, June 1943.

My heart melts when I think of what my mother had to do to whip me into shape for these pictures. Jimmy was much easier. She spent hours bending my thick, unruly hair into curls, trying to turn her tomboy into Shirley Temple, if only for the flash of a camera.

A man came through the neighborhood with a horse trailer and a Brownie on a tripod, and my grandmother fell for it. (So did Jimmy and I.) The ponies were real, (although not so the ducks). Newt Gingrich had a photo of the same sort that he handed out when he became Speaker. He had a gun in his holster.

3

4

My mother was so pleased with the First Holy Communion event that she reenacted it for my grandmother, who couldn't come to Good Shepherd for the actual occasion, and a professional photographer. Buying the dress felt like defeat for my mother, who prided herself on making everything but our shoes. She restored her good humor by finding an old bridal veil and cutting it down to size, thereby saving twenty dollars.

My wedding, September 2, 1972, in the dress my mother and I made. Not all things that end are a failure.

7

Courtney, a flower child, at Gene's parents' vacation house in Borrego, California. In most ways I was a mother like my mother, but I never tried to reconfigure her hair for the camera.

Graduation, June 1992. She made it, and so did I. Kenyon College decided to give me an honorary degree the year she graduated. I had just handed her her diploma and was looking at her father in the first row below.

For years, Kay Graham was a mysterious, imposing Washington figure I avoided for fear of saying or doing the wrong thing. Then one day there she was, tossing salad in my kitchen. In exchange for being allowed to do scullery work, she asked if I would let her have Courtney's wedding at her house.

8

9

This was goodbye to my daughter, as I left to find Jimmy so we could walk down the aisle together. The next time I saw Courtney, she was a wife.

The pair skipping down the aisle from the arbor her dad built.

"Grip and Grins." Politicians raise millions of dollars standing still, for pictures like these. Most reporters throw them in the bottom drawer. But I saved a few.

The Bushes, Kennebunkport, Summer 1991.

Hillary, overcoming any reservations she may have about my coverage of her, being gracious to Courtney at the family picnic, Summer 1995.

My only State Dinner invitation, for Prime Minister Tony Blair, February 1999. Courtney was my date.

15

16

17

The Bushes had just hosted the Starlight Foundation for children. W. went for a jog and Laura came in to talk to me.

Christmas 2002. My guest was Courtney's god-mother's son, Sam Empson.

With Tim Russert, the unelected Mayor of the Press Village, on *Meet the Press,* June 24, 2001.

A still shot in midair, with my CNN Gang, in 2001. We appear live, every week, from Washington.

through government contacts than a hands-on executive. He's had to explain his past support for OPEC's pinching off supply to boost prices and his company's overseas policy of Americans-only rest rooms. He dithered for weeks over the company's parting gift to him of about $20 million before pledging to forgo part of it should he win. He skipped voting in 14 of the past 16 elections in Texas and cited pressing "global concerns" when it was pointed out.

He has warmed a bit to his task. He occasionally comes to the back of the plane to chat with reporters, but he mumbles so much that the press had to set up an amplification device in the aisle to try to catch what he's saying. He joined in singing "Happy Birthday" to his press secretary and was ready with a penknife when she couldn't open Cheney's gift to her, a CD by Peter Gabriel featuring the song "Big Time," a nicely self-deprecating gesture. This gave his wife a chance to joke that she would have to vet the lyrics. Lynne Cheney, a former culture czar and her husband's primary handler, has been more voluble during the campaign than her husband, especially in denouncing Hollywood. Like the independent counsel putting all the dirty stuff into the *Starr Report* to assure its widest possible dissemination, she recited the X-rated material she wants banned. One Sunday on CNN, trying to counter the news that Bush had served on the board of a company that produced slasher movies, she practically sang Eminem's "Kill You." It was quite entertaining.

October 9, 2000

When Politicians Get Prissy

Bush doesn't want the campaign to be ugly or mean. Except when it suits him

It was the gentlest of pokes. "We as a nation can't afford to make Barney Rubble investments in a George Jetson world," Joe Lieberman said last week. But this oblique comparison between George Bush and a cartoon caveman was too much for Bush to let slide. "Americans," he huffed in response, "are tired of the name calling."

Name-calling? This is the same Bush who helped persuade his father to label Michael Dukakis a "bozo" in 1988. Yet he acted hurt again last week after Gore, chatting on Air Force Two, said Bush should "put up or shut up" on prescription-drug benefits. Bush ignored the substance of the remark, saying, "That doesn't sound very presidential to me." His communications director added that anyone who would make a "playground challenge" with "that kind of bitterness" shouldn't be President.

Candidates have always tried to catch the other guy going negative as a pretext for going negative themselves. But now it seems that the party of John Wayne is becoming the party of John Tesh. Bush wails like a cheap car alarm over the most minor incursion—and attacks at the same time. Last Friday he was the first to unleash a frontal-attack ad. And for a year, he's laced every speech with rhetoric aimed at Gore's integrity and concluded most of those speeches with a pledge to "restore honor and integrity to the White House." What's that if not personal?

Bush couldn't get away with crying foul when Gore asks him for his plan for Medicare Part B if the media refs weren't acting prissy too. After Monica, the press is aiming for a campaign that merits a Junior League seal of approval. Gore was labeled "martial" by *The Washington Post* last week for saying, "I hope that my opponent will also present to you specifics of how he would address the problem of children who do not have health coverage today." Viewer discretion advised.

By going on the air first with an ad that essentially attacks character, Bush opens himself up to the charge of violating his own lofty standard. Described by Republicans as humorous, but at best only sarcastic, the ad mocks Gore for exaggerating his role in creating the Internet and for fundraising at a Buddhist temple. Acting shocked that Bush would do such a thing, Gore and Lieberman look as phony as Bush wincing in pain over the Flintstones reference.

Ironically, Gore, who has always relished a fight, is more likely to confine his attacks to issues, while the genial Bush is more likely to get personal, despite vowing to "raise the tone" and avoid "the politics of personal destruction." Bush benefits if the election is a referendum on personality. In a contest for Mr. Congeniality, odds favor the college cheerleader. In a battle over substance, the guy with 24 years' experience has the edge over the one with five.

Last Thursday, a day before Bush's attack hit the airwaves, the Republican was telling an audience that "politics doesn't have to be ugly and mean." But it does—a little—or we won't know what makes one candidate better than the other. They should all just stand up and take—and make—their hits. But Bush wants to have it both ways. When asked in a TV interview whether he'd gone negative, Bush said it depends on what the definition of negative is. Where have we heard that kind of sophistry before?

September 11, 2000

Full Press Courtship

Bush is everybody's buddy on the plane—until you ask too many questions

Politicians aren't supposed to like journalists. We tend to be speed bumps in their otherwise smooth road to being thought of as flawless human beings. Most politicians, like Gore, deal with this by treating each article as a new transaction, a bloodless negotiation between professionals that leaves nothing personal behind. Bush, however, treats each story like a new credit or debit in his family ledger. It's all personal, especially since the 1988 presidential campaign, when Junior acted as the loyalty enforcer. The Bushes fed hot dogs and lemonade to the reporters at Kennebunkport, even took a special few out on the cigarette boat. But these gestures were always a quid pro quo. If you were not "loyal to all Bushes" after that, you fell off the list for interviews, horseshoes and movies in the family quarters. The next time you held out your hand, it might not be shaken.

What happened on Labor Day, when Bush was captured by an open mike calling *The New York Times's* Adam Clymer "a major league a—hole," was that George W. got caught doing publicly what he usually does privately. If you are the candidate of "raising the tone," it won't do to use epithets that can be printed only with dashes. If gravitas is the main quality you sought in a running mate, it doesn't do to have Dick Cheney, in an Ed McMahon moment, agreeing, "Oh, yeah, he is—big time." And if you need the press to confirm your image as a nice guy, it's bad to be seen singling out one of their membership for minor transgressions. Bush's insistence that he only apologize for being heard, not for being vindictive, reminds people that he has a mean streak and that his discovery of God and self-discipline are rather recent.

Although trivial in the end, the outburst was a setback in Bush's wooing of the press. He routinely comes to the back of the plane to pinch cheeks and hand out nicknames. He asks about the budding romances of the reporters on board; his favorite scribes get their bald heads palmed. The care and feeding is four star. Sleep was plentiful, thanks to Bush's light schedule, which protects his naps, nights and weekends.

Such a genial host has the quiet effect of curbing pointed questions. Who wants to bring up politics, religion or money at a family dinner or when there are DoveBars on demand? One day in Pittsburgh, after Bush and his press pack filled the plane with talk of jogging routes, pickup trucks and heifers, it was the reporters on the ground who pressed Bush to clarify his mushy position on abortion and whether he could prove, given the absence of official documents, that he had actually put in all his time in the National Guard. The charm vanished, the lips pinched, discussion ended. As he so often says when crossed, who are we to judge what's in his heart?

Lately the coverage has shifted dramatically. Gore is schmoozing more, and Bush looks sour when he's running behind. The press that panned Gore's convention speech has discovered that the 97-lb. weakling is an Issues Superman, a hunk on the rope line, and a good kisser. Stories ran last week quoting Newt Gingrich to the effect that Gore was "instrumental in creating the Internet." What's next? Will we find out there really is "no controlling legal authority"? In contrast, Bush's verbal tics are suddenly evidence of an addled brain not up to debating. Before, he was a breath of fresh air; now he's trotting out old supply-side economics.

For Gore, good press relations are not crucial. Running on issues, he needs the press only to tell voters what he thinks. Bush, running on personality, needs the press to tell voters what he is like. It better be that he's a nice guy, since that's at the core of his bid for the presidency.

September 18, 2000

The Oprah Primary

Who won? Gore explained his famous kiss, but Bush planted one on the host

George W. Bush just had his first good week since the convention, and there's only one explanation: *Oprah*. She can sell books, why not slumping candidates? In the dog days of his a—hole aside about Adam Clymer, Bush swore he would switch to campaigning on issues. But that was a short-lived promise to silence critics worried about how quickly Gore had closed the charm gap. On *Oprah*, Bush was on friendly, issue-free terrain, where he gained ground just by planting a big one, big time, on the queen of daytime talk. The week before, Gore too had done well on *Oprah*, but the kid who asked for extra-credit assignments was not made for the confession format. Gore goofed by merely shaking hands ("No kiss?" Oprah wondered aloud). Worse, he pulled the curtain back only on Tipper's depression, rather than serving up any dark night of his own soul.

Bush, on the other hand, delivered the emotional arc Oprah's fans tune in for, speaking of God and his battle with alcohol. The money shot was a tear in his eye, better even than Clinton's lip biting, as he described Laura's difficult pregnancy. His eyes still glistened after the commercial break.

His staff members were so excited by his performance that they spun themselves into a whopper, telling reporters they had been swamped with favorable calls from viewers around the country. Problem was, the show hadn't aired around the country; it had just finished taping in Chicago.

Have we come to the point that appearing likable on *Regis* and *Oprah* is as important as doing well in the debates? Really, how much do we have to like the guy whose job is grappling with international crises? It's not as if we're going to be invited over for hoedowns on Saturday night. Even Clinton could squeeze in only 404 sleepovers a year.

The talk shows do occasionally push candidates into that potentially revealing place that lies between their programmed selves and who they really are. We've seen that Gore is not as stiff as we thought, and Bush can hold his own when not scripted. But don't think these appearances are ad-libbed. Appearing on *Regis*, Bush went through a wardrobe change so that he could walk onstage dressed exactly like . . . Regis. Thank God Kathie Lee retired, or he might have donned spandex.

As Bush found out, you can get hurt by straining to keep up with a trained comedian. When Bush appeared by satellite last spring on *Late Night*, Letterman lobbed a seeming softball about his saying he was "a uniter, not a divider." Bush said, inexplicably, "That means when it comes time to sew up your chest cavity, we use stitches as opposed to opening it up." The audience booed. What could he possibly have been thinking? A few days earlier, Letterman had cried while recounting his heart surgery.

America's chat culture, with its false intimacy and scripted spontaneity, often gives the candidates just one more facile disguise. If the ability to emote on *Oprah* is the standard for the presidency, then 90% of the country is qualified. But if you're more worried about your Social Security check than congeniality, flip to C-SPAN.

October 2, 2000

"We Raised Him for It"
Gore's father wanted his son to finish what the family had started

Our parents mess with our heads long after the first gray hair appears. As much as Al Gore insists he is not living out his parents' dreams for him by running for President, he has followed dutifully in his father's footsteps since he learned to walk. When his son took office in 1992, his father boasted, "We raised him for it."

What the elder Gore didn't say was that his son was raised to go further than the vice presidency, to finish what the parents had started back in 1938, when Gore Sr. won his first congressional seat at age 30. That alone was a remarkable feat for the son of a hardscrabble farmer, who had to work the fields in dirt-poor Possum Hollow, putting himself through a state teacher's college and then a no-account law school. He met another striver, Pauline LaFon, who worked at a coffee shop to pay her way through Vanderbilt law school. They married and merged their formidable ambitions.

Pauline became the brains and heart of his campaigns. He won office after chucking his long speeches on reciprocal trade in favor of playing "Soldier's Joy" on the fiddle. Fourteen years later, Gore Sr. boldly challenged the state's venerated Democratic Senator Kenneth McKellar and whupped him. That made Gore Sr. a formidable presence even before he shouted, "Hell, no," to Senator Strom Thurmond when he tried to intimidate Gore into defying the federal desegregation orders.

A living legend can be a terrible thing to live up to, but by all accounts, Al Jr. was an earnest acolyte. His second-grade teacher said he was so mature that she wondered whether "he was a child or a man." He listened raptly as his father held up the phone while John Kennedy bullied the steel industry, sat through hearings on the transportation bill that would create the interstate highway system, and was invited onto Vice President Nixon's lap when he presided over the Senate. At St. Albans, an elite prep school, Gore was a diligent student and athlete. Once when the other boys were roughhousing on a class trip to Andrews Air Force Base, the little man asked the chaperone whether it was time "to be rowdy."

Gore Sr. sent Al away most summers to toughen him up. On the 250-acre family farm in Carthage, Al would rise at dawn to feed the cattle, slop the hogs and clear tree-filled fields by hand. Pauline, no slouch herself, once chided her husband for pushing Al so hard, saying it would be possible for a boy to grow up to be President even "if he couldn't plow with that damned hillside plow."

However formal the father-son relationship, it was strong enough that Al went off to war for him. When most kids wouldn't come to the dinner table wearing a clean T-shirt, Al signed up for Vietnam to diminish the impact of his father's opposition to the war in his unsuccessful fight to keep his Senate seat in 1970.

This couldn't prevent the most devastating moment of Gore's life, his father's defeat by a minor businessman who ran the prototype negative campaign. It was one of the few times his mother saw him cry, and since then Gore has been at pains to avoid his father's mistakes.

Unlike the breezy George W. Bush, who was on a career respirator much of his adult life, Gore has worked up a sweat getting to where he is. He didn't avoid the military, and he beat the old man at his own game by becoming Vice President, an office his father pleaded for, but lost, in 1956. As psychiatrists and Shakespeare would have it, a son comes into his own when he surpasses his father. By that measure, Gore is fully grown.

February 28, 2000

Stretches and Sighs
Gore's fibs may be small compared with Bush's, but they drive us crazy

A few things led me to mistakenly conclude that Gore had won Tuesday night's smackdown. It was clear that Bush didn't fully understand the peril of making Russia our broker in Serbia, especially since Russia remained sympathetic toward the defeated Milosevic. The RU 486 question tied him in knots. He didn't want to remind such a large audience that his official position on abortion is to recriminalize it if he can change enough hearts. So he fudged his earlier statement that he would seek to overturn approval of the drug, saying a President is powerless to do so against the Food and Drug Administration. He got lost in a hypothetical financial crisis and said he would hug his way out of a domestic one. On his signature tax cut, he kept criticizing "the man's" (that would be Gore's) "fuzzy math." But when he couldn't rebut the Gore argument that nearly one-half of his tax cut would end up enriching the top 1% of Americans, it was Bush who was fuzziest of all.

My biggest mistake was grossly underestimating the weight that would be given to any Gore exaggeration. Going in, he had been warned by the press that he had used up his lifetime allowance of melodrama with his sister's deathbed story, with his claim to being the model for *Love Story* (he was in part, the author confirmed, but Tipper wasn't) and with his boast that he took "the initiative in creating the Internet" (although even Newt Gingrich says Gore did so in the Congress). Gore is assumed to be exaggerating even when he's not. We're hypersensitive to the flaw, having just finished seven years with his boss, who really knew how to ice the cake.

Gore served up several juicy targets—that standing-room-only classroom in Florida, Winifred Skinner's picking up cans to buy medicine, his being in Texas during the floods with James Lee Witt. Bush's truth squad quickly put out corrections.

If it weren't for zero tolerance, Gore would have fallen within the margin of political error by scoring 95% for anecdotal accuracy, although the sighing reduced that to below fifty. He looked like Sylvester Stallone, absent the Uzi, as made up by Madame Tussaud. Put him in front of a podium and out of his Dockers, and he reverts to his smartest-guy-in-the-class mode, impressing the teacher with factoids for extra credit, like Serbia plus Montenegro equals Yugoslavia. His excess verbiage actually detracts from the more important point that he might be better handling the crisis in the Balkans.

Reagan, the President who told the tallest of tales, won his debate by employing the famous line "There you go again" against Jimmy Carter, who told the fewest tales. Reagan claimed he took pictures of Nazi death camps and was happy after the war to be able to finally "rest up, make love to my wife . . . ," though he never left the country. Biographers say he got away with it because he was so emotionally accessible. But he was that way only with Nancy (or Mommy Poo Pants, as he calls her in a just published collection of his love letters), not with anyone else, even his children.

Bush is seen as more emotionally open, ingenuously self-deprecating, so his larger distortions—about skewing his tax cuts, raising less money than Gore for his campaign, giving more seniors drug coverage—do not annoy people as much. Embellishment takes a certain amount of calculation, and most of Bush's RAM is used up trying to remember who's covered and who isn't under his own Medicare prescription plan. Bush, who boasts of his preference for one-page memos over books, obviously wanted the bell to ring badly on Tuesday night. He affably admitted he needs help, naming everyone but the Texas Rangers bat boy on the list of experts he would call on in a crisis.

In the end, Gore's fibs, which have to do with his life, should matter less to voters than Bush's fibs, which have to do with our lives. At the end of the debate, Gore was showered with affection from his kids and Tipper, which can't be conjured up for the cameras. His utter inability to extend that emotion outward leads him to make up stories, which he then tells in slow motion, to seem more real. In the process, he ends up seeming less so. It's not sincerity he lacks, it's the insincerity to fake sincerity in a league with Reagan. It leaves him speaking so remotely that we can't feel a word he's saying.

October 16, 2000

Is There a Double Standard?

It's fine to go after the teacher's pet, but no fun harassing the class cutup

In debate two, Gore did not boast and Bush didn't coast. The Governor even brought up East Timor voluntarily—a country whose inhabitants a few months ago he called Timorians—successfully deploying knowledge of the one to suggest knowledge of the whole. For his part, Gore had to forgo his brute-force game and, like a player coached out of a bad backhand but without time to develop a new one, he was left with no swing at all. He agreed with Bush on just about everything, including the Golden Rule, and committed no new anecdotal crimes.

But Bush benefited from a double standard. Residual disdain for the teacher's pet makes it satisfying to catch a smarty pants like Gore in an error, while it's no fun to go after the class cutup. This is not meant to excuse Gore's earlier performance in Boston or withhold credit from Bush for passing an exam on world affairs. But had the standard of accuracy operating in the first debate been applied in the second, Bush would not have fared as well.

For instance, Bush said we should pull our troops out of Haiti, but there are not a lot of troops in Haiti—a scant 34 soldiers by the Pentagon's last count. We don't need to persuade Europe "to put troops on the ground" in Kosovo because almost 85% of the soldiers there now are from Europe. When bombing broke out in Bosnia, Bush did not leap to support it, as he claimed, but said at the time he was "praying," before eventually lending an equivocal voice. He called Nigeria an important "continent." And he may have created a minor international incident by accusing former Russian Prime Minister Viktor Chernomyrdin of pocketing I.M.F. loans, without any solid evidence. Gore let it go, but Chernomyrdin didn't. He warned that "Mr. Bush Jr. should be getting ready for a trial."

On other issues, Bush, in arguing against the Kyoto environmental agreement, seemed unaware of the scientific consensus that pollution does cause global warming. He claimed to be tolerant of gays, but he's on the record as being adamantly opposed to hiring an openly gay person in his administration. And contrary to what he said in the debate, he did block hate-crimes legislation.

Perhaps if Gore had been alive, those mistakes would not have gone unanswered. He'd been unnerved before the debate when his staff had forced him to watch a devastating *Saturday Night Live* parody of his over-caffeinated performance in Debate One. It paralyzed him for Debate Two.

When a smart person like Gore presses a point, however peripheral, it's perceived as calculating and deceitful, not merely wrong. When a less gifted person does it, it's, well, kind of cute. Bush has succeeded in turning his off-mike "a—hole" comment into a joke. The press buys Bush's premise that he is morally superior to Gore, as exemplified by his theme of restoring honor and dignity to the White House. The Bush campaign built Gore's anecdotal exaggeration into a character flaw that renders him unfit for the Oval Office.

At the same time, Bush has avoided exaggerations about his own life by refusing to answer questions about it. He presents a biography in which he was born again at about age 40, when he found Jesus, gave up drinking and struck it rich. This has removed a large swath of his adult life from public inquiry.

But many of the biographical details Gore has provided are regarded as romantic airbrushing, from summers clearing fields on his family's farm in Carthage, Tenn., to his years of living in a rundown apartment hotel in Washington, to actually going to Vietnam so that another hometown kid did not have to go in his place. We prefer to think of him as a pampered prep-school kid growing up in a tony hotel, who went to war solely to help his dovish father in his Senate race. It's a story line that's stuck.

So far, Bush has slipped the bonds of mortal combat. Gore gets pummeled when he deserves it, and when he doesn't. Maybe this week, for the final debate in St. Louis, there will be one standard evenly applied to both.

October 23, 2000

What's Love Got to Do with It?

Bush wants to bring his nice-guy politics to D.C. But that's not how it works

If George Bush wins in November, Ted Kennedy should brace himself for a big hug. In Debate No. 3, Bush made the case that all we need is love. He wished for a law he could sign mandating it and a planet where we would all "love a neighbor like you would like to be loved yourself." Love, not partisan wrangling, will produce policies that will leave no child behind and extend the life of Social Security while permitting yuppies to day trade the trust fund.

How many candidates oppose love or favor leaving a child behind? I'm all for love, especially if it means not having to forgo retirement benefits if those dotcom investments don't pan out. But it doesn't follow that the Contract with America or Newt Gingrich's willingness to let the Medicare agency "wither on the vine" didn't deserve a battle, even a government shutdown. What gives Bush's plea for less partisan bickering its appeal is that the bickering did become personal, thanks to impeachment, and does sound loud, thanks to television. The time when Tip O'Neill argued revenue sharing with Ronald Reagan during the day and drank whiskey with him at night has given way to the city as a sound stage. On cable, every night is fight night: before you tell the other side your objections to a bill, you tell O'Reilly and Matthews. The camera not only makes it harder to work out differences, it encourages them.

Bush didn't speak out against partisan bickering during the most personal manifestation of it two years ago during impeachment, but he wants to end it now, when partisan bickering could clarify the issues. In the last debate, Bush took credit for passing a bill allowing patients to sue HMOs, when he actually fought it. He glossed over the details of what it would take to deliver love—say, in the form of prescription drugs—to ordinary Americans. He seeks refuge in the mantra "I trust the people, not the government."

Sounds harmless, but in Texas that translated into trusting corporate solutions, which resulted in record-breaking dirty air in Houston and children uninsured at an alarmingly high rate. This doesn't mean there's no argument for voluntary efforts over government ones, but Bush has to make it specific, not send a political mash note from his well-meaning heart.

Bush has become so smooth with the Oprah language of caring (against Gore's tin ear for it) that he got the biggest applause of the night on David Letterman last Thursday when he repeated the "trust" mantra. Indeed, when Gore in the debate brought up the Dingell-Norwood bill, a bipartisan effort to solve the HMO problem, he might as well have pulled a shiny chrome instrument out of his back pocket and performed an invasive procedure on one of the Undecideds. In the face of Gore's details, Bush reiterated his good intentions, expressed in a warm bedside manner. "You can quote all the numbers you want. I'm telling you, we care about our people in Texas. . . . Insurance," he sniffed. "That's a Washington term."

Bush's way is to hug his opponents, as he did when he made a house call on the late Bob Bullock, who was the Lieutenant Governor in Texas and ran the state senate. Bush had no choice; under the Texas system, the Lieutenant Governor is as powerful as, if not more so than, the Governor. In Washington, however, there is no single superpower to embrace, and a different ethic. You can share a lot of granola with Tom Daschle and Dick

Gephardt and Charlie Rangel and still not end up with the fraternal and cozy relationships that make the world go round in Austin. Like Bush, the current President believes in hugging opponents to death. But at the same time, Clinton possesses such a chess player's grasp of the issues that Republicans often found their pockets picked.

Gore has Clinton's grasp of issues but little emotional reach. He made Dingell-Norwood sound like some scam rather than the best effort of Congress to balance the needs of patients against those of HMOs. It's called legislation, and until the Constitution is amended, it is how things get done. Love's fine, but let's hear it for bickering too.

October 30, 2000

It's a Crisis! But Largely on Cable
Hold the hysteria, please. There's plenty of time for us to sort out this mess

The pundits, the partisans and a fair number of citizens are treating the Florida ballot dispute like a constitutional crisis on the scale of *Seven Days in May*. Former Secretary of State James Baker, the solemn, senior aide to the Bush camp, says, "Our process is at risk," and we are "on the cusp of having this thing spiral out of control." Bush's strategy chief, Karl Rove, makes a legal battle sound like a civil war. Even a non-alarmist like CNN's Jeff Greenfield likened our democracy to a beautiful antique car sliding over a cliff.

What cliff? If there's a crisis, it's one of the commentariat, that sleep-deprived, hoarse horde frustrated over scrapping non-refundable airline tickets to sunny beaches. They're working double shifts for cable outlets, delighted to have a sequel to Elian in the place where Elian landed conveniently and the satellite uplinks are still hooked up. Sure, some of the Jewish seniors in jogging suits are a little crabby over being called doddering geezers for voting for Pitchfork Pat, who longs for a Christian nation. There are jokes about our need for outside observers from El Salvador. But I haven't heard of any residents of the oceanfront towers in Palm Beach shouldering muskets. So far, the taking to the streets resembles a street fair, with retirees in walkers waving "Re-Vote Now" signs and hawkers peddling "Indecision 2000" T-shirts.

This is just a close election. It's time for America to take a deep, cleansing breath, even an audible Al Gore sigh or two. After that, let's all halve our coffee consumption, put the histrionics in a lockbox and take the time we need to try to ameliorate the unsatisfying results from a questionable ballot that has rendered Florida's 25 electoral votes fuzzy.

You'd think both candidates would see that patience is of the essence. Anyone who doesn't concede an election the moment Dan Rather declares a winner risks being labeled a sore loser. Gore was so eager to surrender in a timely way that he jumped the gun, only to renege later when Florida drifted back into contention. Bush nearly refused to accept the retraction, protesting that little brother Jeb had assured him the Sunshine State was his. To Gore, Jeb wasn't a controlling legal authority. This time he was right.

It's understandable that Bush wants to shut the process down while he's ahead, although it's risky to be perceived as having won the presidency after ballots were thrown out in a state run by your brother. But what is everybody else's hurry? It will be hard enough for anyone to govern without a rush to judgment setting off a cottage industry of the grassy-knoll variety. Do we want *Who Stole Florida?* on the shelf alongside *Who Shot JFK?* Yet when Gore's deputies threatened litigation, Bush spokeswoman Karen Hughes warned that this would be unhealthy for the country. "That's not the way we do things in America," she huffed. Since when? Suing one another is all we do in America. And heaven forbid that someone would look to settle a real legal question before a judge rather than in the court of cable TV, Justices Novak, Press and Matalin presiding. After predicting a Dickensian legal quagmire, the Bush team went to court asking for an injunction to halt a manual recount. The Republic survived.

A relaxed Bush, who might well be on vacation if he thought he'd actually won, worked like a dog putting on a tableau of transition. He may not be President, but he played one on TV, using the Governor's mansion in Austin like the set of *The West Wing,* ushering his make-believe Cabinet through iron gates into meetings. He gave up his usual afternoon video games and naps for lunches with his maybe Vice President on a table set with linens and silver, evoking those famous weekly Clinton-Gore meals adjacent to the Oval Office.

The Constitution we're all in a dither over gives us two months to fix this. No fusion Cabinet, no bonding with members of the congressional opposition will substitute for a genuine, authoritative result we can all live with. Only when we have that result will the winner have any hope of doing more than play-acting at the job. That's worth waiting for.

November 20, 2000

Spot the Characters?

In a national drama like this, there's always someone there to remind us

Democracy: The series has no smooth football star on trial for the murder of his beautiful wife, no American prince plunging his plane into the black waters off Martha's Vineyard and, so far, no Monica. Yet cable is getting sky-high ratings for the first time since Donato Dalrymple, the house-cleaner-fisherman, hid Elian from Janet Reno's SWAT team.

For the moment, at least, civics is cool. This election has brought home how much we treasure the right to cast a ballot we can decipher in a machine that will count it. People racing to make airport connections stop for a gulp of CNN on the latest court ruling letting the hand count proceed. Look, Gore just got 53 votes in Broward! Hey, no certification this Saturday! Bush will have to cancel the Four Seasons ballroom. Celebrating Saturday night would be premature exuberance.

Who would have guessed that the news that antiquated machines routinely miscount votes could compete for audience share with the sexual recollections of a White House intern in a thong? There are no brief outfits in this drama, and only the briefest appearances by the principals. Bush retreated last week to his ranch to nurse a boil, surely a biblical reminder that we'll all need the patience of Job before this is over. The press gave Bush mixed reviews for his candidate-held-hostage look at his ranch in Crawford, but reporters were already a bit cranky after a week at what could be the next summer White House—close to the Days Inn in Waco, but 100 dusty miles from the Four Seasons in Austin and expense-account restaurants, with the closest hot spots being the Dr Pepper Museum and the remains of the Branch Davidian compound. Gore, whose campaign press corps is now home in Washington, fared better, except when they reported he used a TelePrompTer in his own house to make a one-paragraph statement. Does he use it for after-dinner toasts?

Gore's stand-in is Warren Christopher, the man who put the elder in statesman. He's so dull, he ordered Irish coffee during a layover at Shannon Airport with the instruction, "Hold the whiskey, and make it decaf." His very presence undercuts former Secretary of State James Baker's dire warnings that if we persist in this crazy "unconstitutional" recount, markets will collapse, world leaders will wobble and general mischief will abound. In Baker's view, the bipartisan counters are secret croupiers itching to stack the deck, despite there being more surveillance cameras than in a Las Vegas casino and more on-site baby-sitters than in your average day-care center.

The only person who looks like a character from one of the more usual cable dramas is Florida Secretary of State Katherine Harris, a Bush campaign co-chairwoman who mixes the pious certitude of Linda Tripp with the hauteur of a *Dynasty* protagonist. She once performed in a Sarasota nightclub, getting audience members to join her in flapping their arms to music in a peculiar art form called chicken dancing. Until the Florida Supreme Court enjoined her from certifying the vote, Harris was briefly the most powerful woman on the planet. She decided she alone would certify the winner last Saturday without all the hand counts. To grasp the enormity of what Harris was up to, imagine James Carville as a political appointee of Governor Roger Clinton's, deciding to shut down a legal recount of an election with a 300-vote margin and award the victory to Roger's brother Bill.

For his part, Baker uses litigation to delay hand counting while inflaming the public against the delay that hand counting will cause. Laws in Texas and Florida recognize that hand counts are more accurate than machine counts. Last Thursday all Republicans seemed to have the same "Trust machines, not people" talking points. Touch the ballots too often and they'll crumble like the Dead Sea Scrolls. The stunt of the day was to hold an imaginary ballot to the head and mimic Johnny Carson's Carnac the Magnificent. Like ancient papyrus and chads, jokes do wear out with repeated handling.

What's fraudulent is the very notion that one side's political operative could single-handedly decide a disputed election. If this were a horror movie, the audience would be mentally shouting, "Stop this woman! Call the authorities!" To many, an "I voted" sticker is like a badge of civic honor, a talisman erasing all that was messy and rancorous in the campaign before. Casting a vote helps each of us accept the legitimacy of the sum of all votes cast, one of democracy's gifts, delayed but soon to arrive.

November 27, 2000

Joe Versus the Volcano

A reprieve to count again

Among Joe Lieberman's worries last Friday was how late the Florida Supreme Court's ruling would come and how early it gets dark these winter days. He had consulted his rabbi about whether he could concede on the Sabbath. As it turned out, Lieberman had to worry not about a concession speech, but about whether to indulge in a moment of relief.

Since Election Day, Lieberman has been the recount absolutist. The moral certainty that drove some of his Senate colleagues to distraction—when he voted his conscience instead of his party—has provided crucial ballast here. Al Gore, known to change his story, his message, his demeanor and his clothes under pressure, has resisted the pressure to get it over, in favor of getting it correct. This has meant that Lieberman, considered a happy St. Bernard in the Senate—"as moral, decent and honorable a man as I've known there," said Senator John McCain last Friday—has seen his image morph overnight into a Rottweiler. Conventional wisdom holds that a position can't be principled if it is also self-serving. As Lieberman waited to go on *Larry King Live*, I asked him how it feels to go from media favorite to just another pol. He quoted the late Senator Richard Russell, "You fight until hell freezes over. Then you fight on the ice."

The recount may yet go forward in a race in which the margin of error vastly exceeds whatever the margin of victory ends up being. Lieberman faults the media as much as George W. Bush's spin machine for the hole his side finds itself in. And he has a point. At first I thought the media's desire to come to a conclusion, whether or not they came to the truth, was partly the result of dirty laundry, unrefundable airline tickets and weekends spent doubled up in scarce hotel rooms. But it's actually the passion to be first, even at the cost of being wrong, as election night proved.

Gore has been cast in the role of sore loser whose congressional support could evaporate in an instant, a supplicant trying to win in court what he didn't win at the ballot box. And every day the media persist in calling the race anew. A reporter will read the latest polls showing that a majority of the American people don't mind waiting for a thorough recount and then open the next segment with the question "When, in the name of the American people, will this madness end?"

By contrast, the notion of Bush's conceding never comes up. Tallying votes is seen as tantamount to anarchy. Citizen counters, as corrupt and dexterous as Las Vegas dealers peeling from the bottom of the deck, will steal the election. Never mind that manual recounts are routine and that Bush himself is asking for one in New Mexico.

The Bush team called Friday's ruling a constitutional crisis. But it is a crisis only if they throw a constitutional tantrum. It's properly assumed that a Bush win after a recount will elicit a Gore concession. It's also assumed that a loss for Bush will occasion a power play by the legislature in a state controlled by his brother and, if need be, a power play by his brother.

Americans don't like games won by faulty scorekeeping or sore winners.

December 18, 2000

Save the Last Dance for Me

Al Gore's concession speech was almost as good as the rave reviews would have it. Quoting his father about how defeat shakes the soul was the right touch of poignancy. Saying he would be mending fences in Tennessee admitted how much it hurt to be rebuffed at home. Invoking the clichéd "It's time for me to go" so elegiacally displayed the mordant, subtle humor of one who accepts that life is mad. Finally we glimpsed the Gore who, according to those who love him most, always existed. But the encomiums were overdone by a commentariat that praises freely only when it comes to bury. Gore went gently into that good night because, as *New York Times*man Thomas Friedman put it, someone had "to take a bullet for the country."

Rob Reiner was present for the dying of the light. He had stopped over at the Gores' for a roast-chicken dinner after hosting an event for his I Am Your Child foundation. He was polishing off his lemon tart when word came that the U.S. Supreme Court ruling was imminent. They flipped on CNN in the dining room, and Reiner watched transfixed with Tipper and three of the children, while Gore got on the phone with his lawyers. "There we were getting the opinion, slow page by slow page, over the fax machine, as CNN was reporting on us getting the opinion. It was *The Truman Show*." At first, Reiner said, Gore was encouraged that while there was an equal-protection problem, it could be fixed by making the standard for counting votes uniform. But he was crushed when the Court imposed a deadline by which it couldn't possibly be accomplished.

Gore wanted to sleep on it. But no amount of sleep could soften an unsigned opinion tossed over history's transom like a ransom note penned by Kafka. You have to wonder if the Supreme Court, instead of reading election results, is now in the business of making them. The Court warned that its ruling was custom fit: "Our consideration is limited to the present circumstances . . . equal protection . . . generally presents many complexities." You bet it does: like flawed machines that disproportionately failed to record legally cast votes in inner-city precincts. Or the purging of voter rolls by a firm hired by Bush's brother that disproportionately disenfranchised blacks.

For Gore, this is the right tragedy, the right male-pattern baldness, the right time in life to occasion a full-fledged midlife crisis. With his first dream dashed, he could reach for a second act more suited to his gifts. For his own peace, it might be better if the second act he hopes for is not a second chance. Even though he won the popular vote and, for all we'll ever know, the electoral one as well, his own party is complaining that had he won bigger, he wouldn't have needed to be worried over a few thousand un-counted ballots. Democrats don't like their losers, even good ones.

December 25, 2000

Waste Not, Want Not—Not!

Conservation is for wusses. Dubya's boys believe that thrift is un-American

There is a certain kind of person who thinks a certain other kind of person is a sissy. The first kind thinks it's a birthright to fill up the Silverado, put a cold one in the cupholder, crank up the radio and drive off into the wide-open spaces. Mass transit is for pointy-headed Easterners, and every room should be as cool as a meat locker. Don't have enough energy? Drill for it like a crazed dentist. If that doesn't do the trick, let's blast for coal and rebuild Three Mile Island. These are people from out West, where no one will be fenced in by $3-a-gal. gas. You may recognize the type. They're in charge now.

There's another sort—let's call him Conservation Wuss. He might hug a tree but not necessarily. Some of his ilk are skinflints, in the Puritan-Calvinist tradition, clipping coupons (for cents off on laundry detergent, not bonds) and using fluorescent light bulbs. Others are poor folks, trying to stretch a buck. They all see the value of heat pumps and buying low-flow shower heads and cars based on how many miles per gallon they get.

There are lots of Conservation Wusses on the crowded, constricted Left Coast, but there are many more everywhere than Cheney, in his about-to-be-released energy plan, acknowledges. He sniffs at conservation as a "sign of personal virtue" and not much more. Yet in Seattle, the first place to make coffee a separate food group, Conservation Wusses have saved the equivalent of a new power plant over two decades. In the late 1970s, in-stead of merely investing in new plants, Seattle City Light focused on in-centives to change consumption patterns and invested in boosting efficiency. While much of California is sweltering, its groceries spoiling, its office buildings dark—and paying dearly for the privilege—Seattle has saved enough juice to power the city for a good year and a half at rock-bottom prices.

Conservation is cool beyond the cappuccino-sipping communities. Much of Big Business is ahead of the administration. Automakers may lack the single-mindedness that regulation may bring, but they have been making ever more economical cars. Ford and GM are dueling it out over whose emissions are lower and whose SUVs will get more mileage. Toyota and Honda are spending billions on hybrid-engine cars, while companies like GE and Whirlpool are developing more efficient low-BTU mousetraps, like dishwashers, that can be programmed to click on in the middle of the night. A few bones thrown its way, and business would surely do more.

But the Cheney plan looks as if it will slash funds on the conservation side by as much as half, while vastly increasing amounts for drilling where the caribou roam. Only a few decorative items, like turning animal waste into energy, remain. To rationalize building 1,300 new power plants, Cheney cites Energy Department studies showing demand outstripping supply. Yet studies out of the same department suggest that basic conservation measures could cut growth in demand nearly in half. When Ari Fleischer was asked last week whether the President would be asking citizens to change their lifestyle given that we consume more energy per capita than any other people on the planet, he said, "That's a big no."

Hanging over all is the specter of Jimmy Carter in his sweater lowering the thermostat to 68 (degrees). There were worse fashion statements in the '70s than that *Mister Rogers*–inspired cardigan, but what ridicule the man took for urging citizens to layer their outerwear! While we remember the *Saturday Night Live* parody of Carter's efforts, polls at the time showed that people responded well. Lots of other problems contributed to the Carter malaise, but the image persists of that presidential appeal not being presidential. Just ask Dick Cheney: In his world, real men don't turn down the thermostat.

May 21, 2001

Courage and Cleaning

I'd been planning to write about how things have changed in the new world order post–September 11. I'm reading up on Islam, consulting obscure publications like *Jane's Defense Weekly*, becoming familiar with Humvees and M-16s now that they are all over downtown. I call members of Congress to see what they know. And I clean.

Actually, I clean more than I call. I took the small attachment to the vacuum, the one not worth the aggravation to use ordinarily, and sucked up every cobweb in my house. Even that nether region under the radiators would pass the white glove test. This wouldn't be worth mentioning, except there's a lot of it going around. Sen. Richard Shelby lives on my street and we marveled Tuesday morning about how the street was spilling over with black trash bags. A lot of closets being cleaned out. I told the Senator about my own and how I'd blitzed the kitchen cabinets, tossing stale spices and ancient condiments, and then trimmed the ivy around the windows, which I then washed. "There's a lot of nervous energy around. Gives you a sense of control, doesn't it?" he said, climbing into his car he'd just washed.

Seeking order in the midst of chaos is one source of the nervous energy. But what's disturbing a lot of people is a deeper question that rises not from the evil we've seen but from the goodness: thrown into the same circumstances, would we behave as well as those who performed feats of courage and kindness? Would I risk my own life to help a colleague? A stranger? Would I, like the maintenance worker in the basement of the World Trade Center, leave the relative safety of my office below for the 44th floor to help people down?

Here is the other thing about the heroism: These were for the most part the back-office people of the financial and government world. The Masters of the Universe work uptown. How people behaved was in many cases inversely proportional to their position in the corporate hierarchy. WTC security guard Esmerlin Salcedo was in no peril on the day of the attack since he was attending a computer class at a safe distance away. But when he heard the first strike, he raced from his class to his desk at the command center on the B-1 level. He walked fellow worker Roselyn Braud to an open exit and told her to run for her life. The last time he was seen he was helping another guard to safety. The 36-year-old father of four earned $10.51 an hour. He has an $80,000 life insurance policy but his survivors may not be eligible for survivor's benefits because he wasn't officially "on duty."

There's an air of surprise at how so many working stiffs rose to the occasion, but there shouldn't be. The surprise comes in part because those celebrated, elevated, lionized and lavishly compensated in recent decades are people like Jack Welch and Bill Gates, Roger Clemens and Tom Cruise, not firefighters and teachers and nurses and paramedics. Had you seen a fireman interviewed on prime-time TV before this week, before 300 of his fellow firefighters died saving others and before his boots melted on his feet after digging 24 hours at a stretch in ruins that could still crush him? I don't remember any. Instead, we are served a steady diet of glamorized businessmen. Welch is hailed as an icon of our time simply for driving up the stock price of General Electric.

I thought of this as I watched the airline executives come to Congress to ask for a massive infusion of cash, which they got Thursday ($5 billion in emergency cash and $10 billion in loan guarantees). They should get help for the unforeseen harm which hit them, but the airlines were in deep trouble before September 11. U.S. Airways was so rickety that its chairman had recently sought to save himself with a merger with United Airlines. This week, he announced that 11,000 employees would lose their jobs, without any of the cushions usually associated with undeserved job loss, but not so the chairman. By leaving before November 12, he would split with two other executives a $45 million severance package.

The Pew Research Center released a report today in which nearly three-quarters of Americans say they have felt depressed over last week's terrorist attacks, nearly half have had difficulty concentrating and one-third are having trouble sleeping. Almost 70% of those say they are praying. I'm doing some of that, along with the scrubbing. I discovered yesterday that many others are seeking solace in sugar. At the Safeway, there wasn't a pint, not one, of Ben & Jerry's, not even a default flavor like vanilla. The manager said he'd never seen such a run on ice cream.

September 20, 2001

A President Finds His Voice

Bush began to look like a leader when he threw out the script

A man ain't supposed to cry. A hundred movies and books and the bylaws of the Republican Party say so. Answering a reporter's question Thursday morning in the Oval Office, he teared up and said, "I am a loving guy, and I am also someone, however, who has got a job to do. . . . This country will not relent until we have saved ourselves and others from the terrible tragedy that came upon America."

This transcendent moment erased two days in which Bush blinked his way through TelePrompTered remarks like a schoolboy reciting his lessons. In one of those staged events that are designed to look candid but fail utterly, he paced behind his desk during a photo-op phone call with Mayor Rudy Giuliani, accepting the mayor's invitation to tour his city's wreckage. Bush looked like a nervous teenager making weekend plans, especially in contrast to Giuliani, who was magnificent during New York City's darkest hour. But this very bad Bush moment was immediately followed by the first very good Bush moment, in which he showed the humanity and resolve—choke up, swallow and keep going, just like everyone else—the public needed to see.

It's a lot to ask of any man to go from the moral equivalent of war to a real one in nine months. In this land of plenty, we tend to treat everyday problems like major crises. Until Tuesday, the measure of Bush rested on whether he or the Democrats would be the first to open up a lockbox that doesn't even exist. The bar for his success was keeping the looming recession shallow and short.

Now the stakes are as high as they can get. No wonder Bush looked the way he did Tuesday. He disappeared for precious hours in a bunker in Nebraska, which cost more precious hours the next day, as his aides tried to quiet criticism from his allies on the Hill that he should have returned immediately to the White House with a false story that the Secret Service made him do it.

When Bush listened to his p.r. team and worried about his image, he was at his worst. When he listened to his conscience, turned his back on evangelists Jerry Falwell and Pat Robertson, who had suggested that the bombings might be God's wrath on gays, lesbians, feminists and civil libertarians, he was the leader we need. When he mourned victims, comforted survivors and rallied the nation from the rubble, he began to discover his best self.

Bush choppered into lower Manhattan Friday to stand at the center of the terrorist winter, surrounded by men and women working day and night to help the living and recover the dead. He had come to thank the people the whole world wanted to thank—the cops and firefighters, the pipe fitters and welders who had left their jobs uptown to pull up the ruins downtown, the paramedics working 36-hour shifts. As much as anyone or anything, it was the images of these people doing their grim, ceaseless work that kept the country together. Bush was at home among them.

When the cameras went off, he met with 200 family members of missing and dead police officers and firefighters. There was no plan. Hurting people just came up, pressing their stories, their pictures and themselves on him. Bush let the tears flow freely. "It was Clintonesque," a staff member later said, the one thing Bush vowed he would never be.

Oh, the silly things we used to worry about before Tuesday. Clinton was ridiculed once upon a time as "Mourner in Chief," but he didn't own the office until the tears ran down his cheeks as he comforted the survivors of the Oklahoma City bombing.

Now Bush has to get us all to put on hard hats, give up comfort and certainty and indulgence for something larger than ourselves. It's not going to be as hard to start this war as to continue it in a country that's a guerrilla's dream and a general's nightmare, and to rebuild it afterwards.

During the campaign, we were assured that even if Bush was not seasoned, he was surrounded by those who were. But every history book tells us how war renders a President an island unto himself. As Senator Harry Reid observed after leaving a White House meeting in which Bush was surrounded but singularly responsible, "For the 535 of us in Congress, there's always one of us standing around to lean on. He's there alone."

Bush's father had the same people around him during Desert Storm, but he bore the solitary burden of a President at war. On Friday at the Washington National Cathedral, after the President delivered his homily, Bush senior reached over to squeeze his son's hand, his eyes not looking at him but raised toward the heavens. Like few others, he knows that the President is on his own.

September 24, 2001

How Rumsfeld Rallies the Troops
Suddenly, the formerly media-shy defense secretary is everywhere

Last Friday, as he now does every day around 6 a.m., Donald Rumsfeld went out to say "good morning" to the soldiers, rescue workers and Red Cross members dealing with the ruins on the west side of the bombed-out Pentagon. It seems quiet as a tomb now that the shrieks of sirens and emergency vehicles are gone. Men in white suits, masks and gloves have been slowly sifting through piles of rubble, reducing it to smaller and smaller piles in hopes of identifying the dead. As Rumsfeld returns to his office, dust on his shoulders, employees who wouldn't have approached the Secretary now stop, shake his hand and say thank you.

Until the attack, Defense Secretary Rumsfeld was the stealth Cabinet member. In green-eyeshade mode, he'd buried himself in a top to bottom review of the military. He was at war with the bureaucracy and skeptics of his plans. He kept Congress at arm's length and turned to retirees for military advice. Now he's Washington's version of Mayor Giuliani, not just racing to the scene of the attack on the military's heart but also taking care each day to either give a televised interview or show up at the Pentagon press room to give aid and comfort to a country hungry for news and reassurance. "It's important to be seen now and it simply wasn't before when he was working on the review," explains Assistant Secretary Victoria Clark of the Secretary's frequent appearances. He can be a little Clint Eastwood ("If we cock it, we throw it") and a little professorial (he's famous for the "Rumsfeldian pause," an existential moment when he breaks stride to let the wheels turn). He explained last Thursday that he was searching for a new vocabulary to deal with the post–September 11 planet. In the middle of a briefing, he stopped dead in his tracks to write himself a note about something he'd forgotten to tell Russia's Minister of Foreign Affairs Igor Ivanov. He admitted easily that the original name for the operation, Infinite Justice, was likely to offend Muslims and should be changed. On Tuesday, the operation to get Osama bin Laden was christened Operation Enduring Freedom.

His first call of the day from his stand-up desk wrapped in his cardigan is to Secretary of State Colin Powell and NSC Adviser Condoleezza Rice to coordinate what they will do that day and what they will say about it. In by 6 a.m. and rarely home before 11 p.m., Rumsfeld is the Commander-in-Chief's commander, calling up reservists and signing deployment orders, all the while burying the dead and rebuilding headquarters. Rumsfeld has to make it possible for the President to go after the Taliban should they not turn over Osama bin Laden. His deputy, Paul Wolfowitz, would also like to be ready to go after terrorists in Iraq. When Bush did not mention Iraq in his speech before Congress, observers thought Iraq was surely off the table. But others say that if the former Navy pilot Rumsfeld, whom Kissinger called the best in-fighter he'd ever seen, agrees with Wolfowitz, and there's no reason to think he doesn't, Saddam Hussein should be worried. This, despite the fact that Secretary of State Colin Powell is against widening the war to Iraq, since the broader the coalition you need, the narrower your target should be.

The attack on the Pentagon has proved the head of the Pentagon right in his assessment of how mean, lean and nimble the military of the 21st century will have to be (laid out officially in his *Quadrennial Review* due September 30). Or mostly right if you don't count his $8.3 billion request for the missile defense shield, useless against what we now face. Tracking down terrorists in caves calls for a highly mobile force, for "brilliant" bombs that can be guided by soldiers on the ground, for hand-held computers linked to satellites that can send coordinates to anyone in the area. The very attack on Pentagon headquarters by an unconventional enemy using unconventional means has silenced critics who were saluting him with their right hands and undermining him with their left.

This war, even as Rumsfeld mobilizes the troops, will share little with that of the Greatest Generation. It's not your dad's war when the enemy attacks you where you live with $2 knives and an airline ticket, and then goes into hiding, not in a specific country but a cave. There will be no Rosie the Riveter, no influx of stenographers from the farms, no dearth of nylons or rationing of sugar. This is the Richest Generation, after all.

The most visible signs that an army moves on its stomach are in the Pentagon parking lot, where Share our Strength has delivered 500 pounds of charcoal briquettes to grill 8,000 pounds of chicken donated by Tyson's to the clean-up crew. There's enough Gatorade for several battalions. Like Giuliani on Monday, soon Rumsfeld will have to give grim news to families who have posted signs and pictures, balloons and flowers, along a makeshift Vietnam Wall outside the Pentagon. To the loved ones of 124 of the missing (189 missing altogether), their remains may never be found, no matter how long the men in the white masks search.

September 26, 2001

Patriotic Splurging

One evil act has spawned a million acts of kindness. But here in Washington it has spawned a hundred acts of greed as well. Lobbyists for planes, trains and automobiles, fast food, hotels and real estate have swarmed over the Capitol seeking a piece of the $75 billion stimulus package. Those with the best chance of scoring are those with the best chance of jogging consumer spending. The President favors consuming our way out of this slump as well, urging us to "go to Disney World" and eat high on the hog, as he did for the cameras at Morton's steak house.

While that effort is easy to caricature, it's hard to refute. The President's first job may be to send troops to capture Osama bin Laden, but his second—if we're not all going to find ourselves up the economic creek—is to send vacationers to Florida and diners to three-star restaurants.

But boy, does it strike a sour note. In the aftermath of one awful moment, we've finally come to understand what our parents meant by a cause larger than ourselves. We're hungry for a way to help the war effort, honor the dead and help the survivors. We're not shunning the perfect marbled steak at Morton's for want of a tax break, but because it feels wrong with planes being shot at in Afghanistan.

The fact is there's going to be no grand mobilization for which we can sacrifice. It's not our parents' war, with its visible monsters, quantifiable victories and necessary sacrifices. The Greatest Generation got to save old tires, dig a Victory Garden and forgo sugar. The Richest Generation is being asked to shop. Last week Republican Senator Jon Kyl proposed a "Travel America" tax credit to encourage us to check into the Bellagio or lie on the beach.

The irony of this strange war is that just as we see the limits of what money can buy, buying becomes our patriotic duty. Perhaps we'd need to buy less if we could learn to accept less upward mobility and slower growth. In the meantime, we'll have to feel our way to being a Better Generation. With the collapse of the World Trade Center, the curtain closed on the decade of wretched excess heralded when Wall Street's Gordon Gekko proclaimed, "Greed is good." When a plea went out on Sept. 12 that the rescue workers needed socks, thousands of pairs flooded ground zero. Word came to send money instead. The money poured in, but the socks kept coming. The task in this new decade is to find a place for all the socks we have to give.

October 15, 2001

Unleash the Pitcher Within!

Snatch the President from his spinners, kill the TelePrompTer, unleash the Everyman within—and George W. Bush knows how to buck up a country. Last week, after getting intelligence that set off a second high alert, Bush ignored the advice of his Secret Service and traveled to Yankee Stadium for the first home game of the World Series. Alone on the pitcher's mound, not an agent in sight, with thousands rooting for him, he took his own sweet time and delivered a clean strike.

By making an appearance at this high-value target (and not dribbling one into the dirt the way his father did at the Astrodome in 1986), Bush defined the new normalcy better than the many other voices in his administration have done. Our terrorist ombudsmen have produced as many catatonic citizens as informed ones, bogging us down in a quagmire of nose swabs, bomb-damage assessments and vague warnings. When one of them says go about your business calmly but be on the lookout for anything suspicious, people lose their calm and flee indoors, where at least they know the NutraSweet is not anthrax. Bush aides admitted last week that briefing saturation had "muddled" their message. Shouldn't those talking agency heads (save Rumsfeld, whose briefings should be replayed in perpetuity on C-SPAN) get back to headquarters and catch us some terrorists?

If people were moved by encyclopedic knowledge and compound sentences, Al Gore would have run away with the debates and the election. Bush's gift of pre-verbal authenticity comes at a time when the most articulate among us have been rendered speechless. Three days after the attack, this man of few words picked up a bullhorn to reach the men of action at ground zero. A few days later, he was criticized for sounding like Dirty Harry channeling Winston Churchill—but his vow to take bin Laden "dead or alive" had an appealing clarity. And last week an impromptu Bush put the war in perspective after introducing the Nigerian President in the Rose Garden. Squinting into the sun, Bush promised that "we're on the hunt" and we're "going to chase them down," then advised impatient Americans to get over their need for "instant gratification."

Given his strengths, why would his staff set up three major addresses this week instead of letting Bush be Bush? The TelePrompTer is not Bush's friend. Other than in his address to Congress, Bush's voice hasn't been captured by his speechwriters, and no matter how august the setting, smoking out the "evildoers" sounds like a teenager playing a video game. Formal addresses, like high alerts, have diminishing returns. F.D.R. never gave more than four fireside chats a year during World War II.

Perhaps any pol would know to use a World Series game being played nine subway stops from the World Trade Center to teach a lesson in American resolve. Bush says that when he owned the Texas Rangers, the Yankees were the team that most often broke his heart. But he knew that this time the toss of a ball at the House that Ruth Built would mend more hearts than anything he could possibly say.

November 12, 2001

A Pillow Away from the President
Laura Bush's sense of calm spills over to him, and so to a nation

Hillary Clinton wore us out, something the current First Lady will never do. As soothing as a warm bath, Laura Bush came into the Diplomatic

Room of the White House at 11 a.m. last Wednesday, after being up since 5:30 a.m., when the President brought her coffee and papers in bed, and fresh from hosting a Starlight Children's Foundation event. She was squeezing in 45 minutes with *TIME* before getting ready for two Christmas receptions (at which she would shake 900 hands in four hours) and prepping for a *Meet the Press* interview.

Meet the Press? Who'd have thunk it? There she was, the first First Lady to mix it up with Tim Russert, not to mention with Mayor Rudy Giuliani, over whether the President was put on earth to lead us after 9/11 (intermittently Rudy's Catholic view of his mayorship) or whether God is less specific (her modest Methodist take). The least ambitious First Lady in recent memory, save perhaps Mamie Eisenhower, Mrs. Bush recalls the pact she made upon her engagement: She would join her husband on his daily jogs; he would never ask her to give a speech. "We're even now," she says as the President goes off for his midday run—without her. "We've both broken our prenuptial promises."

On 9/11, Mrs. Bush was headed to the Capitol for a Senate education hearing when the second plane struck the World Trade Center. Committee chairman Ted Kennedy recalls seeing her looking "so alone" as she walked down the hall toward him. As she tried to reach her daughters, mother and husband, she was struck by the fact that she was watching, with Senator Kennedy, the worst tragedy since his brother John was assassinated. Together they went to the Caucus Room to calm the press. Kennedy says, "You take the measure of a person at a time like that. She is steady, assured, elegant." That night, she and her husband were finally in their own bed after hours at a secure location when a panting Secret Service agent burst into the room, saying there was an unidentified plane in the airspace. "I couldn't see a thing without my contacts, so I held on to my husband to go down to the basement," she says. "Before they could get the lumpy foldout couch made up, they identified the plane. I got back to sleep, but I can't say the President did."

For the first weeks, Mrs. Bush was happy that there was no "immediate retaliation." Revealing a strain of pacifism, she says, "I knew the President would do the right thing, but like a lot of women, I was hoping that was going to be nothing." A few days before he authorized the bombing of Afghanistan, the President confided his decision to Mrs. Bush. They stuck to their plan to have close Texas friends go to Camp David that weekend (lest the terrorists win), although they would now be joined by the national security team (who helped the President put together a jigsaw puzzle of the White House).

Mrs. Bush is unlikely to make an outright political statement. Indeed, she hardly seems interested in making a fashion statement (though she lifts the hem of her brown slacks to show a stocking-free leg: Women Against Panty Hose, Unite!).

Before 9/11 the First Lady was happiest reading *The Very Hungry Caterpillar* to kindergartners. She is no co-President but has become a part-time surrogate for her husband, appearing on *60 Minutes*, three times with Larry King, addressing the National Press Club and giving the radio address on November 17, while continuing to work hard for education. Kennedy says she's devoted and selfless. "At various panels, I ask if she doesn't want to speak first and leave. Instead, she comes early, listens to everyone else and speaks last. I can't tell you how rare that kind of effort is."

Still, Mrs. Bush seems to prefer the personal to the political. She will have 27 for Christmas at Camp David, where, to the relief of her family, she will not be cooking (she loves to read cookbooks, not follow them). Before wrapping it for Jenna, Mrs. Bush hastily read *Still Alive: A Holocaust Girlhood Remembered*, by Ruth Kluger, about "an interesting mother-daughter relationship. They're all interesting," she says, adding that the twins like to comment on her appearance ("Mom, your hair moves as a unit!"). She has hinted that she might write a book about Barney the Scottish terrier if she could "get that $8 million advance or whatever it is," a reference to her mother-in-law's bestseller about Millie. Asked what Barbara Bush thinks of her daughter-in-law's surpassing her in the polls, Laura pleaded, "Please don't tell her."

It matters who's a pillow away from the presidency. David Gergen writes in *Eyewitness to Power* that a chipper President Clinton would arrive in the morning only to get a call from Hillary, after which "his mood would darken." The Bushes keep a lid on criticism. "In politics you always have an opponent. It shouldn't be your spouse," she says. It's impossible to judge a marriage from the outside, yet it's hard to picture Mrs. Bush ever darkening the President's day. The peace she carries with her spills over to him, and so to us.

December 31, 2001

THE CLINTONS

JUST BECAUSE ANYONE CAN GROW UP to be president doesn't mean anyone who gets to be president is a grown-up. Bill Clinton is a case in point. His adult side devoted his huge brain to grasping the art of governing, scarfing up every detail of the body politic from the cost of delivering prenatal care to Indians in Montana to the composition of every competitive congressional district in the country. An impressive list of his accomplishments played across the giant screen at the 2000 Democratic National Convention as the soon-to-be ex-president Clinton wended his way through the labyrinth corridors of the Staples Center: the balanced budget (passed without a Republican vote) that set off the longest economic expansion in peacetime history, a tax cut for the poor, and a tax increase on the wealthy that replaced deficits with surpluses as far as the eye could see. While making it do more, he shrank government to its smallest size since the Kennedy administration. He signed the Brady Bill, an assault weapon ban, and NAFTA. He fostered peace in Ireland, Bosnia, and the Middle East. All of it was done in the face of roadblocks and unrelenting pressure from the opposition party. Although Representative Newt Gingrich and special counsel Ken Starr used everything at their disposal to destroy Clinton, he outlasted them.

The other Clinton is a self-indulgent kid who wants what he wants when he wants it. In Arkansas, he was the big-brained smoothie with one eye on the White House and the other on the girls, a split-screen existence that made him decide not to run in 1988. By 1992, he thought Chelsea was old enough to take whatever attacks came his way. He was one of the first to declare his candidacy to take on the seemingly unbeatable President George H. W. Bush, whose approval rating hovered around 90 percent.

When I got to the Governor's Mansion in Little Rock to interview Governor Clinton in 1991, his first concern was to put a gauzy narrative spin on the milestones of his life, to fit his troubled childhood into a log cabin myth. He belabored his humble beginnings the way only someone who's convinced he's escaped them does.

Clinton had a pile of trouble. His father died in an accident before he was born. He lived with his grandparents until his mother got a nursing job in the little town of Hope. Later he had to protect her from an alcoholic stepfather. But rather than be defined by how hard growing up was, he became an adult without truly growing up. He said he was the most talkative kid at school, and who could doubt it? Not one to crack the books, he nonetheless did well. Things that didn't come easily, he took a pass on. In high school, friends say he was too undisciplined and flabby to play sports, so he opted to play sax in the band. He skated through college, borrowed Hillary's notes at Yale Law, and lost his first political race because he ran an uneven campaign.

The pattern never changed. Clinton would work hard for something, only when he thought it wasn't his for the taking. Then he would take it for granted again until he saw trouble and straightened up. Losing his first re-election bid in 1980 was a bracing life lesson. As only a whiz kid could, he'd assumed he'd been elected Governor for Life in 1978. No one could tell him anything—not that he shouldn't raise auto registration fees, not that his wife should take his name. He worked harder next time, listened and got elected. He got re-elected and got sloppy, having extramarital affairs that were the stuff of gossip. If I'd been more suspicious back then, I would have wondered why he was quite so chummy with his security detail. It wasn't some egalitarian urge; they were on the take morally, following a Don't Ask, Don't Tell policy on philandering. The seeds of Troopergate were there in front of me. I missed them.

A president gets to have two sides. Americans love seeing their presidents at play, letting their hair down: JFK sailing off Hyannisport, FDR playing with the dog, the swashbuckling TR wherever he swashbuckled. But those scenes must be balanced by an equal and opposite side: the buttoned-up Master of the Universe. Clinton didn't balance his weak salute, the frequent pit stops at McDonald's, or the short shorts exposing white thighs with sufficient gravitas or White House formality. Every day of the week was casual Friday. There were far too many pictures of Styrofoam cups, too few of Diet Cokes served on a silver tray.

The bias of most reporters is not a preference in political parties, but the one that's visceral. An interview can go bust because someone reminds you of the guy in high school who sweet-talked you out of your chem notes, or because the subject stares into your eyes in the overly sincere, moony way of the student council president. With Clinton, it was the sweet talk, the eye lock, the lip biting. He could have caught a fly, his mouth was open so much, as if he were astonished at the wonder of it all, when the wonder might be nothing more than a ribbon being cut at the opening of a government office.

Once when I was flying around Arkansas in a four-seater with Clinton in a terrible thunderstorm, he leaned forward and put his hands on my knees to comfort me. "There, there," he said. "I've been in a lot worse. I landed in a rice field one time." You'd think a candidate who'd avoided Vietnam wouldn't risk bringing up rice fields, but the ladies' man is so used to basking in approval, he doesn't sense when the paddy is about to give way under him. He always believes his act is working.

If Clinton's life had once been hard, it had long ago turned easy. The air of the teacher's pet hung about him. He gave the impression, to paraphrase Mel Brooks, that it was good to be king. Running a small state means that many of your subjects know you. Some get jaded by the proximity, but many more remain enthralled. As he traveled about, the seas parted for him. No wonder he thought he could fool people. No wonder the strip search by the national press corps in the presidential campaign was a shock to his system.

Back then, Hillary was a working mother with outsized ambition but normal sized ego. Friends would have you believe she was an amalgam of Betty Crocker, Mother Teresa, and Oliver Wendell Holmes, rising before dawn and hopping into an environmentally correct car with her perfectly behaved daughter to perform good works. But Hillary was more complicated than that. She'd come to Arkansas reluctantly, convinced by Clinton she didn't need shots to visit and that being a big fish in a small pond could have its own rewards. Little Rock did yield a fuller family life than New York or Los Angeles, where law firms hum until midnight, and becoming a mother and becoming a partner are at odds. Hillary thrived, climbing the legal ladder while managing to get home for dinner, drive the car pool and attend school plays. Like Clinton, who thought he was the smartest person in any room, she thought she was the smartest lawyer in the state, and might have been. A small-town practice allowed her to cut her legal teeth where the stakes were lower, while being married to a big-shot governor opened the door to a world where the stakes were higher and she would someday play.

The two made quite a pair, the marriage a merger as much as a relationship. Their brains were their calling cards, and they let no one forget they could have competed in any East Coast firm but had chosen Arkansas instead. They could both talk you to death. Clinton would ask, "Did you see my welfare reform proposals?" You could say yes and wait to be quizzed on the content, so he could fill in the inevitable blanks with statistics from the latest census report. Or you could say no and sign on for a lengthy disquisition on income redistribution. The man listened with his tongue.

Hillary, too, could talk anyone into the ground. One night very late in New Delhi, India, Joe Klein, then at *Newsweek*, and I got a joint interview with the First Lady. She ate up our time with chatter about the Taj Mahal and the ambassador's gardens—all about as newsworthy as someone showing you slides from their summer vacation. About midnight, an aide showed us the door, literally. Our time was up. Valiantly, Klein reeled her back in with a question about health-care reform. As we descended into the swamps of single-payer insurance and Klein's very own plan for universal health care, I leaned against the open door—and fell asleep. I woke up when my notebook clattered to the floor, embarrassed that jet lag had struck so hard, but unworried that any news had been committed.

All that chatter helps Hillary take the personal and make it impersonal. Last summer, talk show host Chris Matthews was in critical condition at Sibley Hospital in Washington, stricken by malaria, and just after he was out of intensive care, Hillary called. But after a half-minute of personal conversation, she launched into a treatise on malaria, its causes and its cures, its prevalence in the Third World and what Congress should do about it. All this to a deathly ill man, who might have welcomed a joke, or two, or a piece of news from the cloakroom of the Senate. Not that he didn't appreciate the gesture.

At first, Clinton went around touting how the country could "buy one, get one free." This didn't poll so well. Hillary turned out to be a mixed blessing and a lightning rod for criticism. Some of it was standard misogyny, some of it was taking the show to Broadway with too few tryouts in New Haven. Whatever the reason, the promise of a co-presidency wasn't flying, and it was dropped from Clinton's speeches. But Hillary couldn't be dropped, and one day, responding to the suggestion that her brilliant career was the result of being married to a governor sending state business her way, including that of shady savings and loan operators, she got off the now infamous line about not staying home and baking cookies, a phrase that would haunt her the rest of the campaign.

But no matter if Hillary wasn't polling well. Clinton needed her once Gennifer Flowers gave her story to a tabloid and held a press conference. One false move by Hillary—a skipped event, a cold shoulder—and instead of being the Comeback Kid in the New Hampshire primary, Clinton would have been all washed up. Being a smart lawyer was beside the point. It was Hillary standing by her man on *60 Minutes* that made Clinton president.

How grating that was for both of them: the president, because he owed her so much; Hillary, because she thought better of herself than being the little wife. Count the number of presidential candidates any year and it will nearly coincide with the number of wives who looked into the bridal mirror and saw a different kind of First Lady staring back, a full-fledged partner, not a potted plant.

Hillary wouldn't be the compliant helpmate for long. The Clintons were hardly in the White House a minute before the two-for-one was revived. He owed her big time. In naming Hillary to head up the largest domestic initiative of his administration, Clinton was unapologetic. There would be no nepotism joke to lighten the moment, no JFK saying how he had wanted to open the door of his Georgetown house and whisper, "It's Bobby" for attorney general. Clinton made the announcement in the Roosevelt Room, Hillary at his side, wearing her headband and her full name in time for the network news. Rodham was back!

Health care would fail. Perhaps no one could have pulled it off, but in failing, Hillary displayed some attributes that would define her: micromanagement, secrecy, a penchant for big government, and a resistance to collaboration. Those who had tried to reform health care in the past had nothing to tell her. Congress was an inconvenience to be dealt with at the last moment.

After health care reform died, Hillary went underground, ending up where she thought she would never be, writing a book about baking cookies and having teas in *An Invitation to the White House*. She joined preservationists on a Heritage Tour with fashionista Ralph Lauren, urging that communities restore American landmarks.

But by 1998, Hillary was busy again standing by her man. Monica delivered her pizza and how Hillary felt about it was completely beside the point. However immature her immature husband had been, she would have to show maturity in limiting the damage. It was a delicate line to walk: If she showed no anger over Monica, Americans might have felt the need to punish the president themselves on behalf of their First Lady. Show too much anger, and the country would have had to come to the aid of a damsel in distress and thrown the bum out. Her challenge was to be wounded, but not so much that she would have to leave the marriage, and to be loyal, but not so much that her feminist credentials ended up in a ditch. She had to be steadfast in her defense, but not foolishly so. Too much of any single thing and everyone would have gone into free-fall.

Hillary was helped in her response by Ken Starr, who always went too far. She blurted out the thing about the vast right-wing conspiracy, but every day Starr would do something worse, from threatening to arrest Monica when she thought she was meeting her friend Linda Tripp, to calling Monica's mother before the grand jury to rat on her daughter. Starr burrowed into every nook and cranny of Clinton's intimate life, as if he were on trial for rape. Starr's inquiry was a miscarriage of power and the House Judiciary Committee hearings a travesty, members dressing up questions about sex as questions about perjury, all on live television. In this spectacle, Hillary had much to be grateful for.

Where was common sense? Where was Howard Baker? Where was the off button? True, Clinton soiled a blue dress, a cigar, the study off the Oval

Office, and his own family. But Starr and the House managers, as the judiciary members called themselves, spoiled the Constitution. It's painful to remember how caught up we all were the week the Monica story broke. On the White House lawn at three in the morning, so many klieg lights beaming on so many reporters, it looked like daytime. Rain had turned the front lawn, where network cameras are set up, into a swamp. Stand-ups were done on layers of plywood overlaid with Hefty bags overlaid with newspaper. Clinton could have declared war on Great Britain and we wouldn't have gone more crazy.

But if the reaction was out of hand, but so was the behavior. Clinton supporters, like James Carville and Paul Begala, railed against the press and the denizens of Washington as either prudes or members of the Establishment who never liked Clinton and had leapt on his transgressions to prove themselves right. True, the Establishment didn't take to Clinton, the way it didn't take to Carter, but the non-Establishment of Camp Hill, Pennsylvania, was as appalled as the chattering classes in Washington. As for the prudish, you don't have to be a Salem preacher to object to a man being so tawdry that he would have sex with a girl his daughter's age when that very daughter was at home two floors above doing her schoolwork. It wasn't that he did what so many have done before and will do again, but how high the stakes were, the way he did it, and with whom. Hadn't the presidency forced him to grow up? Wasn't being president worth not doing what you want when you want?

As Carville was defending the president, the president wasn't, a friend now says, racked with worry, as I assumed, but seething with anger, every public performance an act of will not to give his enemies the satisfaction of seeing him in turmoil. During this period, he was alone in his lie, without a confidant, unless you count Dick Morris, who had some inkling that the worst was true. Clinton asked him to poll the public on how they would feel if it turned out that he had indeed had an affair. When Morris told Clinton he would be run out of town, Clinton, according to Morris, said, "Well, we'll just have to lie, then."

And lie he did. How did he go on, each passing day bringing him one day closer to everyone finding out that he'd done the thing he'd sworn he hadn't? How could anyone go nine months with that inside? Should he tell Hillary to soften the blow? Could he stand the humiliation when it all came out? It took as much strength to get through those two years as it took weakness to get into it.

*   *   *

In the wider world, the Clintons' fortunes moved in opposite directions: the worse things got for Clinton, the better they got for Hillary. She could see her future partly still hinged on his. Joint ambition held as the family took off for its summer vacation to Martha's Vineyard. After the humiliating visit of Ken Starr to the White House and Clinton's speech to the nation in which he apologized—or not—for his "inappropriate" behavior, it would have been wrong for Hillary to hold the hand of the president, knowing by then that *we* knew *she* knew. Still, standing by her man had gotten her to the White House in the first place, and she couldn't stop completely. Chelsea, perhaps at age eighteen a little old to be holding the hands of her parents, nonetheless serving as the connective link with both. Hillary never touched her husband, even ducking under his arm at the entry to the Marine One helicopter. The First Lady stayed grounded in reality while subtly improving on it. Wearing sunglasses, she looked like an aggrieved widow, not a betrayed wife. It was a boffo performance.

And a performance it was. Gail Sheehy reported later that Hillary had been faking it. Sheehy talked to an aide who was on Air Force One going to the Vineyard. The aide told Sheehy that Hillary laughed and joked all the way to Massachusetts.

*　　*　　*

Ah, those Clintons: insincere, slippery, maddening, careless, self-centered, and indulgent. If only Gore had been more like them, he might be president today. He wouldn't have lost Clinton's Arkansas or his home state of Tennessee (which Clinton carried in 1992 and 1996). There would have been no Supreme Court calling a close one against him.

It looked like such a beautiful relationship, those Boys on the Bus, a marriage of like minds sharing a burning commitment to making themselves, and the world, a better place. What a charming, engaging couple they made as they took off on the Campaign America bus, fresh from a spectacular convention in New York. Like two giddy teenagers, they finished each other's sentences. They could almost taste the White House.

The happy couple would make it to 1600 Pennsylvania Avenue, but Al and Bill would not live happily ever after. Monica strained the relationship to the breaking point, and the last straw came at Clinton's first cabinet meeting after the news broke that he had had an affair with an intern. Nine months earlier he had assured his cabinet it wasn't true. In August 1998, with DNA on the blue dress proving it was, the president had some 'splaining to do. He called his administration to the Yellow Oval on the third floor of the residence, and it was here, two cabinet members recall, that Gore snapped. He just couldn't let Clinton get away with it anymore.

Part of it was that Clinton, as usual, slathered the meeting with words. He started out apologizing, but it was lost in new age jargon and resentment toward his prosecutors. It became a rambling "I'm okay, you're okay" exposition of why his public accomplishments, which had boosted everyone's net worth, made up for his private life. If presidents were to be judged by the latter, Clinton said, "Nixon would have been a better president than Kennedy. Kennedy's personal life never interfered with his greatness." What was supposed to be a mea culpa to the cabinet he'd lied to ended up with Clinton comparing himself favorably to the most beloved president of the last forty years.

Gore, who had stood in the Rose Garden and predicted that Clinton would be judged one of our greatest presidents, was standing by his man no longer. In his hectoring, slow-speaking voice, Gore said it would not be possible for Clinton to regain the respect and trust of those in the room he had so grievously disappointed if he didn't "surrender his anger."

Gore had been so slavishly loyal that some present thought he was taking part in a show trial in which he had been told to throw some fake punches and draw some fake blood so that the room would feel that its collective anger had been expressed by the vice president. But it wasn't a charade. The president bristled. Gore fidgeted. One cabinet member said the chemistry that had existed was "poof, gone," and what remained was cold mutual resentment.

The couple would never repair the breach. In the divorce, Gore did not get custody of the booming economy. He got custody of Clinton's character. Gore ran for president alone.

In their first meeting after Bush's victory, Gore, whose body was back in the West Wing but whose heart was still counting chads in Palm Beach, explained that keeping Clinton at a distance was a rational response to polls showing swing voters were still mad as hell over the year of Monica. Clinton, who had rewritten that episode as My Defense of the Constitution, shot back that had Gore embraced him and the booming economy he'd created, he would have won. Like estranged lovers arguing over who left the cap off the toothpaste, they came to no agreement over who was at fault for the loss. Gore had never openly confronted Clinton, except for his outburst at the cabinet meeting and his subsequent refusal to be seen with him. Clinton said he was shocked to learn that Gore was so "knotted up" over Lewinsky, who was, as Gore aide Carter Eskew put it, "the elephant in the living room." Poor Gore. Hillary could ignore the elephant and win, even though the elephant was in her bedroom.

As in so many things, one person in the relationship gets hurt more than the other. Gore must wonder what it would be like if he'd been more like Hillary. Does anyone think Hillary would be the senator from a state she'd visited only as a tourist, but for Monica? Has anyone ever benefited more from sexual favors she didn't dispense?

Gore laid low for a long time. It wasn't until the book *Joined at the Heart* was published that Gore re-emerged. In fact, he became so available you could barely turn on the TV without seeing him, tanned, rested, and cable ready. His two previous reemergences—when he criticized Bush on tax cuts, but wouldn't say whether he would rescind them, and when he criticized Bush on Iraq but wouldn't say what he would do—bombed.

Other than those two speeches, Gore was like Waldo: Where's Al? Scarcity artificially inflated his value, as did dangling his decision about running in 2004, as if he hadn't made up his mind but might at any second, on any show. How else would an author whose book couldn't even make it on to the Advice and Miscellaneous bestseller list get on the David Letterman show? He said he was ready to "speak from the heart and let the chips fall where they may," but instead spoke like a semiconductor chip. Trotting out "will he or won't he" landed plum exposure on Larry, Connie, and George. But he soon slipped back into kindergarten cadence, the jokes got stale, and his declaration that he was relaxed and unscripted looked scripted. Playing Hamlet on TV as if he were undecided about running got tiresome. How long could he drag it out?

Long enough to get a gig hosting *Saturday Night Live.* Ever since Clinton played his sax in shades on Arsenio, paying a visit to the pop-cultural icons is desirable if not required and *SNL* is one of the Stations of the Cross. But there are limits, and Gore would have done well to remember the pasting Clinton took for discussing his choice in underwear on MTV. All you could do was watch in wonder as he strutted and fretted his final hour upon the stage at NBC, opening with an ungainly kiss of Tipper, a parody of the already parodic kiss of the 2000 convention.

The show was a reminder of Gore's weakness. Depending on who's directing, whether a political consultant or a producer at NBC, he lurches from one guise to another. He isn't just going to be more forceful, he's going to be an alpha male in earth tones. He isn't going to change his debate demeanor; he's going to go from Rambo to Mister Rogers in a week's time and back again. He isn't just going to go on *SNL*, he's going to take a page from *The Bachelor,* appear in brief shorts soaking in a hot tub, clutching a glass of champagne and make fun of his former running mate as a "yes man." What would possess a man to do that? Not running. The next day he announced his decision.

Gore can't be Gore publicly because he can't find the real Gore to be. In Nashville, with his family, doing other things, writing other books, he can be himself. There's always 2008, with the chads and the hot tub behind him, with Bush back in Texas. It's not out of the question. Even Nixon came back.

But in 2008, Gore will have an even more treacherous prospect than the specter of a rematch with Bush—a rematch with a Clinton. You might have thought the partnership adultery would sever would-be husband and wife, not president and vice president. Clinton never cheated on his vice president but it's that estrangement that's permanent. The Clintons, as politicians, will never be put asunder.

Contrast the Gore-Clinton cabinet meeting with Clinton's first with Bush, as he welcomed him to the Blue Room for coffee the morning of Bush's inauguration. Bush and Clinton have little in common—not intellectual curiosity, not attention span, not ideology. Yet the sports jock and the rock star clicked, as they saw the scamp in each other. Clinton told friends later, "Bush really connects. It's a mistake to underestimate him." And Bush said, "I don't always respect the guy, but you gotta like him." And they had a laugh at Gore's expense. Bush asked Clinton if being called "the Shadow" by Bush during the campaign had spooked his vice president. Clinton said that it must have. Why else would Gore have banished the president from the campaign? They both chuckled.

After the longest good-bye in history, a pure Clintonian reluctance to give up the stage, the Clintons left for Chappaqua. Bush was practically in bed after his inaugural balls before the Clintons climbed the stairs of Special Air Mission 28000, one of the two 747s that rotate as Air Force One. Clinton was leaving on a high, despite flaps over a bridal gift registry, $28,000 worth of furniture taken by mistake, and his wife's outsized eight-million-dollar book deal. Soon Clinton would be found to have violated one of his most sacred duties, granting pardons to worthy felons, which meant, to Clinton, felons with some connection to his fund-raising or his in-laws or his stepbrother.

With the Clintons, transactions trump relationships. Forget that and you could end up in prison (Hillary's law partner and deputy attorney general, Webster Hubbell, whom the two never called once he went off to jail), dead (Hillary law partner Vince Foster, who committed suicide because he couldn't play the "blood sport" of the White House), abandoned (countless nominees who ran into resistance), or devastated (the staff with ulcers, broken marriages, and legal bills from defending Clinton). The Clintons have not helped defray attorney's fees incurred on their behalf but have raised millions for their own bills and applied for reimbursement from the government for Whitewater-related expenses. The best way to survive the Clintons is to treat them as they treat others. The most successful exit from the administration was executed by George Stephanopoulos. He quit, wrote a revealing memoir about the Clintons, and landed a plum job as anchor of ABC's Sunday show, *This Week*.

Loyalty is something the Clintons demand but rarely give. In the midterm elections in 2002, the honorable thing to do would have been for the Clintons to remain neutral in the New York gubernatorial primary between Clinton's former cabinet secretary Andrew Cuomo and State Comptroller Carl McCall. But fearful of hurting Hillary's base in the African American community, and of Cuomo establishing a power base of his own, the pair maneuvered Cuomo out. If Cuomo, while in Clinton's cabinet, had abandoned Clinton in the midst of impeachment, Clinton may well have been driven from office. It would have taken only one cabinet member to crack for Democrats to fold like cheap umbrellas.

Nothing kills the Clintons—not impeachment, not abandoning their friends, embracing their enemies, switching sides, or letting off felons. Clinton once said that in Al and Hillary he had found the perfect partners. But there is only one lasting union in Clinton's life as he spends his days plotting his return to power by standing by his woman. The pair survives, comes back, thrives. In his quest to redeem himself, Clinton sees his best chance not with a Gore in the White House but with a Clinton.

Bill Clinton: Front-Runner by Default

Bill Clinton has the unlined, open face of a man who has had it too easy. True, his father died before he was born, and he grew up poor in the southwest Arkansas town of Hope (pop. 10,000). But Clinton was Hope's Doogie Howser, succeeding at everything he tried, the darling of his teachers and one of the first from the area to go to college. He got his bachelor's degree at Georgetown University, won a Rhodes scholarship to Oxford, then went on to Yale Law School, where he met his wife, Hillary. By 1978, 32 years old and back in Arkansas, he was the youngest Governor in the country.

Two years later, Clinton was the youngest ex-Governor in the country. In Pea Ridge and the Ozarks, the voters resented the notion that this whiz kid had returned home to put shoes on everybody and introduce them to book learning. Says Carrick Patterson, former editor of the *Arkansas Gazette*: "They thought he had gotten too big for his britches." Clinton admits that he took too much for granted. He hiked license-tag fees. The fact that his wife used her maiden name and that the family was not a member of any organized religion did not help. By 1982 Hillary Rodham was answering to Hillary Clinton and the family was worshiping regularly at Little Rock's Immanuel Baptist Church. But mostly Clinton was two years older and chastened. He was re-elected, with 55% of the vote.

Are things once again going too smoothly for Clinton? At 45, he has a decade in the statehouse behind him. After Mario Cuomo took himself out of the race for the White House, Clinton became his party's media-anointed front-runner. He may soon discover that the worst thing that can happen to a candidate is to be too far ahead too soon. The political press corps, which prides itself on how quickly it can knock the stuffing out of those who would run for President, has gone into a deep swoon over his candidacy, from which it will sooner or later recover. For the moment, reporters seem entranced by Clinton's persona: a good-government geek saved by a self-deprecating sense of humor. As chairman of the Democratic Leadership Council, a group that wants to yank the party back to the center, Clinton's idea of a well-spent weekend is one given to working on welfare and education reform. Yet when he was introduced at a forum in New Hampshire as the smartest of the candidates, he quipped, "Isn't that a little like calling Moe the most intelligent of the Three Stooges?"

Last summer, when rumors swirled about Clinton's alleged extramarital affairs, some reporters thought they might have another Gary Hart in their sights. But Clinton deflected the inevitable "have you ever" question at a Washington breakfast meeting with journalists. With Hillary sitting next to him pushing scrambled eggs around her plate, he said their 16-year marriage, like others, had had its ups and downs, but "we believe in our obligation to each other." So far, an army of reporters has failed to uncover a smoking bimbo.

In the first televised debate among the candidates, Clinton acted as though he were the returning champion on *Jeopardy!* while the others, especially Jerry Brown, behaved as if they were on *Let's Make a Deal.* Clinton, seated on the end, maintained an air of detachment, speaking only when called upon by quizmaster Tom Brokaw. He managed to squeeze in concern for the middle class about as often as Bob Kerrey referred to his war record.

Unlike many Southern pols, Clinton does not have a Velcro personality, attaching country ways at home, then peeling them away in the fund-raising parlors of Norman Lear and Pamela Harriman. He makes $35,000 a year (supplemented by his wife's salary as a lawyer). He has been wearing off-the-rack clothes since the word got out that one of his suits cost $800.

Clinton looks happy at the risk of seeming insufficiently serious. His version of a campaign handshake ranges from a bear hug to a full body slam. As he plays host at yet another fund-raiser and poses for one more picture at a campaign breakfast with a woman dressed as if it's cocktail hour, he can be as ingratiating as a frat-house president during rush week. He told a voter during his last Governor's race, "I was afraid you might be tired of me by now." The farmer replied, "I'm not, but everybody else I know is."

The whole country got a chance to get tired of Clinton in 1988, when he glazed the eyes of the delegates at the Democratic Convention by droning on for 33 minutes. The audience broke into cheers when he finally got to "In conclusion . . ." After Johnny Carson joked about what came to be known as "the Speech," Clinton wangled an invitation to appear on the show and play his saxophone (badly).

Now his campaign performances are polished and full of specifics. When Clinton delivered a speech at Georgetown in October, there were whoops as he lambasted the greedheads on Wall Street and the drug dealers of Mean Street, and again when he laced into George Bush for dividing the country by using the oldest tactic in the book: "You find the most economically insecure white people, and you scare the living daylights out of them."

As Governor, Clinton threw most of his effort into early-childhood intervention and education. Social Security numbers are recorded on birth certificates to help trace deadbeat fathers. He increased teachers' salaries but insisted on a controversial competency exam. Parents who don't show up at teacher meetings are fined $50. Starting in 1993, failing students will not be allowed to get a driver's license. Clinton has expanded Head Start and launched school-based health clinics (where condoms are distributed, much to the outrage of the religious Right). While other governors have taken rich states and made them poor, Clinton has taken a poor state and made it a bit richer, without crowing about an "Arkansas Miracle."

As President, Clinton says, he would take much of what he has tried in Arkansas, add money and stir. He would increase taxes on those earning more than $200,000. He would apply to all corporate executives a variation of the rule devised by Ben & Jerry's homemade ice cream: Any income above 25 times what the lowest-paid worker in a company earns would be taxed at a higher rate. (Take that, Jack Welch.)

Clinton has shown a little foreign-policy leg on trade missions abroad, and he was the only Democratic candidate to support the Persian Gulf war unequivocally. He thinks the isolationism and protectionism being thumped by several Democrats as well as Republican Pat Buchanan are shortsighted. He prefers to move the discussion back to domestic policy as quickly as Bush gets onto a plane to avoid it.

A mean streak, unlike happiness, is something money can buy, as Bush demonstrated when he hired Roger Ailes to de-wimp him in 1988. Clinton's hired gun is James Carville, the Democratic version of G.O.P. spin doctor Lee Atwater.

Carville's first job may be to ward off overconfidence by spinning the candidate's own expectations lower. That will not be easy in the face of all the head-swelling raves coming in—even from Republicans. In December, Clinton was invited to breakfast by 60 California executives, several of whom had contributed as much as $100,000 to the 1988 Bush campaign. A few are hedging their bets this time around by pledging money to Clinton.

December 30, 1991

All Eyes on Hillary

You might think Hillary Clinton was running for President. The first student commencement speaker at Wellesley, part of the first large wave of women to go to law school, a prominent partner in a major law firm, rated one of the top 100 lawyers in the country—there is no doubt that she is her husband's professional and intellectual equal. But is this reason to turn her into "Willary Horton" for the '92 campaign, making her an emblem of all that is wrong with family values, working mothers and modern women in general? Republicans think so. Hillary has been such a constant target of G.O.P. campaign barbs that Bill Clinton recently wondered aloud whether "George Bush was running for First Lady."

The foundations of the anti-Hillary campaign were carefully poured and were part of a larger effort to solidify Bush's conservative base. Republicans dug up—and seriously distorted—some of her old academic articles on children's rights. Rich Bond, the chairman of the Republican National Committee, caricatured Hillary as a lawsuit-mongering feminist who likened marriage to slavery and encouraged children to sue their parents. (She did no such thing.) Richard Nixon warned that her forceful intelligence was likely to make her husband "look like a wimp." Patrick Buchanan blasted "Clinton & Clinton" for what he claimed was their agenda of abortion on demand, homosexual rights and putting women in combat.

Hillary finds herself held up against what is probably the most tradition-bound and antiquated model of American womanhood: the institution of the First Lady. The President's wife, as Eleanor Roosevelt once wrote, was to be seen and not heard, a discreet adornment to her husband's glory. Never mind that Mrs. Roosevelt broke most of her own rules with her high-profile tours and a vocal interest in civil rights. Most of those who followed remained true to the traditional backseat role. Those who ventured too close to the policymaking arena—Rosalynn Carter sitting at the Cabinet table, for instance—were harshly criticized. There is some reason for concern: The President's spouse is potentially the second most powerful person in government yet is beyond accountability. Still, for reasons that are both social and generational, Barbara Bush will almost certainly be the last of the traditional First Ladies. Whoever follows her is likely to shatter the mold—particularly if it is a woman with the professional achievements, the career ambitions and the activist bent of Hillary Clinton.

Still, Mrs. Clinton would have done well at the outset to have conformed more to the traditional campaign rules for aspiring First Ladies: gaze like Nancy Reagan, soothe like Barbara Bush and look like Jacqueline Kennedy. By not doing so, Hillary played into the hands of her critics. At first she seemed insufficiently aware that she was not the candidate. Instead of standing by like a potted palm, she enjoyed talking at length about problems and policies. At one coffee in a living room in Manchester, N.H., people were chatting amiably about the cost of groceries when she abruptly launched into a treatise on infant mortality. She sometimes took longer to introduce her husband than he did to deliver his speech. She, and he, should have known that quips like "People call us two-for-one" would arouse the traditionalists.

Her image as a tough career woman probably peaked in March, when Democratic gadfly Jerry Brown charged that her law firm benefited unfairly from her marriage to the Arkansas Governor. After she shot back, "I suppose I could have stayed home, baked cookies and had teas," minds snapped shut on Hillary faster than you can say sound bite. (Almost no one reported the rest of what she said: "The work that I have done as a professional, a public advocate, has been aimed . . . to assure that women can make the choices . . . whether it's full-time career, full-time motherhood or some combination.")

Ironically, Hillary's desire to shield her daughter from the glare of publicity fed suspicions that she valued the role of high-powered lawyer over that of wife and mother. Instead of using Chelsea in photo ops in New Hampshire, where a sweet family portrait might have helped counter the Gennifer Flowers story, Hillary kept her daughter back in Little Rock with her grandparents. To this day, Chelsea has not been interviewed and only rarely photographed.

All this made Hillary a perfect foil for Barbara Bush, the composed matron for whom hard-edged feminism is as foreign as an unmade bed. That she looks and acts as if she is above the political fray only makes her a more potent force within that arena. Her most conspicuous activities are politically neutral, like hugging sick babies, promoting literacy and ghostwriting best-sellers for her dog. Twice as popular as her husband, she can have it both ways when she wants. No one would think to label America's favorite grandmother cynical when she lets it be known that she is pro-choice, while her husband is trying to make abortion a crime. Mrs. Bush has also worked hard to conceal her role in the White House, which can be every bit as ferocious as Nancy Reagan's, especially when she believes the President is not being well served. She can turn on a bulldog disposition when warranted. "You people are just not as important as you think you are," she once growled to a group of journalists she thought were tormenting her husband.

Although Mrs. Bush initially said Hillary bashing should be off limits, she reversed herself later on the grounds that Mrs. Clinton had spoken out on public policy. The President agreed and got in a few swipes of his own about Hillary's legal writings.

The main reason for the backlash is obvious: By taking after Hillary the way they did, the Republicans unnecessarily angered moderates, who saw the attack as one on women in general. By going after women who work, they got at the elite Murphy Browns—a small contingent—but also snagged the middle- and working-class Roseannes, creating solidarity among both groups, who aren't confident enough in their new roles to take a presidential strike force with equanimity.

Scratch the surface of any mother and she wonders if she is doing it right, whether she works full-time, part-time or not at all. A note from the teacher saying Junior is having trouble with long division can make a trial lawyer wonder if she should write briefs from the kitchen table. Ask a stay-at-home mother at a cocktail party what she does, and she looks at you as if you just asked if you could have one of her fingers as an hors d'oeuvre. She is wondering if she will ever be able to get back into the job market again, and is worried that if her children don't turn out a lot better than those of the woman doing arbitrage deals down the block, she will have wasted her life.

While the Republicans were busy painting Hillary as an overly ambitious careerist, she seemed to be consciously modifying her style. In the past few months, she has softened her image, grinning and gripping like a mayor's wife and baking cookies to show she is not a harridan. She has even learned to stand at the back of the stage and look at Bill with a convincing imitation of Nancy Reagan.

In person and off the podium, Hillary Clinton is neither a killer lawyer nor the adoring spouse of the bus tours. Riding in the backseat of a car during a New York campaign swing, she wolfs down popcorn while worrying about whether Chelsea got her booster shots. She jokes about only making the teams for sports like volleyball and softball—and laments that she didn't have the foresight to concentrate on profession-enhancing pastimes like tennis and golf. While Bill can go for long stretches of time on the road, she says she has to head back frequently to Little Rock to "make a cup of tea, hang out with Chelsea, take an afternoon nap. If I don't get back there, I don't feel grounded."

While not the life of a party, Hillary tends to get into the spirit of an evening. She's the one to "try the new meal—hippopotamus stew—or order the blue drink," says television producer Linda Bloodworth-Thomason. Most socializing is done at home in the kitchen and around the piano. (All three Clintons play the instrument, says Hillary, "but none of us is what you'd call good.") They play Pictionary, Scrabble and a cutthroat card game called Hungarian Rummy.

There is no mistaking that Hillary is a strong and determined woman, used to dominating whatever situation she is in by force of mind. Although the campaign plays down her role, she is the talent that test-drives the Governor's ideas, punches holes in his theories, comments on his speeches and often identifies the weak spots in his campaign operation and helps get them corrected. She is one of the people who can convince him it's better to make three points in a speech rather than six, and the only one who can make sure he gets to bed on time rather than shooting the breeze with staff members into the wee hours, as he likes to do.

First Spouses have always had some influence on the President, no matter how much that influence was hidden. Woodrow Wilson's wife, Edith, was the virtual President during her husband's long illness. And it is impossible to imagine Presidents from George Washington to George Bush not listening to the counsel of the one person in the world upon whom they can count to have their joint interests at heart. Bush is a better President for having Barbara Bush at his side. And why shouldn't Bill Clinton have the benefit of Hillary Clinton's counsel? Perhaps it is time to admit that "two for one" is the deal we've always had, and a good one, at that.

September 14, 1992

A Different Kind of Fire

Hillary Clinton is poised to reinvent the role of president's spouse—but if her own political biography and experience of the campaign are any guide, she will proceed with caution

For America, Wednesday was the first day after the election of a new President. For Hillary Clinton, it was the first day to define the most ill-defined job in America. After a decade of getting up early, popping into her blue Oldsmobile and driving her daughter, Chelsea, to school before heading to work at Little Rock's leading law firm, and after a year of nonstop, around-the-clock campaigning, she now has time for a second cup of coffee. Of course, her new position has its privileges: she gets to live in the country's most famous house, jet on Air Force One to visit heads of state and throw parties with the most impressive guest lists in the world. Someone else sees to the details.

But if it's a fairy-tale existence in some ways—the closest a democracy comes to having a queen—the position is not without its frustrations for a woman who could be king. There have been accomplished women in the East Wing, but there has never been one who would qualify to be White House counsel, if only her husband were not President.

The question is whether being First Lady will change Hillary Clinton or Hillary Clinton will change the role. There is speculation that Bill Clinton will find a way to employ his wife without igniting a protest. A new generation of leaders brings with it new assumptions about the roles that women—or wives—should play.

On the other hand, the Clintons may move carefully. When the Governor talked about "buy one, get one free" and possibly appointing Hillary to the Cabinet, her popularity took a dive. "People have changed their attitude about Hillary," says pollster Peter Hart, "but if they see her reinforcing one of their earlier negative feelings they won't like her." Last week Hillary said she wanted to continue to be "a voice for children," which fits within the choose-a-cause deportment of First Ladies past.

"The Hillary problem," as some aides call it, mixed the personality of the teacher's pet with the grimness of the first generation of women lawyers, afraid to crack a joke about a client for fear of being sent back to the typing pool. To some, her marriage looked like a merger. Former candidate Michael Dukakis only read about Swedish land-use planning in his spare time; the Clintons talk about similarly dense topics with friends over dinner.

Throughout the months of scrutiny, Hillary took the criticism seriously enough to change, but not personally enough to wilt. Her critics contend that she underwent a personality transplant, allowing handlers to substitute the interests of Martha Stewart for her own.

Washington remains the heart of tea-pouring country, where Senate wives still hold Red Cross blood-bank drives and political wives give up high-powered careers to advance their husbands'.

It is natural in a democracy for people to worry most about the influence they cannot see—which helps explain the uproar when their worst suspicions are confirmed by what they do see. Some commentators went off like a cheap car alarm when Rosalynn Carter's fingers grazed the doorknob of the Cabinet room. Columnists conjured up Lady Macbeth when Nancy Reagan introduced policy-by-horoscope, and when she nudged her husband at a press conference on the hostages and urgently whispered, "Tell them you're doing the best you can."

As she flies into Washington for the inauguration, having studied closely the biographies of past First Ladies for guidance, Hillary Clinton may vow not to go to Cabinet meetings and take notes, declare a tablecloth crisis or order up a set of gold-rimmed china. She may find a way to chart a new course. But however circumspect, she will make her own mistakes. And if history is any guide, for reasons as old as Adam and Eve, some Americans will punish her for them, all out of proportion to their significance.

November 16, 1992

At the Center of Power

The First Lady wants more than clout. She wants to have a life too.
Can she find the formula?

Hillary Rodham Clinton knew life had changed forever when her daughter, Chelsea, got sick one night in February and asked her mother to fix one of her favorite dishes. No sooner did the First Lady pad down the hall to the kitchen on the second floor of the family quarters, open the refrigerator and begin cracking eggs than a steward appeared magically at her elbow. He wanted to help by whipping up an omelet. At the risk of hurting his feelings, the most influential woman in America explained that the eggs had to be scrambled and that she had to scramble them.

Such are the days and nights of Hillary Rodham Clinton. In exchange for taking on the burdens of the world, including the most ambitious and powerful role a First Lady has ever assumed, all the practical considerations of daily living have been removed—whether she wants them to be or not. As she sits in the library on the first floor of the residence after holding a reception for community volunteers on the South Lawn, a butler brings her iced tea on a silver tray, and with him the unmistakable formality of this old house with 132 rooms. She finally eats lunch that day at 3:30, looking almost too exhausted to chew, and admits it's been a "pretty stressful three months."

Exhausting, yes, but also remarkable and historic. In her first 100 days, she has redefined the role of First Lady in America more than anyone would have imagined a year ago. By the end of this month, she plans to deliver a proposal for the largest piece of legislation since Social Security, a health-care plan that will affect one-seventh of the American economy. Her tackling of a nearly $1 trillion-a-year problem is accompanied by the sound of glass ceilings breaking as women empowered by the Clinton Administration rise to new positions of influence and opportunity: the new Attorney General, Janet Reno, celebrated a decision to allow female pilots and sailors to go into combat, women accounting for one-third of nominees to top administration jobs.

Hillary is the first First Lady to have a major assignment by which she can—and will—be judged. As leader of a task force with a staff in excess of 500, she has traveled across nine states, held 50 congressional meetings and met with everyone from nurses to Native American spiritual healers.

To millions of women, Hillary Clinton's career-and-family balancing act is a symbolic struggle. Never mind that she has plenty of help, including more top officials on her staff than Al Gore. Hillary still has something in common with women everywhere: a day that contains only 24 hours, and responsibilities that extend way beyond what happens in the office. Family duties fall primarily to her—from attending soccer games and helping Chelsea with her homework to shopping and organizing birthday parties. She's also looking after her mother, who is staying at the White House while recovering from the death of Hillary's 82-year-old father, Hugh Rodham. The First Lady's plea is familiar to any working woman. "We are trying to work it out that we have some more time just for ourselves. The job eats up every spare minute."

The next few months will offer little respite. In the midst of the final marathon sessions to complete the task force's recommendations, the once rosy picture for pushing health-care reform through the Congress has turned bleak. House Ways and Means Chairman Dan Rostenkowski went so far as to ridicule her nascent plan as the "domestic equivalent of Star Wars." (She still had him over for dinner that night.) A growing cabal of administration officials has urged the Clintons to delay their health-care plan, arguing that the President can't risk overloading the system by sending both his economic and his health packages to Capitol Hill. But she is undaunted. The past two weeks have been a blur of 16-hour days, meetings for two and three hours at a clip with the health-care task force, interrupted by congressional briefings. She insists, "There is no delay in what we're doing."

At the same time, the First Lady plays an up-front, active part in the presidency, from domestic affairs to political strategy to speechwriting, bringing to the table two decades of experience and no apologies. In all but foreign affairs, she has emerged as First Adviser, being called in on the spur of the moment to a meeting of 15 senior staff members in late April, for example, to assess the problems of the first 100 days and the defeat of the President's stimulus package.

While the whole world is watching to see how she pulls off her expanded role, she is also responsible for the traditional duties of a First Lady. Ceremonial events, like dinner for the country's Governors or tea with the King and Queen of Spain, don't stop because there is a deadline on managed competition. Paint chips and fabric swatches also fall under her jurisdiction. She is redecorating the private quarters to suit her informal style, which favors quilts and rocking chairs. She has already moved a table and white wicker chairs into the kitchen upstairs so that the family can eat breakfast and dinner in a cozier manner than the imposing dining room would permit. And she has had bedside phones installed that do not require going through a switchboard. "He sleeps here and has his phone," she says, indicating one side of the queen-size bed. "And I sleep there and have mine." She furnished her husband's private study next to the Oval Office with a stand-up desk, a CD player, framed campaign buttons and a large portrait of herself.

The First Lady ran into controversy by trying to keep the task force's meetings behind closed doors. A group of doctors and industry insiders sued the White House and a federal judge ruled that some of the meetings had to be open.

The First Lady has earned grudging respect on Capitol Hill, in part because she makes house calls. During her first visit, 30 Democratic Senators listened carefully, although most of them would rather have been having gum surgery. Her every misstep was discussed, from an overly familiar manner to her middle name. Minority Leader Bob Dole disputes press reports that Hillary blundered when she called him Bob. "Last time I checked," he said, "that was my name." He calls her Hillary.

Outside her health-care mission, there is probably no title that could convey the scope of her role, although "Counsellor to the President" was batted around for a long time. As always, she is her husband's most trusted confidante, best friend, toughest critic and most ardent cheerleader. She is open but vague about how much they share. "He'll say, 'What do you think about this?' or 'Give me an opinion about that.' It's kind of give-and-take, pretty informal." And then there is complete access. "During the day I can see him anytime I want to. I can look out the window and see him," she says, smiling as she turns her head toward his office. "He's right there."

When the presidential door closes, Hillary is behind it if she wants to be. "The President sits in the middle of the table, the Vice President right across from him, and Hillary wherever she wants," says an aide. "And the refrain we have all gotten used to is, 'What do you think, Hillary?' " When the President's economic address to Congress was scraps of paper on the conference table in the Roosevelt Room, she stepped in and pasted it back together again. Aides are gradually becoming more open about Hillary's breadth. One says it goes like this: "A speech that needs a rewrite, get Hillary. A speech that needs to be given, get Hillary. The President has a problem he wants to chew over, get Hillary. The point is you never go wrong getting Hillary."

With the power to make appointments comes the blame when many have gone unmade. While the Clintons have dithered over whether the chief of protocol job should go to a man or a woman, events that should have garnered goodwill for the pair have sparked resentment. The most disastrous incident occurred at the most important affair so far, a White House reception in honor of the opening of the U.S. Holocaust Museum. Scheduled to be there at 4 p.m., the President arrived 2½ hours late. By that time, Polish President Lech Walesa, entertainer Mandy Patinkin, House Speaker Tom Foley and others had long run out of anything to say to one another and were squishing in the mud under a tent in a driving rain. Many of the older guests, Holocaust survivors, had left in disgust.

When Hillary is going about her day, she acts like any other professional with a demanding, brain-crushing job. Her office in the West Wing is one of the least imposing, furnished with a blue-beige-and-red-striped sofa, a table submerged in paper, a small desk and a window looking out on a red tile roof. She goes through paperwork like butter, trying not to touch the same piece twice. Says her deputy, Melanne Verveer: "I'm efficient, and she makes me look like a daydreamer."

In general, she stays away from irony, since humor has to watch its step in politics, avoiding off-the-cuff repartee that can look bad when repeated.

Her whimsy runs more to lip-synching "Baby, I Need Your Loving" and giving a tour of the White House the way Alistair Cooke might guide visitors around Windsor Castle.

Even so, some people are scared to death of her, one aide saying she's both "formidable" and "frightening," with all the protective, wifely instincts of, say, Nancy Reagan, but on top of that very smart, so that "nothing gets by her, nothing." Hillary took a hand in making office assignments for the West Wing. "We were looking at this floor plan and, presto, she had a layout it would have taken an industrial engineer weeks to figure. Not everybody was happy, but she got it right."

Hillary's open involvement in policymaking disturbs some Republicans and others who feel duped by the Hillary Lite that emerged in the latter stages of the campaign after polling found that voters were fearful of what pollsters termed an "empowered Nancy Reagan." A Republican consultant told a network newscaster that his job was to make sure Hillary Clinton is discredited before the 1996 campaign. Each day anti-Hillary talking points go out to talk-show hosts. The rumor machine is cranking out bogus stories about her face (lifted), her sex life (either nonexistent or all too active) and her marriage (a sham). Many of the stories are attributed to the Secret Service in an attempt to give the tales credibility. She denies the yarn about her throwing a lamp (or Bible or vase), then wonders about the sources. "Why are they telling lies about me? What is it about me?"

Hillary has yet to adjust to the notion that every waking moment of a First Lady, and some of the sleeping ones, are public property. Friends say Hillary fenced off a zone of privacy right after the notorious broadcast of *60 Minutes*, when, she claims, almost every frame of tape showing her at her best was left on the cutting-room floor. After that, friends say, she adopted the attitude that the less of her that is known, the less there is to pick apart.

Her reticence is a departure, given the open life she lived for a decade in the Governor's mansion in Little Rock. She drove her own Oldsmobile, waited in line at the movies and had the church choir over for picnics in the backyard. She purposely sent the household staff off on weekends so she could go to the grocery store on Saturday mornings. She comes from a family so bizarrely intact that the whole group went on the Clintons' honeymoon to Acapulco. In a state where Gloria Steinem was considered by some a communist, Hillary started out being regarded as a stuck-up feminist from Wellesley who wouldn't change her name, and ended up a popular First Lady.

Now, Hillary wants to preserve some part of the prosaic quality of life so Chelsea doesn't grow up believing food magically materializes on her plate.

While Hillary generally shrugs off criticism about herself, the treatment of Chelsea is another matter. Hillary took out after *Saturday Night Live* producer Lorne Michaels and his writers for "having nothing better to do than be mean and cruel to a young girl," after they ran a skit making fun of her daughter.

Yet Hillary is in a position no First Lady has ever experienced. As the icon of American womanhood, she is the medium through which the remaining anxieties over feminism are being played out. She is on a cultural seesaw held to a schizophrenic standard: everything she does that is soft is a calculated cover-up of the careerist inside; everything that isn't fuzzy is a put-down of women who stay home and bake cookies.

In her Texas speech, her voice halted as she quoted the admission by Atwater that he had acquired all the wealth and prestige he had wanted and still felt empty. "What power wouldn't I trade for a little more time with my family? What price wouldn't I pay for an evening with friends." Last Thursday evening as the sun was going down, the President emerged from a meeting on Bosnia to join his wife. They hadn't seen each other for a few hours, and in the shadows behind the door of the diplomatic entrance, he touched the side of her face and took her hand before they came out to say good-bye to the 500 members of the health-care task force gathered on the South Lawn. He thanked them, and then turned and said, "I'm indebted once again to my wonderful wife." It's a line uttered by politicians since the Republic was formed, but he may just mean it.

Perhaps in addition to the other items on her agenda, Hillary Rodham Clinton will define for women that magical spot where the important work of the world and love and children and an inner life all come together. Like Ginger Rogers, she will do everything her partner does, only backward and in high heels, and with what was missing in Atwater—a lot of heart.

May 10, 1993

Shear Dismay

For Bill Clinton, little things like a fancy haircut and a tempest in his travel office loom large

A President can do just about anything he wants, which is why he is under constraints to behave so well. As much as the bills he introduces, the speeches he gives and the Executive Orders he signs, a President is defined by the small acts at the margin that burn themselves into the national consciousness: Jimmy Carter with his killer rabbit and lust in his heart, Lyndon Johnson displaying his surgical scar, Richard Nixon strolling on the beach in his wing tips. In years to come, the biggest small thing of the Clinton presidency may turn out to be the $5,500 Haircut.

Itemized, that's $200 for the haircut and $5,300 for the plane. While Cristophe of Beverly Hills, Calif., snipped the presidential locks, Air Force One idled at Los Angeles International Airport with a full crew aboard for close to an hour. The Secret Service says it put no hold on traffic; nonetheless, reporters claim two runways were closed and at least two flights delayed. His Bubba barber of 17 years, his off-the-rack suits, the Governor's mansion with its tattered volleyball net—these have given way to a Belgian-born hair stylist, Armani jackets and a private jogging track.

Few citizens begrudge a President some luxuries, but it has to be done in the context of respecting the folk who sent you. The New Democrat who cared about the people who worked hard and played by the rules, who eschewed the cultural elite for a decaf at McDonald's is now perceived as being concerned more about gays in the military, abortion-rights activists, and loading up his Cabinet with millionaire lawyers, than with Middle America. "The President should remind himself," says presidential scholar Stephen Hess, "that the people who elected him get their hair cut, not styled, by barbers named Ed, not Cristophe, and they pay in cash, not personal-services contracts." The speed of passage of the haircut from Beltway to Burbank monologue set a new indoor record.

The haircut hubbub even had a complex sideshow: the disclosure that the administration had abruptly fired seven longtime employees of the White House travel office, which handles trips for the press. The move should have been a public relations plus—rooting out shoddy accounting practices and gross mismanagement in an office with large amounts of unaccounted-for cash and noncompetitive contracts. Instead, how the White House handled the affair overshadowed the affair itself. The White House can replace any political appointees it wants to, with or without cause, but it should ensure beforehand that its pink slips do not produce red faces.

When it turned out that a distant cousin of Clinton's, Catherine Cornelius, would become interim director of that office, the press bombarded the White House with charges of cronyism and hubris. The release of the audit of the office by the accounting firm Peat Marwick documenting serious abuses and the FBI's decision to move forward with a criminal investigation did not reduce the reporters' outrage.

The White House failed to take into account that the travel office had a powerful protector in the press, which has long been pampered by the plush level of accommodations. The reporters appreciate the way their favorite drinks are served the minute they sit down in first-class seats. Family members can come along for a flat $100; any purchases made during trips get hauled back free. A reporter's fingers hardly ever touch luggage.

Past presidencies are filled with cautionary notes that should warn a public official off any non-Jeffersonian actions. George Bush's attempt at just-folks normalcy was undermined when he turned a blind eye to his chief of staff flying military jets to private appointments, and closing the waters off Kennebunkport, Maine, while he pounded through the surf in his cigarette boat. Ronald Reagan could pull off the common touches as only a B-movie actor could, but his wife offset those by ordering a set of hand-painted china inscribed "NANCY" and a closetful of unpaid-for designer creations. Nixon dressed up the White House guards like something out of a Sigmund Romberg operetta.

The most consistent image of the White House so far is the parade of celebrities being whisked in and out of the iron gates for private audiences with administration officials. Barbra Streisand played her new CD for the President first, made calls from the study next to the Oval Office and dined with Janet Reno. Christopher Reeve and Billy Crystal got environmental briefings from two Cabinet Secretaries. A group of Hollywood celebs was invited for a Saturday-morning briefing on health care. The overnight guest list for the Lincoln Bedroom sometimes reads like the register at the Hotel Bel-Air.

White House officials realized there was too much Wilshire Boulevard and too little Main Street, and for two weeks there were no sightings of anyone whose birthday is announced by Mary Hart on *Entertainment Tonight*. But it was Clinton who broke his own edict first by giving Quincy Jones a guided tour of the flying White House just before the presidential haircut. The next day, when Clinton was going to the Hill to push a tax bill that asks the middle class to pay more, the driveway in front of the mansion was clogged again with stretch limos bearing people who think sacrifice is a day when the personal masseuse doesn't show up. Sinbad, the comedian, held his own impromptu press conference in front of the West Wing, explaining his deeply held belief that it was every American's right to have his hair done daily. Rap star M. C. Hammer was also on the premises but unavailable for comment.

Hollywood has always been White House–struck: Michael Jackson moonwalked through the Bush Administration, and Frank Sinatra danced cheek to cheek with Nancy Reagan. So far, Clinton has resisted naming a Shirley Temple Black as an ambassador or an Arnold Schwarzenegger to a presidential commission. But he needs to prove that Roger Clinton got all the rock-star genes in the family and that he intends to govern more like

Harry Truman than Oprah Winfrey. The most perceptive question pollsters ask is whether the respondent believes that the President cares about people like you. Unless Clinton is pursuing a 40% strategy, he might consider spending more time in Arkansas than in L.A., and in a barber chair, not a traffic-stopping runway salon.

May 31, 1993

Where Hope Ends

The apparent suicide of a close friend and adviser leaves the Clintons in mourning and Washington with a painful question: Why did he do it?

"Before we came here, we thought of ourselves as good people." This was one of the few observations Vincent Foster Jr., the 48-year-old deputy White House counsel, allowed himself to make about how Washington had chipped away at his psyche after he joined the Clinton Administration. Last Tuesday afternoon, six months to the day since his boyhood friend had taken the oath of office and everything seemed possible for the men from Hope, Foster passed through the iron gate of the White House in his gray Nissan, crossed the Potomac River to a Civil War fort preserved as a national park. He put his father's antique .38-cal. Colt revolver in his mouth and ended his life, leaving those who knew him in stunned and uncomprehending grief.

The President, whose friendship with Foster began four decades earlier in Hope, Ark., learned of his death at about 10 p.m. After cutting short a live interview with Larry King in the library of the residence, he immediately called Hillary, who was in Little Rock. He then ordered an unmarked van to take him to Georgetown to visit Foster's wife, Lisa. He stayed there for several hours, then returned for a vigil with friends at the White House, where he said, "We did a lot of crying and a little bit of laughing," remembering the man Clinton called his Rock of Gibraltar. "When I was told what happened," he recalled, "I just kept thinking in my mind of when we were so young, sitting on the ground in the backyard, throwing knives into the ground and seeing if we were adroit enough to make them stick."

The knives hardly ever stuck, Clinton said, but the friendship did. The President brought his oldest friend, who was also his wife's colleague at the Rose law firm, to Washington with him. One of Little Rock's most brilliant litigators, Foster was trusted by the Clintons, says Arkansas lawyer Joe

Purvis, "not just for one or two projects, but leaned on in almost every facet" of their lives. As deputy in the counsel's office, he was among those who attracted much of the criticism in the early days of the administration over insufficiently vetting nominees and the abrupt firing of seven members of the travel office. He had become a target of *Wall Street Journal* editorials about "legal cronies from Little Rock," although he laughed it off, says a colleague, calling it "b.s. stuff." He was the one, Clinton recalled, who bucked up others, always the protector who never seemed in need of protection himself.

The death left the White House staff wandering around glassy-eyed in disbelief, with those who knew him best searching their memories for the offhand remark, the telling anecdote, that would illuminate what Foster kept hidden. Skip Rutherford, an aide to Chief of Staff Mack McLarty, recalls a conversation a week earlier when Foster said, "No one back in Little Rock could know how hard this is." Purvis remembers Foster's description of his days. "You try to be at work by 7 in the morning and sometimes it's 10 at night when you walk out just dog-tired. About the time you're thinking, 'What a load,' you turn around and see the White House lit up, and the awe of where you are and what you're doing hits you. It makes you realize it's worth it."

The official account of Foster's death has done nothing to answer the questions about a man charmed in his life and so devoted to his wife and three children that he once admitted that "two days alone in the house" without them drove him crazy. There was no note near the cannon where his body was slumped, or in the car parked 200 yards away.

Foster's morning had been spent in routine meetings and at a Rose Garden ceremony to announce the nomination of a new FBI director. Foster returned to his second-floor office with his boss, Bernard Nussbaum, and had a sandwich at his desk. Nussbaum recalls an upbeat conversation when Foster poked his head into the office a little after noon. That afternoon Foster's wife was at her new house with her friend Donna McLarty, telling her that Vince's distraction—no one called it a depression—had lifted during a getaway weekend on Maryland's Eastern Shore.

It is unknown what Foster did between about 1 p.m. and 6:04 p.m., when the U.S. Park Police, tipped off by an anonymous caller, found his body. And despite the President's acceptance of Foster's death as an inexplicable suicide, the Justice Department is coordinating an investigation to consider foul play, blackmail or any other possibility.

As Foster's life was drawing to a close, lawmakers were on their feet cheering the President's only public speech at the Capitol since his February economic address. While it had been a rough six months for Clinton, the sustained applause rang in his ears, and the President and his aides felt optimistic. But Vince Foster, on that peaceful bluff overlooking the Potomac, could not hear the cheers or feel the optimism. He had already crossed to the other shore.

August 2, 1993

On Hollywood and Vineyard

The natives are restless as Bill, Hillary and Chelsea begin their summer vacation

Finally, on the afternoon of his 47th birthday, seven months after he took the oath of office, the President came to rest on a New England island so small it has no traffic lights. Martha's Vineyard, a 100-sq.-mi. haven of quaint shingled houses, quiet country gardens, yacht-studded harbors and stunning beaches, has many attributes to recommend it, not the least of which is that its inhabitants are sufficiently celebrity-trained so that no one stares into opera diva Beverly Sills' grocery cart at Cronig's or gawks at Jackie Onassis riding her bike near her house in Gay Head. A President— no big deal.

A live-and-let-live attitude toward the famous is one reason Martha's Vineyard won out over a number of other vacation possibilities, like Jackson Hole, Wyo. (too isolated); Florida, where Hillary's brother Hugh lives (too hot); California (too shallow, although Hillary and Chelsea vacationed in Santa Barbara for a few days on the way back from the Tokyo summit); and Telluride, Colo. (too small). Not that the decision came easily, or could have been carried out if seven-day-advance-purchase airline tickets were a factor. Unlike most Presidents, Clinton is a man without a country house— no Kennebunkport or Gettysburg farm, no Pedernales or California ranch.

Moreover, he doesn't seem to kick back as well as Republicans. Richard Nixon had no trouble repairing to San Clemente for 31 days in one sitting, and Ronald Reagan clocked 200 days at his spread by the first year of his second term. Clinton doesn't even take off weekends, and he delayed making holiday plans as if he were putting off minor surgery. Some people wondered if a man who had not got away for four years on a regulation vacation would make it five, and if the dreaded word "working" would be appended to "vacation" even before one began.

Enter Vernon Jordan, a man determined to have fun, as Press Secretary Dee Dee Myers put it. Jordan had vacationed on Martha's Vineyard for 20 years, and he pointed out that it met all the First Family's requirements: it has beaches (Massachusetts is one of the few states that permit private ones), a golf course (18 golf carts were shipped in for the Secret Service), a good price (former Defense Secretary Robert McNamara donated his house), populism (the Clintons could eschew the main residence for the guesthouse) and enough celebrities to be interesting without being rarefied.

But while the Vineyard might be perfect for the Clintons, there was some apprehension that the First Vacationers would not be perfect for the Vineyard, a tiny community already stuffed to the gills with artists, writers, journalists, psychiatrists and academics so set in their reverse-chic ways that no newcomer could hope to adapt. These are people who congratulate themselves for not choosing to vacation among the canapé-consuming classes in the Hamptons who use *summer* as a verb. Hunting, fishing or networking without a license is punishable by a $300 fine and deportation to the mainland.

The birthday party was such a jolly, casual evening, according to one guest, that the ordinarily shy Chelsea felt comfortable enough to toast "a wonderful father." Hillary toasted him as well, remarking on the incredible year gone by since he turned 46 and their new life in Washington. She ended by looking across the room to her husband's table, raising her glass and saying, "I love you, Mr. President." The party didn't break up until 1 a.m., unheard of on Martha's Vineyard, where, as Beverly Sills puts it, "10 p.m. is midnight."

By Thursday afternoon, as hope began to fade for invitations, attention shifted to Friday night, when Katharine Graham would be having a previously scheduled dinner to which the President had been added. There was much grousing that Graham's Republican houseguests, Henry and Nancy Kissinger and Larry and Marlene Eagleburger, were eating up valuable table space, while certified liberals like Walter Cronkite, Carly Simon and Jules Feiffer were going begging. When columnist Art Buchwald had netted no invitations by Thursday afternoon, he decided to be satisfied with "having dinner at the house of someone who is invited to have dinner with the President."

In between sailing with Jackie and dining with the Kissingers, Clinton has dozens of other invitations to sort through. The Vineyard chapter of the N.A.A.C.P. has asked him to speak, the Oak Bluffs selectmen want to present him with a medal and the Wampanoag tribe has invited him to a pow-wow. The Edgartown city fathers may have had the best idea. Knowing the President's weakness for town meetings, they have invited him to one scheduled for August 25.

So far, the President seems content to sit still for a while, and the country should be grateful for whatever it is in the Edgartown air that will make Bill Clinton unwind. Everyone needs to be beyond the phone and the mailman, to go to a place where NAFTA, if mentioned at all, is thought to be a new kind of pasta, and health care means taking the waters off South Beach. He can no longer harp about soaking the rich in a place where the rich are soaking.

August 30, 1993

What Was That Again?

Among those of us who have resisted growing up, it's an article of faith that we can put off growing old. We work out, we eat poached salmon, we devour alternative-medicine nostrums while gobbling antioxidant vitamin supplements, just in case. We don't ask the first baby-boomer President for much—not for universal health care, not for campaign-finance purity, not even for a tax cut. But we do count on him, as the emblem of our age, not to give in to the ravages of time.

He was re-elected in part because he complied. He looks improbably young. His hair may be gray, but it's all there. He runs without gasping for air, and he's managed to lose 20 lbs. when it's all too easy to gain twice that. So the news on Friday that the President was fitted with hearing aids hurts. Bifocals are one thing, Miracle-Ear quite another. For once, the many baby boomers covering Clinton feel his pain.

After Clinton's annual physical at Bethesda Naval Hospital, White House spokesman Mike McCurry announced the presidential ear trumpet. "It's called high-frequency audio loss, and it's a boomer malady," McCurry said. "Helicopters probably made it worse for Clinton, but loud music does it to most of us." Clinton, of course, actually had horns blowing directly at him during his years in the school band. He should have practiced safe sax.

While his hearing loss comes early for us, it may not be a minute too soon for Clinton. Presidents have long used their infirmities to deflect attention from their mistakes. Funny how Lyndon Johnson unveiled his appendectomy scar during the Vietnam quagmire. Woodrow Wilson's stroke muted criticism of his failure to bring the U.S. into the League of Nations. When Reagan joked about getting shot, his popularity shot up. His favorability leaped again after he waved cheerily from his hospital room, fresh from having had polyps removed from his colon. That feel-good moment saw him through Iran-contra. We liked that he was out of the loop.

But some Presidents struggle to keep their physical frailties secret. Eisenhower called his first heart attack digestive upset. Kennedy played touch football with overcompensating vigor rather than give a hint of his Addison's disease. Bush got no sympathy for throwing up in Japan. Dole's remarking that "some of the things that we read about don't return as quickly as advertised" after prostate surgery just reminded us he was old.

Clinton can't use poor hearing to explain his failure to discern the roar of Whitewater, but it has possibilities for his current troubles. Experts agree that hearing loss is most pronounced at social events. All those coffees? He never heard a word that John Huang said. Was Roger Tamraz talking about a pipeline—or *Nightline?* Those pleas from Harold Ickes to make fund-raising calls? He turned a deaf ear.

Clinton would be well advised, however, not to try that hand-to-the-ear thing when reporters are shouting questions. Sympathy for your frailty will carry you just so far, even among aging reporters who might not be able to hear your answers anyway.

October 13, 1997

Ken Starr, Gumshoe

Last week America learned there was probable cause to believe the President betrayed his wife, his daughter and his country. Whether or not it is finally proved that he had an affair with a 21-year-old intern and then tried to cover it up, he behaved irresponsibly enough to enable prosecutors to expand what started out as an investigation of an Arkansas land deal into a fishing expedition for intimate details of his daily—and nightly—life.

What gives this the overtone of Greek tragedy is how utterly avoidable it was, if the President had exercised the slightest bit of restraint. Already given a lot of slack by voters who believed he was an adulterer but elected him anyway, the President had only to comply with the minimal standard of presidential marital conduct: Don't have sex in the White House with a woman not your wife (no one thought to add "intern").

In these sexually perilous times, we all know lawyers and businessmen who won't meet in a hotel room with a colleague of the opposite sex. But Clinton, fighting accusations that while Governor he exposed himself to a female state employee, is now accused of behavior so reckless, so arrogant, so tawdry, that if the charges turn out to be true, he should be ashamed to show his face, much less brag that he is going about "business as usual." None of the rest of us can. We feel his shame.

Thanks to Clinton we have two other problems: having to explain to the kids over Cheerios not the significance of the first Papal visit to Cuba by the most famous celibate in the world, but just why it is that a perky anchorperson is talking about something called oral sex. The second, perhaps more lasting problem, is the legal precedent set by this ballooning investigation. Until last week, the criticism of independent counsel Kenneth Starr went largely to his unchecked power. Former Republican independent counsel Joseph diGenova calls the whole setup "a constitutional monstrosity." Now we watch as a prosecutor gunning for a President uses tactics to dig up dirt that would make *NYPD Blue*'s Detective Sipowicz blanch. Starr not only pulled a sting on a former White House intern but reportedly planned to wire her to run one on the President himself, as if he were John Gotti.

Consider Starr's response when Monica Lewinsky's "friend" Linda Tripp brought him 20 hours of surreptitiously recorded conversations. He wired Tripp, listened in and then three days later instructed her to lure Lewinsky to a Virginia hotel for lunch. Instead of a sandwich with Tripp, Lewinsky got a raft of agents swooping down on her. They took the stunned Lewinsky to a set of rooms and commenced an on-again, off-again interrogation that would last 10 hours. Her lawyer, William Ginsburg, said she was "crying and screaming and yelling. . . . They told her if she left she'd be subject to immediate prosecution." He described it as "a treatment for *NYPD Blue*."

If a prosecutor appointed to unravel a land deal (remember Whitewater?) bootstraps himself into a civil suit and thereby compels testimony about the most intimate matters, we will soon have a government that can get to anyone. Everyone has something embarrassing to hide. When we aren't all dealing with a President we're ready to string up, this unfettered intrusion may be what haunts us most. What a Hobbesian choice: lie and face prison or tell the truth and face public humiliation. The perjury follows, even though the act—reprehensible though it might be—did not flow from official duty. No one should lie, but Big Brother shouldn't ask. This all comes by way of a prosecutor who before he took the appointment was ready to file an amicus brief supporting Paula Jones. Now he's her amicus, all right; the course of her case is in Starr's hands as much as anyone else's.

You don't have to have a moment's sympathy for the President to know that this convergence of Jones, Starr and the FBI is not right. As Starr disgraces the Judicial Branch and Clinton the Executive one, things once lost—like respect for privacy, the presidency and proportion—cannot be retrieved.

February 2, 1998

Inside the Magic Bubble

Around Washington, those in awe of the President's resilience say that if Bill Clinton were the *Titanic,* the iceberg would have gone down. On Thursday night, he lived out that metaphor when he hosted Britain's Prime Minister Tony Blair at a formal dinner in the East Room. Like a brightly lit ocean liner on a dark sea, the White House floated above the scandal for five hours, as 240 guests clinked glasses and basked in the glow of being rich, of being powerful, of being there.

It was eerie. Just getting the most coveted ticket in Washington—to dine with those two powerful heads of state—lent the evening an illusion of invulnerability: that all is right in the world because all is right at this moment. There was the President, charming and being charmed by the bicoastal Masters of the Universe: Steven Spielberg, Barry Diller, Jack Welch, Warren Buffett, Tom Hanks, Ralph Lauren, John F. Kennedy Jr., Tina Brown, Anna Wintour, Barbara Walters, Peter Jennings. Bad luck seemed as far away as it must have seemed in the ballroom of the *Titanic.* How can anything be wrong when Stevie Wonder and Sir Elton John have come to sing to you?

But shortly after dinner, in a white tent over the West Terrace, as Wonder began "You Are the Sunshine of My Life," an aide handed Clinton confidant Harry Thomason a printout off the Internet of a next-day *New York Times* story about Betty Currie's testimony. The sight of Thomason hunched over in the dim blue light with Clinton adviser Rahm Emanuel, straining to read, set off a buzz among the reporters. Abruptly, Peter Jennings left. Stop the music: Clinton may be done in—and by his own secretary.

So often scandals come to this. The fate of those on the upper deck hangs on the mettle of those below. History belongs to Henry Kissinger and Madeleine Albright—until it devolves to Dwight Chapin and Rose Mary Woods and Betty Currie. But if Linda Tripp has come to be the Iago of the piece, full of malice, Currie occupies a place of goodness. One of her closest friends says Currie won't "forget" what she'd rather not remember. If she knows something awful happened in the Oval Office, Clinton should be worried.

As she plows through the press mob or watches as the lawn of her suburban bungalow is chewed up by a stakeout, the anguish visible on her face comes from her knowledge of Bill Clinton, the man up close, not the President we write about from afar. No doubt she's been a victim of his carelessness, as so many have, but she has also been the recipient of a hundred kindnesses. When her brother and sister died suddenly and young in the space of six months, Clinton dropped everything to go to both funerals.

The band played on last Thursday as the President and First Lady danced till 1 a.m. to "My Girl" and "In the Mood." Later reports would suggest that Currie's testimony would not sink Clinton, after all. For now, the ship of state sails on.

February 16, 1998

No. There's a Trap Waiting

"I don't know anybody at the top of the system . . . who really wants to see the President hurt," said Senator Orrin Hatch, who could inflict some of that hurt. "[If] he does come forth and say, 'I made a mistake . . .' [to] protect his wife and daughter . . . and then ask for . . . some sort of consideration, I think we would bend over backward to try and give him that consideration."

That's so sweet, but so unlikely. I've heard those words many times. Come to think of it, I've said those words many times, even though I've hardly ever seen it work out. The best example in my life came when my parents heard about a bunch of 15-year-olds who had talked their older friends with licenses into letting them drive around the local shopping-center parking lot after hours, creating havoc. "Just tell me if you've ever been down there," my mother urged. "It will be worse if I find out from the security guards or other parents." So I 'fessed up to that heady, behind-the-wheel spin from rows A to N. It's possible things would have been worse if an independent counsel had forced the truth out of me. But for copping to that escapade willingly, I wasn't allowed to get my learner's permit until I was 17.

Although everyone talks about the perjury trap that Ken Starr's grand jury holds for the President, the confession trap is just as big a hazard.

This doesn't mean coming clean isn't the right thing to do—just that it isn't the panacea some make it out to be. Imagine if Clinton were to confess, reversing his finger-wagging denial. Even if he said he did it to spare his family, the support he enjoys among a majority of Americans would sink like a stone. It's one thing to have an abstract notion that he actually had an affair and covered it up (and to have that leak from Starr's grand jury). It's another to hear it from his own mouth, to have the fig leaf of doubt removed and be forced to confront our own moral laxity in being willing to overlook it.

The implicit bargain struck with the Comeback Kid was that in exchange for his one get-out-of-jail-free card on the Gennifer Flowers business, he would never, ever fool around in the White House. If he has broken that bargain, forget some mealymouthed I-caused-pain-in-my-marriage explanation. Now that he has caused pain in the country, the noninhaling, I-didn't-get-an-induction-notice escape artist must give a detailed accounting on prime-time TV.

For drama, it would be hard to top a mea culpa. Just for Monica's appearance last week, white canopies sprang up outside the courthouse to shade hundreds of reporters and their coolers of soda and take-out food, their lawn chairs and boom boxes. Add a few prize bulls, and it could have been a county fair; add a bride and groom, and you could have thrown a wedding. Journalists may not relish seeing a President brought down, but what will we do for excitement once the biggest scandal of our time ends?

The only confession that works without fail is the religious kind, the bless-me-Father-for-I-have-sinned sort. For five Our Fathers and five Hail Marys, you get absolution. Confession and forgiveness really are divine, not human, and certainly not political. That's why it's called a sacrament.

August 10, 1998

Thanks, but Hillary Doesn't Want Your Sympathy

Last Friday, Hillary Clinton walked out to the White House lawn and celebrated her husband's 52nd birthday as if it were his fifth and he deserved a pony and a trip to Disneyland. Joking about how old he was getting, she led more than 100 staff members in a rousing chorus of "Happy Birthday."

How does she do it and, more intriguingly, why, when the only reasonable reaction to the pain her husband has caused her is to take that spice cake with the buttercream frosting and plant it in his face? At the very moment she was being Harriet to his Ozzie at the garden party, aides were inside considering just how much the President would have to say to satisfy calls for his head and yet preserve some semblance of dignity for his wife and child.

People think it takes so much out of Hillary Clinton to play the loyal wife that anyone who thinks she might also be a loving one is dismissed as a gullible dupe. To many viewers, Hillary's full-throated defense on the *Today* show in January, in which she blamed her husband's enemies for the scandal, was pure spinning for her man. But it was easy for her to believe that the same amalgam of right-wing moneymen, zealots and Clinton haters who had launched investigations into (and made movies about) whether Vince Foster was murdered could be behind a starstruck groupie suddenly in the clutches of both Ken Starr and Paula Jones' lawyers. Certainly, if she believed the charges against her husband, the lawyer in her would never, ever have conceded to Matt Lauer that an "adulterous liaison" with an intern, "if proven true, would be a very serious offense."

Whatever her suspicions over these past few months, she did not have any need to hear the whole truth from her husband until the reality of his testifying in front of Starr sank in last week. Anyone who saw her emerge from Marine One last Thursday, after a ceremony for the Americans killed in the embassy bombings in Africa, wondered if some of the agony on her face wasn't for the ordeal ahead. Ever since Chelsea was 6, Hillary has protected her daughter by convincing her that some of her father's political opponents would smear him to beat him. This week one of those opponents would be sitting in the Map Room, two floors below Chelsea's bedroom, learning from Clinton himself that some of the smearing might in fact be true.

As this drama has unfolded, the admiration that eluded the First Lady for years is now hers, as she climbs to a 60% approval rating. Two weeks ago, when she and Chelsea and some friends walked into a Washington restaurant for dinner, first one diner and then others stood and applauded, until the whole room was cheering. Her husband would have worked the tables, but she took her seat. For the disciplined and private Methodist, the brainy lawyer from Yale who hasn't asked for sympathy, having people feel sorry for her is just one more indignity to bear.

August 24, 1998

Now Say It Like You Mean It

Clinton was once the master of the apology act. So why can't he fake it again?

For three weeks, Bill Clinton has been on a World Apology Tour. It started in the Map Room, moved out to sea to a friendly island off the People's Republic of Massachusetts, then went on to the Kremlin and ended in Ireland. Not once, though, did he hit a pure, clean high note. In Dublin he finally coughed out an "I am sorry," but grudgingly, as if he were repeating something for a dense and demanding bunch of whiners.

It has been an odd spectacle for those who expected Clinton would be sorry enough that he'd been caught, to be sorry enough to be contrite. The Speech That Would Put This All Behind Us failed by not putting an apology in front of us. As disappointment poured in—not just from the media elite but from his supporters—an expanded apology was promised. The press went on red alert, hoping to cover a full Jimmy Swaggart. But when the vacationing President chose to mention forgiveness—in a chapel, no less—it was in the third person and past tense.

He may have done further damage. By invoking Nelson Mandela, who did nothing to deserve his captors, Clinton suggested he had done nothing to deserve Kenneth Starr. It was as if Clinton had been fighting for freedom, rather than boffing an intern in the Oval Office. Practitioners of the nonapology like the passive voice. Newt Gingrich, who pleaded guilty to ethics violations, was sorry "to whatever degree in any way that I brought controversy or inappropriate attention to the House." Senator Alfonse D'Amato said he was sorry "if I've offended anyone," when he knew full well whom he had offended with his buck-toothed, "no tickee, no laundry" mimicry of Lance Ito.

Last week Representative Dan Burton, a vicious critic of Clinton, broke new nonapology ground when he expressed pre-emptive regret for what a *Vanity Fair* reporter might have found in some 200 interviews. Burton suddenly remembered he had been separated from his wife three times. The next day his memory was jogged again when he learned that an Indianapolis paper was set to report that he had had an affair and fathered an illegitimate child. He wouldn't say more because of "everybody's heart being ripped out" and because "enough is enough." Sound familiar?

Linguistics professor Deborah Tannen says that men hardly ever apologize because doing so "shows weakness"—the next thing you know, some stronger type is clubbing you over the head and taking over your cave. That may be why Clinton, in Moscow, felt he had to defend his refusal to apologize for his refusal to apologize. He said he reread his speech and thought it was just fine. Clinton also volunteered that he was "heartened" by the understanding he'd found in "leaders around the world," a fresh take on the "in France this would be no big deal" defense. You would think Clinton was a recent émigré from Paris, completely taken aback by the customs of the natives.

Clinton's supporters argue he should get credit for not giving a faux-earnest Apology on Demand. But why would Clinton now, after seven months of sustained lying, suddenly choose honesty? His Slick Willie side has always known that the most important quality a politician can have is sincerity. And no politician is better at faking it than he is. In 1980 Clinton was a failed one-term Governor until he apologized for raising car-tag fees and got his wife to drop that "Rodham" business with her name. In 1992 he became the Comeback Kid, miraculously saving a crashing candidacy by quickly apologizing for causing pain in his marriage. So why on August 17 couldn't he lie about being sorry in order to satisfy a huge TV audience looking for a reason not to impeach him, fearing that impeachment would hurt the country as much as it would hurt him? For whatever reasons of pride and arrogance and poll numbers, the magic word didn't seep out of him until Friday, before far fewer people.

What an irony it would be if the man who won the presidency after claiming he was being unfairly penalized for a woman he didn't sleep with, a draft he didn't dodge and a drug he didn't inhale would lose it over an apology he didn't make quickly enough. This one was wheedled out of him while he showed the reluctance of a child who finally gives in and says, "O.K., O.K., I'm sorry. Are you happy now?"

He's a better politician than that. But never mind. When the Starr report comes, if it is as damning and detailed as expected, the drama of when and how much he apologized will be seen as an insignificant sideshow. The main event may be so devastating that no matter how sorry he is, the Comeback Kid will have no comeback.

September 14, 1998

The Shadow of Her Smile

It was nearing midnight in the solarium, the informal room on the third floor of the White House. The Mexican food had been cleared away, and a few dinner guests were hanging out waiting for the President to come back from taking a phone call. Just as he was returning, the First Lady noticed out of the corner of her eye that the TV was on, tuned to the David Letterman show. Casually, she leaned over, picked up the remote control and switched the set off before the President could hear a barrage of scandal jokes.

It's hard to believe she would need to protect him from the Top 10 Reasons Monica Is a Babe. But Hillary's gut response is always to defend the President against incoming fire. What's different this past month is her failure to go on the offense. For the first time, she hasn't scraped the staff off the floor, quarterbacked the Hail Mary pass or given her own statements. And when she said, just before the worst performance of his life on August 17, "It's his speech. Let him say what he wants," it wasn't helpful, nor meant to be. What a time for a work slowdown. The First Lady may not be able to save the President the way she saved the candidate, but she surely will hurt him if she doesn't stand by him once again, and not like some potted plant. Within days after the Lewinsky scandal broke, Hillary was on the *Today* show shouting her husband's praises. But for weeks now, there have been only perfunctory remarks during icy cameo appearances, bad body language and her failure to refer to the President with her usual "my husband" at a Moscow event.

Like so much coming out of the White House, Hillary's anger could be one more piece of spin, which makes it hard to interpret her switch to a hyper-smiley face during a flurry of public appearances at the end of last week. If Hillary had been faking anger because that's what any normal person would feel, she did it well. Rather than say anything herself, she issued a chilly statement of forgiveness through an aide. The administration seemed eager to disclose that the Martha's Vineyard vacation was a time for "healing." It certainly wasn't a time for fun. She sulked behind sunglasses, stared straight ahead and answered in monosyllables. There were no late evenings singing around the piano with Carly Simon and Beverly Sills, no going out every night till all hours, no golf. The guest house where the President spent most of his time alone was akin to the woodshed.

Like most marriages, the Clintons' is a mystery, only more so. How can she stand his repeated betrayals? Does she yearn for power that much? The Clintons nearly separated in the late '80s, after the then Governor had an affair. But several years ago, a friend noticed that the marriage was much improved. "Hillary liked living above the store. He was under a kind of White House arrest, almost always home for dinner with her and Chelsea."

It's this proximity that fuels the current Capitol parlor game: What did Hillary know, and when did she know it? Writer and television producer Linda Bloodworth-Thomason says it's ludicrous to think that Hillary knew her husband had been involved with Lewinsky in her very own house and defended him anyway. "Anyone who thinks Hillary knew what happened before the two of them had their conversation wasn't there that weekend. The second floor of the White House was a somber place." Until then, the President had told Hillary that he had befriended Monica and that she had taken his attentions the wrong way. In the face of so many awful rumors, including one that the Clintons murdered Vince Foster, the Monica accusation was just more gunk from the sewer.

The aftermath of the confession was brutal. Hillary spent several days in her room, talking only to her mother, who was staying at a cabin in Pennsylvania, going to church and then meeting, along with Chelsea, with Jesse Jackson. Hillary has also taken to vigorous workouts. "She's so enthused about her state-of-the-art exercise equipment," says a former aide, "that she talks about it as if she's hosting an infomercial." When you've lost control of so much around you, you can at least get thin.

By Friday, Hillary had resumed the "my husband" business in her introductions and adopted a modified Nancy Reagan gaze as she listened to the President at Friday's prayer breakfast, although a friend jokes that if the President apologizes one more time, Hillary will kill him. Aides are pushing her hard to go on TV to shore up the President. But if she reads the report and has any feelings left at all, the only honest reaction will be to let him twist slowly in the wind.

September 21, 1998

Our Nattering Nabobs

Hearings have ceased to be useful. They are now an extension of television

If the age of scandal is peaking with the possible impeachment of the President, it also shows signs of sputtering out. Scandals are now likely to claim the accuser as well as accused. Henry Hyde will be written about not for his three decades of public service but for failing to rise to his moment in history. Remember the invincible Senator Alfonse D'Amato who kept predicting the discovery of a smoking gun in his Whitewater inquiry? New Yorkers did, and he's outta here. Serial investigator Representative Dan Burton was re-elected, but not before he was nailed for an extramarital affair during which he fathered a child.

Televise a hearing today, and it ceases to be one. It becomes a chance to pillory your opponents, play-act morality and audition for your 15 minutes of cable fame. People not only choose sides, they also choose roles. Representative Lindsey Graham's early turn as Hamlet turned out to be a search for an unoccupied spot on the opinion spectrum that might land him on *Meet the Press*. He found a "legal technicality" that allowed him to vote against one article, earning him the valuable CONSERVATIVE BUCKS HIS PARTY headline in *The New York Times*. Members don't want to cede airtime to witnesses, so they toss hand grenades disguised as questions. Who has time for answers when members are determined to be home and rested for Christmas?

There were pure meta-television moments. Early on, Clinton spear carrier Representative Robert Wexler said he had a rebuttal to impeachment gonzo Representative Bob Barr—but was saving it for an appearance that evening on *Crossfire*. Blurting it out at the hearing, he said, "wouldn't be fair to the program." The minority counsel prepared an *America's Funniest Home Videos* clip consisting of Ken Starr saying over and over that he couldn't recall, remember or recollect.

The tone of the proceedings plays into the strategy of Majority Whip (and Speaker for Now) Tom DeLay. His aim is to define impeachment down, depicting it as nothing more than censure. What's the big deal, he said, if the more responsible Senate would never do anything so ridiculous as convict? The House is home alone! This doesn't really get rid of the guy, so let's impeach!

The only thing worse than DeLay succeeding is Clinton escaping the noose once again. Despite reiterating in the Rose Garden that he's really, really sorry, the hole in his soul where a conscience should be would lead him to interpret a failure to impeach as proof that he was unfairly persecuted. Remember the famous litany of the 1992 campaign where he was being unjustly penalized for "a woman he didn't sleep with and a draft he didn't dodge." And don't forget about the drug he didn't inhale. Next week he could be complaining about "a lie he didn't tell about that woman, Miss Lewinsky, whom he didn't have sex with," and, O.J.-like, vowing to spend the rest of his life searching for the real soiler of the blue dress. Look how he acted right after Democrats did better than expected in the November elections. Instead of seeing that reprieve as the remarkable kindness of strangers, he saw vindication. He was unyielding in his answers to Congress' 81 questions, and he missed his last opportunity on Friday to act like more than a criminal defendant protecting himself from the remote possibility of indictment. Even his allies were fed up with him.

So much in Washington now seems less than it was—the Lincoln bedroom, the independent counsel, the truth. And now, impeachment. Don't you have to believe that the President should be removed from office to vote for it? Hyde insisted Friday that was "exactly not true." But there's no asterisk beside your vote explaining that you just wanted to scare the guy to death, and you are sure that Wise Men in the Senate will put on the brakes. Impeachment is coming to look like just another weapon in the scandal wars. They're not really removing a President; they're just pretending to—on TV.

December 21, 1998

The Clinton in Us All

Those who hate him seem to bear more than a passing resemblance to him

My favorite commandments are the easy ones. I don't covet anyone's spouse; I don't want to kill anybody. A day of rest? No problem. But I'm in a constant struggle with the commandment Republicans have chosen as the one needing the full force of government sanction: Thou shalt not lie. I know honesty is the best policy, but I've been known to try the second-best policy when I have to justify the fact that the Christmas tree isn't up or that I haven't watched every minute of the historic debate *TIME* magazine pays me to cover.

But that's me. Republicans apparently never, ever tell a lie. Moreover, they don't count the other sins as sins unless compounded with a lie. Mother Marita Joseph didn't see it that way. Who would have thought the family-values party would be saying, in the interest of distinguishing Clinton's behavior from its own, "It's not the adultery, stupid; it's the lying." When it seemed last Thursday that the world couldn't spin any further out of control, here was Speaker-elect (although not for long) Bob Livingston announcing that because he wasn't "running for saint," his occasional affairs shouldn't be held against him. He called what he did "straying," said he had "sought spiritual counseling" and "received forgiveness" from his family. Sound familiar? Lest this remind anyone of you-know-who, he asserted, "These indiscretions were not with employees on my staff, and I have never been asked to testify under oath about them."

Not quite an instant classic in a league with "It depends on what your definition of is is," but it had promise as hairsplitting of a high order. For one thing, no one had charged that Monica Lewinsky was hit upon against her will, as Livingston implied. And the Livingston rationale ignored his good fortune in having Larry Flynt, not Ken Starr, with his subpoenas and a grand jury, pursuing him. Thus Livingston could cling to the claim that in a sting operation run by a desperate prosecutor, he was the kind of guy who would have come clean. But the ultimate parsing in Livingston's comments was contained in his description of who it is he had slept with. He hadn't strayed with an employee, he said, skipping over the issue of whether his indiscretions might have caused a different set of problems. That discussion might have required too much parsing, and so he quit.

In any case, this is the kind of legalism we hate Clinton for, and it misses what matters. The worst part of cheating on your spouse is what it does to your marriage, not what it does to your oath taking. To take such an important element of yourself and give it to someone else is to live the biggest lie imaginable, whether or not it's repeated in court. Lately there's a tendency to dismiss adultery lightly if no official lying is involved. Henry Hyde describes a long affair with a married mother of three as a youthful indiscretion (he was 41); Dan Burton says his affair with a state employee and the secret child it produced is O.K. because he pays child support; Helen Chenoweth excuses her affair with a married man who was a business associate because she wasn't married and it took place before she was elected. What message does that send the children?

And the rule for Republicans seems to be that lying under oath about things other than adultery is not actionable. Hyde explained this standard best when excusing lies in the Iran-contra affair. It did not make sense, he said, to "label every untruth and every deception an outrage . . . in the murkier grayness of the real world, choices must often be made." Ronald Reagan could remember very little about his efforts to arm the contras, but when confronted with facts indicating that he'd been told about it, he insisted his "heart and [his] best intentions" proved otherwise. After Ollie North bragged about his own lying and got off on a legal technicality, the G.O.P. wanted him to be the Senator from Virginia.

Clinton isn't above the law, but he should be above doing what he did. Livingston's resignation and the impeachment of Clinton teach children exactly the wrong lesson: that other people's deepest secrets can be plundered for political gain. Clinton is weak, not evil. He violated the commandments, not the Constitution, and should be solemnly censured for it. In this season of Christmas, perhaps some Wise Men will appear in the Senate.

January 4, 1999

Monica, We Hardly Knew You

We spent a year imposing identities on her. Now we meet her for real

When Monica left her videotaped deposition at the Mayflower Hotel last week, she was her usual Garboesque self: a shock of black hair, a fashion statement and silence. Unlike her pursuers on Capitol Hill, who brake for cameras, she plows determinedly through the crowd—never a comment, never a pose, never a clue. This encourages others to cast her in whatever role suits their favorite story line: starstruck ingenue, thong-flashing temptress, duplicitous home wrecker, *Vanity Fair* vamp or troubled product of a broken home in need of ministering, the kind a President can give.

The latest label was "young," affixed by Republicans coming out of the Senate Cineplex. It was the first successful talking point to emerge from the caucus: factually unassailable and subliminally suggestive of the heart of the President's darkness. How could he have taken such advantage, been such a sexual predator? As *Monica the Movie* began Saturday morning, there was less of a buzz in the chamber than a quiet nostalgia. Everyone knew it was time to embrace the seventh stage of scandal—acceptance that it would soon be over. It was one of the last times all 100 Senators would be together, one of the last times the gallery would be this crowded. For all the partisan posturing, the Senate hallways have been as sociable as a county fair.

Journalists say they hate the Monica story, but they actually love its narrative drive, its beyond-the-Beltway characters and the voracious appetite it has spawned in New York City editors for a Washington dateline. Its demise will mean the end of the newsroom as college dorm, with ordered-in food, endless talk of sex, and all-nighters. Next week we will be back to Medicare reform. No one will read us; no one will write. Brian Williams won't call.

Monica flickers onto the screen, and she's young, all right, with the lingering baby fat and the uhs and you-knows of a teenager. But what the Senators mean by "young," she isn't. She's older than many women my age. She comes across as composed, self-possessed and unbroken. I guess that if Bill Clinton had it to do over again, knowing what he knows now, he wouldn't (although he has two years left, so I'd put no money on it).

But Monica might. You don't have sex, or a reasonable facsimile of it, with a man who has his own standing army in order to relieve existential loneliness or find a soul mate. You do it for the record books, the thrill of it all: Sex in the study next to the Oval Office while the most powerful man on earth discussed military action with a member of Congress might have been what she had in mind when she packed those "presidential kneepads."

Onscreen, Monica is as savvy and funny as the lawyers questioning her. When House manager Ed Bryant tells her she is going to have to talk "or else we can go home," Monica replies, "Sounds good to me." When Bryant says "I want to refer you to the first so-called salacious occasion . . ." Monica: "Can you call it something else? . . . I mean, this is—this is my relationship."

Lights out, Ed. *Hasta la vista*, Bob Barr and Bill McCollum and the rest of you. For your final, willful act, you have inadvertently begun the rehabilitation of Monica Lewinsky, giving her the opportunity to reject bitterness for wistfulness, she of the "mixed feelings" who gently tweaks you as her steady gaze holds back more than she gives. She doesn't have the usual mementos—the wine bottle to put the candle in, the rose pressed in the diary—just some trinkets stashed under a bed, a satchel of subpoenas and a book deal. It didn't work out the way she'd hoped, but somehow she comes across as someone who got what she wanted anyway.

February 15, 1999

Sighs and Whimpers

Bill Clinton has always thrived amid enmity. So what will he be like without a crisis?

Over his long, tumultuous career, Bill Clinton has shown himself to be a man who can live without friends but not without enemies. He thrives in a storm, not in sunshine. Before Ken Starr, Clinton stood isolated from Democrats, having triangulated and compromised himself out of their good graces. That was fine when Starr was just investigating a moldy land deal. But when he turned his high horse onto the low road of presidential sex, Clinton knew things were different. For the first time, he needed congressional Democrats more than they needed him. And Democrats, fearing the right wing might really be gaining ground, answered his call. It was the beginning of a beautiful friendship that peaked last Friday, when all 45 Senate Democrats stood by their man.

But what will happen now that the danger has passed? Will Clinton drop his new friends, put Dick Gephardt and Tom Daschle on hold while he speed-dials Trent Lott to cut deals to build the legacy he craves? A former confidant remarked, "He's the kind of guy who's there for you when he needs you."

When Clinton spoke briefly in the Rose Garden after the vote, he looked, finally, grief-stricken and empty, like a mourner left alone with the empty Jell-O molds and casserole dishes after the funeral. The adrenaline was gone, the friends dispersed. His wife, welded to his side through most of the bitter fight against Starr, was pointedly absent in its Rose Garden aftermath. Her refusal to shut the door on a run for the Senate in New York could almost be taken as an announcement that she's open to a de facto separation, a psychological divorce.

Surely 1999 won't be a repeat of 1998—who could survive it?—but it could be a throwback to 1997, when Clinton's broken leg matched his busted-up spirit. Dreams of universal health care had been downsized to an extra day in the hospital for major surgery. The state attorneys general, not Clinton, were leading the war on tobacco. His heart wasn't in campaign-finance reform. He was reduced to bite-size governing and musing about his relevance.

Starr got his juices going then. In rising up to foil his foes, taking to the ramparts when most of us would take to our beds, Clinton has left behind him the political corpses of Al D'Amato, Bob Livingston and Newt Gingrich and the wounded reputations of Starr, Henry Hyde and their colleagues. Who will replace them? What enemy will rouse him now?

February 22, 1999

Hillary's Antiwar Movement
The First Lady settles in New York. Is that one way of making peace with Bill?

Do they have kids? That's what we always wanted to know when a moving van pulled up in my old neighborhood. Back then, the arrival of the Clintons would have prompted other questions. Is she married? Then where's her husband? And who are all those tall men in the dark glasses?

As always, nothing is simple with the Clintons, who have given almost as many answers about their living arrangements as they did about the billing records. Originally, the President wasn't going to show up in Chappaqua until next week. But with news cameras trained on the five-bedroom, four-bath residence, the President hastily bailed out of the Middle East peace talks to forestall video of Hillary spending her first night alone. The next morning, in their end-of-driveway press conference, the First Lady made like a young bride, ecstatic to be unpacking gewgaws from Arkansas circa 1983. This helped fend off thoughts about her as a carpetbagger in need of a new zip code, or worse, as the first First Lady to abdicate.

For the moment, the Clintons diverted attention from the fact that they are the first presidential couple to officially take up separate residences and that this most reckless of Presidents will now be Home Alone. By turning compliance with New York's residency requirements into a Lifetime movie, the Clintons have given new meaning to keeping up appearances. We're being asked to believe that "they" are staying married, that "they" are moving to New York, when by many people's definitions, "they" are doing neither. The headline in one New York paper was HERE TODAY, GONE TOMORROW as the President returned to Shepherdstown, W. Va., for the Israeli-Syrian talks. Among their possessions, you could see a couple of rugs, a kitchen table and a large bed. Don Imus wondered whether the plastic would ever come off the mattress. I wondered whether there would ever be enough living in the living room to fill up such a huge space.

But the media pictures on the front porch may at least remind people of Hillary's bright and winning side, apparent in her early listening tour but obscured by a series of errors: the bungling of the Puerto Rican clemency issue, a messy mortgage that had to be scrapped after it raised ethical questions, and her unfortunate embrace of an Arafat. Most recently, her campaign spokesman loudly denounced presumed rival Rudy Giuliani as "shameless" for starring in "I Love New York"–type ads, sponsored by the tourist bureau. Problem is, they aren't taxpayer financed, and it drew attention to her soft-money donations (more than $300,000 from corporate donors and wealthy private citizens) and her own blurring of the lines between official and campaign business. Most candidates have to take the shuttle between Washington and New York. She flies on Air Force jets.

Fortunately for Hillary, Giuliani's domestic life is no Norman Rockwell painting, either. As the Clintons were playing out their own soap opera, Rudy's wife, Donna Hanover, was announcing that she had signed on to play a recurring character on ABC's *One Life to Live,* an example of bad art imitating life. Hanover long ago dropped her married name and stopped attending political events. Having garnered all the credit there is to get from saving the city, the mayor has some controversies of his own to overcome: police-brutality cases, his crackdown on the homeless, his feud with the just departed school chancellor. Hillary can turn the race around if she "makes the race about Rudy and not about her." In other words, pray for snow and another tasteless museum exhibit.

The photo ops of the First Couple on Old House Lane may serve to bring down the curtain on the past two years in the White House. Once again, Hillary is nodding her head at everything the President says. Monica has found a job hawking a diet program. Linda Tripp is a "new man," as David Letterman observed, after her massive plastic surgery. Ken Starr is back at his law firm. Clinton is busily working on his legacy.

The amazing thing is not that we don't know whether the Clintons are a couple but that they themselves don't seem to. The President hemmed and hawed his way through a question about how they would manage to find time together. What even the adults in my old neighborhood wouldn't have been able to fathom is how the new woman down the block has passed through life's most traumatic events—marital meltdown, the death of her father and best friend, Whitewater and more than a year at the center of a crisis that laid bare her intimate life—and craves no down time to catch her breath. Picking through the charred embers of the conflagration of the past two years requires more attention than your average candidate can spare. But that may be just the way she wants it.

January 17, 2000

Who's That First Lady?

Bill's sins made Hillary human. Without him, she's just another boring pol

Taking the platform in Los Angeles last week, Hillary Clinton showed she has mastered the ballet of politics. She extended her arms like Evita to take in the cheers of the crowd, sweeping back and forth across the stage, the mistress of all she surveyed, breaking stride only for the hackneyed wave and point—with astonished delight, as if she'd just spotted a bunkmate from sleep-away camp. But once the supportive circle of six women Senators left the podium and the applause subsided, Hillary simply couldn't make music. To her the Staples Center was the world's largest day-care center, and she the patient teacher, mouthing bromides in the singsongy style that Al Gore made famous. Along about the third reference to helping children, the audience began to drift. By the time she was saying thank you (for what she didn't say), many had lost the will to live. If the film introducing the President hadn't been mesmerizing, the walk dramatic and Elvis determined to leave the building quaking, the chill she cast might not have lifted. Democrats I talked to in the hall just don't know who Hillary is on her own. Yes, she's smart and would have made something of herself had she not married Bill Clinton. But without his sins, we wouldn't know she's human. Had she not become the Wronged Wife before deciding to run, does anyone think Hillary's Senate candidacy would be the least bit plausible? She hated the sympathy, but without it she would never have recovered enough from grabbing health-care reform for herself and then bungling it.

The first First Lady to totally give up her White House duties, establish a separate residence (even a separate skybox), Hillary, without the President, is all work but no warmth. Can't we just award her the Senate seat? She has followed the owner's manual on how to be a candidate. She kisses babies, wears funny hats, eats blintzes, visits diners (and doesn't forget to tip) and has been to so many senior citizens' homes it's a wonder her hair isn't blue. She's not exaggerating when she boasts of visiting all 62 counties. She probably knows the precinct captains in Poughkeepsie.

But she still can't catch a break with suburban women. It isn't only her hunger for the job; she just doesn't come across as genuine. It is hard for people to tell what's true when you can't talk about the things most important to you and have to put a smiley face on one of the toughest political marriages in history. When she says she felt like a newlywed unpacking boxes in Chappaqua, it rings hollow. Does she really relish the prospect of rattling around in the huge empty house on her own? When she says, "It takes a village," doesn't she really mean, "It takes mandatory universal health care, if only you people had listened"? When she shook so many hands in the Puerto Rican Day parade that veins were bulging in her wrist, all the while earnestly asking, "How are you?," it sounded tinny, like a hotel operator inquiring, "How can I direct your call?"

Many Democrats in the hall have given up trying to figure out what's real and what's Memorex. Several weeks ago, Hillary told Elizabeth Bumiller of *The New York Times* that she had, after all, been quite active behind the scenes of the administration. I tend to believe that's true, but the truth is closed off to Hillary after six years of denying that she ever set foot in the West Wing, preferring to concern herself with preserving historic sites, fussing over state dinners and writing a book on entertaining. You can have only so many guises.

The President's such a campaign junkie that he pushed a speechwriter out of her chair to tap out Hillary's official announcement speech on February 6 in Purchase, N. Y., then gazed rapturously as he listened to his handiwork. Too bad he was too busy with his own speech at the convention last week to improve hers.

How many people, after being broken in half in front of the whole country, would choose to run for office rather than seek a calm visiting professorship somewhere? If she doesn't ask the people in the hall to believe her, but asks them to believe she can accomplish what they believe in, she may yet pull it out. She's such a survivor, CBS should have cast her on the show.

August 28, 2000

Capitol Hill

If time doesn't heal all wounds, a Senate seat just might. After a dogged campaign, the First Lady gets a chance to work on a legacy all her own

While some women get a diamond necklace or a trip to Paris from an errant spouse, Hillary Clinton got herself a U.S. Senate seat. And unlike Al Gore, she soaked up the President's help. Now with the Middle East peace in tatters, impeachment in the first paragraph of his obituary and Al Gore's status uncertain, Senator Clinton is a legacy the President can cling to.

But not too closely. After keeping quiet at Gore's insistence for six months, the President may have to zip it for six more years. Senator-elect Clinton personally choreographed her victory celebration. She stood between her new colleague, senior New York Senator Charles Schumer, and Chelsea, with the President banished to the side. There would be no Tipper-Al embrace for them. He wiped away a tear. She shed none. His staff explained, "It was her night." There will be no co-senatorship.

Although New York has a 2 million–voter Democratic advantage, there were obvious drawbacks at the beginning. Surely a sitting First Lady couldn't abandon the White House for a place in the suburbs of Westchester County to run for office in a state she had only visited. New York is celebrity friendly, but her fame ran more to Evita than Mother Teresa in a co-presidency of more failures than triumphs. Before impeachment, Hillary was one of the more unpopular First Ladies. She bungled the administration's biggest domestic project—health care—after wresting it from Gore's portfolio. Her fingerprints were everywhere, especially on the scandals (from Whitewater to Travelgate). In every crisis, her reflexive response was to blame others, rail against enemies and stonewall, unless called before a grand jury, at which point she would be overcome by short- and long-term memory loss. It wasn't until the President found himself under siege that her popularity took off. By the end of impeachment, she realized that, Sally Field–like, people really liked her, so she decided to run.

Clinton made mistakes early on as a campaigner, many of which came from trying to pretend that her birthplace of Chicago was an outer borough of New York City. It bordered on the sacrilegious to don a Yankees cap when she had been a well-known Chicago Cubs fan. It remained such a toxic moment that she couldn't risk taking the D train to the Subway Series to join in the purest of Big Apple moments. Rather than the usual grip and grin, she embarked on a listening tour, looking at times like Margaret Mead visiting the Samoans. A Big Apple neophyte, she bungled interest-group politics with a notorious flip-flop on clemency for unrepentant Puerto Rican terrorists.

Fortunately, while Clinton was making her worst mistakes, she was running against a distracted Mayor Rudy Giuliani, whose negatives were as high as hers and who played out his marital crisis on the 6 o'clock news. When Giuliani finally dropped out to fight prostate cancer, the Rottweiler was replaced by a puppy dog named Rick Lazio from Long Island, a four-term Congressman with a picture-perfect family who had nursed his father through a stroke. He reminded some, physically at least, of a young Dan Quayle with brains. He was so frisky at a Memorial Day parade, trying to shake as many hands as possible, that he literally fell on his face. He had to introduce himself to voters with a fat lip.

Lazio pitched most of his effort at emphasizing what he wasn't: a carpetbagger or associated with that infidel in the White House. While he made those two points, Hillary was dandling hundreds of babies upstate, where Lazio was as much of a carpetbagger as she was. Clinton told a friend, as she was well on her way to racking up visits to all 62 counties, that upstate New York was a lot like Arkansas. And indeed, she seemed at home there, mastering the arcana of dairy-price supports and economic revitalization. Clinton commiserated with those left behind by the current boom. She could still leech the life out of a large audience with her platitudinous speeches; but at diners, schools and community centers she was able to connect one on one. Among nurses, teachers and social workers, she was a goddess who understood what they were up against. Rather than faulting her for muffing health-care reform, they rewarded her for trying.

The carpetbagging charge faded because Clinton was there so much. She even gave up time in the glittery New York outpost of Martha's Vineyard to vacation amid the blackflies of Skaneateles. She was the first up and last to bed, handshaking her way through county fairs and college campuses, just plain outworking her opponent. And as much as yuppie women may have been skeptical of Hillary's motives, upstate women of a certain age greeted her like Oprah, an avatar of spiritual renewal touching down in Poughkeep-sie. They turned out for her, stayed afterward, lined up for autographs. Her first victory lap began upstate in Albany, Rochester and Syracuse.

Clinton's victory depended on some intangibles. Time heals wounds—perhaps not Hillary's inner ones, but those nursed by some voters against her for the mess she was part of in Washington. Other voters may have believed she shouldn't be made to suffer—or that she suffered enough—for her husband's sins. New Yorkers want someone bigger than life, and Little Ricky was no match for a vanity candidate like Hillary.

Clinton may finally have what she wished for, however lonely it may look with a husband building his library in Little Rock, a daughter in California, and a frequently empty house in Chappaqua. New York has provided the stage for the diva to triumph over the evil forces arrayed against her. Instead of expiring in Act III, she has hit high C.

But Washington calls for deference to one's esteemed colleagues, even from its prima donnas, if you're to deliver the bacon to the folks back home. When Hillary offered that she hoped to form "bipartisan coalitions," Republican Majority Leader Trent Lott snapped, "I'll tell you one thing: When this Hillary gets to the Senate—if she does, maybe lightning will strike and she won't—she will be one of 100, and we won't let her forget it." She couldn't ask for more than to have Lott behaving badly. If it weren't for men, including her husband, making a martyr of her, would we be calling her Senator?

November 20, 2000

Living Well Is Her Best Revenge

Hillary's new Washington digs are as grand as her ambition

Elvis is not leaving the building. Neither is Mrs. Elvis. Bob Dole was on to something when he once joked that it would take a SWAT team to get the Clintons out of the White House. After secretly checking out houses as storied as the Auchincloss mansion in Georgetown, the couple agreed last Friday to buy a six-bedroom, seven-bath, $2.8 million colonial on a third of an acre in an exclusive neighborhood. Secluded and quietly elegant, it has a spectacular garden in back, with a pool tucked in amid hundred-year-old trees. Nearby is the Naval Observatory, the British embassy and Vernon Jordan. The Clintons are so close to the vice-presidential mansion they will be able to see Allied Van Lines pull up and cart the Gore possessions off to a modest residence in suburban Virginia, and watch the Cheneys move in.

The Constitution says you can't have a third term, but it doesn't say you can't have a second act, and the Clintons have decided to break with tradition and have an ex-co-presidency a zip code away from the Rose Garden. Hillary wanted an instant Washington salon, as grand as her health-care plan, with as many rooms as her ambition. There will be no cramped weekday existence for her, like the members who live large in their home states but modestly in D.C. Senator John McCain stays in a thin-walled Crystal City high-rise, with jets from National Airport shrieking overhead. The senior Senator from New York, Charles Schumer, bunked for years with four guys. Others sleep in their offices and shower in the gym, as House Majority Leader Dick Armey used to do.

A President dies twice, the first time when taking leave of the White House, with its massive power and all its trappings—the marble splendor, the world-class chefs, the Navy stewards bringing your Diet Coke on a silver tray. A temperature-perfect limo waits at the door. You have intersection control. Barbra Streisand croons just for you.

Although the Clintons can't take the butlers with them, they may take things that caused them so much trouble. Each Clinton has a character flaw that gets in the other's way. His is a sloppy self-indulgence. Hers is a haughty grandiosity—the tendency to think that because she is devoted to doing good, she is entitled to do well. Biographer David Maraniss reports how she complained about not having a pool at the Governor's house in Little Rock. There wasn't a lot of surprise in Arkansas over the disclosure of her shady cattle-futures investment or their Whitewater deal.

Hillary's needs are expensive and immediate, which is why she is financing the beginning of her new life with a controversial $8 million book deal. Bill Clinton will soon bring in even more. His dream isn't DreamWorks, as rumored, but to save the Third World—to be Jimmy Carter, except with more money and without the carpenter's apron. A Washington lawyer will broker a book deal, and he may also talk to agents in Manhattan eager to package this most mediagenic figure into a brand: big-ticket speeches taped to become one-hour specials; missions to Africa turned into PBS series.

Meanwhile, as the President stays up late into the night urging a peace settlement on Arafat, Hillary's concerns are more domestic. Friends have long been relied on to contribute to the Clintons' campaigns, their legal-defense funds and their library. *The New York Times* got wind of friends' wanting "to treat her like a bride" to help launch her First Lady afterlife. Earlier, cooler heads had prevailed to nix an actual shower. Now, friends say, there's something of a silent one taking place, whereby those who want to help out can learn what china (Spode) and soup ladle (Fabergé) to buy, preferably before the Senate gift ban kicks in January 3.

For the Clintons, just because something isn't done doesn't mean it can't be. For them there will be no retreat to a Santa Barbara ranch, no exile to Saddle River, N.J.—in fact, no leaving. Staying will make it all the easier when, and if, in the next grandiose leap, Hillary leads the Clinton restoration to follow the Bush one. She'll be just a zip code away.

January 8, 2001

A Shower of Gifts for Hillary and Bill

Why did the Clintons troll for freebies they can surely afford?

Last month, when newspapers reported that Hillary Rodham Clinton had registered for gifts like a bride at a department store, many of her friends insisted Hillary simply wouldn't do something that tacky. Now that the President and First Lady have filed their annual financial-disclosure report, we have proof they would. Amid the DVD player and chandelier were $22,000 in china and $18,000 in silverware. Only one gift looks like a quid pro quo: furniture valued at $7,375 from Denise Rich, the ex-wife of Marc Rich, the fugitive tycoon pardoned last week.

The rest just smells bad. Most of us look at the platter from Aunt Katie with a wave of affection. Can you really get a warm glow from a place setting sent by a contributor you barely know who's angling for your attention? I'd stack my dishes on the floor before I'd accept a china cabinet from Walter Kaye, the insurance mogul who delivered intern Monica Lewinsky to the West Wing. What's most revealing here is not the gifts themselves—although it is hard to picture one adult giving another a sofa—but how horrified people were at the very suggestion that Hillary would lean on supporters to furnish her house. The Clintons have long dismissed the criticism of those in the vast right-wing conspiracy whom they don't respect. But how do you dismiss the views of those you do respect—who insist you would never sink so low, until they are silenced by proof you did?

Even as Hillary was registering for the china and silver, she understood that the day would come when she would have to admit to the world what she had done. In the absence of a law (the Senate gift ban didn't take effect for Hillary until January 3) or an active conscience, you might think shame would rein in the Clintons. How many people would park in a handicapped space if they knew the next morning's paper would carry a picture of it?

Most Presidents are felled by failures of their office—Carter by the hostages, Nixon by Watergate, Johnson by Vietnam—but the Clintons have been brought down almost entirely by their sexual and financial escapades, the former his, the latter hers. Hillary's lapses have been explained away by her husband's low pay in Arkansas. Yet by most standards, the Clintons lived large in Little Rock; she was a partner in one of the city's leading law firms, they called the Governor's mansion home and had only one child to put through college. Still, she got the family enmeshed in a shabby get-rich-quick land deal and cattle futures, which led to the Whitewater investigation, which led to Ken Starr, which led to impeachment. The most interest Governor Clinton ever showed in Whitewater was when he famously dripped sweat on James McDougal's office chair after a jog, stopping by for a look at the books at Hillary's behest. Ever angling, the Clintons actually took a tax deduction for donating used underwear (boxers or briefs not specified) to charity.

Hillary doesn't realize that finally she is rich, with her $8 million book advance and married to a man with massive earning potential. Just in salary and pension, the Clintons bring in about $300,000. So why did they debase themselves for gifts as if they were struggling newlyweds starting out? Some on the givers' list told NBC they weren't "wanting to give her special farewell presents," as a Clinton spokesman claimed. They said they had been contacted by political supporter Rita Pynoos, who is married to a California developer, to send the gift registry a $5,000 check. Hillary trolling for soup ladles she could easily afford is as irrational as the Fifth Avenue matron who filches a vial of perfume from the counter at Bergdorf's. Only Freud could sort it out.

Maybe the specter of giving up "Hail to the Chief" and motorcades puts you back in the nursery, frantic that your mother isn't going to warm your milk. But how can you ever have a home when it's partly filled with loot from strangers? There may be no connection between the disgraceful pardon Clinton gave Marc Rich and the coffee table Denise Rich gave the Clintons. But I'd never be comfortable putting my feet up on it.

February 5, 2001

Showtime at the Apollo
Still the Crowd Pleaser in Chief, Clinton could teach Bush a few bars

How many times can the comeback kid come back? As many times as he needs to. Last week Bill Clinton emerged from his self-imposed post-pardon-scandal exile to open his new office on 125th Street in Harlem, with its $350,000 annual rent (his first choice, Carnegie Towers in midtown, would have cost taxpayers $800,000). It was full-frontal Clinton—winking, mugging at the most mundane remarks, pointing excitedly into the crowd as if he had just spotted a long-lost friend or a donor. Except for Senator Chuck Schumer, stage center, trying to boogie with the homeboys, it was picture perfect, a routine ribbon cutting turned into exuberant street carnival. Cable dropped its coverage of the current President giving a speech in favor of coverage of an ex-President opening an office. *The New York Times*'s headline the next day: A HERO'S WELCOME.

These moments of redemption are the narcotic Clinton craves, the high that makes the Gennifer Flowers, Whitewater, Monica and Marc Rich valleys a necessary part of life. Where better to feel the love than the city of second acts, a place so crowded and alive that his bottomless need for human contact can be satisfied every time he walks down the street? Jackie Onassis went there because the locals are blasé about celebrity; Clinton went for the ones who aren't blasé, who pay the high rents for the frisson of seeing Gwyneth Paltrow sipping a latte at the corner café. Sure, it's hard to give up traffic control and Air Force One. But he makes himself a movable feast, providing sidewalk entertainment to a surprised group of rock fans waiting for the Dave Matthews Band in front of the RIHGA Royal hotel. A frequent sight on the New York–to–Washington shuttle, where the prevailing ethic is no eye contact, Clinton works the aisles until forced to take his seat.

Some of the criticism of Clinton at the time of his departure—the White House vandalism, the stripping of Air Force One—turned out to be grossly exaggerated by President Bush's aides. But enough of the other stuff was serious—the White House gifts shipped to Chappaqua, the parade of pardons—that his cooling-off period had to be longer than planned. So he communed with Buddy for six months, venturing out in the SUV for his morning coffee, playing a lot of golf. Hillary had some issues of her own to deal with—her pardon-mongering brothers, the gift registry, pocketing a book advance before Senate rules forbidding it kicked in. She went to ground, found her inner workhorse and rose 12 points in the polls. She had her first headline victory last week, Bush's pick for Consumer Product Safety Commission chair. Speculation that the Clintons would divorce soon after leaving the White House now vies with speculation that Bill might someday be the first First Gentleman.

Clinton envisions an ex-presidency like Jimmy Carter's, minus the tool belt. This week he will produce the first in a series of benefit concerts for AIDS in Africa with Kenny (Babyface) Edmonds, enough of a hip-hopper for teens to notice but not so much to remind people of Clinton's bad-boy genes. He is also helping earthquake victims in India (one trip and $10 million raised so far) and linking up small businesses in Harlem with the big ones in midtown.

Of course he's cashing in like no other President has done before. This week he takes his pick of a dozen book deals, all offering advances, according to a publishing source, "beyond the papal range"—which means he beats his wife's $8 million. Domestic speech offers are matching international ones, $100,000 to start.

Bush has benefited over the past six months from not being Clinton; a grateful nation got some rest. But Clinton's re-emergence is a reminder that it's nice to see a President mixing it up outside the Rose Garden. Clinton's body language says, I wish I had two more hours to spend with you; Bush's says, I can't wait to get home. Bush brags about the searing, dry heat at his remote Texas ranch, where he will spend most of August hanging with his heifers. Real men don't go to Martha's Vineyard, where the softie Clinton will once again mooch a house off friends to swing among the swells. There must be some middle ground between these two. Bush is promising to make a few sorties out among the people during August to whip up enthusiasm for his presidency. He should review a tape of Clinton in Harlem to see how it's done.

August 13, 2001

OH SAY, CAN YOU RUN FOR PRESIDENT?

*I*F ANYONE CAN GROW UP to be president, it follows that anyone can run—and run again. The more the merrier and repeat offenders aren't penalized. Candidates, even ones in it for the thrill of it, get famous and fame in America almost always comes with rewards: a bigger TV contract, more clout for your magazine, a book written about you, your very own think tank.

But should the fact that anyone can *grow* up to be president mean that anyone can *run* for president? I give you Donald Trump, Alan Keyes, Pat Robertson, and Morey Taylor (1996) as examples that the answer should be no. You say Morey who? He was the tire magnate from Ohio who was so remarkably ill suited to running that *The New Republic*'s top political correspondent, Michael Lewis, wrote a book about him as a prime example of the genre. Does it really help an already cynical electorate, voting in smaller and smaller numbers, to be bombarded with an assortment of characters in search of temporary fame and matching federal funds? There can be too much of a good thing, too many candidates with shaky credentials and mixed motives, chasing a distracted electorate. Picture the debates in 1996. If given a pop quiz, could you name the folks occupying the stage? I couldn't. I forgot Gary Bauer, and I was covering it!

I'm tempted to say the more the merrier. Just the way Seinfeld needed Kramer, one candidate needs another to bounce off of. By another, I mean one, or two, maybe three. Until the excess of candidates was cleared out in 2000, George W. Bush was so shrouded by others that Senator John McCain, the viable alternative, could barely take a shot at him. Seven dwarves entered the Democratic primary in 1988, eight Republicans showed up to compete for the prize in 2000. A few of the candidates were engaged in brand extension (the Pats, Buchanan and Robertson, were primarily TV personalities who became bigger TV personalities after running). Some were businessmen with time on their hands (Donald Trump, Steve Forbes), others were moralists (Alan Keyes and Gary Bauer), and one wasn't getting enough attention in the Senate (Orrin Hatch). The debates were like an episode of *Survivor,* where the audience is waiting to see who will be voted off the stage.

A couple of factors have produced a glut of amateurs: the decline of the parties, which lets just about anyone *in,* and the rise of cable television, which lets just about anyone *on.* Moreover, those already in power have made themselves vulnerable to amateurs by buying in to the outsider game. America is in love with the underdog, and who captures the myth better than the amateur politician struggling to prevail in a field of slick pros.

Republicans play that game better than Democrats, arguing that big government is the problem, even as they fight to get control of it. Reagan perfected the cry of getting government off our backs, and Newt Gingrich plumbed its depths with his Contract for America (or Contract *on* America, as critics called it), a primer on how to hijack Washington, disperse its power to the states, or make it vanish altogether.

It's a short-term strategy, however. An amateur who wins once turns into the very thing he despised. Political virginity is hard to reclaim, even with a million-dollar media consultant. It's especially entertaining to see an outsider who campaigned entirely on term limits (Representative George Nethercutt defeating Potomac cave dweller former House Speaker Tom Foley) run for reelection saying there should be this one teeny, tiny exception for him because somehow he'd escaped becoming the Capitol denizen he loathed such a short time ago.

How do these guys explain not going home, opting instead to stay until they're navigating the hall of power with the help of a walker? Nethercutt said he'd made a "mistake," complimenting himself on having the "integrity to acknowledge it." Some are just being generous and kind; as Representative Tim Johnson of Illinois said, "My constituents were the ones who would suffer." Others know what God wants. When Representative Tom Tancredo of Colorado announced he would be reneging on his pledge to serve two terms, he said, "God has a plan for everybody and I am doing my best to do what I think he wants." Who would have known that God would have a position on term limits? Or Tom Tancredo?

Others reclaim political virginity through résumé deflation. Remember Lamar! (his punctuation) Alexander? Currently a Senator from Tennessee, Alexander was considered a front-runner in 1996 for the Republican presidential nomination because of his wide experience in government. But you'd think he'd had a wicked past for all he did to hide it. He campaigned like a country boy, making a plaid shirt and boots his signature costume, playing country music in a general effort to erase his previous Washington address. The former Secretary of Education sank like a stone.

The outsider game is even sillier when played by two insiders. In 1988, Bush the First, with a government résumé a mile long, suffered from the perception he was an elite prepster (and a wimpy lapdog) who didn't care about domestic problems. He desperately needed to become a man of the people, a subset of the outsider, so he discovered a passion for country music and pork rinds. This helped defeat a nerdy liberal from Massachusetts, who argued against recitation of the Pledge of Allegiance and shared an area code with Harvard.

But it didn't work in 1992. Bush is a blue-blood WASP whose idea of solving a domestic problem, as Senator Thomas Harkin said in 1991, "is to fire the maid and yell at the butler." When Bush found himself challenged in 1992 by a lowborn customer like Bill Clinton, Bush with his striped grosgrain band watch on one arm and reaching for pork rinds with the other, just didn't fly. If you make pork rinds the symbol of something good, the guy who comes along and gobbles them for breakfast will eat your lunch.

The real estate equivalent of pork rinds is the ranch, which Reagan used to such great effect in 1980, not only to make the frontiersman's argument that government should get off our backs, but to scrub Hollywood from his résumé. Bush the Second used Prairie Chapel, his ranch, metaphorically before there was one. It was just under construction as he presented himself as the lone cowboy come to save the town from fast-talking gunslingers (or from a slow-talking one, like Gore). He spent nearly three months of his first two years in office among the dudes and dust of the prairie to make sure the Guccis and gotcha of Washington didn't cling to him. He talked about reconnecting with real people as if he'd been with aliens on Mars, rather than returning to 1600 Pennsylvania, where he'd been at home as the son of a president. He repeated "return to the heartland" so many times during those visits to Crawford that he sounded like a pitchman for Corn Flakes.

It's easy to see why the insider wants to make something else of himself. His story is a hard sell. The cowboy on the white horse makes a solid, experienced public servant like former majority leader Bob Dole look like Senator Bob Dull (although he's the best ex-senator since Mike Mansfield). As accomplished as he was, Dole had trouble getting any traction against Clinton in 1996. Yes, Clinton had some things going for him: a great economy, an hiatus on the Paula Jones scandal, and Monica had yet to appear; he'd passed a balanced budget, and reformed welfare. But the president also had some vulnerabilities: It looked as if he could be rolled by the Congress and a warlord in Mogadishu, scandal was nipping at the heels of his cabinet (the deputy attorney general and Hillary's law partner and close friend Web Hubbell would go to prison), and firebrand Newt Gingrich was making him look "irrelevant." He was no longer the progressive, problem-solving governor of Arkansas: what was wrong with Washington now had his name on it.

But when Dole talked about what he'd accomplished in Congress, it sounded like a lecture on how a bill becomes a law. It's near impossible to bring a crowd to its feet describing how Republicans nailed subsidies for ethanol. And an insider doesn't just come with a parliamentary personality, he comes with a voting record he has to defend. Dole had thirty years of votes to explain, not to mention comments like "Democrat wars." No one ever called Ross Perot to account for the rosy picture drawn in EDS's annual report.

In 2000, Bush took a McCain vote and twisted it so that instead of killing a vote against a bill full of pork barrel projects, it looked like a vote against breast cancer research. McCain is a strong advocate for breast cancer research. His mother has the disease, so it was a particularly noxious charge to use against McCain, who was only casting a vote against government waste. But the accusation went up in late ads that left no time for McCain to respond. That's what he gets for being in Washington.

Unlike the amateur candidate who likes nothing more than talking about himself (and may have gotten in the race for the express purpose of doing so), Dole was in for reasons other than vanity. When Dole said anything about his heroism in World War II, he spoke in the third person, divesting it of its power. When pushed by his staff to be more direct, Dole said, "Bob Dole was wounded in the war like so many other veterans here tonight. Like Bob Dole, you all love your country. Vote for Bob Dole." Such humility, noble in a person, is death to a candidate.

If politicians have helped make the outsider king, the wealthy businessman has made himself king of the outsiders. With the financial wherewithal to skip the costly primaries that weed out weak sisters, the businessman arrives on the political scene like Mighty Mouse come to save the day. The businessman candidate, generally a Republican, presents himself as the silver bullet solution to whatever problems the body politic has as a result of the country being run by professional politicians. He's met a payroll, fired people, shown a profit, and satisfied his shareholders, or so he claims.

What's your average pol done? Raised taxes, rolled logs, accepted contributions from questionable characters, and chaired the Subcommittee on Capital Markets, Insurance, and Government-Sponsored Enterprises. Perot and his ilk plead innocent on all fronts. Invariably an adherent of Thomas Carlyle's famous dictum, "The history of the world is but the biography of great men," your average CEO has no trouble saying he's great— just ask him. He comes with his own PR department and transportation, often a Gulfstream. A platform? No problem. A campaign consultant can quickly build one, if not of sturdy two-by-fours, then of some medium-density fiberboard that will last the length of the campaign: a little Medicare reform here, a lot of "growing" the economy there, a ten-point program to save Social Security (or privatize it, choose one), and you're campaign-ready. While he's at it, a full-service consultant can sand off the rough edges, buff the family values and remove from *Nexus* magazine profiles that show undue partygoing or jet-setting. Good hair, a wide smile, and a few Tocqueville quotes casually rendered help, but are not essential.

When free media runs out, businessmen have pockets deep enough to flood the airwaves with paid ads. In their respective campaigns, Perot and

Forbes bid up and bought out ad time in primary states so that there was none at any price for the slowpokes, who'd had to wait until they'd raised the money. And since public administration is messy and corporate governance less so (since it's autocratic and largely hidden), the CEO is able to hammer home the point that he's the guy who can get things done, not like those lugs building consensus and operating by committee. The ivory tower CEO knows how to keep his board eating out of his hand and how to delegate the mundane details of his job to a vice president. He'll be prepared to efficiently deploy the one due him under the Constitution.

Although the parties don't want unaffiliated rich guys crashing the presidential races, they scour the country at the Senate and gubernatorial level looking for them. A bored gazillionaire won't put the arm on limited party funds or waste precious time dialing for dollars. The wealthy candidate places a one-minute call to his banker to arrange a wire transfer. There were so many of these critters running in the last cycle that the cliché "Experience money can't buy" popped up in political ads in *five* races—to little avail. The Senate is ever more the millionaires' club: Herbert Kohl, Peter Fitzgerald, Maria Cantwell, James Exon, and Jon Corzine, all wealthy businessmen with no public experience. A rich candidate occasionally fails, like California's Michael Huffington, who spent $27 million doing so. He did, however, create a career for his now ex-wife, Arianna, as a true compassionate conservative. Republicans scored a big win in 2002 when multimillionaire Mitt Romney won a hotly contested race for governor of Massachusetts.

While Perot proved loopier than that crazy aunt in the attic he kept talking about (where did he get the notion that men in black helicopters had been sent by Bush to disrupt his daughter's wedding?), he at least had some basis other than sheer ego for running, unlike more recent contenders. Perot ran on the idea that deficits as far as the eye can see are bad and that the giant sucking sound we might be hearing if NAFTA were passed would be jobs going to Mexico. Steve Forbes ran on the idea of a flat tax. Donald Trump ran on no ideas at all.

The Reverend Jesse Jackson may keep his outsider status forever. He's done so well while doing good that he is both businessman and candidate with a cause, although one who wants to run more than he wants to be president. Early on, he earned the reputation of being a solo act, alienating even his colleagues in the civil rights movement. He prefers ad hoc decision making to planning, and leaves subordinates behind to tie up, or frequently not tie up, loose ends. Some days his staff couldn't tell you where he would be an hour hence. Travel with Jackson and you might not see anything but foil-wrapped nuts for twelve hours while the reverend changed his schedule to accommodate a visit from former Superwoman Margot Kidder.

Jackson didn't really want to be vice president, either. When he met to talk about the number-two spot with Dukakis in 1988 (and leaving aside Dukakis's poor people skills), Jackson's aides cited the fear he would be blamed for any loss as his excuse for not taking the interview more seriously. Jackson preferred the consolation prize: his own plane and money for a "Get Out The Vote" effort.

Jackson frequently says he wouldn't have been considered an amateur candidate if he weren't black. But if being black held him back initially, it propelled him forward later—over bumps that would have derailed a white candidate. Government agencies charged that Jackson's PUSH could not properly account for more than $1 million in federal grants (Jackson struck a deal to repay $550,000). His Rainbow Coalition has been accused of shaking down corporations for money, although he says it's all legit. He has practiced diplomacy by wet kiss with some of the third world's most controversial characters. He's called New York City Hymietown, and associated with Louis Farrakhan, who's called Judaism a gutter religion. What other presidential candidate could have run with those negatives?

Running as an amateur is a gateway drug, setting off an adrenaline rush the political neophyte seeks to repeat. But the coverage the press gives the political ingenue is a onetime thing; you can never get the same high again. The second or third time (think Jackson, Perot, and Buchanan), you begin to look pathetic. Still, I doubt we've seen the last of Alan Keyes or Gary Bauer.

Amateurs beget more of the same. If he can do it, why can't I? The Reverend Al Sharpton's candidacy for president is inevitable. Running on the basis of what, and from where? On the occasions that he votes, he does so in New York, but what else does he do there? Until Sharpton apologizes for ruining D.A. Stephen Pagones's life by pushing false charges of Tawana Brawley's rape, he should be barred from public life. Arnold Schwarzenegger, aka the Kindergarten Cop, is also considering public office, like Reagan running first for California governor to set the stage to run later for president. Oddballs running is not a victimless crime. Several things kept the most admired political figure in America, Colin Powell, from running—his wife's worries, for instance—but surely the prospect of sharing the stage with someone like the Terminator is one of them.

For proselytizers, running for president is a boon for their causes. It's so much more fun to embark on a campaign with its promise of national exposure and the roar of the crowd than to send out yet another direct-mail solicitation or preach to the already converted in church basements. But is it good for America? Where's the smoke-filled room when you need one?

Celebrities run—or toy with running—because they want to be taken seriously, hope to break out of the Hollywood ghetto, are bored, or all three. Editors hunger for the offbeat political story. As Warren Beatty mulled a run, his every meeting and trip to Starbucks was tracked. He'd played a presidential candidate in the movie *Bulworth,* so why not be one? Phil Donahue, famous as the talk show host who once wore a skirt, got considerable coverage just for mulling a twirl around the dance floor. The fact that he once publicly *thought* about running for the Senate from Connecticut gave him more credibility when he *thought* about running for the presidency. Like Pat Buchanan's quadrennial candidacies, just the dalliance can boost your marketability. Buchanan and Donahue both have new talk show gigs.

There's no category that covers Minnesota governor Jesse Ventura, who was threatening to run for president soon after his improbable win in the governor's race. Ventura, the only governor to have an action figure modeled after himself, decided not to seek reelection; in a press conference so full of bitter recriminations that it rivaled Nixon's exit in 1966. Ventura sulked off, but not before saddling Minnesotans with huge deficits and a sour taste. He too used the gig to get a better gig in his chosen field of boa constrictor, rhinestone-studded world wrestling. He landed an XFL television contract and then his own talk show. He may yet come back to run for president—as a rich businessman.

Mercifully, we should be seeing a respite in the cult of the CEO: the heroes of the nineties have become this decade's bottom dwellers. The self-satisfied CEO gazing out from the cover of a glossy magazine has been replaced by the CEO with wrists cuffed, in full perp walk. Absent pinstripes and power tie (removed as a suicide risk), being led by the nose to be arraigned and fingerprinted, the businessman looks more like a drug dealer than a Master of the Universe.

In the silver lining department, the CEO implosion (even adulterous Jack Welch lost his glow when his estranged wife revealed he grabbed everything but his own nuclear device as part of a grotesquely inflated retirement package) means we won't have Ross Perot clones to kick around anymore. It's hard on reporters, but good for the country.

More Than a Crusade
This time Jackson is making new friends while keeping the old

Four years ago, a Jesse Jackson campaign stop would have been incomplete without a stretch Cadillac, driven by a funeral director or minister, filled with local VIPs riding from one event to the next. This year the Jackson campaign has an entourage of staff and Secret Service, plus a fleet of official vehicles to handle such chores. The local limousines are dinosaurs in the 1988 campaign, a nuisance the Secret Service would like to banish. But Jackson holds on to them, although they often ride empty except for one proud driver whose fingers no one in the Jackson campaign wants to pry from the steering wheel.

The riderless limos are not the only sign that the 1988 Jackson campaign is a far cry from the seat-of-the-pants, roller-coaster operation of 1984. The dilapidated Lockheed Electra turboprop (which later crashed) has been replaced by a DC-9, complete with computers. Schedules, just vague advisories in the last campaign, which ran on Jesse Jackson time (three hours behind all known time zones), are sometimes adhered to. Church choirs warming up the crowd are still crucial, but now, so are the hard-nosed strategists busily color-coding districts on wall-size maps. "Eighty-four was a crusade," says Ann Lewis, a longtime Democratic Party pro. "This is a real campaign."

But the most significant change in the Jackson campaign is the attempt to expand beyond its black base. In order to add working-class whites to his rainbow coalition, Jackson has renegotiated loans for farmers in Iowa and Missouri. He has fought for the right to unionize plants in New Hampshire and Maine. He stood with disgruntled workers in Dubuque and Marshalltown, Iowa. He joined environmental battles in New Hampshire. One of the few black men some whites in these states had ever seen up close turned out to be running for President.

The worry within his campaign is whether the white stripe in his rainbow can grow without shrinking the other colors there first. Having announced a standard for himself as a candidate capable of attracting broad support, Jackson will now be measured by his ability to do so. No wonder, then, that Jackson last week diverted his attention from getting out the vote in black districts and ventured into white districts in Kentucky and North Carolina that were mere flyovers in 1984.

To forge a black-and-white coalition in such places, Jackson aims his populist message at working people of both races. He wants to raise the minimum wage, institute comparable-worth wages for women, build affordable housing and to "stop drugs from coming in, stop jobs from going out."

His trip to Asheville, N.C., last week allowed Jackson to return to a town 60 or so miles from his birthplace and recall how he played segregated football games nearby during the 1950s. Jackson drove home the point by bringing along his white press secretary, Asheville native Liz Colton. Unlike 1984, Jackson repeats over and over that this is not a black struggle. The poorest Americans, he says, are white and female. "We can't just lift black boats," he said to a black audience at Winston-Salem State University last week. "We must lift all boats."

The modest success of this message, however, contains an irony, one that is discomforting to the Jackson campaign: It seems to appeal to affluent white liberals more than to the poor white workers. Some of Jackson's strategists are urging him to take advantage of the situation, but the purists warn against altering his message; a coalition involving students and liberals, they say, will turn out to be more ephemeral than one embracing poor and working-class whites.

Jackson's performance in the South next week, however impressive, will not thrust him into the nomination. Even the optimistic scenarios of his advisers do not give him much chance to continue his success when the election moves away from the South and the number of white candidates splitting the vote has been reduced. But it is increasingly likely that the Democratic nomination will end up involving some bartering, and Jackson now seems sure to arrive at the table with one of the largest piles of chips— as many as 700 delegates.

That in itself is destined to mark a fundamental change in the nature of black politics in America. During the 1970s, the civil rights struggle was transformed into a political movement that gained power in cities and towns across the country. Next Tuesday, Jackson has the potential to bring this power to bear at the presidential level.

March 7, 1988

Loose Buchanan

Pat Buchanan's announcement that he was running for President was exactly in character. He was at pains to say how much he likes George Bush.

He was communications director in the Reagan-Bush Administration and has dined with the current First Family in their private White House quarters. But Buchanan has his reasons for launching a full-frontal assault against the fellow Republican he likes so much. For Buchanan, Bush is insufficiently Buchanan-like—not nativist, rightist, homophobic, authoritarian or anti-Israel. Like many ultraconservatives, Buchanan is unfailingly kind and generous to people regardless of their background. But he can be just as cruel to the groups to which they belong. To him, gays are "sodomites," the poor are "freeloaders," and immigrants from anywhere but Western Europe are a threat to the American way of life. Buchanan's remarks about Jews in particular are so provocative that his fellow panelists on TV political talk shows—including Al Hunt of *The Wall Street Journal*, Morton Kondracke of *The New Republic* and *Washington Post* columnist Mark Shields—have felt the need to say publicly that their colleague is not an anti-Semite.

That issue came up during the debate over whether the U.S. should use force to expel Saddam Hussein from Kuwait. Buchanan charged that there were "only two groups that are beating the drums for war in the Middle East—the Israeli defense ministry and its amen corner in the U.S." *New York Times* columnist A. M. Rosenthal accused Buchanan of anti-Semitism and "blood libel" (a reference to the canard leveled by bigots since the Middle Ages that Jews kill Christian children and use their blood to make Passover matzo). Rosenthal's attack was so outrageous that Buchanan survived the storm.

Now the man Buchanan reveres as his "spiritual guide" has taken Buchanan to the woodshed. In a 38,000-word essay in the *National Review*, William F. Buckley Jr., the godfather of conservatism, writes, "I find it impossible to defend Pat Buchanan against the charge that what he did and said during the period under examination amounted to anti-Semitism, whatever it was that drove him to say and do it; most probably an iconoclastic temperament."

That iconoclastic temperament has also driven Buchanan to give sympathetic attention to crackpot Holocaust revisionists. He made intemperate comments during his crusade to prove the innocence of John Demjanjuk, a retired Cleveland autoworker convicted by an Israeli court of having helped murder hundreds of thousands of Jews as a Nazi death-camp guard known as Ivan the Terrible. Buchanan has also claimed that diesel engines do not emit enough carbon monoxide to kill anybody, much less 850,000 people at Treblinka; that the U.S. should not have apologized to France for protecting Nazi war criminal Klaus Barbie; and that Arthur Rudolph, the ex-Nazi rocket scientist forced to leave the U.S. after the Justice Department accused him of brutalizing slave laborers at a Nazi rocket factory, was "railroaded."

Those views go beyond being merely pugnacious. Four years ago, Buchanan came close to running for the presidency with the slogan "Let the bloodbath begin." It is still his motto.

December 23, 1991

The Thorn in Bush's Right Side

A conservative who speaks his mind, Pat Buchanan stands about zero chance of winning, but he is certainly giving the White House fits

Politicians are candid at their peril; a gaffe occurs when one of them inadvertently says what he actually thinks. By that standard, presidential candidate Patrick J. Buchanan is a veritable gaffemeister, insisting that Watergate was "a bunch of Mickey Mouse misdemeanors," Congress is "Israeli-occupied territory," and Ollie North is "a hero." Buchanan's pasty face crinkles into a smile when he recalls penning phrases like "pusillanimous pussyfooters."

Buchanan, 53, has not trimmed his verbal sails since beginning his effort to oust the traitorous George Bush, whose cave-in on taxes was "the Yalta of the Republican Party." He uses Bushspeak à la *Saturday Night Live*'s Dana Carvey to lambaste the President for breaking his tax pledge and begs Bush to debate him "at the country club of his choice."

His regular stump speech extolling isolationism, protectionism and fiscal stinginess is seasoned with attacks on "boodling" Congressmen, upholstered think tanks cooking up cockeyed new programs, and softheaded Trilateralists who would bail out Chinese communist Deng Xiaoping, the "85-year-old chain-smoking communist dwarf," but let Macy's go into Chapter 11. This may not be the stuff to win over the country, but it could be enough to reclaim the Republican Right.

At first, Buchanan says, he thought his America First ideas would inspire "something more than a supper club but less than a third party." By December, Bush's popularity was moving south, the economy was worsening, and Bush wasn't doing anything about it. "There were more sightings of Elvis in New Hampshire than [of] the President," Buchanan said. Buchanan jumped in on December 10, and now, two months later, he is clocking in at 25% to 30% on most polls, assuring that he will send a message, if not a bomb, to the White House.

Buchanan was already well-known as co-host of *Crossfire,* regular on *Capital Gang,* occupier of what came to be known as the "Yahoo chair" on *The McLaughlin Group,* and syndicated columnist. His monthly newsletter, sent to 30,000 true believers, made him a multimillionaire.

But now Buchanan has given up the protective cocoon of celebrity life, a world in which he traveled by Mercedes (so much for buying American) from his pillared mansion in McLean, Va., to the CNN studio where, as one staffer says, "he never actually had to come into contact with the bozos who think the way he does." He has taken up traveling by minivan, begging for donations, and bedding down at Holiday Inns. The speeches he used to give at about $10,000 a pop are being delivered free in overheated living rooms in New Hampshire.

A little suffering fits the Buchanan Weltanschauung that too much happiness in this life could reduce the chances of salvation in the next—and that has helped him pull off his aggrieved underdog pose. From inside the Beltway, even before there was one (he was born the third of nine children in a comfortable Washington neighborhood), he has nonetheless successfully positioned himself as a scrappy outsider.

Buchanan's passed along his devotion to Joe McCarthy, Douglas MacArthur and Francisco Franco and his belief that a sharp right to the jaw was an excellent way to make a point. "Wild Bill" made his sons hit a punching bag 400 times a week and cheered when Pat bloodied the nose of a first-grade bully. He once held young Pat's hand to a lighted match to demonstrate what eternal damnation would be like.

After eighth grade, when the fancy sons of lace-curtain Irish lawyers and lobbyists departed in tweeds and cashmere for Georgetown Prep, Buchanan proudly went off in his blue serge suit to Gonzaga, an inner-city school run by tough Jesuits, where the basketball nets were made of chain, the decor consisted of a crucifix on the wall and grudges against those who had it too easy were encouraged. A nonconformist who dared come to school with a day's growth of beard would be collared by Father Aloysius McGonigol and dry-shaved until his face bled.

Buchanan missed his best opportunity to escape the boundaries of religion and culture drawn by his father by opting to Georgetown University. He was suspended for a year after he punched two policemen who stopped him for speeding. As he romanticizes the episode, "I was ahead on points until they pulled out the nightsticks."

After working in his father's office and at a summer job delivering mail (he jokes that he fed people's Social Security checks to their dogs), he graduated third in his class from Georgetown, got a master's degree at Columbia's Graduate School of Journalism and landed his first job at the now defunct *St. Louis Globe-Democrat,* writing ripsnorting editorials that bashed bleeding-heart liberals. In 1965 he went up to Nixon at a reception and reminded the "old man" that he had caddied for him at Burning Tree Country Club (where they relieved themselves in the woods) and urged Nixon to run for President—with his help.

In 1969 Buchanan went to work in the White House, where he met Shelley Scarney. They married in 1971, and like many couples without children, they are inseparable, to the point that Buchanan barely ties his shoes without her. His scheduler, secretary and chauffeur, she trails along behind him wheeling a suitcase full of mail, setting up a mobile office wherever he happens to be. When he stopped drinking a few years ago, so did she. Loyalty—to his father, the Latin Mass, Brylcreem and the party of Robert Taft—is all.

It is hard for friends and colleagues to square the private Buchanan with the public one: the Rottweiler who has turned nostalgia for the days of Ike and Elvis into attacks on anyone who is not white, male, Christian and straight.

When asked whether he's anti-Semitic, Buchanan says no, that he tries to be "good" in the Judeo-Christian sense. He is calm about the primary, in part from knowing that on the issue that matters most, neither he nor the voters will have the final word.

February 17, 1992

Good-bye to Whatever Man
The press loved Bob Dole. He was one of us

It was okay when Spiro Agnew and Richard Nixon blamed liberal media bias for their troubles. But to hear that from Bob Dole, after all we did for him, it really hurts. Bob Dole knows that Bob Dole is being unfair here. To the extent that the Washington press corps likes anyone, it likes Dole.

Forget the simple man from Kansas. Bob Dole is one of us—hothouse specimens of the genus *beltway,* with nearly identical customs, habitats and native costumes. We ate the same Senate bean soup (on the menu since around 1903 and still only $1 a bowl) and grazed at the same receptions. We overlooked the fact that he seldom spoke a complete sentence or used a personal pronoun—and I'm not just talking about I, but also he, she or it—recognizing that he had so mastered his craft that the mother tongue was no longer a sufficient form of expression.

Dole saying in Hill Esperanto that S.R. 32 had been marked up and would be fixed in committee was music on the Sunday-morning talk shows, for which he held the record for appearances. When he cut deals, he told us he was doing it, so no big deal. When we wrote that Dole was mean for zinging that tinny lapdog George Bush (so labeled by George Will), we meant it as a compliment. So he could be snide and cynical—just like us! No big deal.

It's true that when Dole resigned and traded in his tie for leisure wear, we were temporarily thrown off balance. But we snapped right back when he said that if his resignation had leaked, he wouldn't have done it. Now, that's our guy. When he threw red meat to his right wing, he winked and said he was hitting "wedge issues" so we would know that he knew how craven it was. By the time he was handing out deodorant to reporters on his plane for the 96-hour torture tank, Dole had resumed his visits to the press section in back, which had been cut off after a summer of gaffes.

Until the end, he kept railing against *The New York Times.* But when you think of what they could have run in the daily "In His Own Words" section—and I'm thinking of "When he [Strom Thurmond] ate a banana, I ate a banana" or when he said in a glass factory, "Blow in, blow out, blow whatever"—he got off easy. By the way, the word *whatever?* He got it from us.

Funny how the little things we shared turned out to be liabilities among those real people we hear exist outside the Capitol, like full sentences and stories of picture-perfect holidays (not a Christmas tree in the lobby of a Bal Harbour, Fla., condo or mail-ordering frozen steaks to his only child, back in suburban Virginia). Dole lives in a three-room apartment in the Watergate, where room service is just a call away, with a wife who looks younger than his daughter. The Doles are apart so much they fax each other their schedules—the kind of yuppie coping the peripatetic press can identify with. We'd forgotten that outside the cocoon of the Senate, his life might look shrunken and inadequate.

Dole finally calmed down, remembering that it was the press that had anointed him the inevitable candidate in the first place. Don't know how he feels; probably won't say. But from us: Sorry, Senator, we won't have you around anymore. Really. Mean it.

November 18, 1996

The Rules from 1996

Like the women who buy dating guides, candidates yearn for surefire advice—and comb each campaign for tips

Out go the lights on the '96 campaign, and it's time to ask what we've learned. The voters couldn't have learned a lot, unless they were unaware that education is good and drugs are bad. Future candidates, however, will take away meaning. For instance: Don't discuss entitlements in the heat of a campaign. It's like putting metal in a microwave. Small fires break out, and dousing is not only exhausting but may also elicit promises that cannot be kept and make serious reform even more difficult. This is why Washington invents commissions.

By all means, smile. The candidate sporting a silly grin beats the one wearing a scowl. Yes, Richard Nixon glided to a dark victory, but there's an exception to every rule. Consider Jimmy Carter after he discovered malaise. Consider George Bush after the economy slipped. Consider Bob Dole. And, by the way, it is the economy, stupid. People vote their ATM cards and money-market accounts. Other lessons, for good or for bad, peculiar to this campaign:

Find a cartoon character. Happily, by 1996, the caricature of 1994, the Angry White Male, had gone on Prozac. Unhappily, he was replaced by the ubiquitous Soccer Mom, who was treated even more simplistically. After all, no one followed the A.W.M. to the grocery store to watch him buy his six-pack. But pundits rummaged around in the S.M.'s sock drawer for clues to how she would vote and wondered whether her choice of oversized mini-vans was a sign of male envy, like those huge shoulder pads in the power suit of the '80s.

Character has lost its attraction as an issue now that it no longer means sex. Once the press and the candidates realized that harping on sexual indiscretions ran the risk of Mutual Assured Destruction, the character issue was reduced to the impossible—and tedious—task of weighing one man's soul against another's. There was a brief respite provided by Dick Morris, whose idea of triangulating involved toes. But otherwise, nothing. Sex may finally be out until someone can show a connection between a model sex life—Nixon, Carter—and a successful presidency.

Primogeniture must go. To make room for younger, stronger candidates without dissing your elder statesmen, consider something like the Oscars' Irving Thalberg Lifetime Achievement Award. Snag some headline entertainer like Jay Leno sufficient to attract network coverage, and air the same hagiographic film that would otherwise be shown at the convention. Better that the candidate end his career in prime time, droning on about his second-grade teacher, than at sparsely attended airport rallies, shouting epithets into the wind.

Money can't buy you love. Thanks for this lesson go to Senator Phil Gramm, who announced before the first vote was cast that he had won the money primary with his $20 million and so everyone should get out of his way. At the straw poll in Florida, he had the best barbecue and the best band, spending $76,000. About $4,000 a month went to a "crowd builder." Not since John Connolly spent about $13 million and won only one delegate has money done less.

Money can buy you love. Both candidates believed in spend now, pay the FEC fine later. By the time "fugitive DNC fund-raiser" worked its way into the conversation, Clinton had a double-digit lead and promised to do something about the problem—later. Fortunately for Clinton, Dole was no better: He'd already blocked campaign-finance reform and stuffed his pockets.

Keep it simple, but not too simple. Steve Forbes was put on the political map by his flat tax. He was taken off by it too. Filing on a postcard lost its allure once the middle class realized the top bracket would benefit first and most. For the rest it was good-bye home-mortgage deduction.

You can be too good to be President (see Senator Richard Lugar). You can also be too bad to be President, and as a consequence, have the first real scare in your congressional race in years (see Congressman "B-1 Bob" Dornan). And you can be too phony to be President (see Lamar! in the shirt playing the piano).

Your enemies are as important as your friends. Clinton's enemies: Joe Camel, the N.R.A. despoilers of the Grand Canyon. Dole's enemies: teachers, the N.A.A.C.P., Katie Couric, minimum-wage workers. And with friends like Newt, Dole couldn't really afford enemies. All those double-date press conferences during the budget negotiations looked like a buddy movie with Newt the star and Dole the sidekick. If Newt were really Dole's friend, he wouldn't be running around the country swinging a plastic bucket to symbolize all the money the revolution saved on congressional ice deliveries while Dole was trying to make the country forget there ever was a revolution.

Hire the most amoral, faithless, money-grubbing, shameless philanderer you can find. Dick Morris brought family values to the debate, moved Clinton to the mushy middle and acted out his boss's worst proclivities so that Clinton didn't have to. But exercise extreme caution when trying this at home—particularly if there are photographs.

Small is beautiful. The presidency is a big thing. But in the era of downsized government, little things are fertile terrain for a feel-your-pain incumbent. And what bigger pain than raising a teenager in a vulgar world—thus, the V-chip, school uniforms and curfews. Compassion legislation: feels so good, and it's oh so cheap.

Charisma is no substitute for conviction. America loves an Odd Couple, if their most profound disagreement is over how often to vacuum: twice a day or never, and then only on television. But Bob Dole and Jack Kemp are no Felix and Oscar. They differ on fundamental matters like immigration and affirmative action. The photo-op vice presidency played well at the convention, but by October it was clear the marriage could not be saved, even for the sake of California's 54 electoral votes. Never wed someone with whom you already have irreconcilable differences.

Don't quit your day job. You need a job to get a job. And you shouldn't pretend you were nothing more than a simple man from Russell, Kans., for the past 35 years. In the process of disavowing his presence in the belly of the beast, Dole also gave up credit for his legacy of passing moderate, bipartisan legislation, a record of real accomplishment.

Never annoy a billionaire. Here's the deal, see? It was clear Perot wasn't going to get into the debates, what a waste for Dole to be the one to block it. After that, Perot would have to be crazy to entertain Dole's proposal that he drop out of the race, which may be why Dole gave it a whirl. A leak allowed Perot to garner more press attention than he had since he started. What a dang fool idea. The weird and goofy billionaire even got to call Dole weird and goofy. Like a possum calling a poodle ugly.

If polling is good, focus groups are better. They're cheaper, they're faster, they're simpler. Forget that they are made up of the kind of people willing to sit for a couple of hours in a stifling room drinking burned coffee for $50; politicians are slavishly devoted to them. Dole got his cockeyed idea that people would rather leave their children with him than with Bill Clinton from a focus group. But the user addicted to the practice is Clinton (à la Morris), who tested every subject save whether a switch from a Big Mac to a Double Cheeseburger would attract your more mature voter. In the next race, consultants will be looking for volunteers willing to have electrodes permanently implanted for minute-to-minute reactions to consultants' ideas.

Perhaps each new campaign just seems to be the worst when you're actually living through it. The best thing to do about the rules this campaign yielded will be to break them next time around.

November 11, 1996

My Evening with the Donald

Are we ready for a man who likes palaces and pre-nups?

"I could be married in 24 hours," insists twice-divorced would-be presidential candidate Donald Trump, as if the all-night convenience store had brides on Aisle 3 for the politician who finds he's running low on family values. He twists the gooseneck lamp in the back of his limousine to shine it on his companion, Melania Knauss, a model just back from a photo shoot for *Sports Illustrated*'s swimsuit issue. "Is this the next First Lady of the United States or what?" he asks. She beams under the tiny spotlight, showing teeth like a prize filly at the state fair.

Well, perhaps. At a time when a wrestler who looks down on organized religion but dreams of being reincarnated as a piece of lingerie can become Governor of Minnesota, it's not totally outlandish for an Elle Macpherson clone to be measuring drapery for the East Wing. I have come to New York to see if Trump, the umpteenth person to form a presidential exploratory committee this year, is as big a jerk as he sometimes seems to be.

Not that being a jerk automatically disqualifies a person from becoming a candidate: anyone with airfare and a website can jump in. But he's the first real estate developer with a skyscraper-size ego to run, a man famous for prompting Marla Maples' tabloid headline BEST SEX I'VE EVER HAD, and for refusing to shake hands for fear of germs. As he shakes mine, I ask him if he's over this phobia. "I don't mind shaking the hand of a beautiful woman," he croons. "It's worth the risk."

With an answer like that, how big a jerk can he be? But what about the vision thing? Every candidate needs one. He's for tax cuts, against affirmative action and pro-choice; he fears that if we outlaw guns, only outlaws will have guns and thinks campaign finance is a complicated issue but simple enough for him. He's "prepared to spend what it takes, $20 million to $40 million," he declares. Does he really have the cash, having gone neck deep into debt in the early '90s? "I could be very liquid very quickly, and I wouldn't have to sell a thing." Take that, Steve Forbes.

But who is going to vote for the king of broads and blackjack, pre-nups and palaces in a year when the public is looking for a grown-up as an antidote to Bill Clinton? "All my construction guys love me. The guy who picks up the bus at the Port Authority, gets $50 in chips, a ticket for the all-you-can-eat buffet and takes the missus to the Trump Taj Mahal, he loves me," says Trump.

He boasts that he already owns the southern White House, which means he won't be mooching off rich friends on Martha's Vineyard. "I bought

Mar-a-Lago [a Palm Beach, Fla., estate], which Marjorie Merriweather Post willed to the government to be used by Presidents," he says. He brags he paid only $8 million, a steal at the time.

But if Trump's prepared with the real estate, he's less prepared with the foreign policy. He may have to pull as many all-nighters as Republican front-runner George W. Bush. Trump does know the difference between Slovenia and Slovakia, but some of his writings bring the hawkish general played by George C. Scott in *Dr. Strangelove* to mind. "I would let Pyongyang know in no uncertain terms that it can either get out of the nuclear arms race or expect a rebuke similar to the one Ronald Reagan delivered to Muammar Gaddafi in 1986," he wrote two weeks ago in *The Wall Street Journal*. Bombs away! As for Castro, Trump wrote that the Cuban leader should be tried for crimes against humanity as "the most abnormal political figure in our hemisphere." Hmmm. Isn't a politician who doesn't shake hands a little abnormal too?

Over Labor Day weekend, the Reform Party's highest public-office holder and a kingmaker, Minnesota's Jesse Ventura, tracked Trump down in Las Vegas and encouraged him to run, telling him he could draw from the same disaffected groups as Ventura did. The two stayed in touch, and last week Ventura called to say he could come to New York. Trump said, "Come to dinner at my place [Jean Georges at the Trump International Hotel]. I'll bring Melania." Ventura said, "Great. I'll bring Woody Harrelson."

To each his own. Trump scoffs at the usual reasons for launching a third-party bid. He says he's not just looking to get his hands on the party's $13 million in federal matching funds or to have a podium at the debates or to gain spoiler status. "I'm not running for some measly 22%. I will only do this if I can win."

October 18, 1999

Next: The Forbes Bump

If it happens—and the publisher's money and crowds suggest it could—then it's good for McCain

For a long time, I've dismissed Steve Forbes as the poster boy for the candidates who don't matter. Sure, he managed to come in second in the Iowa straw poll. But it was a 90 (degree) day, and he benefited from having an air-conditioned tent and short food lines. Some days, money can buy you love.

But money can't buy presidential stature. Forbes, despite spending millions, is stuck with the uncomfortable person he is. In one ad in which he gazes from a movie-set White House at the real one, with emotions running the gamut from bland to vanilla and a smile unconnected to his eyes, he conveys exactly the opposite of the Mount Rushmore effect: he's doomed to be looking endlessly at the one mansion he can't buy.

By attracting crowds in Iowa Forbes slowed Bush. "They like my conservative message out here," he says from his bus, *Victory Express II,* where the cooler is always full and the snacks are never ending.

Since John McCain is not competing in Iowa, Forbes gets to take on Bush directly. Forbes, who usually sounds like the disembodied voice that tells you to "press 1" to be connected to the next available operator, is actually animated when he talks about Bush's failing the latest pop quiz. "Everyone would understand if he didn't know the No. 2 in Uzbekistan. But not knowing important world leaders underscores that people don't know whether he has a grasp of foreign policy. Or any other issues for that matter."

Forbes can stay on Bush's case with enough money to buy TV ads until the end—enough to buy a TV network—if he wants. He's shown he will spend from his $450 million fortune what it takes. If Forbes peels off conservative votes, it increases the chances of a McCain nomination. The Senator from Arizona should go to Iowa and help him campaign.

November 15, 1999

By Their Quirks Ye Shall Know Them

In last week's debate, Al Gore reissued his challenge to Bill Bradley to swear off those empty 30-second ads in favor of twice weekly debates. Twice weekly? Who does Gore think he is, the host of *Who Wants to Be a Millionaire?* The Democratic duo's last appearance—with its "No, I didn't," "Oh, yes, you did" tone, interspersed with stock lines from speeches—left me wondering whether the debates haven't reached the point of diminishing returns. Long idealized as the noblest form of political discourse, debates are today about as overproduced, overprogrammed and devoid of meaning as the much reviled ads. I stopped counting the canned phrases when I hit 26.

On the Republican side, some critics say the problem is too many candidates. From Alan Keyes' keening against the "howling moral void" to Orrin Hatch's cracking wise about how Steve Forbes is so rich he couldn't lift his wallet.

To extract a fresh thought, restive reporters will try anything—surprise, confrontation, rudeness. Nowadays, consultants even vet the campaign music: Bush's squad recently killed "Cat's in the Cradle" after realizing the lyrics were about a son who grows up to be just like his remote father. It would take nothing short of sodium pentothal delivered at the podium to get Bush to clear up his conflicting statements on abortion. Tell us—do you really mean it when you say you will keep the Republican platform, which would ban all abortions? Are you saying farewell to soccer moms? And no one is more scripted than Forbes. I'm not saying his vacant stare is reminiscent of the Manchurian Candidate. But I wouldn't risk flashing the queen of diamonds at him on the campaign trail.

In an effort to crack the candidate's defenses, the Associated Press sent out a whimsical questionnaire asking each candidate to name a few of his favorite things. Keyes refused to answer any questions at all. Too busy filling the moral void, perhaps. Bradley dodged a few. Some replies seemed focus grouped. Asked to list the last book he had read, Donald Trump named *A History of the English-Speaking Peoples* by Winston Churchill. I want to be around for the pop quiz on Chapters 1 through 3. Pat Buchanan—he of the recent soft-on-Hitler p.r. crisis—blithely offered up that he's reading *Day of Deceit: The Truth About FDR and Pearl Harbor* and that his first car was a German DKW, known as Das Kleine Wunder. Not a trace of handler input there.

Although Bradley had resisted revealing his favorite book, he said in the debate that he liked Joseph Conrad's *Victory* and even speed-quoted a section. He cautioned that it told us nothing about him other than that he had read the book.

Au contraire, Professor Bradley. So it's old Joe you've been channeling this campaign? Your reluctant venture into the belly of the political beast is a journey into Conrad's heart of darkness. You can bet none of the others are doing such heavy lifting. Bush likes Robert Parker mysteries. Now that sounds a lot more like Bush than the Dean Acheson biography he claimed to be reading and was hard-pressed to summarize.

Lots of things fit. Bradley, the thinker, likes long drives on his day off, while Gore, the fighter, prefers water skiing. Bradley picked the sugar-free, protein-laden cashew as his snack of choice, while his colleagues admitted to mainlining cupcakes and Three Musketeers bars. Gore, the Harvard-educated, alpha male in training, named *Shakespeare in Love* as his favorite movie, while Hatch chose *Simon Birch,* a peculiar film about a dwarf who believes God selected him for a heroic mission. In another life, Hatch says, he would like to be in the CIA. It may be just as well we lost him.

Stranded on a desert island, Bush would take his fishing rod and a Bible, while McCain hopes for a satellite dish, perhaps because he had to rely on memory to entertain his fellow prisoners of war with narrations of *Stalag 17* and *One-Eyed Jacks*.

These tiny glimpses are tantalizing. But how do we get a deeper look, induce any of these Clockwork Oranges to come unsprung enough to show a little of their own lives before we entrust one of them with the life of a nation? Bradley boasts he's comfortable in his own skin, but how would we know, since he doesn't let us get under it? Does Gore of the earth tones even dress himself? As lame as the debates are, don't expect to see Bush mixing it up with Forbes and Keyes should he dispense with McCain. He'll revive his earlier excuse and suddenly have a lot of awards ceremonies to attend with his wife. He temporarily shut down press conferences after a reporter got too close to the bone. Voters have learned the hard way that character matters, that you need to know who someone is much more than you need to know what his tax plan entails. So, candidates, unhand yourselves. We hardly know you.

February 7, 2000

PART THREE

Saints and Sinners

SOMETIMES I THINK I SHOULD PAY SOMEONE for my job, not the other way around. There's not much more fun to be had in life than to go see what all the fuss is over Katharine Hepburn or Rush Limbaugh, to see if Arthur Sulzberger, the young editor of *The New York Times,* is up to running the Gray Old Lady, or to check in with Gloria Steinem. And you don't have to grow up to do it.

There was no interview I looked forward to more than mine with Hepburn. The only time I was more anxious at *Time* was after eating a piece of bad fish at my welcoming dinner and having to produce my first piece in the magazine the next day. Neither turned out well, and to this day, a charred slab of yellowfin tuna or the opening credits of *Guess Who's Coming to Dinner* make my stomach churn. The upside of bad experiences is that in my job, I get to write about them.

There's no particular unifying theory of what ended up in this chapter. Some stories here most writers would pass over. But if I had to give the pudding a theme, it would be that some people are worth writing about even when they don't screw up; others are worth it only when they do.

Some of these folks are on a list I keep of "People Who Must Be Stopped." How did John Mack end up with a cushy job on Capitol Hill after beating a girl to a bloody pulp in the back room of a chain store? How about those Menendez brothers, Exhibit A of how the soft and indulgent upbringing of Beverly Hills can rot the soul. They are the embodiment of arrogance, murdering their parents and complaining about being orphans. They used their inheritance to hire lawyers who would spoil them in the way they were accustomed to, right down to providing catered meals and casual wear designed to make them look like frat boys who'd taken a prank too far. Then there's O. J. Simpson, who started out fine but got rotten from too much coddling. He went from athlete who'd worked for what he'd gotten to cosseted TV star to aging celebrity who thought his wife deserved to be pummeled.

And how about Martha Stewart? She gives cover to those of us who find the gloomiest day can be brightened by baking a loaf of bread or calling twelve friends to come for roast chicken (although a drink with an umbrella in it can have a similar effect). Sure, Martha was a household Nazi, and she stomped on people as she climbed the diva ladder, but a lot could be forgiven for her perfect shade of sage green paint. Too much spoiling is as bad for adults as for children, and when Martha got to the top, she went bad. Everyone went along with everything, even her tantrums. Not surprising then that when she came under suspicion for insider trading, her first instinct was to deny it and do so with details that would require corroboration by pliant minions. She wouldn't have assumed that because her stockbrokers and assistants had always said yes to her, they would continue to do so, even when under oath.

What a bad choice. Had she simply 'fessed up at the beginning, she would still be the imperious queen of all she surveys, tending her free-range chickens and feeding the roses as CEO of a Fortune 500 company that hadn't lost 75 percent of its value.

Martha's not alone in thinking she could get away with anything because she always has. So many of those who fall precipitously depart the world of mere mortals for the world of "yes, I'll get right on it." When your luggage is Fed Exed ahead, your temperature-controlled limo purrs at the curb, and you never have to wait in line (or wait at all), you come to think there's got to be a press agent, a lawyer, or an aide to fix whatever might go wrong.

Leona Helmsley spoke for so many others more discreet than she when she said, having run criminally afoul of the IRS, that she always thought tax laws "were for the little people." If Pete Rose hadn't begun to believe his press clips and groupies, would he have gambled on baseball? No matter how heinous his conduct, Rose never imagined he would be banned from the Hall of Fame. If not for overarching greed and arrogance, would Tyco chair Dennis Kozlowski, who was given at company expense $18 million of Impressionist art to hang on his penthouse walls, chisel the state out of the taxes on it? It's not always money. Newt Gingrich was flying so high as architect of his own revolution, the former Speaker thought nothing of the

House impeaching Clinton for having an affair at the very same moment he himself was having an affair with a Capitol Hill staffer. The difference between the two was that Gingrich left his second wife for a third.

Lying is so often the thing that gets people in trouble, rather than the thing itself, and the higher on the ladder, the bigger the lie you think you can get away with. Clinton, of course, told a real finger-wagging whopper, for which I reluctantly gave him half a pass in "Liar, Liar (page 63)." It was an ugly choice to have to make between a president of the United States stonewalling about his puerile and humiliating dalliance and an obsessed prosecutor questioning him about it in his house with his wife and daughter upstairs and publishing every prurient detail on the Internet. This is not what the Founding Fathers had in mind. Clinton could be a jerk but against the bully, Ken Starr, he was the little guy, and for that one moment, worth rooting for.

That Killer Smile

Lyle Menendez, whose rich kid's tan has long since faded from his face, broke his pose as the grieving son to peel a thin smile from his limited supply. It was his response to the judge's announcement of the second deadlocked jury in the case of the two brothers on trial for murdering their parents. Menendez's attorney, Jill Lansing, later boasted about how she had introduced doubt into a case the prosecution had once hailed as open-and-shut murder in the first degree: "I don't think anybody at the beginning believed the possibility that they were abused or motivated by fear. Obviously, a great number of people believed that was the situation at the end." She added: "I think there are a lot of abuse victims . . . empowered by this case. They could see themselves as victims as opposed to being responsible for their situation." Victimology has turned out to be the winning tactic of our era. In the Menendez case, the law has been so stretched that an "unreasonable" belief that one is in danger of serious harm—one no sane person would harbor—can be sufficient grounds for self-defense. How did we go from a society that brooked no excuses to one that embraces every explanation; from a society that distinguished right from wrong to one that understands all and punishes nothing? In less understanding times, two boys who chose the maid's night off to pump 16 rounds of fire into their parents as they ate ice cream and strawberries in the family room in front of the TV and are on tape admitting they did so would be serving life sentences by now. But under California law, you can tie up a court for six months, eat up the resources of the criminal justice system and use your murdered parents' $14 million estate to pay for a top-of-the-line legal representation if you unreasonably believe your parents were going to kill you for fear that you were about to expose their abuse.

The age of the culprit as victim began with the Twinkie defense, which freed the killer of San Francisco Mayor George Moscone and Supervisor Harvey Milk; too much sugar made him do it. More recently Damian Williams, videotaped beating trucker Reginald Denny during the Los Angeles riots, was found not guilty because he got caught up in the moment. Lorena Bobbitt convinced a Virginia jury that being physically and sexually abused by her husband, forced to have sex when she didn't want to and failing to "have orgasm" drove her to cut off his penis. She only has to see a psychiatrist.

But victim chic has found its finest expression in Lyle and Erik Menendez. The brothers admitted what they had done only when the existence of a tape their psychologist had secretly made became known. On it they said they had killed their parents because it was what was best for their mother, who had been cheated on by her husband. So what could the jury have made of the fact that they reloaded to shoot her point-blank in the face when she refused to quit crawling away?

For months, of course, the boys' strategy was lying, from the frantic, tearful call to 911 saying, "Somebody killed my parents," to the loving eulogy at the memorial service, to the hiring of a bodyguard in case they were next on the Mafia hit list. Then they came up with the theory of self-defense-cum-child-abuse.

But the more important technique employed was that of the modern talk show. Erik's lawyer, Leslie Abramson, held her jury riveted. She mastered the art of tough love so well that in her postmortem disgust with Jose and Kitty—who were tried and convicted of the most heinous crimes without being able to confront their accusers—the jurors wanted to go wherever she did. By dragging the case out for six months, the defense was able to give the jury time to work through their problems with what the boys had done. In this 12-step program, the jurors were led through a recovery process whereby they could see that the sons could only begin their healing process once they got their parents out of the way.

Each day the defense team came into the small, windowless courtroom as if it were a foster home and they were surrogate parents, making sure these orphans were seated comfortably, picking lint off a shoulder, huddling close during recess. The brothers eschewed the suits worn by most defendants seeking respectability in favor of the open-necked Oxford shirts and crew-neck sweaters of all-American college boys, not two grown men who could have left home if life was so intolerable.

In the jargon of the trial, the parents were guilty of enabling their sons to be bad boys without consequences. Plush Beverly Hills High, which the boys attended, comes complete with an indoor parking garage for BMWs and Mercedes-Benzes. When Lyle's father presented him with an Alfa Romeo—a gift for learning to drive—the boy called it a "piece of shit" because he wanted a Porsche. Within days of killing the old man, he bought one for $70,000. The jury looked shocked only twice: when Lyle's cool voice came out of a boom box telling the therapist he would miss his dog as much as his parents, and when Erik said he felt love for his mother when he placed the shotgun in her cheek and blasted away her eye and nose. The brothers went from parents who understood too much to a jury that did.

At a time when the public is clamoring for a get-tough policy on crime, juries are being led to empathize. During the trial, Lyle, who wears the most authentic toupee money can buy, put on a mask of pain. Last week he smiled.

February 7, 1994

The Victim, You Say?

By my count, O. J. Simpson has been called an American hero about 4,392,979 times since being charged with murdering his wife. Even the U.S. Senate got in on the chorus. In chamber on Friday, the chaplain offered a prayer for O.J.: "Our hearts go out to him. . . . Our nation has been traumatized by the fall of a great hero." To this moment, I have not heard Nicole Simpson referred to as much of anything at all. A victim, you say? She has become even smaller in death, as her ex-husband grows larger than life. As a noncelebrity and a woman, she looks headed for a very unfair trial.

Consider the 911 tape released last week, which should have had the unambiguous effect of bringing the most die-hard O.J. fan to his senses. Instead of the silky-smooth patter of the blue-blazered N.F.L. sportscaster, the self-deprecating wit of the motivational speaker, here comes the coarse rant of a man who owns his ex-wife. He rampages through her home, breaking down a door, and you can hear how terrorized Nicole is, even as she begs her ex-husband to hold his voice down to keep from frightening the children. But so firmly entrenched is his image, so unformed hers, that the tape had the perverse effect in some quarters of helping to explain his conduct and incriminate her. Hey, she had a boyfriend. What's more, she entertained him in the living room O.J. paid for. Her antics provided fodder for an article in the *National Enquirer* that made him look like a cuckolded male entitled to exact revenge. That's something men calling into sports talk shows can sympathize with.

Was this what lawyers had in mind when they concocted the heat-of-passion defense? Radio host Rush Limbaugh with 20 million listeners had an on-air epiphany, when he played the tape for his listeners and found out it was another man that O.J. was furious about. He broke down a door, big deal. He didn't break her.

It shouldn't be so hard to humanize Nicole and cut O.J. down to size. He may have held the record for yards rushing, but he also holds it for celebrity afterlife. Only in the deflated coin of the realm would Simpson have been considered a hero. He was an athlete who turned a brilliant career running a football into a minor one flacking rental cars and NFL football. Much is made of the amiability with which he performed these duties, but accommodating fans is how a faded athlete convinces a company like Hertz to keep paying him top dollar for pushing midsize cars with unlimited mileage.

Domestic violence remains not really a crime—especially among the men who commit it or sympathize with those who do. The word *domestic* modifies and diminishes the word that follows so much that it's a different, lesser, violence. Beating up a stranger gets you jailed; beating up a wife lands you in therapy.

Society now is all too ready to blame the victim, while simultaneously making a victim of the perpetrator. In O.J.'s so-called suicide note, he is the victim. Before this is over, Nicole will be the bitch who ate Brentwood and asked for everything she got. As for O.J.? He was only human.

July 4, 1994

Divorce, Kennedy-Style

A new book and another scandal may finally hit the Kennedys where it would hurt—in the ballot box

When you look at the third generation of Kennedy men, much of what remains of a once powerful dynasty is good teeth, good hair and the best public relations a trust fund can buy. Some of the boys grew from being spoiled and bratty—belittling the help, once chasing the cook up a tree at Hickory Hill—into full-blown debauchery, driving fast, drinking hard, club hopping like wild men. Most of this got spun by family retainers into the playful high jinks of a raucous clan. But the escapades got seamier over time and the spinning harder: a joyride with Joe Kennedy II left a young woman paralyzed after an accident on Nantucket. Bobby Jr. was arrested for possession of heroin. David died in a Florida hotel of a cocaine, Demerol and Mellaril overdose. William Kennedy Smith was accused and acquitted of rape. Now Michael Kennedy, the sixth child of Robert Kennedy, who once seemed to have his father's quiet passion without the Kennedy sense of entitlement, finds himself at the center of a new scandal—that he allegedly had a five-year affair with a girl who baby-sat his three children at the family home in Cohasset, Mass., beginning when she was 14. At the same time, Joe II, a six-term Congressman planning to run for Governor, is trying to weather a just published book, *Shattered Faith,* by ex-wife Sheila Rauch Kennedy that depicts him as a narcissistic bully and protests his efforts to have their 12-year marriage annulled.

In Kennedyland, where everyone is his brother's keeper, the blowback from Michael's scandal and publicity surrounding *Shattered Faith* have sent Joe's popularity sinking. In *Boston Herald* polls, 17% of voters said they are less likely to vote for Joe based on Michael's problems alone, and one in four has a less favorable view of Joe as a result of the book. The heretofore impossible in Massachusetts seems plausible: an office a Kennedy wants could be kept from him.

The baby-sitter story broke in *The Boston Globe* on April 25, just as Michael and Victoria Gifford Kennedy, the daughter of ABC sportscaster Frank Gifford, were officially separating. The paper reported that Victoria had discovered Michael in bed with the baby-sitter in January 1995, an incident Michael blamed on alcohol. He then enrolled in a rehab program. But apparently the two continued to be seen together around the wealthy seaside town and, according to a report in the *Herald,* even went on a whitewater rafting trip, organized by his closest friends, and shared a tent. Victoria seemed to ignore the swirling rumors about the continuation of the relationship, which is apparently a family tradition. In *The Kennedy Women*, Laurence Leamer writes that patriarch Joe stuck Gloria Swanson in Rose's face "so close that she could see the pores on her skin," yet Rose acted oblivious, for "as long as nothing was said . . . life could go on as before."

Joe's scandal didn't have to happen. He had divorced in 1991 with no electoral downdraft. As Irish luck would have it, he had married a woman much like the woman who married dear old Granddad: silent in the face of a raw pursuit of power and pleasure. When the marriage ended, Sheila didn't utter a peep, not even asking for alimony. For the sake of the children, she stayed in the Boston area, moving into a rundown house in Cambridge, which she renovated. When Joe soon took up with an aide in his office, Beth Kelly, Sheila said nothing; when he married her, Sheila wished the couple well.

But being a Kennedy means never having to leave well enough alone. Joe wanted to remain in the church, so he was willing to say that because he'd lacked "due discretion," he had never really been married. When Sheila got a curt notice of the annulment proceeding from the Boston archdiocese, she proceeded to fight. In an interview she explained that nobody "has ever been able to convince me that an annulment was in the best interest of the children, so the argument that was used to keep me in line before didn't cut the mustard this time."

Like a recession, a scandal is best early in an election cycle. A *Globe/WBZ-TV* poll last week found that Joe Kennedy was viewed negatively by 39% of voters. In the 1994 Senate elections Ted Kennedy's negatives were above 50%, yet he easily won re-election, thanks in part to a second marriage that restored his soul. Local analysts believe Joe will regain his lead. To paraphrase Senator Kennedy's speech at the Democratic National Convention in 1980, the teeth still sparkle, the hair is thick and the dream will never die.

May 12, 1997

Empress of "How-to"

Martha Stewart's face is everywhere but on a Wanted poster: in her magazine, on four videos and a dozen books, on TV (twice a day), unofficially on the Internet, at Kmart and in her catalog (Martha by Mail). In an interview, conducted as she shuttled among her farm in Westport, Connecticut, her two Hampton beach houses on New York's Long Island and her Manhattan office, she says her aim is nothing less than to take over Christmas. "It is our intention to own areas in communication. I don't mean to sound egomaniacal, but Perry Como used to own Christmas on TV. By own I mean monopolize and influence."

She already claimed a chunk of Christmas in 1995 with her "Home for the Holidays" TV special featuring Hillary Clinton. Many people ceded Easter to her after 1994, when she counseled readers to celebrate by taking a fresh ham, roasting it for five hours and serving it garnished with organically grown grass that had been cut early that morning with the dew still on it. Never mind that most of her magazine's 5 million readers still buy the honey-baked version at Boston Market or, horrors!, take it out of a can. Even the subscribers who don't work may think twice before taking on her October 1994 project: "It occurred to us at Martha Stewart Living that we had never really focused on the pleasures of raising backyard livestock."

If Martha Stewart relied on people actually doing what she suggests, as opposed to just watching her do it, she would be very poor indeed, instead of the multimillionaire empress of elegance. The secret to Martha is that the perfection she is pursuing is so out of reach to anyone without a staff, or who sleeps more than Martha's four hours a night, that there is no obligation to actually do it. Being in Martha's thrall is like buying a treadmill and instantly feeling fit, though it serves mainly as a coat rack; acquiring the Martha oeuvre makes you think you will conduct a beautiful domestic symphony one of these days—when the kids grow up, when you lose your day job and the lunkhead you married who will only eat meat loaf and ketchup. The magazine and television show bearing her name have a Merchant Ivory movie-set glow. Actual people, as opposed to imported guests, would really mess it up.

So why is Martha so much more influential than, say, Alice Waters, the Chez Panisse chef who transformed restaurant cooking? It's because Marthaland is a one-stop shop, for everything from bed to kitchen to garden, where one thing builds on another. She pulls all this off with total earnestness, except when she's paid to be ironic by American Express, lining her swimming pool with a mosaic of cut-up credit cards. Otherwise, she stays in character: that of a demanding schoolmistress who will be coming around to test for trace elements of bottled dressing in your *salade niçoise*. When Bryant Gumbel tried to poke a bit of fun at her during her baking segment on *The Today Show*, she blithely ignored him. If she doesn't take cake decorating seriously, who will? Martha's dominance partly derives from the fact that she's bossy and knows what's good for us. The universal zinger for a household shortfall is, "That's not how Martha would do it."

Which is another element of her success: Rather than bring the subject matter down to the audience, she is bringing the audience up to the subject matter, making it worthy of the effort it requires. Sure it's easier to identify with Gloria Steinem, who admits she lived in her apartment for four years before realizing the oven didn't work. By making the impossible pur- chasable—at least in magazine and catalog form—Stewart is now simply Martha: cooking, sewing, gilding, planting, wallpapering and painting her way into every corner of your house—and your life. And Christmas? You'd better watch out.

June 17, 1996

Martha of the Spirit

Sarah Ban Breathnach is to the soul what that other domestic goddess is to the home

It's July 29 and I'm going to see Sarah Ban Breathnach, whose name is pro- nounced Bon Brannock. She is the author of *Simple Abundance: A Day- book of Comfort and Joy,* a five-hundred-page meditation to help women find fulfillment by appreciating what they already have. It has been on the bestseller list for seventy weeks, with 2.2 million copies in print. (A com- panion journal zoomed onto bestseller lists last month—astonishing.) *Sim- ple Abundance*'s entry for today is "The Home as a Hobby," in which the author suggests that cleaning out the basement, if seen as a pastime, would be fun instead of drudgery. Tomorrow she wants you to get rid of "Habits That Steal Precious Moments," so that instead of reaching for a glass of wine, you are satisfied with sparkling mineral water, if it is served with a wedge of lemon in a pretty goblet. Never mind that after removing mildewed mattresses and broken toys, many of us will want a glass of some- thing stronger than club soda, even if it's poured into the Mason jar we've just emptied of rusty nails.

This is Martha Stewart for the spirit, and like the doyenne of impossibly complicated domestic arts, Ban Breathnach is exhausting in her particu- lars yet somehow soothing in her totality. Few devotees of Martha Stewart are going to build a Palais de Poulet, then match their wall colors to the aubergine eggs laid by her free-range chickens. And it's unlikely that *Abundance*'s 2.2 million copies are in the hands of many people who actually hauled junk out of the basement last Tuesday. But Ban Breathnach is right: you would *feel* better after clearing a space for yourself, so much so that just thinking about it is enough to lift the spirit.

With so much self-help mush out there, some journalists see authors like Ban Breathnach wearing a *"kick me"* sign. When I come to visit, she readily agrees to show me where she writes her first drafts, even though it's in bed. And anticipating my next line of questioning, she offers that indeed money does make some things easier but that it "doesn't protect you from life's sufferings. Tears are the same whether they fall on silk damask or cotton." She has proof. She and her husband, a government lawyer and the mayor of Takoma Park, Md., have just separated.

Back in 1991 when she started writing *Abundance*, Ban Breathnach was angry and envious. She had survived a freak but serious accident—a ceiling tile had fallen on her head in a restaurant. The thought of continuing to write books about Victorian doilies and manners filled her with dread. She turned to a survey of philosophy, religion, history and poetry, and one day made a list of 100 things that were good in her life. The way to jump-start happiness, she decided, was to stop looking for what she didn't have and look instead at what she did have: breathing the same crisp spring morning air as the richest person in town, loving your kids as much. Just because that's what all the major religions preach and your mother told you a hundred times doesn't mean it doesn't bear repeating. She'd found the topic for her next book.

Ban Breathnach began to chart the journey from resentful to contented. She filled her writing with references to Buddha and the Bible, Rebecca West and Zsa Zsa Gabor, the humbling nature of hair, the joys of sleep as opposed to sex and how to compensate when you have neither.

Her sensibility is feminine, not feminist. Few of her quick fixes involve gross motor skills, like tennis or kickboxing. Perfume, crayon drawings and a hot bath are her nostrums of choice. She honors work, even if she doesn't grapple with the crushing choices that face women whose childbearing years and peak career years coincide. She doesn't say how you can stop for the pot of tea when the car pool, the grocery store and the new ad campaign all beckon at once.

Abundance sold steadily by word of mouth for months before it found the one reader who counts more than any other—Oprah Winfrey. She invited Ban Breathnach to be on her "People I'd Like to Have Dinner With." Three weeks later, the book landed the number 1 spot on the *New*

York Times bestseller list. As behooves an author whose animating principle is being grateful, Ban Breathnach produced a sequel, *The Simple Abundance Journal of Gratitude*, dedicated "For Oprah with Love. Thank You."

Journal is a masterpiece of brand extension: a series of blank pages that have intermittent homilies from Winston Churchill to Bob Hope to Laura Ingalls Wilder. On each day, the buyer is to write five things the buyer is grateful for in a $12.95 diary. *New York Times Book Review* editor Charles McGrath declined to put the book on the Advice, How-to and Miscellaneous list (where *Abundance* now reigns), explaining, "I don't think the bestseller list should reflect merchandise."

As for the stressed-out journalist, I'm grateful to be done with this week's writing. Today's instruction is to lie under a tree and look up at the sky. How about that mineral water and a slice of lemon? Maybe that will do the trick. Simple abundance, one day at a time.

August 11, 1997

Clean Queen

With her book *Home Comforts,* Cheryl Mendelson has legitimized finding joy in the art of keeping house

Before I read Cheryl Mendelson's *Home Comforts,* I kept a lot of secrets. I didn't tell anyone that every day I take an old toothbrush to the crud that collects around the faucets, that I rarely talk on the phone without a bottle of Windex and paper towel in hand as I walk around wiping off fingerprints. Housework is the third rail of feminism. Do too much of it, and you are out of the sisterhood. Talk about it, and you will find yourself discounted at work and shunned at parties.

But Mendelson, with her graceful, witty best-seller on making a house a home, has made it acceptable for a generation of women and men to come out of the (uncluttered) closet. It is okay to find joy in a full refrigerator, an empty hamper and clean, well-lighted rooms. Just as it took Nixon to go to China, it took a lawyer (she graduated from Harvard) and philosopher (she has a Ph.D.) to legitimize housework. Mendelson once believed that only chumps did not order in, contract out or let it go as they pursued being buff, polished and ready to master the universe. Then one weekend when guests were coming, she blitzed her apartment, making beds with hospital corners, putting out fresh flowers, fixing pasta. She was astonished to find that the psychic reward was high.

Her interest in the domestic grew as she settled into a second marriage and motherhood and began to work only part-time, teaching legal philosophy. She pored over her collection of old-time housework manuals and consulted innumerable experts, from firefighters to microbiologists. Eight years later, she had more than 800 pages that are the final word on how to get out any stain, how to sweep a floor (to the center) and how to remove candle wax (apply ice until the wax crumbles). After reading her book, you will throw out your old sponges, always have white vinegar handy and become slightly paranoid about mold and dust mites. Her reigning philosophy is that the right way of doing something is almost always the fastest.

Cheryl is not to be confused with Martha. She will not tie ribbons around 300-thread-count linens that someone else irons. (Mendelson says percale is fine and folding will do.) She will never crow over serving eggs laid by her own Araucana hens. Cheryl does not substitute crafts for life, and she has help only once a month or so. In her cozy Manhattan apartment, bikes are parked in the dining room, and the fridge door is a mess of notes, schedules and magnets. "Who can feel at home in a place where the demands for order are exaggerated?" she asks.

Mendelson says she does not get as many cold shoulders in social settings as she once did as both genders discover the limits of careers and the promise of home. "It's housekeeping that turns your home into a vital place where you can be more yourself than you can be anywhere else," she says. "Housework is not drudgery. You don't know drudgery until you've parsed a commercial contract."

September 17, 2001

Stealth Warriors from Washington

Elections 2002: In North Carolina, Liddy goes "local" in her bid to beat an ex-Clinton aide

Elizabeth Dole gets ready for every event as if she's having tea with the Queen. At a rally in a tobacco warehouse so humid we all feel like chain smokers, Dole appears in a bubblegum pink suit with beige pumps and stockings. If someone were to, say, spill barbecue sauce on her, a mint green spare is hanging in her Buick sedan.

This is the Liddy we came to know during her brief presidential race in 2000, when not a hair or verb was out of place. She's trying to be looser now as she runs to replace retiring North Carolina Senator Jesse Helms against former Clinton Chief of Staff Erskine Bowles. After her stump speech about religion, the troops, jobs and schools, and an hour of meet-and-greet, I ask Dole, 66, why she isn't sweating. She hunches up her shoulders and motions for me to reach inside her jacket. "Feel the back of my neck," she offers. "I'm drenched." I take her word for it.

The script this time is that Dole is unscripted. I catch on after three people, including Dole herself, tell me how she jumped on a Harley to roar into an auditorium at Duke University, which, of course, was entirely scripted. The crowd is not terribly specific about why they like her, but they do love her. One says Dole is "so much like Jesse," another marvels at how Dole's "mother over there in Salisbury is 101 years old," while a white-haired gentleman gushes over "what a pretty lady she is." He puts a yellow "pride in tobacco" hat on her head. She takes it off.

No one talks about her remarkable career in Washington, perhaps because she rarely does. Any mention of three decades serving three Presidents and thawing Lean Cuisine for husband Senator Bob Dole at their Watergate apartment is drowned out by her frequent recital of local credentials in resurgent drawl: her 1994 North Carolinian of the Year award, her degree from Duke and, of course, her mother, whose house she recently bought, making Dole the best kind of North Carolinian, a landowner. "My roots are deep. I've been here constantly," she says repeatedly, as if being graded on attendance.

Politicians are the only folks who practice résumé deflation—the price of regaining political virginity. Bowles doesn't trumpet his presidential service, even though he won bipartisan praise for getting a balanced budget and steadying the ship of state during Monicagate. The closest he has come to playing the inside game was to import former Secretary of State Madeleine Albright, purified as she once toured North Carolina with Helms. While it might help with African American voters, Bowles says he won't be hosting his ex-boss.

At a breakfast with Bowles in Raleigh, I wonder if the race is between Stiff and Stiffer. Bowles, 57, who dresses and speaks like the banker he was, stresses Dole's opposition in 1989 to an increase in the minimum wage. In a state chock-full of seniors who didn't make it to Florida, he is scoring points with Social Security, while Dole, like Bush, would privatize, after a fashion. She now proposes that a modest 2% go into private investments, but some worry even that amount could cripple the system.

Bowles, who trails Dole by just four points, wants to hash out their differences in as many as eight debates. She wants fewer. So far, they have agreed on one, on the night the World Series opens.

On the issues, the battle lines are clearly drawn. Bowles supported the Family and Medical Leave Act (Dole opposed it, though she now says it has value); he's pro-choice (she's pro-life); he's for coverage of prescription drugs (she's for some coverage); he supports the Brady Bill and closing gun-show loopholes (Dole, on Oprah two years ago, was against assault weapons; in gun-happy North Carolina, she is not).

Of course, Bowles could wear the pink suit and still not flank her on gender. Women greet the Harvard Law grad and former Secretary of both Labor and Transportation like a rock star. By hiding a steel magnolia under a sweet one, she puts powerful men at ease while racing past them, a trait many women could use.

Dole got flustered when I asked, "Where's Bob?" (Maine, maybe.) She couldn't remember if she'd seen a fax of his schedule that day. He is a far more enthusiastic supporter this time around than during her presidential run, when he contributed to her primary opponent, Senator John McCain. She notes that at least she knows where the family dog is. "Bob left Leader with me," she says. "So I don't have to sleep alone." I take her word for it.

October 14, 2002

A Doctor Prescribes Hard Truth

C. Everett Koop, America's Surgeon General, has an opinion on everything healthful, but he nonetheless enjoys meat and martinis

He is, by Washington standards, a little strange. First, there is the uniform draped with gold braid. Before he became famous, it prompted people at airports to pile him with baggage and ask what time the flight was leaving. Then there is the big, clunky hearing aid that he takes out and fusses with right in the middle of a conversation, as if it were a pipe, the canvas tote he uses as a briefcase, and his habit of loudly cracking his knuckles. On top of that there are the Old Testament beard and the preacher's voice that make him seem like Moses come down from Mount Sinai to deliver Commandments 11 through 20. Smoking? It's an addiction that will kill you. Sex? Only in marriage. AIDS? The best preventive device is a monogamous relationship; the second best, a condom. Deformed newborns? Save them. Sex education? In the earliest grade possible.

You name it, Surgeon General C. Everett Koop has an opinion, which he will give you with great certainty at high speed. There has never been a Surgeon General like him, not even Luther Terry, who slapped warnings on cigarette packs 24 years ago. It's a fair guess that Terry was never air-kissed by Elizabeth Taylor, was never the butt of jokes in Johnny Carson's monologue, was never a visitor to the set of *Golden Girls* and never lectured Hollywood producers about showing safe sex in their programs. Antismoking is a small part of Koop's crusade; AIDS, child abuse, domestic violence, pornography, old people, drunk driving and Baby Doe regulations have made Koop one of the most visible officials in Washington. Now at airports people offer to carry his bags.

The 13th Surgeon General almost never got a chance to don a uniform. When Koop, a retired pediatric surgeon, and his wife, Betty, moved to Georgetown in early 1981 to await his confirmation, they became proof of the old saw that if you want a friend in Washington, buy a dog. The process, expected to take a few days, turned into nine nightmarish months of name-calling and personal attacks, as liberals stalled his confirmation. He was called a right-wing crank, a prolife nut, a religious zealot, Dr. Unqualified (*The New York Times*), scary (California Congressman Henry Waxman) and Dr. Kook. The intensity of the attacks was fueled by pro-choice advocates who feared his opposition to abortion. In addition to being the author of several books, Koop was known for an antiabortion film he produced in which a thousand black and white dolls were scattered over the salt wastes of the Dead Sea to represent millions of aborted fetuses. Koop, who became an evangelical Presbyterian in his 30s, explains his views against abortion and against withholding food and medical care from congenitally deformed newborns simply: "If you had led my life, you would understand." As a pediatric surgeon for 33 years, Koop saved many babies no bigger than his hand. In the course of treating 100,000 patients, Koop saw many so-called difficult cases become happy and productive children. One of these was Paul Sweeney, born in 1965 with twisted intestines, facial deformities and a cleft palate. Koop operated on him 37 times. For the final operation by another surgeon in 1983, Koop returned to Philadelphia in full dress uniform to wheel his former patient into the operating room. Sweeney recently graduated from West Chester University in Pennsylvania.

Accustomed to the godlike treatment accorded surgeons, Koop was stunned by the viciousness of Washington, which has neither gods nor heroes. Every day he would go to his temporary office on the seventh floor at the Department of Health and Human Services. Every day the phone wouldn't ring. His wife, uprooted from Philadelphia, waited in their small sublet wondering whether to unpack. One day Koop returned to find tears rolling down her face, a critical newspaper article on her lap. He considered leaving, but Betty persuaded him to stay. The two had been through a lot—long years of medical school, Koop's fractured vertebra and stomach surgery and, worst of all, the death of a son—and they stuck it out. Finally, in November 1981, he was confirmed.

Koop was expected to be a figurehead with little authority and few duties, but he quickly shook things up. He insisted that the commissioned corps of public-health officers wear uniforms. Then the 6-ft.-1-in., 210-lb. doctor, whose taste for red meat and martinis keeps him from losing his paunch, pronounced the U.S. a country of fatsos. When Koop found out that the tobacco companies had fought hardest over the years against the government's calling nicotine addictive, he cited the fact high up in his Surgeon General's report that nicotine is addictive. "They absolutely hated it," he gloats. He said sending cigarettes to the Third World was "the export of death, disease and disability."

He is not above gimmicks. Pushing his slogan "A Smoke-Free Society by the Year 2000," he adopted a kindergarten class whose students pledged not to start smoking ("Like Communists," he says, "you have to get them when they're young"), and everywhere he goes he hands out buttons saying "The Surgeon General Personally Asked Me to Quit."

But Koop might have remained just another bureaucrat if it had not been for AIDS. As the disease grew to near epidemic proportions, the administration had to do something. Conservatives breathed a sigh of relief when in 1986 the President handed the job to the Fundamentalist Christian Surgeon General.

Koop took to the task with an open mind, consulting government experts like the National Institutes of Health's Dr. Anthony Fauci and inviting more than 25 groups, from gay activists to the Southern Baptist Convention, to his office. He wrote 26 drafts at the stand-up desk in the basement of the brick house he rents on the campus of the NIH. He numbered the copies he took to a meeting at the White House and collected all of them to prevent leaks. The next day he released the report at a packed press conference.

Administration conservatives were stunned by the report's candor. They were particularly outraged that he did not preach abstinence alone and actually uttered the word *semen*. "The White House doesn't like the C word. But if you don't talk about condoms, people are going to die. So I talk." Liberals were amazed that Koop had produced a reasoned report with such compassion for homosexuals, whom he had once called antifamily.

Koop says no one should be surprised, that the report is consistent with his moral view that you can hate sin but love the sinner. "I am the Surgeon General, not the chaplain, of all the people, and that includes homosexuals," he says. He outraged conservatives again in January. Although opposed to abortion morally, Koop concluded, following an 18-month study undertaken after President Reagan promised right-to-life leaders a report, that the evidence just wasn't there to condemn the practice as psychologically harmful.

Despite his success in Washington, Koop's real calling is medicine. At 15, he would take the subway on weekends from Brooklyn to Columbia-Presbyterian Hospital in Manhattan, pinch a white lab coat and take a seat in the balcony of the operating room, transfixed for hours by amputations and appendectomies. Back home, while his father was at the office, he persuaded his mother to help her precocious only child round up stray cats and dump them into a sterile trash can with an ether-soaked sponge so that he could perform exploratory surgery. He brags he never lost a cat.

He went to Dartmouth and Cornell University Medical College, and surprised many people when he decided to specialize in pediatric surgery, a low-rent field in those days, when the real brains were going into neurosurgery. "Children weren't getting a fair shake in surgery, getting giant incisions like their grandfathers' and being sewn up like a football when a tiny hole would do," he recalls. Koop's training consisted of going to Boston Children's Hospital and peering over the shoulders of surgeons there.

Koop quickly became known as a tireless and dedicated doctor. When a peptic ulcer threatened to keep him out of surgery for months, he treated himself at night, filling an IV bottle with milk and clamping it onto the bedpost. With the help of his wife, then pregnant with their first child, he would push a tube through his nose and down his throat so the liquid could drip into his stomach while he slept. More than once, the jury-rigged system failed, and the Koops woke up in a soaked bed.

Koop was named surgeon in chief at Children's Hospital of Philadelphia in 1948. There he perfected techniques for correcting undescended testicles and undeveloped esophaguses, skills that he compares to threading together two wet noodles at the bottom of an ice-cream cone with your eyes closed. His first brush with fame came when he separated Siamese twins joined at the abdomen and pelvis. Dr. Judah Folkman, a professor at Harvard Medical School who trained under Koop, says, "I remain in awe. He was beloved at that hospital, worrying over patients as if they were his own children." To criticism that he tinged his medicine with religion, Koop says, "There are no atheists at the bedside of a dying child."

Koop learned this firsthand in 1968, when his youngest son, David, a junior at Dartmouth, fell to his death in a mountain-climbing accident. "I thought I knew what parents went through, but I had no idea," he says. "I felt bone-crushing grief."

Washington has made its peace with him. Most of the friends he lost in making the decision on AIDS have come back. The city that worships at the gray altar of ambiguity found there was room for a man of black and white.

April 24, 1989

Charlie Hustle's Final Play

An unrepentant Pete Rose is banned from his beloved game

When the dust settles on the deal struck between baseball and Pete Rose, it will still be nearly impossible to explain his banishment to the kids who love the game. Rose's bargain was the work of lawyers; its contorted logic was utterly devoid of the simplicity and finality that make the game so refreshing. It was a fine-print compromise that both allowed baseball commissioner A. Bartlett Giamatti to announce that Rose was banned from baseball for life for betting on his own team, and allowed Rose, an hour later in Cincinnati, to say, Hey, it ain't so. Although the 14 others expelled from baseball over the years have never again set foot on a major league diamond, Rose insisted he would be back.

A blue-collar guy from Cincinnati who played with the enthusiasm of a 7-year-old on the field—and exhibited the same level of maturity off—Rose may actually believe it. Exiting with his chin stuck out was probably the only way Rose could go. He was blessed by the gods not so much with talent as with an insatiable drive to win, a competitor stubborn enough to play long beyond his prime until he could break Ty Cobb's batting record. A rookie who ran to first base when he was given a walk, a bruiser who plowed so hard into an opposing catcher during an All-Star game that he separated the man's shoulder, Rose was too vain and too arrogant to beg for mercy from a former Ivy League classics scholar like Giamatti.

Seven volumes of evidence, including a stack of betting slips in his own handwriting, shouted that Rose would gamble on any game, in any sport, at any time. Nothing shames him. Not a 1979 paternity suit that he did not contest, the messy unraveling of his marriage in 1978 or striking an umpire in the chest, for which he received a 30-day suspension in 1988. Criticism in the press about his friends in thick gold chains and diamond pinky rings who placed wagers for a living did not faze him. Even now, the night before

Giamatti's announcement, Rose was hawking autographed baseballs on Cable Value Network at $39.94 a throw and selling uniforms with his old No. 14 on them, the same number he used with his bookie.

Star athletes whose crassness is tolerated when they are winning—Rose once made a scene in the Stage Deli in Manhattan because there was no sandwich named after him—are often stunned when the indulgence ends. When a reporter at the press conference asked Rose why he was accepting the most severe punishment possible if he had not bet on baseball, Rose was speechless. He turned to his lawyer, Reuben Katz, shiny with sweat beside him, who could only natter on about the fine print of clause F. Katz had fought for language that would allow Rose to stand before the microphones and speak about his banishment as if it were a slump he would soon pull out of.

Rose will almost surely never earn a living in baseball again, but he is likely to continue to make a living off baseball by merchandising his relics. In 1985, the year he broke Cobb's record, he arranged to collect royalties on T-shirts, beer mugs, pennants and plastic figurines of himself. On the lucrative baseball-card show circuit, where one show promoter has clocked him signing his short name 600 times an hour, Rose earns as much as $20,000 an appearance. He was broke or unsentimental enough to sell the bat from his record 4,192nd hit.

So far, Rose has resisted the refuge of the Betty Ford defense, so popular among addicted celebrities, that his compulsion to gamble made him do it. But he could not resist dragging his family in. He said he had never looked forward to a birthday as much as his new daughter's first (August 22, 1990), since it would signal his first opportunity to apply for reinstatement to baseball, thus inadvertently revealing her place in his life relative to the game.

Whether or not Rose is voted into the Hall of Fame when he becomes eligible in 1992, he may have achieved the kind of immortality that goes beyond fading type in the record books. America may celebrate winning, but what really fascinates the country is a fall from greatness. Bill Buckner's fielding career is overshadowed by the memory of an easily hit ball rolling inexplicably, eternally, through his legs in the 10th inning of the sixth game of the 1986 World Series. Rose in his 24 seasons set records for hits (4,256), games played (3,562) and 200-plus-hit seasons (10). He was the National League's Most Valuable Player in 1973, the World Series MVP in 1975. He won the National League batting title three times.

But it is Rose's unfathomable squandering of his own ability, his willingness to surrender his history for the rush of the bet, that will make his memory endure beyond any portrait hanging in a gallery in Cooperstown.

In the end, it wasn't the courts, or a pointy-headed commissioner out to get him, or his bookie friends squealing on him, but just himself that took baseball from him.

September 4, 1989

A Bad Case of HEPBURN

"How dare you keep me waiting? Are you that stupid?"

Not a good beginning. Not good at all. An interview with Katharine Hepburn is not easy under the best of circumstances, even when her publisher has set it up to publicize the paperback release of her best-selling autobiography, *Me: Stories of My Life*. It is going to be awfully hard to ask what she was thinking of carrying on a 27-year affair with the married Spencer Tracy if she keeps her back turned to me the whole time. Apologies are definitely in order.

"I'm sorry I'm late, really I am."

"You are not sorry. You are stupid."

Well, 10 minutes late is unfortunate, yes, but a deal breaker?

"I've been waiting a half hour for you," she says, rounding up by 20 minutes the delay. "You're an idiot."

As a lifelong fan, I keep waiting for the comic heroine of *The Philadelphia Story* to enter. Wouldn't Tracy Lord have chastened Dexter with a blithe reprimand and moved on? If not humor, what about understanding and empathy? But these, the critics found, were the very qualities she had trouble conveying, which limited her to light comedies and, in later years, to playing starchy, irascible eccentrics. Hepburn was dogged for years by Dorothy Parker's famous put-down of her performance in the Broadway play *The Lake:* "Katharine Hepburn runs the gamut of emotion from A to B." If her parents, heirs to the Corning Glass fortune, had not bought her out of that flop and she had not secured the rights to *The Philadelphia Story*, she would not be summoning reporters to her house today.

She is so determined to be sure this effrontery does not go unpunished that she has forgotten the book altogether. Instead, like the college professor who fiddles endlessly with his pipe before explaining why you are flunking his course, Hepburn decides to tend the fire in the second-floor drawing room of her Manhattan town house, for which she says (later, when she is speaking) she was offered $2 million. I look around at her watercolors, the antique duck decoy, some African artifacts, and memorize the pattern in the Oriental rug while she slowly removes the screen from the fireplace, chucks in a couple of corn husks, stokes the embers a bit here and there and shoves the wood around.

Both of us are staring into the flames now and have yet to make eye contact. My regret at not having camped on her doorstep all night hangs heavy in the air. The silence gives us time to reflect: me on all the other times my lateness has been costly—a part in the sixth-grade pageant, a starting place on the field-hockey team; her to conjure up fondly her own perfect record of punctuality. "I've never been late once in all my years in the theater," she says. "Four hours. You should have allowed four hours. Anything less is dumb. I was 15 minutes early today."

Fifteen minutes early to your own house? At one time, she was known as arrogant and overbearing, with above-average narcissism and self-regard even for a young actress. But over time and with a few flops under her belt, she was supposed to have mellowed. "Adorable," "charming," are the words she uses to describe her gradual transformation.

"So why did they send someone from Washington, anyway?"

We've now spent more time on this inquisition than was eaten up by traffic at LaGuardia. Short of couples therapy, will nothing get us out of this trough? Maybe the Washington comment is a way out, a four-lane expressway to freedom.

"You're right. They should have sent a correspondent from New York. Let's reschedule, and someone who can be 15 minutes early will come."

Hepburn turns around and heads toward the window to close it. She has noticed how cold it is in here despite the roaring fire. "Well, you're here now, aren't you? Might as well sit down."

All this time, and a simple threat to leave was all that was needed to break the logjam. A bully respects a bully. In her book, Hepburn speaks candidly of being "totally selfish," "a me, me, me person." To Ludlow Ogden Smith, her husband of six years whose only mistake was that he loved her, she admits to being an "absolute pig." He tried everything to please her, went so far as to change his name so that she wouldn't be known as Kate Smith. "Isn't that the way it is?" She shrugs. "Luddy loved me and would do anything for me. I loved Spencer and would do anything for him. So often these things are unequal."

When asked how someone so full of rectitude could fall in love with a married man, she says, "You don't pick who you fall in love with. There are so few people to love. It's hard for one adult to even like another. Almost impossible." No argument there. But what about Spencer Tracy's wife, Louise, home with their deaf child? "We never lived together. He stayed in one house on George Cukor's estate, and I stayed in another nearby." Does that nicety of real estate explain why many members of the press came to romanticize her affair? "I never talked to them. Never. They could write what they wanted, but without any quotes from me, though. So they lost interest."

She offers lunch and I gratefully decline, in the interest of not being late for my next appointment. But she insists. "You kept me waiting so long, it's now lunchtime. I'm starving."

No one wants that. Better to be force-fed toasted ham and cheese than to give her cause to start up on the late thing again. She is in her trademark khakis ("Look at this hole, from gardening at Fenwick"), black turtleneck, sweater tied over her shoulders. The Gap should pay her royalties. "It was the only sensible way to dress. Anything else was silly. Fussing over clothes. Idiotic."

Hepburn calls Norah, her housekeeper who got the job, Hepburn recalls, because she did not sit until Hepburn did, with a loud grunt of the sort not heard outside a barnyard or a soccer match. "Eeuuuuuunhhhh!" A deep breath and another grunt. "Why," Hepburn turns to confide in me, "do they only hear you the second time?"

Finally, we are on the same side. I'm upstairs, Norah's downstairs. Hepburn has someone new in her sights. When dessert is slow in coming because Norah is waiting for the homemade Irish lace cookies to bake, Hepburn muses, "What do you think she is doing down there to that ice cream, making it?"

Hepburn still swims, "to be irritating," all year off Long Island Sound but points to a bum ankle that forces her to crawl over the rocks to get out of the water. "Imagine the obituary, Actress Drowns in Six Inches of Water." Only for a second do I imagine this. I ask her, generally, about dying. "No fear. I love to sleep. I picture it as just a good long sleep." She likes being alone. "I have such a great family that I haven't had much need for friends. Guests come for dinner at 6 and have to leave by 8."

After her divorce, she was involved with the agent Leland Hayward and Howard Hughes, but it was Tracy "who was on to her," who gave up nothing for her and who consequently won her devotion. She stopped doing everything that irked him, even altered "qualities which I personally valued. It did not matter. I changed them." Despite making it safe for women to wear pants, she is not a have-it-all feminist on the subject of children and career. "You can't do both. It's a choice. If you want a career, which I did, why bring a child into the world who won't get the benefit of your total attention? You can't concentrate on more than one thing at a time."

Hepburn is no more introspective in person than she was in her off-the-top-of-her-head, sentence-fragment memoir. Hepburn does not like people who "make a fuss." When she found her 16-year-old brother dead, hanging from the rafters by bedsheets, she cried later because it was expected of her. The apparent suicide was never discussed.

She waits until the last chapter to talk about Tracy, who she says initially believed the rumor that she was a lesbian. She never knew how he really felt about her and wonders now if she "should have straightened things out." He would have felt less guilt, and the divorce would have been "ennobling to [Louise]." Regrets? Only that she did not become a writer, because it is so easy. "No makeup. No costumes. I wrote in bed every morning. Whatever came into my head. Someone types it up, and you have a book. I have no idea what it says. I've never read it."

This, like wearing an old green raincoat fastened with a big safety pin to auditions to show that she didn't care whether they liked her or not, is something of a pose. There is an audiotape of her reciting *Me,* so she has read parts of it at least once.

She suddenly stands. "You have enough, I'm sure." As is her custom, she leaves without saying good-bye.

June 29, 1992

The Times of His Life
With a friendly exuberance, Arthur Sulzberger Jr. tries to put a younger face on his family paper

Someone who grows up with his own gas pump and dog cemetery, and is heir to the greatest newspaper dynasty in the country, has to work hard at being a regular guy. For Arthur Sulzberger Jr., who succeeded his father as publisher of *The New York Times,* this means taking public transportation, not owning a country house or a car and touring Europe by secondhand BSA 175 motorcycle. His signature sport is not golf or squash but rock climbing. The new *Star Trek* is his favorite program. He has taken on cleaning up Times Square and working at homeless shelters rather than organizing charity balls. If the restaurant choice is up to him, it is usually inexpensive and convenient to a subway stop.

But despite the camouflage, if he were taken prisoner by the *Daily News,* his cover would be blown when he couldn't recite the rules of stickball. His wardrobe is suspicious as well. With his double-breasted jackets, pink suspenders and purple-striped shirts, he dresses as if Paul Stuart grabbed him by the French cuffs when he was young and has not let go.

The burden to be like everyone else when he so obviously isn't requires immense energy and makes him seem hyperactive. That he engages so earnestly in the effort is one of the more endearing things about him. As Sulzberger returns by subway from jury duty, talking about it as a great adventure rather than an onerous task, he bounds into the company cafeteria for a late-afternoon yogurt and a chance to wave to a few troops. If there is a hand among the 300 in the newsroom he hasn't shaken, it is not for lack of trying. "I'm a journalist who gets off at the wrong floor now," he is fond of saying.

Unlike his father, who reportedly witnessed a fiery car crash at Le Mans and neglected to call the news desk, he knows his way around a notebook. While an undergraduate at Tufts, he worked at *The Boston Globe* and the *Vineyard Gazette*. After graduating, he worked at the *Raleigh Times* in North Carolina and the Associated Press in London before joining *The New York Times* as a reporter in the Washington bureau in 1978.

David Binder, his editor there, remembers him as "an invading army. He worked harder than anyone and had fun at it besides." No other cub reporter would have played along so willingly when Binder, trying to prevent Sulzberger from going home on time and spoiling a surprise birthday party, asked him to get quote after quote about the Panama Canal treaty. "I said, 'Arthur, why don't you call Ellsworth Bunker and see what he has to say?' Arthur got a quote from Bunker a few minutes later. Then I said, 'What about Averell Harriman?' He got a quote from him. Then another elder statesman, and another. Finally I let the guy go."

In 1980 Sulzberger moved to New York City and had to prove once again he was more than the boss's son. Columnist Anna Quindlen says, "From the moment he walked in the door, there were people desperately trying to dislike him. It proved to be impossible." He did everything but deliver the paper—and as night production manager, he came close to doing that. He covered city hall, then became an assignment editor, "the single most exhausting job I ever had." This was when he learned the importance of walking around, often without his shoes on, practicing his theory that participatory democracy is the best way to manage people. Says a Metro reporter: "I wasn't afraid of him, and I'm afraid of just about every other editor here."

Once Sulzberger became deputy publisher in 1988, he felt for the first time "the job was mine to lose." His confidence increased, and the Letter-manesque wise-guy side of his personality receded. Reporters noticed a deeper affection growing between him and his father, "Punch." One editor observed, "Arthur took on some of Punch's winning characteristics—his self-deprecating humor, his listening rather than talking." (He did not find it humorous, however, when people tried to stick him with the obvious diminutive "Pinch.") When, just after being named publisher, he said that it gave him comfort to know that his father would remain as company chairman and be there to counsel him, colleagues believed him.

Sulzberger leaps out of his chair in his 11th-floor office with its view of Broadway on the slightest pretext: checking with his secretary on whether he calls his father "Dad," "Punch" or "the chairman" (in public, it's "the chairman"); grabbing a book by a management guru he admires; pointing out the stand-up desk where he reads the paper at 7 each morning. At a birthday party at the 300-acre family estate in Connecticut (where the family dogs have their own memorial park), it poured all day, but, like a camp counselor with a shrill whistle, he insisted that everyone jump into the pool and play volleyball.

Some who lived through the "reign of terror" under executive editor A. M. Rosenthal say that Sulzberger's single greatest achievement has been instituting a philosophy that values people almost as much as their copy. "Fear is not the best way to get things done," he says. This works better on the business side, he admits, where he has been able to wipe out layers of middle management, and less well on the editorial side, where executive editor Max Frankel joked on the day Sulzberger was named publisher that the newsroom would remain a monarchy.

Nowhere has Sulzberger's expansive attitude been more apparent than in his treatment of gays. Rosenthal was called "homophobic" by the *Advocate* for refusing to use the term *gay* in print, among other things. One reporter lived in total secrecy, fearing the consequences if Rosenthal found out he was gay.

Sulzberger made a point of giving the *Advocate* his first interview after being named publisher, and he sent to the first national meeting of the National Lesbian and Gay Journalists Association a videotaped speech in which he supported domestic-partnership benefits at the *Times*. Jeffrey Schmalz, who covers politics for the *Times*, says Sulzberger clearly lets it be known that he won't tolerate discrimination. "I collapsed in the newsroom and went to the hospital with what later would be diagnosed as AIDS. Arthur checked up on me almost every day. When he saw me for the first time after that, at a book party, he walked straight across the room and gave me a big, long hug. That's how Arthur leads."

Unlike his father, who had his job thrust upon him at age 37 when his own father was paralyzed by a stroke, Sulzberger has followed a carefully calibrated path to the top. At the tender age of 14, he decided to leave his mother's house and go live with his father. He knows how hard that must have been on his mother, but, he says, "she didn't cry in my presence." He moved uptown to an elegant Fifth Avenue apartment that included his father's second wife, Carol, so demanding that she once told the wife of the Paris bureau chief to get the chintz curtains cleaned immediately. An adolescent boy, however well house trained, can seem like an invasion of Visigoths. "It wasn't easy for either of us," Sulzberger says, "but she handled it with great sophistication."

Shortly after that, Sulzberger had his only burst of rebellion, letting his hair grow long, wearing his father's old green Marine jacket on most occasions, and getting himself arrested in peace demonstrations. During Thanksgiving break from college, on a trip to Topeka to visit his mother and her third husband, he met his future wife, Gail Gregg, literally the girl next door. The two married in 1975 and shortly thereafter moved to London, where they worked for competing wire services. She often beat him on stories. Being related to a Sulzberger is not the best career move in New York unless you want to work at the *Times,* so Gregg decided to go to art school. She has a studio over a bagel shop and has a growing reputation as a serious painter.

They live well but not grandly in an apartment on the Upper West Side, where their two children go to private school. They socialize mainly with family and non-*Times*men. "When I moved to New York, I decided for my own mental health that my closest friends should be outside the *Times.* They can afford to be honest with me." This policy is not popular with colleagues who used to be close to him.

Sulzberger's biggest challenge is to attract to an old gray newspaper those who now get most of their news from MTV. The splashiest effort to pull in these twentysomething readers is Sunday's section, "Styles of the Times." When he unveiled it for the Washington bureau at a brown-bag lunch, Sulzberger joked that young readers had better like it because all the older ones would drop dead when they saw it.

Not dead, but perhaps a little numb, as the paper of record takes on a clothing store specializing in "bondage trousers," described as a lace-up crotch contraption for skinheads and dominatrices, or covers a smoke-filled party given by *High Times,* a magazine devoted to legalizing marijuana. The debut front-page piece, "The Arm Fetish," which analyzed "the body part as fashion accessory," was followed by others on "The Lipstick Wars" and health clubs (they're popular). Like an American abroad speaking slower and louder to be understood, the type is extra large and the sentences are extra short. The overall effect is of a grandmother squeezing into neon biking shorts after everyone else has moved on to long black skirts.

The section is evolving; it adds value for those who want to read it. "No one has to read the whole Sunday paper but me," says Sulzberger.

During the board meeting last January, at which his father announced that his son would get the keys to the kingdom, the drama was heightened when the famous clock on the Times Building suddenly went dark. Now it is ticking again, as Sulzberger gallops out of the building, talking about the new plant, covering Brooklyn as thoroughly as Beirut, the outer suburbs to conquer, Pulitzers to win. Without a sigh—he is not a sigher—he turns down 43rd Street to catch the bus and says, "I've got time."

August 17, 1992

My Dinner with Rush

"I've had 4,635 stories in which I was mentioned in the past year without giving any interviews," says Rush Limbaugh, who is definitely counting. Over a plate of shrimp, rigatoni and an assuming Bertani Catullo 1990, Limbaugh isn't happy to be doing this one with a "reporterette" who hasn't tuned in enough to know that he's moved off abortion and other social issues and is focusing on fiscal matters. He warned the new Republican Congress in December, "Some female reporter will come up to one of you and start batting her eyes and ask you to go to lunch and you'll think, 'Wow! . . . I've really made it.' Don't fall for this. . . . This is not the time to start trying to be liked."

No, it's not, as I found out at Patsy's, one of Rush's favorite Manhattan restaurants, which he enters through a side door. He's here against his better judgment, since the Mainstreamliberalpress insists on misunderstanding him. "I'm not a hater, not one of the angry radio guys. I'm an entertainer with a conservative agenda who wouldn't have 20 million listeners if I spewed venom. Yet you liberals lump me in with all the others," he says, lumping me in with all the others. This is surprising, since I have a history of giving Rush the benefit of the doubt—which he admits. But instead of finding him more sanguine about his place in the world—which is on top of it since his team swept the November elections—he is less so.

Could it be the bear market in liberal shibboleths? Without Joycelyn Elders, midnight basketball and the Hillary Rodham Clinton socialized-medicine task force, are the easy targets gone? Not at all. "Just look at Dick

Gephardt trying to run against Clinton for President, saying the way to get rid of welfare is to spend more on it, and coming up with a flatter tax than the Republicans," he says. "I tell people don't kill all the liberals, leave enough around so we can have two on every campus; living fossils, so we will never forget what these people stood for."

But, surely, people aren't going to tune in with the same amount of glee to hear Rush praise Newt, even approving the then $4.5 million book deal as a good example of capitalism. But he insists he's not cozying up to power. "I'm not friends with these people; I want to be free to criticize if need be, if they back off on term limits or a balanced budget." The new Speaker and Rush have spoken, he guesses, only "seven, eight times at the most." Rush has kept less distance from the new members, who have been called the "Dittohead Caucus" and dubbed him the "Majority Maker."

Rush after the revolution is much like Rush before the revolution, an outsider content to stay there because it gives him a clearer shot and because, after all this success, he still thinks he won't find acceptance on the inside. Rather than be part of the Speaker's festivities, he took the week off to golf in Hawaii. Unlike so many rich guys who have used their new fortunes to remake themselves with Fifth Avenue apartments, houses in the Hamptons and charity balls, he lives the kind of small-town life he would have lived had he stayed in Cape Girardeau, Missouri, only with more possibilities for ordering in ethnic food. After dinner, he is dropped off at a nondescript high-rise on the Upper West Side, with two bedrooms and no dining-room table. Having gone on numerous diets, he is now satisfied, he says, to "maintain" his current weight, which is one attitude the President might be sympathetic to. He doesn't go to museums, the theater or the movies. He prefers to buy videos rather than rent them, so he doesn't have to take them back. (His latest purchase was *Philadelphia*.) For a social life, he has "the Mosbachers—that's it as far as New York society goes—and they're friends." The one thing he likes about Manhattan is that everything can be delivered.

Lucky for him, he didn't have to go out to find his third wife, Marta, whom he met on CompuServe. They married last Memorial Day weekend at the home of Supreme Court Justice Clarence Thomas. The only time he gets really irritated is when he is reminded of his comment two years ago about whether, as a family-values kind of guy, he was interested in having a family. He replied he would think about it, after he had a wife. "So, yeah, now maybe I'm thinking about it," he snaps, "but what does that have to do with anything?"

The routine gets to him at times: the seven newspapers at 7:30 a.m., the relentlessness of being on. "Some days I don't care if anybody knows what I think. But you get up and do it, you're a pro. I defy you to tell me when I'm having one of those days."

He's definitely not having one of those days on Thursday, when he takes time out from celebrating his 44th birthday to broadcast his spin on my interview before it appears, criticizing me for trying to get him to criticize Newt, criticizing me for not criticizing the Democrats, criticizing me for being a reporter. "I tell you, folks, it's another glorious reason why you're fortunate to have me as your host because the real story here is how the Democrats are falling apart, and you will not find this in the Mainstream-liberalpress."

January 23, 1995

Newt's Bad Old Days

When Newt Gingrich was fighting his way through a horde of reporters into Border Books in Phoenix, Ariz., last Wednesday, it didn't take too much imagination to reduce the temperature by 70 degrees, raze the palm trees and picture another gray-haired politician caught in press gridlock in Manchester, N.H., in 1992, right after Gennifer Flowers made her charges against then Governor Bill Clinton.

Now it's Gingrich's turn, and it's Anne Manning, a former campaign worker claiming in *Vanity Fair* magazine that she had an affair with Gingrich while he was married to his first wife. In the current climate, that's all it takes to open the door to the kind of microscopic scrutiny politicians from Gary Hart to Bob Packwood have endured. At first Gingrich quipped Gipperlike that he couldn't hear the questions, then he refused to respond to anything in the article; finally, he resorted to calling a reporter "obnoxious." The next morning, in a radio interview, he suggested that Manning is politically motivated. "I knew . . . if we're going to have a revolution to replace the welfare state, we better expect those people who love it to throw the kitchen sink at us."

Manning—who said she had spoken to *Vanity Fair* because when Gingrich "talks about family values and acts righteous about stuff like that, it just gets my back up"—is hardly a shill for the American welfare state, nor are Gingrich's former campaign treasurer and another aide who both went on the record with Sheehy about Gingrich's various affairs, but never mind.

Stonewalling the press in matters sexual often works, but it doesn't stop the frenzy of interest, which is particularly high when the person in question has set himself up as the putative leader of the family-values revolution. He even blamed Susan Smith's drowning her children on the Democrats' ethics, until it was revealed that Smith's stepfather was a leader of the local Christian Coalition.

In his book, Gingrich rails against sex outside marriage and celebrates family life. Although his own life is closer to *Playboy*, he pines for the morals of the '50s as specifically portrayed in the pages of *Reader's Digest* and the *Saturday Evening Post* from 1955.

Neither has much in common with *Vanity Fair*, which is one reason Gingrich likes them. Some troubling realities of that era, such as segregation, were not acknowledged amid the heartwarming Americana served up by the *Digest*, which featured "Unforgettable Characters" (an Arctic explorer), animals ("What Snakes Are Really Like") and business derring-do ("Dr. Geiger's Little Magic Box"). In this well-ordered world, mothers stayed home and fathers, who smoked Lucky Strikes, worked. They worried about their daughters going off on dates and about the menace of Red China, but not much else.

Not only was this gauzy portrait of America misleading (births to teenagers reached record highs in the mid-'50s, unsurpassed even now, and a third of marriages ended in divorce), but it especially wasn't like that for Newt Gingrich. His grandfather was born out of wedlock and raised in a household in which his real mother posed as his sister. His father was a Navy man who left right after Newtie was born and who later allowed him to be adopted by his stepfather in exchange for not having to pay child support. Newt's mother, Kit, said in the interview that she is manic-depressive. The senior Gingrich proudly recounts smashing Newtie against the wall when he was 15. Gingrich's half-sister, a lesbian activist, is writing a book about all this for Scribner's.

As for Gingrich's adult relationships, the *Saturday Evening Post* would never have printed this story, either. His first marriage to his high school math teacher ended bitterly when it was reported that he visited his estranged wife's hospital room after her surgery for uterine cancer to discuss the terms of their divorce. He had to be pursued for adequate child-support payments, although he writes in his book that "any male who doesn't support his children is a bum." In a 1978 congressional campaign against Virginia Shafard, Gingrich, the "moral standards" candidate, charged that if she won, she would leave her family behind in Georgia. He won and left his family behind in Georgia.

These days, he spends far more time with Calista Bisek, a former congressional aide, and Arianna Huffington, who hosted a $50,000-a-plate dinner for him, than with his second wife, Marianne, who has never actually moved to Washington and who has been candid about their marriage's being "on and off." Newt once gave the marriage 53-to-47 odds of lasting— and that was before Marianne said she wasn't going to stand by her man if he decided to run for President. "He can't do it without me," she told *Vanity Fair*, and if he does, "I just go on the air the next day and I undermine everything."

In fact, the only factor that might allow Gingrich to overcome his own "family" problems, if he does run, is that Bob Dole, Phil Gramm and Pete Wilson also left their first wives. And that's the stuff of *Vanity Fair*.

August 21, 1995

Alas, Poor Gingrich, I Knew Him Well

All ego and scapegoating, he had no one to blame but himself in the end

Newt is not going to miss me, but I'm going to miss him: his knowledge of Prussian history, his unerring sense of what the Duke of Wellington would do in any situation, his grandiose sense of walking in the boots of Winston Churchill. A global visionary, he wrote he was going to "articulate the vision of civilizing humanity" and, when that was done, "define, plan and begin to organize the movement . . . to help people . . . pursue happiness."

The speakership has affected him like a camera: it added 30 lbs. to his girth and 60 lbs. to his ego. After a trip to Asia, he came back and bragged that Mongolians in yurts were devotees of his Republican revolution. At the center of the cosmological charts he doodled was, no surprise, himself. Former Congresswoman Susan Molinari wrote that Newt told her "I get up every morning and say to myself, 'This is the day I shall die.' "

Friday was the day he died a Washington death, becoming just a guy in a suburban tract house in Marietta, Ga., carrying out the trash. With Nixonian petulance, he rejected suggestions that his party tanked because he had put all its eggs in Monica's basket. No, he said, it wasn't him, it was the media's "All Monica All the Time" madness that kept him from getting his message out. He woke up Wednesday morning but still didn't smell the coffee. He told Katie Couric on the *Today* show, "Look at all the hours that Tim Russert spent . . . on [Monica] vs. the number of hours on Social Security."

A quick check with Russert reveals that he offered Gingrich the entire hour of *Meet the Press* the Sunday before the election to discuss—you guessed it—Social Security, along with tax cuts, the budget and education. Gingrich declined. In truth, it was fear of increasing scandal fatigue that prompted Gingrich's biggest blunder of the campaign: devising, testing and spending $10 million on TV spots reminding voters of what a snake the President was—a subject the electorate was trying to forget.

What else was there to do but grasp at scapegoats when, in the blink of an eye, the discussion moved from "Can Clinton Survive?" to whether you can. At the time the intern story broke in January, Gingrich's revolution was sputtering. Gingrich looked to Monica as his deliverance from having to come up with a new, new Republican revolution. Oh, the eager, summer-in-Washington look of her, the goofy beret, those chubby cheeks. And a presidential embrace captured on videotape! At last all that heat he endured for shutting down the government was paying off: interns had to fill in for paid staff, and one of them wore thong underwear.

November 16, 1998

They're Shocked, Shocked!

The Washington press corps feigned surprise that radio host Don Imus offended the President, the First Lady, Speaker Newt Gingrich and others at the Radio & TV Correspondents Dinner last Thursday night. There were some funny moments, and intermittent silences, as Imus, the evening's emcee, took jabs at the Speaker's gay half-sister, Clinton's alleged extra-marital activities, Senator Bob Kerrey's artificial leg, and offered X-rated details of a TV journalist's marital difficulties. Imus went easier on people who visit his show (Tim Russert, Bob Dole, Cokie Roberts) than on those who don't, such as Bernard Shaw (an anchor desk away from going postal) and George Will ("the kind of guy who dresses up on weekends in clothes that make him feel pretty"). The press asked for what it got. Just like the White House Correspondents Dinner later in the spring, this affair seeks out performers to act as surrogates to tweak, if not debase, people in power.

But for the first time, the correspondents association sent a formal letter of apology to the President. "What did the organization think they were getting when they invited Imus? I fault them," said Tom Brokaw. ABC's Jackie Judd, one of the dinner's organizers, said, "We wanted some discomfort, but not that much." After the show, White House press secretary Michael McCurry called C-SPAN to ask that it not re-air the event. In a press release C-SPAN countered that the public had a right to see "what all this fuss is about." ABC's Cokie Roberts, an Imus regular, said, "He always separates his raunchiness from the political part of his show. I thought he would have sense enough to do the same here. Now none of us can go on his show again."

Roberts was one of the few who would go on record; the others fear reprisals. "Imus can trash you for a solid week," a network correspondent said. Imus says he followed his only instructions, which were to make fun of everybody and tell no organ jokes. "Did they expect me to say one thing on the radio and then go to Washington and be a weasel? When the First Lady laughed at my opening, I thought I was home free." He didn't know that a few sex jokes later, NPR's Elizabeth Arnold whispered to Mrs. Clinton that she would join her if Hillary wanted to leave. The First Lady hung in: she's heard worse.

April 1, 1996

The General's Next Campaign

Colin Powell finds a cause worthy of his star power—calling on America to volunteer

Presidents are expected to do good works at the end of their term, except perhaps for Gerald Ford, whose wife does that for him while he plays celebrity golf. But General Colin Powell is going through the process in reverse. Having postponed running for President, he is channeling his immense popularity into promoting volunteerism. He will serve as general chairman of the Presidents' Summit for America's Future, which kicks off with an Olympian opening ceremony in Philadelphia on April 27. Joining him on the steps of Independence Hall will be co-chairmen Bill Clinton and George Bush. (Jimmy Carter and Gerald Ford will also appear during the three-day event.)

It's hard to think of a better use of celebrity than inspiring the rest of us to get off our collective duff. But the project is not without some risk. We all know what the road to hell is paved with. And Powell's crusade could be seen as giving succor to Republicans who would like to leave it to volunteers to reweave the tattered safety net. "Nonsense," he says. "This is no replacement for government help. We're partners." Waving toward the capital skyline outside the window of his suburban office, he adds, "It's hard to cut the politics out of things in this wonderful town of ours. But this is not a bipartisan effort; it's nonpartisan."

Powell wasn't an easy hire. Since his decision not to run, a lot of people have wondered what it would take to get the general out of semiretirement, off the phone (he is a well-known phone and fax abuser) and away from the mail (he answers every letter). Even his wife, Alma, was thinking he ought to get out of the basement more. He had a stack of offers from corporate boards, foundations and academia that if laid end to end would circle the Pentagon and make the Republican who actually did run weep. Then Ray Chambers, a philanthropist who has devoted the past decade to salvaging kids in Newark, N.J., asked Powell to look at an idea to convene a national, star-studded event to promote volunteerism.

Powell (a board member of the United Negro College Fund, Howard University, the Boys & Girls Clubs of America and Gulfstream Aerospace Corp.) is actually Powell Inc., which he runs from his house in McLean, Va., and a boxy little office nearby that's decorated with Army memorabilia, a print of Teddy Roosevelt charging San Juan Hill and a collection of gimme coffee mugs.

Powell has merged his vocation with his avocation: wherever he's invited to speak for big fees, he gives second or third speeches to local community groups. In Scottsdale, Ariz., at a Boys & Girls Club, the kids had questions for him. What size shoe does he wear (12EE), and would he do the Macarena with them? Even if it weren't the official dance of the Democratic Party, Powell, as a notoriously bad dancer, would have been reluctant. He noted there was no music, but the children made some, and he gamely flailed his arms.

For Powell, the challenge isn't to attract offers—he gets a plastic Postal Service bin full of letters each day. The challenge is to separate the ideas that will work from other well-meaning but impractical ones.

Even in the leanest machine, it's hard to avoid such accoutrements of the '90s as logo-design consultants, glossy blue press packets and focus groups that mall-test key words to see which ones grab people's attention. Deaver's p.r. firm, Edelman Public Relations Worldwide, is billing its services at a 20% discount; Deaver is donating his. Powell is not going to put up with the kind of waste made notorious by charity balls and the United Way scandal, in which money was spent to raise more money and lavished on salary and perks. Powell takes no salary.

Before the launch of the project, Powell has already made volunteerism safe for Real Men, rescuing it from its second-class status as women's work. And his timing is impeccable. As politics declines ever further, he has taken on the task of revitalizing civic life, which if successful will only raise the clamor for him to salvage politics as well. Perhaps the odor will get so bad that the presidency will be virtually handed to him, a four-star general of his own all-volunteer army.

March 17, 1997

Once Again on the March
Colin Powell fixed his crusade by working harder and altering his alliances

Colin Powell can do just about anything he wants. He could run for President, run a Fortune 500 corporation, a university or a foundation. The publisher of his best-selling autobiography, *My American Journey,* is begging him to write another. The crate of mail he gets each day is heavy with offers. My favorite is an offer to make a quick million by penning *Chicken Soup for the Black Soul.*

He assures me he won't be turning out an instant chicken-soup book or throwing his name into the presidential or vice-presidential ring. What Powell chooses to do instead is continue to run America's Promise, his "crusade" to enlist corporations, government, nonprofit organizations and millions of citizens into giving every child at risk a chance. Celebrating its second anniversary, America's Promise is on its way to surpassing its pledge to help "2 million kids by 2000." To get away from the mushy anecdotal indices of success, Powell got the accounting firm of PriceWaterhouseCoopers (it volunteered) to evaluate the second year's effort. The firm sampled 91 of the 441 commitments made in 14,000 places and found that 10.3 million children had been "touched," which means served by a "promise partner." The dollar value of the commitments was $295.5 million.

Not a bad showing for someone operating on a shoeshine and a smile, moral suasion and optimism. I was among the skeptics who thought America's Promise couldn't live up to its opening day, when the President, Vice President, all the former Presidents except Ronald Reagan, along with 38 Governors and 100 Mayors and celebs like Oprah Winfrey, gathered at Independence Hall in Philadelphia. Was volunteerism going to be cool? Not just little old ladies with time on their hands but also people in their prime taking precious moments away from their cell phones and Stair-Masters?

That was the plan, but America's Promise hit a few bumps. For weeks the phones were on the fritz, and there were too few people to handle too many offers to help. Powell discovered he is America's Promise. Powell saw that he would need to increase from a quarter of his time to well over half. Wherever he goes, corporate moguls drool over him (and pay dearly—upward of $50,000 per speech—for the opportunity), but it is kids who get him for free who really light him up. As he sings along with a heartrendingly mangled rendition of "America, the Beautiful" by students playing with instruments donated by VH1, the unsentimental general gets misty-eyed. At Colin Powell Elementary School in Grand Prairie, Tex., the kids wanted to talk about the mystery of how those two boys at Columbine with their BMW and pampered lives could have become so hopeless. A child asked the general if he ever got sad. "Something makes me sad every day," he answered, and said that helping others is the best way to work yourself out of it, that if those two lost souls in Littleton had coached a soccer team, visited a hospital, come face-to-face with someone else's little miseries, they might not have "descended into hell." He said, "I don't know a 16-year-old who doesn't have something to give a 9-year-old."

As a journalist, I want to find something to quibble over. Just when I think Powell might be all work and no play, he takes off his standard dark suit for a black T-shirt, a white sport coat and shades and sings "Yakety Yak" at the annual fund-raiser of Best Friends, which tries to keep young girls from drugs and sex with special classes and after-school activities. (His wife, Alma, is on the board.) Spend time with Colin Powell and you can't help thinking, Shouldn't someone this energetic, this smart, this decent, be running for President.

I'd always wondered how Republicans got so lucky as to get the general on their team. It was Democrats, after all, who pushed through legislation ending the discrimination he recalled so movingly, in which he was denied meals at restaurants in the South and forced to drive through several states without being able to stop to use public bathrooms. At a packed press conference in 1995, Powell relieved Democrats with his decision not to run for President (polls showed him handily defeating Bill Clinton) but devastated them with the announcement of his party affiliation. He said he was a Republican because he liked limited government, fiscal prudence and individual enterprise. I think it's also because he came of age in Republican administrations, ending up Chairman of the Joint Chiefs of Staff. To a military man, Democrats are just too messy.

This is how persuasive he is: I got myself down to the District Building to get my police clearance (it took two days; there must be a Margaret Carlson with a rap sheet) so that I could become a volunteer at the Boys & Girls Club. It's the Powell Doctrine of overwhelming force, conquering one couch potato at a time.

May 24, 1999

Oh Say, Can You Sing It?
No, but this is the home of the brave try

Just before Muhammad Ali and Sonny Liston fought for the heavyweight boxing crown in 1965, baritone Robert Goulet lost his preliminary bout with "The Star-Spangled Banner." He made it flawlessly through the first several lines before losing his grip on the lyrics. He later blamed his Canadian upbringing for having to hum the rest before thousands of fight fans and a closed-circuit television audience.

Though it is blared, crooned, strummed, tooted and mumbled thousands of times a year, "The Star-Spangled Banner" is a song almost no one gets exactly right. Some musicians, historians and public officials would like to replace it and Indiana Congressman Andrew Jacobs has introduced a bill that would change the national anthem to the more easily warbled "America, the Beautiful." Critics deride the "Banner" 's lyrics, written by Francis Scott Key after the British assault on Baltimore in 1814, as difficult to memorize, warmongering, and insulting to America's staunchest ally. They also claim that the music is derived from a drinking song popularized at London's Crown and Anchor Tavern. The tune's highs and lows are, well, too high and low. Bass-baritone George London contended the "Banner" is "impossible to sing if you're sober." Opera singers have the best chance to cover the octave plus a fifth. But the soprano who starts a half-note too high will shatter glass and her hopes of auditioning for the Met by the time she gets to the "land of the free." She can forget getting deep enough for the "twilight's last gleaming."

The anthem runs deep in American life, a fixture wherever fireworks explode or a ball is tossed. Although Congress did not make the "Banner" the nation's official anthem until 1931, the military began playing it at ceremonies as far back as 1898. It made its Major League Baseball debut in Chicago during the 1918 World Series, when the band struck it up for no apparent reason and Babe Ruth and the crowd stood at attention. Now it is played before everything from Pee Wee hockey to the Super Bowl.

To put audiences out of their pregame misery, many stadiums resort to canned versions of error-free performances by the Mormon Tabernacle Choir, Robert Merrill (called the "Star-Spangled Baritone" for his ubiquity on the anthem-singing circuit) and the Johnny Mann Singers. But a taped version takes away the thrill of victory and the agony of defeat inherent in every live performance, as well as the singers' inalienable right to get it wrong. Country-and-western star Johnny Paycheck, crooning before Atlanta Falcons fans, faked his way through several lines: "Oh, say can you see, it's cloudy at night / What so loudly we sang as the daylight's last cleaning." An immigrant Hungarian opera singer performing at a benefit showed Yankee ingenuity when he drew on the clichés of his adopted land, belting out, "Bombs bursting in air, George Washington was there." A former Miss Bloomington, Minn., blew her chance to break into the big time when she blew the anthem before a Minnesota Twins game. By the time she got to the "land of the free," she was in the land of the hopelessly confused. "Aw, nuts," she muttered into the microphone, and gave up.

Live performances also provide the chance to make musical history. Singer Jose Feliciano ensured his place in the anthem hall of fame after his bluesy Latin interpretation at the 1968 World Series in Detroit, ending the song with "Oh, yeah." RCA Records pressed a single of it the next day. After that, performers strained to put their personal stamp on the anthem: Lou Rawls (languorous jazz), Aretha Franklin (Motown), Al Hirt (Dixieland) and Frank Sinatra (moody lounge lizard). The prize for the most ear-bending version goes to Jimi Hendrix's screeching finale at Woodstock.

Molto allegro is the desired pace for most performances, to cut down on fan fidgeting and player awkwardness, especially if the game is televised. In 1977 Fenway Park organist John Kiley became an anthem legend for coming in at a snappy 51 seconds. That is still not fast enough for ABC Sports. "The goal," says former producer Dorrance Smith, "is to cut away to a commercial." He didn't have his finger on the mute button during the 1978 World Series in Yankee Stadium, when Pearl Bailey dragged out the song to a record-breaking 2:28.

Like democracy, the "Banner" looks best when compared with its alternatives. "Amber waves of grain" may be more peaceable than "bombs bursting in air," but "America, the Beautiful" lacks drama. "My Country 'Tis of Thee" was stolen, note for note, from the British national anthem, "God Save the Queen." And "God Bless America" has obvious problems with the separation of church and state, but it has de facto status as the anthem of the

Philadelphia Flyers, who won the Stanley Cup in 1974 after Kate Smith inspired them with the ode to the land that she loved. Still trotted out for big
games courtesy of videotape, the late Kate has compiled an enviable lifetime
(and thereafter) record with the Flyers of 58 wins, 12 losses, 3 ties.

If winning were everything, "God Bless America" might carry the day.
Anyone can belt out a respectable version. "America, the Beautiful" is not
much challenge either. But Americans have been gamely trying to master
"The Star-Spangled Banner" without quite overcoming it for 175 years. In
a world that changes every day, that's worth more than lovable lyrics and a
manageable melody.

February 12, 1990

Saddam Made Me Do It

The practice may have begun at a private school in Washington, when a
group of 10th-graders did poorly on a math test. When the results came
back, the class asked the teacher for a makeup exam, explaining how unfair
it was to quiz them on the morning after the first missile attack of the war.
They had lost too much sleep watching CNN the night before.

Children were among the first to see the possibilities in blaming Saddam. They were encouraged by Mister Rogers, who left his beautiful neighborhood to reassure the young during prime time that it was O.K.—indeed,
it showed a certain precocious sensitivity—to be upset about the bombing
in Baghdad. The hand-wringing makes it seem that children have not managed to get through wars before and that death is something that can be understood, if only enough network anchors and child psychologists take to
the airwaves to explain it. Your average child, who sees more explicit violence on Saturday-morning cartoons than footage from Desert Storm, is
not likely to remain alarmed too long over anything that justifies increased
television-watching and provides air cover for a variety of mischief.

Soon, the possibilities in "the Scud ate my homework" spread to those
old enough to know better. True, war is hell for those who fight it, but can
be a handy excuse for those who don't. Adults began invoking it with an ingenuity and appetite that their offspring could only dream about. The Persian Gulf was invoked as a cause of the recession—or as President Bush is
fond of calling it, the temporary interruption in the longest economic expansion in history. Likewise for the two-week closing of the Folies Bergere

in Paris, John McEnroe's dropping out of a tennis match in Milan, the pricing of the video release of *Ghosts* at $100 instead of $19.95 and the New York Giants' refusal to take part in Mayor David Dinkins' Super Bowl victory celebration.

The widespread appeal of blaming Saddam is partly explained by its one-size-fits-all quality. But it also has other attributes prized by veteran excuse makers: it's simple, requiring no complicated, tongue-tying explanation, universally understood, vaguely virtuous and hard to check. War, as the talking heads point out, has unintended consequences, and who's to say having to pay almost twice as much since late January to fly from Chicago to Miami isn't one of them. What corporation worth its public relations department would want to be heard temporizing with an old saw like "The check is in the mail" when a fresh Desert Storm excuse is handy? Trans World Airlines, plagued by high debt and slow traffic since it was purchased in 1986 by Carl Icahn, cited the Persian Gulf in announcing that it would not be making $75.5 million in scheduled payments to bondholders in February. As for the dismal performance of retailers over Christmas, who could think thigh-high hemlines or sticker shock over $100 cotton sweaters and $200 tennis shoes and not combat jitters held consumers back?

Certain linkage is now predictable. In whichever direction the stock market goes and whether it gets there in light, heavy or moderate trading, it does so because of the situation in the Middle East. And the weatherman can hardly get to the local forecast, he's so busy reporting the barometric pressure in Dhahran. But there is still some admirable originality at work: On the day before he was to make a $2.5 million payment to promoters of the George Foreman–Evander Holyfield heavyweight championship, Donald Trump artfully invoked a boilerplate "war clause" in his contract to change the location of one of his Atlantic City casinos. The ploy is unlikely to succeed unless Saddam bombs the boardwalk. Similarly, Sugar Ray Leonard dragged the troops in Saudi Arabia into an interview last Tuesday about why only 4,000 of the 18,000 tickets to last Saturday's championship bout at Madison Square Garden had been sold. He neglected to mention his age (34), string of phony retirements and the obscurity of his opponent, best known for wearing an earring.

If an over-the-hill fighter can make hay out of the war, imagine what archetypal villains of '80s excess like Leona Helmsley and Michael Milken could have done had hostilities broken out a few years earlier. Where was the Persian Gulf when the Keating Five needed it, when the Boston Red Sox lost the American League play-offs in four straight games? Only the oil companies are at pains to avoid linkage. Since Saddam invaded Kuwait, the industry has had a huge surge in earnings. Chevron, which made 2½ times as much in last year's fourth quarter as in 1989's, attributed the uptick to an unspecified "aberration."

If America is lucky it won't have the war to hide behind much longer. In the meantime, certain rules of engagement in the blame game are being codified. As long as there are men and women serving in the Gulf, no one in government, the military, CNN or the take-out pizza business has to apologize for being late, leaving early or canceling out altogether on any non-work-related event, and that includes cocktail-party fund-raisers, rehearsal dinners and dental surgery. As for print journalists, well, a Scud ate the last three lines of this story.

February 18, 1991

And Then There Was One

They were so close, Caroline and her brother, John. When Caroline got married, John gave the first toast: "All my life there has just been the three of us—Mommy, Caroline and I . . ."

And now there is only one of that trio that faced a life so peculiar that only they could understand one another. "They rarely made a decision without checking with the other," said a board member of Harvard's Kennedy School. Jackie sheltered them from the garish glare. "I don't want my children to live here anymore," she said in anguish after Bobby's assassination, fearing America's violence. She was also wary of the immense pull of the hyperactive clan and the demons that came with it. Historian Doris Kearns Goodwin told Jackie at Caroline's wedding how striking the closeness between her two children was, and Jackie said, "It's the best thing I've ever done." They were the matron of honor and best man at each other's weddings, a pillar in each other's lives and that of the country, dividing the labor of carrying on their father's legacy: Caroline taking the library, John the Kennedy School. But as close as they were, they were also very different. If John was an Adonis, she was pretty in that Irish way, all teeth and wavy hair and good healthy vigor. They both worried about how to have a meaningful life in a fishbowl, but John would lead a life that required he bat away the paparazzi while Caroline would have a life in which she could walk her children to school and answer her own phone. She would even intellectualize the quest for privacy in a book on the First Amendment, *In Our Defense*. While John had an effervescent star quality, a glamour about him and his stylish wife, Caroline was incandescent, without a trace of glitz, but glowing from within. She was entirely free of the resentment that attaches to the famous. She never took its perks or used its privileges except in service of the family. After John's smashing performance at the Democratic Convention in 1988, she was asked to serve as chairwoman of the convention in 1992, and she spurned the offer few would have turned down. She more purely embodied her mother's passions: not politics, which was passing, but arts and culture, which were lasting.

If it was hard to be the son of J.F.K., imagine how hard it is to be the daughter of the valiant widow. Caroline had some of the remote, mysterious quality of her mother. When I met her for the first time, I expected to hear that whisper, see a will-o'-the-wisp, but found instead someone with a firm voice, self-possessed and with a day-to-dayness about her. You could picture that she could make her way in Manhattan, hailing taxis and going to the movies and taking her children for ice cream in Central Park, without causing a fuss.

Caroline seemed to subsume her mother, taking up her passions of horse riding and ballet and books. Jackie wanted her children to be serious. She had the historians and intellectuals to dinner, not the crowd from Mortimer's. Barbara Gibson, Rose Kennedy's secretary, remembers Caroline as preternaturally poised and calm. "Caroline was the most trustworthy. I would lend her my car."

Caroline was a good student, attending the Concord Academy, Radcliffe and Columbia Law School. She landed a job at the Metropolitan Museum of Art, which her mother loved and lived across the street from. She rented an apartment on the West Side with three roommates. She partied ever so lightly and dated a writer for two years before meeting an older man, Edwin Schlossberg, an eclectically brilliant polymath, an author and museum designer, whom her mother adored. Schlossberg was 13 years older than Caroline, almost the same age difference between Jack and Jackie. She had as private a wedding as a Kennedy could have, registering her Luneville Old Strasbourg china at Bloomingdale's, marrying at a small Catholic church on the Cape, her cousin Maria Shriver as her matron of honor.

"The best way to get John to do something," said a Kennedy staff member, "was to get Caroline to ask him." At one of their last appearances together, a dinner at the Kennedy Library for J.F.K.'s birthday, a library patron was struck by how happy the two children and their spouses were taking up where Jackie left off. "At the end of dinner, Carolyn was sitting on John's lap. And there were Ed and Caroline, leaning into each other, catching each other's eyes."

As much as Caroline loved her aunts and uncles and cousins, she had chosen last weekend to go rafting out West with her husband and three children. It's hard to picture her bucking herself up in the Kennedy way, throwing herself into games of touch football, sailing off the Cape. She will instead fall back on what her mother so carefully passed along—her normalcy and wholeness—and something her mother never thought she would have needed: the strength to bury someone you love way too soon.

July 26, 1999

What Does Gary Condit Know?

A Congressman is stubbornly silent about a "good friend" now missing

For more than a month, Washington has been intrigued by two missing persons. First came the Missing Intern, Chandra Levy, 24, last seen April 30, when she closed out her membership at a D.C. health club. She hasn't been heard from since she e-mailed her parents on May 1 about flights home for her graduation from the University of Southern California. When her parents couldn't reach her for five days, they called the D.C. police, who entered Chandra's Dupont Circle apartment on May 10. They found no signs of a struggle and everything in order—a packed suitcase, purse and credit cards, a fridge empty except for leftover pasta and a candy bar. Only her keys were gone. The door was locked, as if she had run out quickly.

As Chandra's mother tried to find her daughter, she ended up talking to Washington's other missing person—the Disappearing Congressman. After getting hold of Chandra's cell-phone records in late May and seeing about 20 calls to the same number, Susan Levy dialed it, listened to the soft music and instructions to punch in her number. When she did, she says, she wasn't surprised that California Representative Gary Condit phoned back—she was almost certain his relationship with her daughter was more than professional. But Condit was surprised. They spoke briefly and awkwardly and haven't spoken since.

Condit slipped out of sight about May 10, avoiding reporters who had staked out his office and his apartment in the Adams-Morgan section of Washington. The married Democrat, 53, has not said a word publicly but has issued written statements through his staff. In the first statement, Condit called Chandra a "good friend" and pledged a $10,000 reward from his campaign treasury for her return. Condit has demanded a retraction of a story that the police have evidence Chandra stayed at his apartment. But he doesn't deny that Chandra visited his apartment, only that he didn't tell police she did.

Investigators have all but dismissed suicide or that she ran away (not for six weeks without a trace). Yet they have no evidence of foul play. If there's been a crime, it's a perfect one, so far.

After saying little publicly about Condit for a month, the Levys are now frantic. They believe investigators, obliged to follow special procedures when dealing with a member of Congress (will that be one pair of kid gloves or two?), may not have pressed Condit sufficiently.

Like would-be starlets in Hollywood, interns come to Washington with big dreams and a hunger to be noticed. Monica's neediness and naiveté weren't an aberration. As Clinton was, Condit could be a politician capable of surviving the infatuation of an intern getting out of hand—if that's what happened. Condit is a retail guy in his home district, so sensitive to his constituents' needs that he helps them find apartments in D.C. Unable to say no, he had as many as 10 interns on staff one summer. A workhorse on the Agriculture Committee, he serves the farmers of Modesto, a town of pickups and soda fountains where *American Graffiti* was filmed. He does it so well he routinely wins re-election by close to 70% and was considering a run for statewide office. His district is conservative but hasn't balked at a lifestyle that's surprising for the son of a Baptist minister. His wife, who suffers from a chronic illness, has never moved to Washington. He likes night spots, parties, stogies and rock concerts (he once jumped into a mosh pit). A Harley driver, he posed for raunchy biker magazine *Easyriders* and a calendar called "Hunks on the Hill."

Most of the things folks in Washington fight over are trivial; we don't know what to do when we come up against a matter of life and death. If Chandra was a good friend, wouldn't Condit be more stricken? Isn't he betraying whatever friendship they had by not volunteering every detail about their relationship? The only way his conduct makes sense is if he's slavishly heeding the advice of all criminal attorneys: Say nothing, for it could be used against you.

To paraphrase former Louisiana Governor Edwin Edwards, it takes being caught in bed with a dead girl or a live boy to get a politician in trouble, and that's doubly true in the Age of Monica. There's no evidence that Condit is connected with Chandra's disappearance, but there is a lot of evidence that he is connected to her. Once Chandra went missing, he had an obligation to tell everything he knew about her in a timely way. While the Levys are searching for the daughter they pray is still alive, Condit seems intent on searching for a way out of being embarrassed. A decent man would call the Levys. Their number is on his pager.

June 25, 2001 and July 2, 2001

Three More Months! Three More Months!

I love Rudy. In this I'm not alone. He walks around the city as godlike as a mortal can be. The families of the fallen cling to him. Workers pulling grim double shifts at ground zero get a second wind when he visits. At opening night at the Metropolitan Opera, he gets an ovation Pavarotti would envy. He brings David Letterman to tears and a *Saturday Night Live* audience to life, telling people it's O.K. to laugh again.

So let's forgive Rudy Giuliani for thinking he should be Mayor for Life. But let's also think twice before crowning him. By last Monday, Giuliani had made up his mind that the city couldn't get by without him. He decided to persuade the state legislature to overturn term limits and to seek a third term on the Conservative Party ballot. Friends, especially his companion, Judith Nathan, had convinced him that voters were so grateful they wouldn't mind messing with the electoral laws. But just before his press conference that day, other voices intruded. His friend John McCain warned that the effort to change the rules would diminish Giuliani, make him just another politician. It would revive memories, McCain predicted, of all those "past mistakes, earned and unearned." Who would want to go back to the days of Giuliani's other wars—against street vendors, schools chancellors, art exhibits, political opponents and anyone else who disagreed with him, including his estranged wife, Donna Hanover? Giuliani took McCain's advice to heart—until last Tuesday's primary, when he got 15% of the vote, all from write-in ballots, which are more trouble to fill out than Palm Beach butterflies. On Wednesday, Giuliani summoned the three leading mayoral candidates to his makeshift office at the emergency operations center at Pier 92. There, surrounded by talismans—a picture of Churchill walking through London during the Blitz, a dust-caked mask from his near death experience in the shadow of the crumbling Twin Towers, and a large Tupperware container of Wheaties—Giuliani shook the candidates down: Either agree to give him three extra months in office, he said, or he'd run against them, and win. Well, one thing is for sure: If Rudy is finding time for power politics, things must be getting back to normal.

Giuliani could well win. But the law says he can't run. And the law has always been bigger than any one man, no matter how devastating the crisis. In 1864, Abraham Lincoln recognized that an election should not be a casualty of war, arguing, "If the rebellion could force us to forgo or postpone a national election, it might fairly claim to have already conquered and ruined us."

The terrorists ruined lower Manhattan, where a mass grave still smolders, but they haven't conquered New York City. Giuliani, of all people, should see that wanting to restore the city means having its election go on as planned. Term limits are undemocratic and thwart the will of the people, but democracy requires that people get rid of limits in due course, not in a move by the state legislature for the benefit of one man.

You have to wonder if Giuliani would be such a perfect wartime mayor if he hadn't had his own brush with death. No one would wish all those dark nights of sickness on anyone. But in a man who had often seemed indifferent if not callous to the feelings of others, prostate cancer brought out a gentler side that New Yorkers had rarely seen. As he dropped out of the 2000 Senate race, Rudy acknowledged how suddenly vulnerable to the slings and arrows of life he'd become.

A soulful awareness of the fragility of life and an inexhaustible supply of can-do optimism has been indispensable in getting the city back on its feet without diminishing the horror of its loss. Giuliani can go from empathetic Rudy wrapping a sorrowful widow in his hunched shoulders to traffic warden in a New York minute, barring single-occupancy cars from downtown bridges and tunnels into Manhattan during rush hour. On a typical day last week, he found simple words to console the two children of Inspector Anthony Infante at a service at St. Teresa's in the morning, then managed to control the ego of the Reverend Jesse Jackson in the afternoon as he took advantage of Giuliani's media entourage to nominate himself negotiator in chief. In the evening, Giuliani called on a stricken crowd at Temple Emanu-El to stand and applaud Neil Levin, the head of the Port Authority, who died helping his employees escape. Reverting to tireless cheerleader, he ended his day at Yankee Stadium watching Roger Clemens pitch against Tampa Bay.

To trail in Rudy Giuliani's wake is to feel like the Red Cross ladies handing out aspirin and apples in the temporary commissary outside his office: I wanted to hug him. But that's not the same as handing him an extra four years. As for an extra three months, I wonder if holding the city together at a time when it could have fallen apart doesn't merit the extended time, not as a gift to him but as one for us.

October 8, 2001

Batteries Not Included

Women on Top by Nancy Friday

Nancy Friday's latest compilation of musings from women who responded anonymously to her sex questionnaire—about as representative a group of people as those who call radio talk shows—would not be quite so annoying if Friday didn't insist on patting herself on the back for her courage in pasting them together. Oh, the relief and gratitude women feel now that the Truth Can Finally Be Told by the dauntless Friday, selflessly taking on "the sex haters who will stop at nothing" to silence her.

Pity poor Friday, who has had to endure the hostility of several women friends who cannot stand her success or "bear seeing pleasure, especially sexual pleasure, in another." She has also had to give up being taken seriously by all "the enemies of sex," like the TV anchorman who sits next to her at a dinner party and hastens to tell her that he has not bought her book. "Was he afraid," she asks, "that I might think he'd purchased my book and then gone home to masturbate, he, an opinion maker who appears nightly on millions of TV screens?"

All this sacrifice is made in the cause of bringing us the four-page fantasy of Tara, who dreams of being restrained for an entire night by a man performing acts that produce intense pain, call for plastic sheets and extra-absorbent diapers and include an invasive medical procedure usually done in a hospital requiring the intake of a gallon of ice-cold liquid. Hannah's imagination, to take another example, embraces one horse, one dog, two women, four men, one bottle and two electrical appliances.

Women's fantasies have changed, Friday maintains, since her 1973 book, *My Secret Garden,* in which the leitmotiv was submission. The 150 responses culled from the thousands Friday says she received this time demonstrate that there has been another sexual revolution. Women are now in charge, "on top," as the title says, in sexual posture and every other way. "I will never forget these women," vows Friday, "for they have swept me up in their enthusiasm and taught me, too. 'Take that!' they say, using

their erotic muscle to seduce or subdue anyone or anything that stands in the way of orgasm."

Among the findings that have swept Friday up is that many women like sex as much as, if not more than, men. The last time the opposite was true was in the 12th grade, but Friday finds the phenomenon so surprising that she devotes an entire chapter to it. Another change Friday sees since the fantasies of *Garden* to those of *Women on Top* is the replacement of victim-of-rape fantasies with aggressive perpetrator-of-rape fantasies, although this is belied by the frequency of bondage and bestiality in the book. Women nowadays, it seems, aren't so much dominant as mutually sadistic.

Gone are the appealing men, comfortable settings, clean sheets and room service of prefeminist fantasies. There is no intimacy, comfort or consolation from the sex these women dream of, no momentary sensation of not being alone in the universe. Instead Friday's courageous respondents' heads are filled with thoughts of prisoners, children, animals (farm, zoo and domestic) and so much equipment that batteries ought to be included.

Forget finding anything erotic here. Much of what Friday recounts is so unfathomable—the body has neither the openings nor the agility for it—that it is hardly titillating. The book ends up being ridiculous when it isn't repetitive and boring, having the effect of an affidavit rather than an aphrodisiac. If Friday hadn't padded her pages with psychobabble about women claiming their sexual destiny, and Simon & Schuster hadn't been willing to print anything to make a buck, *Women on Top* would be available only by mail and would arrive in a plain brown wrapper.

December 2, 1991

PART FOUR

Playing with the Big Boys Without Becoming One

I'*VE ROMANTICIZED MY LIFE,* leaving out columns that fizzled, bread that didn't rise, and all the times I wanted to wring Courtney's neck, or she mine. I also left out the potential husbands I didn't marry. It was possible to fall in love, but if the old saw about a good man being hard to find is true, it's doubly so for a good stepfather.

I've dwelled on the big jobs at big publications, assuming that readers, like my mother's bridge partners long ago, are more interested in a magazine that has celebrity journalists on the masthead and throws itself a glitzy seventy-fifth anniversary party at Radio City Music Hall attended by nearly every famous person on the planet.

But the magazine I'm proudest of is the smallest one. In 1985, the *Washington Weekly,* modeled after the *Village Voice,* was born, backed by publisher Mort Zuckerman, *The New Republic*'s Marty Peretz, and Joan Bingham, an owner of the *Louisville Courier Journal* who is now publisher of Grove/Atlantic, Inc.

At first, I wasn't ready to leave Courtney or my kitchen table so I edited part time at the *Weekly* and kept writing pieces for *The New Republic.* But when the *Weekly*'s first editor left, I agreed to take over.

The job made me feel a little like I was back in Camp Hill. We covered Washington as a small town, exposed local corruption (the parking meter scam, businesses fronting for porn operations, dirty restaurants, and dirty deeds). Courtney came to the office after school, to do homework and sell

279

papers from the front porch (for a 10 percent commission). She rarely complained. For the first time, at age eleven, she was allowed to have take-out food, as much moo shu pork and curried chicken as she could consume.

I drafted nearly every writer I knew: Taylor Branch (who would win a Pulitzer Prize for *Parting the Waters*), Rick Hertzberg (former editor of *The New Republic*, currently a *New Yorker* columnist), Tina Rosenberg (an editorial writer for *The New York Times*), and Brooke Gladstone (now the host of NPR's *On the Media*), who put together an events calendar with attitude. We were like family, and the office—a brownstone walk-up above a video store—was like home. We hung quilts, made chocolate-chip cookies, and brought in old wooden swivel chairs nabbed at estate sales. Every issue went down to the wire. We pasted up the pages ourselves. When an ad came in late for some book fair or concert, I'd grab an Exacto knife and start slicing lines out of someone's precious copy to make room. Every Sunday afternoon, we had a picnic and played volleyball.

Just as circulation surged, advertising slumped. The ads from the restaurants and boutiques in Dupont Circle and Georgetown kept coming, but ones from national movie chains and department stores, wary of making yearlong commitments in a slow market, slowed to a trickle. After about a year, the paper shut down. To grieve, we went to the grove in Rock Creek Park where we'd played volleyball every Sunday for a bittersweet good-bye feast that lasted all day.

I've moved offices several times and each time I've lugged along the fifty-two issues of the *Weekly* and stacked them on a shelf within eyeshot to remind me that some things that fail are a success. All those nights of soggy pizza, all those seat-of-the-pants deadlines, all those people are embedded in my heart. My mother would have been at home in that warren of rooms, watching me feel for a fever on the forehead of anyone whose energy flagged for a moment, asking, "Are you sick?" We loved what we were doing and each other.

On closing night, *Time* has the same crazed, collegial feel, padding around in bare feet, catnapping on the sofa, eating dinner at the office, although there's a marked difference in the caliber of food. At both places, togetherness is a requirement of the job. My colleagues from both are among my closest friends.

Are there any friendships more intense than those from junior high or from your first big job after college? We each get only one *Washington Weekly*, like we each get only one seventh grade. One thing the *Washington Weekly* and *The New Republic* didn't do was prepare me for big-time journalism. They were Mom and Pop operations compared to *Time*.

*   *   *

My first glimpse of the underbelly of a big institution came in the mid-1990s when the Washington Bureau office manager of thirty years was shunted aside so that a friend of one of the executives could take over her job. *Time* usually celebrated such bloodlettings with a show party known as a "pour" for the presence of drink and the absence of food. I myself once drank a festive toast to a bureau chief pushed out by an editor in New York who was also the godfather of his daughter.

There would be no pour for Janet (she is still too ashamed to have me use her real name). She had first been afraid to let anyone know she'd been told to leave. But gradually her humiliation lifted enough to let anger drive her to see a lawyer, and she filed suit.

At the time I was deputy bureau chief and Janet's supervisor, so I was deposed under oath at the offices of *Time*'s outside counsel, Akin Gump. I'd been interviewed informally, so the lawyers were not surprised when my answers defended Janet (as did others, like former columnist Hugh Sidey). Silly matters were raised: Did she keep a change of clothes hanging on her door, did she actually change clothes in the office? (By the way, we all changed clothes in the office, since we were there night and day.) They even asked, "Did she flush the toilet?"

As the session drew to a close, one of the lawyers pushed a foot-high stack of documents toward me. "Would you like to take a look at these?" It was a pile of expense account reports. Not Janet's. Mine. Is there anything uglier? Yikes.

I was paralyzed like a character in an Alfred Hitchcock movie. One minute the birds in the trees are singing, the next they're flying too low and chirping too loudly. I was going to be pecked to death. I wondered if I would have to go back over every trip, every meal, every cab then and there, deprived of food and water until I broke down and admitted everything. I hadn't brought a lawyer to the deposition. Why would I? I am one, by the way, but didn't think I'd need a practicing one since this wasn't supposed to be about me.

I was asked about a White House trip they seemed to think hadn't been billed properly. I explained the bizarre press office accounting and how it had all washed out in subsequent reports. But the implication was clear: If I was supporting Janet, I must be in cahoots with her so that she would cast a blind eye on my expenses. In fact, she cast no eye on them at all, since she just passed them along to green eyeshade types in New York. As for those New York accountants, they were so thorough I doubt a paper clip eluded their sharp eyes. If those guys had been called in to examine AOL's books before Gerry Levin agreed to buy it, *Time* wouldn't be left holding Steve Case's worthless paper. They might have caught the cooked books that landed the company in such hot water with federal authorities the merged company had to make the largest restatement of earnings—$100 billion— in corporate history.

There was no discrepancy in my expense accounts or in Janet's steward-ship of the bureau. As mysteriously as these criticisms of Janet appeared, they disappeared. The lawyers settled and Janet walked away with a large sum of money. That's the good news. The bad is that when the guys wanted to hire a crony, they were willing to trump up accusations against a decent, loyal employee to get rid of her, an experience from which Janet has never recovered. When I told the story of the deposition to friendly editors in New York, expecting outrage, I was told to be a big boy and get over it.

Perhaps I should have left then. But I was no profile in courage. So what if the expense account and world travel, the access and the recognition, came at the cost of a corporate culture less like a magazine and more like IBM? I was too ambitious and too comfortable to give it up.

Given that I was staying, I should have taken the advice to be a big boy, but I'd thrived without becoming one. The politics of the Washington bu-reau could be dicey—too many correspondents chasing too few White Houses—but I had generous colleagues and was lucky to carve out a niche where I wrote a column about politics broadly conceived, from the Hill to the agencies to the White House. For eight years, the Clintons were a gift that kept on giving. I also got to write profiles about what makes *New York Times* editor Arthur Sulzberger or Rush Limbaugh tick. Some days, I felt I should pay *Time* for letting me do my job.

I had only one other unfortunate experience at *Time*. I think of it as "My Lunch with John Huey," which might have turned into "How I Became the Last Woman Columnist at *Time* Magazine," but didn't. Huey arrived at the magazine in July 2001 from a successful stint as editor of *Fortune* maga-zine. More than that, he was a close friend of editor in chief Norman Pearl-stine, who elevated him to be his equal as coeditor in chief of all Time, Inc., magazines. He was heir apparent.

My first inkling of Huey came shortly after he arrived and I was asked to write a personal reminiscence of *Washington Post* publisher Katharine Gra-ham. A week earlier, Graham had gone off to Herb Allen's annual retreat for the media in Sun Valley, promising me as she left "to bring back a mogul." She had not remarried after her husband died but was determined that I should once Courtney was grown.

Moments after a lively lunch with a bunch of pals that included Tom Hanks, Graham fell on her way back to her cabin, slipping into a coma from which she never recovered. When asked to write her obituary, I cau-tioned New York that I might know Graham too well, but I was told that was what was wanted. *Newsweek* would be putting Mrs. Graham on the cover. All *Time* would have would be my essay.

That week, Jim Kelly, managing editor of *Time,* was on vacation in Saltaire, Fire Island. Because I wanted to be sure I had struck the right note, I e-mailed Kelly a copy of my piece. He sent back a note saying it was "beautiful," high praise from someone who's given to mumbling "nice" for a piece that wins a National Magazine Award, and "It will write itself" when he assigns a tough piece with a short deadline.

The number two editor in charge in Jim's absence put the piece to bed late Friday night. But the next morning, I had a call from him, saying that the folks upstairs (translate Huey and Pearlstine) didn't like it because it failed to deal adequately with the impact of Graham's death on the family-controlled publishing empire where there were Class A and Class B shares, or with publishing dynasties. He didn't think it could be fixed.

But I did. I called publishing experts. I called board members. I called former *Washington Post* editor in chief Ben Bradlee to get his take on the business impact. "Who gives a shit?" he wanted to know. It turned out her death would have no effect on the corporate structure. The baton had already been passed to her son, Donald.

For every word about the business I needed to put in, a word about Graham had to come out. I loved her, but I'd been careful: too much sentiment and the whole thing would go limp as a dishrag. Too little and it might as well be written by the business correspondent. I took out my favorite memory—Graham wrote *me* a thank you note for letting her have Courtney's wedding at her house. I put in enough about publishing to wear New York down. It ran.

Nevertheless, that exercise established a pattern. Soon after Huey arrived, I was writing less than I ever had and I was beginning to feel like a farmer with an agricultural subsidy being paid not to grow soybeans. Still, it would be churlish to complain. Pages were tight, the country was going to war, and Kelly had a magazine to get out. On the other hand, I was worried that I might not be worried enough. Signs of trouble pass me by until it's too late to do anything. When I was in third grade music class, Sister Mary William asked if I would mind turning the pages of sheet music for her. She needed to critique the sopranos, she explained, whom she couldn't hear over my voice. I took this to mean I could hit a clear high C, until Sister told my mother she should consider signing me up for piano lessons. I was shocked. That was the end of my brilliant career as a soloist.

I didn't want to become one of the disappeared at *Time,* with or without a pour, so I called Kelly. He said I was being ridiculous to worry but why didn't I have lunch with John Huey anyway?

It helps to understand that meals occupy the same lofty position in the *Time* hierarchy of rituals that they held in the Bresnahan household. *Time*'s lunches ran to Chilean sea bass and risotto, not meat loaf and potatoes, but the purpose was the same: to smooth things over in pleasant surroundings with good food. If *Time* editors had been staffing the National Security Council last fall, they would have invited Saddam for lunch, sure that any misunderstandings about his weapons of mass destruction could be cleared up over poached salmon and wild rice. I took Kelly's advice and Huey and I went to lunch at the end of November at Michael's, a media watering hole in Manhattan. Huey ordered the Cobb salad, and I ordered roast chicken and french fries.

Huey started by apologizing for lowering my self-esteem. In several formulations, he asked, "Aren't you embarrassed that I don't like your column?" He offered to be embarrassed on my behalf. So what can I do? I asked. "I'm not in the business of fixing people's work," he said. He then told me whom among my colleagues in the Washington bureau he didn't like, which included nearly all of them. He longed, he said, for the days when, with a change of administration, the entire bureau could be wiped out, along with their outdated sources and old ways of thinking. There never was such a day, but I don't doubt he yearned for one.

At the end, I asked him what he was telling me. He said, "I'm saying, why don't you run for the daylight? They love you over there at CNN. Do more TV." Telling that to a writer is like telling someone they have a face for radio.

Still, I shouldn't have overreacted. Huey had every right to pass judgment. He's in charge. But by *Time* tradition, he shouldn't have spoiled a perfectly good expense-account lunch doing it. Although that meal lasted a lifetime, I had yet another that evening—an awards dinner at the Waldorf-Astoria for the Committee to Protect Journalists, where *Time* had taken a bunch of tables. Of all the gin joints in all the world, why did Huey have to walk into mine (or I into his, depending on your point of view), and of all the seats at all the tables, why was there an empty one next to him with my name on it? Two, two, two meals in one day with Huey? It was too late to play the dangerous game of switching placecards. We behaved like strangers and found ourselves mesmerized by folks on either side. Huey later complained that I kept disappearing from the table to talk to every Tom, Dick, and network news anchor in the room. I did.

In retrospect, I had three explanations for Huey's behavior. One, he thought I was a jerk. Two, he was carrying water for Pearlstine. Three, he didn't like women columnists.

The first always has to be given consideration. People don't usually take an instant dislike to me (it takes longer), but Huey was known as a quick study. He'd met me on a few social occasions and on a six-hour plane ride to a media conference in Aspen, where I was on a panel with Charlie Rose and Bob Schieffer. We can all be jerks at times. Perhaps I'd been one at 25,000 feet. Perhaps Huey had sniffed out latent strains of it and was protecting himself from a future outbreak.

As for the second reason, I knew that Pearlstine held a grudge against me, and I admired him for it. I'm a world-champion grudge holder myself, nursing them on behalf of friends against people I barely know. Pearlstine was holding a family grudge—the most admirable type—on his wife's behalf. In 1991, I'd written a review panning the book, *Women on Top*, by Nancy Friday (see page 276). I wasn't the only writer to attack the book, but I was the only writer to do so who would soon find Friday's husband, Norman Pearlstine, as her boss.

Would I have written the review had I known Pearlstine would shortly be appointed editor in chief of *Time*? You can bet your life I wouldn't have. I was still the wuss who stayed after seeing Janet treated so cruelly. Generally, I don't write reviews: Why ruin someone's day? But when I was on a three-month teaching fellowship at Harvard's Institute of Politics, I wrote what- and whenever I was asked as a way of earning my keep in absentia. After reading *Women on Top*, I told my editor that the world would get along just fine without my reviewing it. He said to do it anyway. I'd yet to take the advice to be a big boy, so I did as asked.

The first time I saw Pearlstine post-review, he came to Washington to meet the bureau. I'd first gotten to know him in an earlier life when I worked for Nader and he was covering the auto industry in Detroit for *The Wall Street Journal*. Like any guy who wears X-rated slippers and brags about peeling bananas with his toes, he was easy to like. When a bunch of Nader's Raiders were going to the annual shareholders meeting of General Motors at Cobo Hall in Detroit, Pearlstine invited us to dinner at a Greek restaurant in his neighborhood and to throw our sleeping bags on his floor. Later, he would hire my ex-husband to join him in Hong Kong to start up the Asian *Wall Street Journal*.

As he walked around the Washington bureau, he moved from one group to another in the windowless conference room, getting to me as lunch was served. We shook hands and to his credit he faced the matter squarely, saying, "I'll do my best to get over it."

He didn't get over it after a close friend and editor at *The Wall Street Journal* had made a mildly critical comment about Friday's work. But I never felt any fallout. By then, Isaacson had risen to be managing editor of *Time*. At a book party at the Four Seasons in New York where Walter was playing the part of Kofi Annan trying to get Nancy to speak to me, Pearl-stine pulled him aside and told him to give up. It was never going to happen. And it hasn't.

On the third point, Huey was outspoken on the subject of uppity women. "Let me tell you whose columns I like," he said that day at lunch. He liked Paul Krugman, Charles Krauthammer, and Tom Friedman (well, who doesn't?). He proceeded to tell me who he didn't like, and they were all women, whom I won't mention out of consideration for them, not that they need any protection. Several have won Pulitzer Prizes.

Huey seemed to me that Camp Hill bully all grown up. Little Patrick Higgins didn't want my brother's training wheels, he wanted to see him cry. I don't know what Huey wanted that day at Michael's, but I wanted not to attract the attention of Michael Wolff, the media critic of *New York Magazine,* who was sitting at the next table, so close I could touch him. I feared he might get wind of the unfolding drama, so I beamed happily even when Huey put the arm on my french fries.

Following *Time*'s philosophy, I had lunch at Palio's the next day with Jim Kelly, a layer between me and Pearlstine/Huey. Jim is the son of a policeman from Queens, a product of the Jesuits at Regis High School. He's held on to what was good about Queens and Regis through four years at Princeton. It had been Kelly's idea that I write a column, and over the years we'd become the closest of friends. When his father died, I flew up to sit at his mother's kitchen table in Queens eating food dropped off by neighbors. I'd recently been at his summer house on Fire Island. It was a Kodak moment, sand squishing between our toes as we walked along the ocean, remembering Courtney's wedding a few weeks before, me getting to play for the first time with Jim's son from Vietnam, Luke, daring to say out loud how lucky we were, after all these years, to be working together. I told Jim I wanted to write less. He joked that he'd print two Margaret Carlson columns a week if he could.

At lunch, he suggested I just ignore my earlier lunch. It would all blow over. If I weren't still a girl about such things I would have done just that, and acted as if nothing had happened. We are all subject to changing bosses and tastes, especially at a magazine. Freedom of the press belongs to the person who owns one, and a choice of writers belongs to the editor who runs things, which is how it should be.

My solution was a cooling-off period. This is where this book comes in. I'd first signed an agreement with Simon & Schuster in 1991 to write a book on the Bush family, but my parents died that year and I could barely get myself going day to day, much less get a book to Simon & Schuster. By not producing, I like to think I did Simon & Schuster a favor, since

Clinton's victory in 1992 vastly reduced the appetite for books about the previous administration. Funny, Simon & Schuster didn't see it that way, and Alice Mayhew was insisting I deliver a book by fall of 2002.

That summer I took a sabbatical and rented a cottage on Long Island. I went through nearly two decades of columns and wrote 40,000 words trying to explain them. Aside from wondering who that person who occasionally wrote crazy things under my byline was, it was a good way to spend a summer. I got to see my family whenever I wanted in a cottage as close to my parents' beach house as I could find, right down to the absence of a dishwasher and the presence of a clothesline. My new son-in-law dried the dishes, lugged out the trash, and struggled to beat the Carlsons at Scrabble and Boggle.

I'd forgotten what it was like to be home on a Friday at midnight. I'd not asked myself whether fifteen years at one job is long enough or if there was something else in journalism to do. If my lunch with Huey hadn't spilled into a gossip column, I would never have gotten calls from editors offering me jobs should I ever want to leave *Time*. Much of what was written about my relationship with Huey was wrong. *The New York Times* stated I would no longer be writing a column as a result of my encounter with him. They had to run a correction. Kelly was right when he said the lunch would blow over. It did. And when I got back, my column began running again as if nothing had happened. I had overreacted.

But the lunch taught me something else at last: to be a big boy. And like the big boys, I now have an arrangement, designed by David Boies, one of the very biggest boys, whom I happened to sit next to at dinner one night. He restructured my relationship with *Time* so that I can give speeches, write books, write for other magazines, and take up Huey's suggestion and Isaacson's offer to do more TV. I've signed a contract with *GQ* to do nine pieces next year, and I hope that *G* does mean *Gentleman*. I plan to publish enough columns for both to write another book, I hope, during the summer months in a restful zip code. What it means for sure is that my quotient of Chinese food in waxy containers on Friday nights will go way down.

Because politicians and larcenous CEOs have ruined the line, I'm not going to say this all gives me more time with my family. My married daughter doesn't need help with her math homework. Anyway, my family tells me we spend quite enough time together already.

One thing I want to do is write enough to keep a relationship with the thousands of readers who send in their thoughts. Most of those who get in touch agree with me; those who don't agree who get in touch usually convey their objections with a twinkle in their writing. Of the fraction of the mail that's hostile, only a fraction of that is viciously so. I showed a folder of the worst sort to my CNN colleague Kate O'Bierne, who was embarrassed for her side: Her liberal critics rarely get so personal. She's never gotten a piece of mail that says, "I would like to strangle you with your black stockings." And that's one of the ones I can print.

The largest amount of mail I ever got was over the biggest blunder I ever made. I'd agreed to be on *Imus in the Morning* the day after the 2000 election—that is, before I knew we'd be up all night waiting for Florida to be decided (or undecided). Just before I came on, there was a report that the presidential election was likely to be decided by absentee ballots from military personnel who had chosen Florida as their "state of convenience" because it did not have an income tax. When asked about it, I said how unfortunate it would be if the election were to be decided by a group of tax dodgers.

I'm willing to defend unpopular opinions I actually hold—that future tax cuts which go almost entirely to the well-off should be repealed, that the working class should get a break on payroll taxes, that wealthy people who open offshore accounts, corporations that move to Bermuda, and accounting firms like Ernst & Young devoted to creating ever more elaborate ways around the tax laws be shunned by those who play by the rules.

But I didn't hold the opinion about the military registered in Florida. I'm not against the military, nor do I think they avoid taxes by living in a tax-free state. It's one of the rights they have for the sacrifices they make. My father fought in World War Two and both my father and brother worked for the military as civilians for decades. Our social life that wasn't spent in the parish hall was spent at the Officers' Club at the Mechanicsburg Naval Supply Depot. It's where my mother played bridge, where we held my younger brother's wedding rehearsal dinner, where I occasionally snuck into the pool.

Imus wasn't being his usual gruff self. On the contrary, he tried to keep me from digging myself into a hole and I didn't pick up on it. Was I temporarily possessed by Jane Fonda and Ramsey Clark? Was I just trying to "make conversation," like Jimmy when he doesn't know what to say?

Even before the 693 e-mails started coming in—I answered all except those who wanted to inflict grievous bodily harm—I asked Imus's sidekick Bernard if I could come back on and apologize. Imus doesn't permit apologies and Bernard warned I would be banned for life if I insisted on making one. But I did. It didn't stem the flow of mail, but it did help me. Confession is good for the guilty.

That Saturday, although I risked compounding my error by apologizing to an audience who may not have heard the Imus show, I took the final segment on CNN's *Capital Gang* to apologize as well:

This week my outrage of the week is me. On the Imus in the Morning *program Wednesday, I made a flippant remark about the military that offended many people. I regret it.*

Whatever tax breaks people who risk their lives get, it's not enough. In this life, the military, the police and teachers should get paid the most; lawyers, investment bankers, and pundits the least.

My older brother worked for the Navy for twenty-five years. My late father served in World War Two and worked for the Navy for thirty years. I can't apologize to him. But I apologize to everyone else.

Most of my mail is delightful—thoughtful observations on the Middle East, the last election, or global warming, helpful hints on grooming and suggestions about my social life, as in "Would you like to meet my son?" There are lots of gifts, including a bunch of toothbrushes after I wrote about my grandmother using old ones to clean the crud around the faucets, and a hundred recipes for homemade bread when I mentioned that I baked on the weekends. I even got a vacuum after I complained on *Imus* about mine stirring up as much dust as it removed.

My daughter enjoys the people who stop us at Costco, surprised to find us there, as if I live in that little box in their living rooms and don't need cornflakes and sugar in the large economy size. Discussing terrorism ruins the karma of warehouse shopping, so I steer the conversation to whether buying a year's supply of paper towels is really worth the aggravation of hauling it home and finding a place to stash it. There are regular correspondents who tell me when my glasses are smudged and when I'm wearing too much black or have worn the same thing three times in a row. I treasure all of it.

By the end of last summer, I was getting ready for another of Jimmy's birthdays. He'd done something I'm sure would make our parents happy. He'd become an usher at Good Shepherd Church and done it on his own, since there's no one left at Good Shepherd who remembers my mother ironing the linens or my father calling out numbers at Friday night bingo. Jimmy's established his own presence there and he loves having a reason to make us work around his schedule. After a year of unemployment after the depot closed, he got a job at a Salvation Army thrift store.

I'm always thinking I've seen the best day—the day Courtney was born, or when she graduated from Kenyon College, or the day she got married. At the same time, tomorrow, I'm expecting a million dollars in small bills around the next corner. Like Reagan looking at a room of manure, I see a pony.

One unexpected piece of the future came into focus in early 2003. In a happy turn of events, former Philadelphia Mayor Ed Rendell, who introduced me to his press secretary David Yarkin, whom I introduced to my daughter, who married David a year or so later in Kay Graham's backyard in a ceremony performed by the Mayor's wife, Federal Judge Midge Rendell, is now Governor Ed Rendell of Pennsylvania. He's pleaded with David to come join his administration, and he decided to do so. That means my sweet daughter, who sits at a desk near Mayor Mike Bloomberg from which she watches all of New York pass by, has to give up her job. She'll be looking for one in Harrisburg, Pennsylvania, a place she knows all too well. It's where she spent many Christmases, learned to drive, practiced making pie crust, and, like me, couldn't wait to get away from once her parents were gone. Even if I can't go home again, my daughter will do it for me.

She's resourceful. She'll find a job, although it will be hard to replace Bloomberg. As if heaven made Rendell Governor, an unintended but crucial consequence is that the Governor's Mansion is ten minutes from the house in Camp Hill I grew up in. Courtney will be able to look in on Jimmy, who will be so happy to have his buddy David close by. I can dimly see the day when, if all works out well, Courtney will have children of her own who will be plotting before too long how to get away from such a dreary town.

America is a collection of success stories and most of those stories are about leaving home, whether to a law firm in Los Angeles, a desk on the trading floor of the New York Stock Exchange, or a beat at *Time* magazine. My parents were happy to be fully engaged in the world of extended family and neighborhood and they wanted the same richness for me. They looked with longing at those parents whose kids stayed nearby, preferring that I live around the block, able to drop by on a moment's notice for dinner, than be king of the world hundreds of miles away, too busy to visit.

What I did instead was to leave, but take home with me. I visit my parents every day. On all the big issues and in all the big crises, every person listens for those first voices, of parents and teachers. Every happy person hears them. When I can't hear my parents, I can't write. When I don't listen, I go wrong. I never went so far away from home that their voices don't ring in my ear.

So thanks to my editor, Alice Mayhew, for her uncanny sense of timing, to put fifteen years of what could have been fish wrap between hardcovers. And thanks to Mom and Dad, Jimmy and Edmund, Courtney and David, so many hands crisscrossed beneath me that even if pushed, I can never fall.

Acknowledgments

Thank you to those who take what I put on the page and make it better. For their endurance and way with words, I thank Michael Kinsley, Hendrik Hertzberg, Lee Aitken, Michael Duffy, Matt Cooper, Priscilla Painton, Steve Koepp, Shelby Coffey, Adam Moss, Anja Schmidt, and Alice Mayhew. And they're just the ones required by job description to read copy. I also thank Jay Carney, John Dickerson, Sally Quinn, Catherine Williams, Mickey Kaus, Melissa Moss, Marjorie Williams, Bill Curry, Mort Zuckerman, Mike Bloomberg, and Cathy Isaacson as first readers and my cheering section. When I was reluctant to embark on *Margaret Carlson: The Early Years,* they said, "Do it, just keep it short."

Lots of people had to cut me some slack while I was recalling those early years, particularly my colleagues at CNN: Mark Shields, Al Hunt, Robert Novak, Kate O'Bierne, Tucker Carlson (no relation, I swear), Judy Woodruff, Deborah Nelson, and Bob Kovach. Every week they make studio A a barrel of fun.

For friendship lasting through thick and thin, their promises to be there if ever I should need them, and rescues when I did: Courtney's godmother, Julie Empson and all the Empsons, the Rafshoons, Bradlees, Bennetts, Campions, Champions, Quinns, Pincuses, Matthews, Rattners, Stevens, Thomasons, Glickmans, Gotbaums, Browns, Dingells, Haddads, Kleins, and Lehrers. In making the list, I can be thankful for yet another blessing: how many of my friends are married to friends.

291

For enriching Jimmy's life, thank you to my parents' close friends who still live in the old neighborhood who are there when I can't be, the Atchleys and the Fickes. For making the house and the room I write in perfect, O'Neal Page and Nick Gill.

To Walter Isaacson, my friend who knew I should come to *Time* when I didn't, and to Jim Kelly, who kept me there, my thanks.

And thank you to the O'Connors, Mulveys, McCrearys, Bresnahans who gave me a jump-start in life. And to those who make life so wonderful now: Jimmy and Edmund, Colleen, Moira, and James. For making life sweet every day, Courtney, and the man who makes her happy, David.

Index

About the Author

Margaret Carlson was named a columnist for *Time* magazine in February 1994. Her column, "Public Eye," makes Carlson the first woman columnist in the magazine's seventy-eight-year history. Prior to becoming a columnist, Carlson served as the magazine's deputy Washington bureau chief, and as White House correspondent. She also serves as a panelist on CNN's political programs *Inside Politics* and *The Capital Gang*.

In addition to covering Al Gore and George W. Bush during Campaign 2000, Carlson covered the previous three presidential elections.

Carlson joined *Time* in January 1988 from *The New Republic*. Her career has included stints as Washington bureau chief for *Esquire* magazine, editor of the *Washington Weekly*, and the *Legal Times of Washington*. In addition to *Time*, Carlson also writes a monthly column for *GQ* magazine.

She has one daughter and lives in Washington, D.C.